AMERICAN POPULAR ENTERTAINMENT

Conference on the History of American Popular Entertainment

The New York Public Library at Lincoln Center
November 17-20, 1977

Committee for the Conference

WILLIAM GREEN, Chairman
Queens College, CUNY

MARGARET LOFTUS RANALD, Secretary
Queens College, CUNY

JULIAN MATES, Treasurer
C. W. Post Center, L.I.U.

RALPH ALLEN
University of Tennessee, Knoxville

HELEN ARMSTEAD-JOHNSON
York College, CUNY

BERNARD BECKERMAN
Columbia University

WILLIAM BRASMER
Denison University

RICHARD M. BUCK
Performing Arts Research Center,
The New York Public Library
at Lincoln Center

STUART CHENOWETH
San Francisco State University

SELMA JEANNE COHEN
Dance Perspectives Foundation

MRS. ROBIN CRAVEN
Executive Board,
Theatre Library Association

ROBERT M. HENDERSON
Library & Museum of
the Performing Arts,
The New York Public Library
at Lincoln Center

BROOKS McNAMARA
New York University

PAUL MYERS
Theatre Collection,
The New York Public Library
at Lincoln Center

LOUIS A. RACHOW
Walter Hampden-Edwin Booth
Theatre Collection & Library

VERA MOWRY ROBERTS
Hunter College, CUNY

ESTELLE THALER
Queens College, CUNY

MRS. JOHN F. WHARTON
Theatre Collection,
The New York Public Library
at Lincoln Center

Honorary Committee from The Arts
JOHN BUBBLES   AGNES de MILLE   MORTON MINSKY
JEAN DALRYMPLE   STANLEY KAUFFMANN   MAX MORATH

AMERICAN POPULAR ENTERTAINMENT

Papers and Proceedings of the Conference on the History of American Popular Entertainment

Edited by MYRON MATLAW

Sponsored jointly by **American Society for Theatre Research,**
Bernard Beckerman, President
and **Theatre Library Association,**
Brooks McNamara, President

Contributions in Drama and Theatre Studies, Number 1

GREENWOOD PRESS
Westport, Connecticut • London, England

Library of Congress Cataloging in Publication Data

Conference on the History of American Popular Entertainment,
New York Public Library at Lincoln Center, 1977.
American popular entertainment.

   (Contributions in drama and theatre studies ; no. 1
ISSN 0-163-3821)
   Includes index.
   1. Performing arts—United States—History—Congresses.
2. United States—Popular culture—Congresses.
I. Matlaw, Myron, 1924-   II. American Society for
Theatre Research. III. Theatre Library Association.
IV. Title. V. Series.
PN2221.C65   1977   790.2   78-74655
ISBN 0-313-21072-1

Library of Congress Catalog Card Number: 78-74655
ISBN: 0-313-21072-1
ISSN: 0-163-3821

First published in 1979

Greenwood Press, Inc.
51 Riverside Avenue, Westport, Connecticut 06880

Printed in the United States of America

10 9 8 7 6 5 4 3 2 1

Contents

Contents   *vii*

Myron Matlaw

Preface

The Conference on the History of American Popular Entertainment (better known by its acronym, CHAPE), held at Lincoln Center in New York on November 17-20, 1977, was the first of its kind in the United States. It brought together representatives of the scholarly world, the theatre, and the general public in an investigation of the contribution of popular entertainment to the cultural heritage of this country. The papers and addresses constituted an amalgam of scholarship, analysis, criticism, and history. The reminiscences and re-creations of routines by those who had themselves been, and some of whom still are, active practitioners in the entertainment world provided the living history.

Participants and audiences alike acclaimed this Conference the most auspicious event ever held by its sponsors, the American Society for Theatre Research and the Theatre Library Association—and the most enjoyable scholarly conference in living memory. It opened with an immense two-hour environmental "happening," live acts by juggling artists Hovey and Judy Burgess, a strolling routine by Russell the Clown and Tony (a monkey), and an audiovisual pastiche of concurrently performed activities: nearly fifty vaudeville episodes, a two-hour Emmett Kelly circus film, a dozen silent dance films, and sundry other videotapes and audiotapes of black and white Minstrel Shows, Burlesque Shows, Vaudeville, Ragtime, Ethnic Theatre, Tent Repertoire Shows, Circus, Wild West Shows, Medicine Shows, Dance, and other entertainments—a potpourri of the various topics covered in the Conference itself.

The vibrance and sheer fun emerge even in these published proceedings of the Conference, although the full excitement of the live events is, of course, not wholly retrievable on the printed page. On the other hand, this publication of the proceedings constitutes a permanent chronicle of the erudition, scholarship, critical insights, and reminiscences of the past related by the entertainers.

Reminiscences often romanticize the past, both personal and cultural. Chroniclers of popular entertainment tend to forget to mention or (even worse) they tend to glamorize the vulgar, the stupid, the sleazy sides of these art forms. Fortunately, the papers in this collection are not guilty of such omissions and commissions, however grounded some of them may be in personal reminiscences.

By design, the Conference focused on the major forms of popular entertainment. It centered "around long-neglected aspects of theatrical performance which are currently generating much interest among theatre students and scholars," as the theatre historian Brooks McNamara stated in the program's introduction. He further noted that "unlike folk forms to which they are related, popular entertainments are created not by amateurs but for profit by professional showmen."

Presentations of such live entertainments included Joe Smith's classic vaudeville sketch "Dr. Kronkhite," followed by his reminiscences of his career with Charlie Dale and the Avon Comedy Four; Joey and Judi Faye's reenactments of skits from the Minsky shows—and Eleonore Treiber's all-too-abridged reenactment of a strip tease—and Morton Minsky's panel discussion and talk, giving great insight into the era in which he and his family productions played so important a role; ragtime pianist and entertainer Max Morath's rendition of songs by Bert Williams and his associates, accompanied by commentaries; and the lecture-demonstrations by Chuck Green and Mrs. Buddy Bradley (with piano accompaniment by Sonny Donaldson) of such dance steps as the buck, the wing, shuffle hips, slide, bubbles, and paddle and roll.

Two films shown at the Conference brought to life other popular arts—tent repertoire and the minstrel show. The first of these, *Toby and the Tall Corn*, is discussed at some length in Caroline Schaffner's accounts of past experiences with Neil Schaffner of The Schaffner Players of Iowa. This film illustrates the tent rep, an entertainment that is further explored, from different angles, by Clifford Ashby and William L. Slout. *Yes Sir, Mr. Bones*, the second film, served as an introduction to the immensely successful "Minstrel Shows, Vaudeville, and Burlesque" part of the Conference. This full-length 1951 film features some of the genre's last luminaries recreating the history and charms of two major entertainments of a vanished era, minstrel shows and floating showboats. Other facets of Minstrel Shows, Vaudeville, and Burlesque are explored by Robert C. Toll, Helen Armstead-Johnson, Bill Smith, Ralph G. Allen, Laurence Senelick, Paul Antonie Distler, and Nahma Sandrow.

Another unit of the Conference program dealt with the Circus, Wild West Shows, and Medicine Shows. Marcello Truzzi, Richard W. Flint, George Speaight, and William Brasmer shed light on these little-known subjects. As the conclusion to this part of the Conference, the veteran Medicine Show performer Mae Noell presented a spell-binding "pitch" in her memoir. Also covered in the proceedings were the fields of Dance and Environmental Entertainment. Some of the history of American dance is dealt with in the papers of Jenifer P. Winsted, Gretchen A. Schneider, and Suzanne Shelton. James H. Bierman and Denis Gontard examined two of the primary types of environmental entertainment, amusement parks and theme parks.

The experience of this Conference confirms the belief that American popular entertainment is generating an ever-growing interest among theatre students, scholars, and cultural historians. As is testified in Don B. Wilmeth's bibliographical survey, it is only recently that scholars and critics have begun to study popular American entertainment in earnest and that, at last, there is a real and growing interest in the subject in the academic community. How much is still to be done—and some of the ways in which it may be done—are suggested in Monroe Lippman's keynote address and in Ray B. Browne's summation.

Special exhibitions in various prominent cultural sites in New York City illustrated the Conference's performances, papers, and colloquia and made them even more lively and meaningful. The Vincent Astor Gallery at Lincoln Center featured "Reginald Marsh: The Art of Popular Entertainment," a display of the etchings, pencil drawings, lithographs, watercolors, and tempera by America's great chronicler of vaudeville and burlesque performers, dancers, trapezists, striptease artists, and street musicians. Other exhibitions especially mounted for this Conference in New York City included those at the Songwriters' Hall of Fame and at the Museum of Broadcasting, "Jenny Lind in New York" at the New York Historical Society, and the John Mullholland Magic Collection at The Players.

Chauncey Howell of NBC-TV conducted an interview at the Conference in Lincoln Center on Friday, November 18, which was telecast that evening over Channel 4 during the five o'clock news broadcast; a cassette copy of the interview has been deposited in the Theatre on Film and Tape Collection at the New York Public Library. As a direct result of the Conference, Michael Kerner of CBS-TV developed a program for the *Camera Three* series presented throughout the United States in July 1978 and entitled "A Peek at Burlesque"; it featured participants from the Burlesque unit of the Conference: Joey and Judi Faye, Morton Minsky, and William Green.

Such widespread response to the Conference was more than merely gratifying to its organizers and participants: it testifies to a tremendous and serious interest in this hitherto virtually unexplored subject. The scholarly and criticial papers as well as the other presentations at the Conference, published in the following pages, reveal what popular American entertainment was all about and constitute a unique record of the past. The value of such a historical presentation is self-evident. The introduction of audio and visual mechanical wonders such as radio, film, and television has radically changed popular entertainment—its basis, its forms, and its audience's responses.

Nineteenth- and early twentieth-century popular entertainments are gone. Although they helped to shape the slicked videotaped entertainments of present-day television—of which they are the precursors—they will never again return in their former guise. Perhaps it is as important to explore and preserve a record of that part of the American heritage as it is to deal with the more traditionally studied subjects of our past—the history of our politics and presidents, of our wars and generals. Aside from incidentally shedding light on American social, economic, political, and military history—and the attitudes toward them of the masses, for whom these entertainments were provided—popular entertainments are probably more significant in the sum total of people's lives than are the more conventionally chronicled "great" events in our history books. They certainly were less destructive. And they are more amusing to study.

This published version of the Conference events constitutes a unique history of such popular entertainments. Through the scholarly inquiries by academicians and through performances and reminiscences by members of the entertaiment profession, it helps to re-create our cultural heritage by presenting an overview of popular entertainment and by sorting out the individual forms of the genre. It also traces the relationship of the various forms to each other and explores their uniquely American facets. The Conference itself succeeded in fulfilling the two functions traditionally associated with the best in art: to instruct and to delight. We hope these published proceedings of the Conference will prove to be equally informative and entertaining.

Acknowledgments —————————————

Without the cooperation of the Conference's participants this book obviously would not have been possible. Contributors abided, usually with equanimity and good cheer, with the editor's requests (sometimes nagging insistence) for manuscript submission and changes in order to reproduce, insofar as possible, the actual proceedings of the Conference. For that reason, most of the papers (as well as the illustrations) he received ultimately simplified the editor's work, for which he herewith expresses his thanks to the contributors, individually and collectively.

The editing of the reminiscences and performances from the taped Conference proceedings would have been infinitely more difficult and ultimately less reliable without the help of the various prominent artists and speakers who disentangled the rough and often chaotic typed transcriptions of their presentations. Particular thanks for this work is due to Morton Minsky, Bill Smith, Caroline Schaffner, Mae Noell, and especially to Max Morath and Joey Faye, who took time out from their very active professional careers as entertainers to assist in preparing their Conference presentations for publication. All of them, it should be added, were most generous in permitting the publication of their valuable contributions, which add further luster to this book.

The National Endowment for the Arts in Washington, D.C., a federal agency, provided a financial grant which supported the Conference and helped make possible the publication of these proceedings. Grateful acknowledgment must be expressed also the American Council of Learned Societies, the Field Enterprises Charitable Corporation, The Scherman Foundation, the William C. Whitney Foundation, and the many individuals whose generosity helped make this Conference possible.

All the members of the Committee for the Conference on the History of American Popular Entertainment were helpful to me. In particular, Louis

A. Rachow's able service as Conference historian assisted my work. My deepest gratitude is to the Committee's chairman, Professor William Green. As well as being the genial driving force of the Conference itself, Bill Green was equally unstinting in his guidance and assistance in this project, providing generously of his expertise, his time, and his inexhaustible energy in helping solve the many inevitable problems—scholarly, technical, administrative, and diplomatic—in the editing and publication of this book.

OVERVIEW OF POPULAR ENTERTAINMENT

Monroe Lippman

Notes from an Old Girl Watcher____

When I received the invitation to participate in this conference, it was suggested that I might function as a kind of keynoter. So, as a long-time aficionado of one of America's most popular examples of entertainment—the political convention—I should like to borrow for this occasion its concept of the keynote situation as one in which an ebullient and unquestioning audience receives with wild enthusiasm an address in which the speaker has managed to say practially nothing—and certainly nothing of importance. I pledge to you tonight that if you do your part, I shall certainly do mine.

We have undertaken the consideration of a large subject at this conference. Our major concerns are with those aspects of popular entertainment that are most closely related to theatre; but if, as I believe, popular entertainment is that type of diversion which suits the interests, tastes, pleasures, and pocketbooks of the general population rather than an elite few, we must acknowledge that other forms of entertainment have also been popular at different times in our history. People have always felt the need for some kind of entertainment, and if it has not been readily available in its traditional forms, they have found it in other forms.

Perhaps a personal recollection will help to illustrate my point. I grew up in a small and somewhat remote mining town in northern Minnesota. Being small and remote, it offered little in the way of the usual kinds of entertainment. There was an occasional home-talent minstrel show, during which the audience's greatest enjoyment came from recognizing their neighbors behind the blackface disguises. There was also an infrequent visit from a fourth-rate road company, but we kids of eight or thereabout were seldom allowed to attend. Additionally, of course, there was the circus, but that came just once a year; and there was the street carnival with its sideshows: the dog-faced boy, the spider woman, the wild man from Borneo, and sometimes a fire-eater or a sword-swallower or a man into whom one could stick pins with no apparent effect. But that, too, came just once a year. In between times, the usual types of entertainment were scarce for my generation in that small and remote village.

But being a mining town, it had other advantages. For instance, it boasted significantly more saloons than churches and more than its share of constant inebriates, and it was not long before my dubious companions and I discovered a new and generally satisfying form of entertainment. On Saturday afternoons, we would sit on the curb across the street from the town's most popular saloon and watch the drunks come rolling out between and under the swinging doors, beneficiaries of the special exit treatment provided by the saloon's burly Irish owner. I reveal this questionable practice of my distant childhood not to suggest it as the ideal way for impressionable youngsters to spend their recreation time, but because the story has a moral: that entertainment is where you find it, and if your tastes are not too sophisticated, you can find it in unusual and unexpected places.

Popular entertainment is a universal phenomenon, but I'm not sure that anybody really knows where it came from, although there has been some interesting speculation on the subject. The theory that I find most intriguing, though not exactly scholarly, is that propounded by the late Joe Laurie, Jr. It is his view that it all started in Biblical times. Tongue deep in cheek, he cites as evidence a number of events recorded in the Bible. Thus, he suggests, Aaron was the first magic act, turning a shepherd's staff into a snake. Moses was the first illusionist: he split the Red Sea. Noah had the first big animal act; Daniel, the first cat act; Jonah, the first tank act, and so on and on.[1]

If all this is too fanciful for the serious scholars among you, let me say that there has also been some scholarly conjecture on the subject and there seems to be evidence that such entertainers as magicians, acrobats, clowns, singers, dancers, and trained animals performed in the ancient worlds of Egypt, Greece, and Rome. Particularly popular in Rome were the trained animals, the most intelligent of whom were apes. They proved capable of performing some remarkable feats, including, we are told, even acting in plays—a legacy from which, unfortunately, we have never completely recovered.

In the early years of our own country, the usual kinds of popular entertainment were hard to come by. There were exceptions, but, in general, life in the early colonies afforded little opportunity for entertainment. The hard and continuing fight just to exist demanded the settlers' full time and energies, and wasting time on such nonessentials as entertainment was not merely discouraged, it was forbidden. Later, when the challenge to survival eased up a bit, the colonial South relaxed its restrictions somewhat, but not so the North. There, the Calvinist influence still prevailed, manifesting itself in continued efforts to suppress any form of amusement or recreation for its own sake.

However, although the efforts were persistent, they were not entirely successful, for as the struggle for existence grew less rigorous, the colonists sought relaxation through entertainment. The more traditional forms being largely unavailable, much of the entertainment that they found was centered in the activities in the local taverns where friends gathered, even as now, for a bit of convivial drinking. Also, there were other amusements such as bear-baiting and cock-fighting and the frequently boisterous socializing following such events as corn-husking bees and barn-raisings. Further fun was to be had in such disparate pleasures as dancing and card games, both of which continued to grow in popularity despite the frosty frowns of the more pious.[2]

Those frowns, however, were like sunny smiles compared to the reactions of the bluenoses who found offensive the obvious enjoyment of their less ascetic fellows whose pursuit of happiness led them to that perennially popular entertainment, the ancient and honorable art of girl watching. Many colonists became very adept at it, and, as a matter of not entirely illogical progression, the art sometimes developed to a high level of entertainment. For example, we all know about the charming colonial custom of bundling, which permitted courting couples to climb into bed together, fully clothed, of course, and separated by a centerboard. The reason for this delightful practice, we are told, was to spare the enamored couple the rigors of New England weather while at the same time conserving fuel. However, perhaps not surprisingly, church and court records of those years indicate that it was not rare for some of the more enterprising of the young romantics to discover, with typical American initiative, that the centerboard was not necessarily an insuperable barrier.[3]

The changing American attitudes toward both formal and informal entertainment is apparent in the respective viewpoints of John Adams, our second president, and his son John Quincy Adams, our sixth. The elder Adams held the strict view of the Puritans; he condemned any kind of frivolity and eschewed all forms of amusement or diversion. The younger Adams, doubtless representative of the more tolerant views of his generation, enjoyed entertainment even when it was frivolous. He was a girl watcher of the first rank and even allowed himself to be coaxed into playing parlor games, including one called "pawns," a kissing cousin to a later game called "postoffice," which some of you may remember. That he played the game is clear from his diary, but that he enjoyed it is not, for he wrote of it: "Ah! what kissing! 'tis a profanation of one of the most endearing expressions of love."[4]

Although Adams soon became too occupied with his career to concern himself further with this pleasant pastime, at least publicly, it was during his lifetime that several of the more formalized types of popular entertainment became an increasingly important part of American life. For example, blackface entertainers grew more and more popular, and in the early 1840s, a wriggling, mugging quartet of blackface clowns, calling themselves the Virginia Minstrels, created what is considered the first minstrel show; it was an immediate hit. So widespread did the popularity of minstrels become that within a year a minstrel troupe performed in the White House,[5] thereby setting a precedent for such later entertainment in the White House as that magnificent magic act—Richard Nixon and his Disappearing Tapes.

Another facet of American popular entertainment that expanded greatly during Adams's lifetime was the museum. When that master showman, P. T. Barnum, bought the American Museum in 1841, he laid a solid foundation for the later dime museums that were to feature assorted freaks and other novelties. It was also during this period that the circus became an American institution as well as a European one. Circuses had been established here in the 1790s, but it was some thirty years before they combined the talents of clowns, equestrians, and menageries into one complete show, and thus started on their way to becoming one of America's favorite forms of entertainment.

What did not progress significantly during Adams's lifetime, although the seeds had been planted, were those Goliaths of American popular entertainment—vaudeville and burlesque. Parenthetically, let me say that my references to burlesque are not to the early type built around travesties of well-known plays, books, or institutions, but rather to the later sexier, and usually bluer, variety. Although popularly identified as girlie shows, they also had their share of broad comics, among whom have been some of our most beloved clowns. In a way, vaudeville and burlesque are first cousins, and I suppose one could include revue in this relationship. Not only did their formats bear a kind of family resemblance—although, as in most families there were differences—but some of our greatest entertainers moved back and forth among the three, including two of the most brilliant clowns in entertainment history—Fanny Brice and Bert Lahr—as well as such other performers as Bobby Clark, Bert Walker, Sophie Tucker, W. C. Fields, and Leon Errol, to name but a few.

The burlesque show, as we later came to know and love it, did not exist during Adams's years, although a primitive predecessor may have appeared in the last year of his life. During the 1847-1848 season, the display of the female body, clad in close-fitting tights and posing as statuary in New York variety halls, was titillating male art lovers, who, alas, were thought by some of their less understanding contemporaries to be merely theatrical voyeurs.[6] It is not one of our great national tragedies, but I cannot help but feel a small pang of regret that a former president of the United States, who had been an active and appreciative girl watcher in his youth, should have departed this world without being able to take advantage of the golden opportunity for one last watch, particularly since his youthful pastime had attained the lofty level of art appreciation.

Like burlesque, vaudeville also failed to reach a definite form during that period. In fact, it was really just taking its first steps toward its future prestigious standing as the most popular form of theatrical entertainment known in this country. The road to this exalted position was long and arduous, for in a very real sense much of vaudeville grew out of America's expansion. As the country pushed west, entertainment followed, and early vaudeville flourished in some disreputable places, its chief habitat being waterfront dives and frontier honky-tonks from the Bowery to the Barbary Coast. In many of these joints entertainment was merely a means to an end, the end being to divest the patrons of their money by the most effective expedient possible. Because most of the customers were miners, cowboys, sailors, prospectors, or adventurers, whose time was spent largely in the company of other men, it quickly became apparent that the most effective expedient was women. If they failed to cajole the customer into generosity by coquetry, they were not above plying him with liquor until he reached the point at which he could be rolled without too much difficulty.

The same dubious ethical standard applied to the traveling medicine shows and circuses, whose methods were perhaps less violent but not appreciably less unscrupulous. They, too, had an overriding passion for acquiring the customers' money and were rarely deterred by compunction. The medicine shows were extremely proficient at convincing the yokels that their health might be gravely imperiled if they did not buy the life-saving cure-alls offered as a panacea for all the known and most unknown diseases. By the time the suckers discovered the duplicity, the medicine show, of course, was long gone, leaving the patsies angry and poorer, if not always wiser.[7]

Nor did circuses suffer any qualms about gypping the customer. In addition to their unofficial sponsorship of pickpockets and other grifters, they not only permitted, but rewarded, similar questionable practices. For example, E. F. Albee, later to become czar of vaudeville, was blessed with a happy combination of qualities: industry, intelligence, eloquence, and a complete lack of conscience. This combination made him very useful to the circus that he ran off with at seventeen, and, in a short time, he became an "outside man"—a sort of combined barker-cashier in an outside ticket booth. With his glib tongue and an elastic code of ethics, he soon developed into an expert short-changer, a talent that he never allowed to get rusty, if we can believe the later claims of many vaudevillians.

It is not surprising that the multitudinous victims of this kind of chicanery developed a strong distrust, sometimes amounting to hatred, for anyone associated with the performing fraternity. Entertainers had never been great favorites of the clergy, but now they were targets of such virulent attacks from the pulpit that they became objects of abhorrence to many God-fearing men and women. It was not unusual for boarding house owners to post signs reading "no dogs or actors allowed," although some later relented and allowed dogs, presumably on the theory that they could be housebroken.

Entertainment in the honky-tonks, of course, was intended for male audiences, who were not noted for their delicacy of taste. The only women present ordinarily were those called entertainers, and since their entertainment techniques constituted a veritable encyclopedia of what every young girl should never learn, it is easy to understand the questionable moral quality of the entertainment. Part of it was very, very blue indeed—and that was the clean part. Unfortunately, the rowdy tone of honky-tonk entertainment persisted in vaudeville for a long time.

In fact, it was not until 1881 that a definite attempt was made to establish a vaudeville house that would present only clean entertainment—a real family theatre in which women and children could feel comfortable as well as men. This radical notion was conceived by Tony Pastor, and its achievement took some doing, for the long years of suspicion and fear that grew out of the honky-tonks had created a kind of apprehension that was not easy to dispel. However, through perseverance, maintenance of a decent moral tone, and especially the giving away of fine door prizes such as silk dresses, Pastor was able to attract ladies to his theatre and so create for vaudeville the image of respectability that it had never had. Once this image was established, the popularity of vaudeville grew so prodigiously that within twenty years there were some two thousand theatres around the country playing vaudeville exclusively, and attendance was estimated as about 10 to 1 over any other form of entertainment.[8] People flocked to it everywhere, seeking escape, laughs, thrills, excitement, novelty. Rarely were they disappointed, then or in the later years.

My own introduction to vaudeville occurred when I was about twelve or thirteen, and it was a case of love at first sight. I had given up my saloon-watching hobby some time before—abruptly—upon my mother's horrified discovery of it. Not altogether unreasonably, she felt that even in that mining village there ought to be some more normal avenue of entertainment open to a healthy youth. And, as was frequently the case, she was right, for it was not much later that I discovered that long-established entertainment medium—girl watching. Now it is true of girl watching, as it is of any art, that given the basic talent, the more the aspiring artist works at it, the more skillful he becomes. When I saw my first vaudeville show, I was still enough of a novice to find pleasure in watching just any old girl. Vaudeville changed all that.

As a devotee of vaudeville, as well as revue and burlesque whenever possible, I soon discovered that watching just any girl was not nearly as rewarding as watching special girls; and what better opportunity for watching special girls than in those entertainment media? What better way of improving one's girl-watching standards than by exposure to such gifted special girls as Gracie Allen, Marilyn Miller, Gypsy Rose Lee, Gladys Ahern, Eve Sully, Elsie Janis, and the Duncan sisters, to name a mere handful? and I must add, with a deep bow to burlesque, that sensational tassel twirler with the incredible control, Carrie Finnell.

Gratifying as it was, however, girl watching soon became a minor reason for attending a vaudeville house or a revue or even, though to a lesser degree, burlesque, for vaudeville and its cousins offered a potpourri of entertainment successfully designed to suit all tastes. I consider myself lucky to have been around for at least a few of their golden years. Where else could I have known such widely different styles of comedy as those displayed by Dr. Rockwell, Lou Holtz, Joe Cook, Willie Howard, Smith and Dale, Moran and Mack, Phil Silvers, Professor Lamberti, and dozens of others? all funny. Where else could I have heard the top singers and seen the top dancers of the entertainment world? Where else could I have seen Ethel Barrymore in *The Twelve Pound Look*? Or Al Mando and his lazy dog, or Dunninger, or Thurston, or Houdini, and so on almost ad infinitum? In short, where else could I have seen so many of the greatest American entertainers of their time? I cannot but agree with Marian Spitzer who, though referring specifically to The Palace, could have been speaking for the entire vaudeville family when she said, "Never in theatrical history was so much offered to so many at so little cost to them."[9]

There are those who mourn the death of the kind of entertainment provided by vaudeville, revue, and burlesque. In my judgment, such mourning is premature. Only the formal formats are gone, not the kind of entertainment and certainly not the talent. For old entertainers never die, they just move to Las Vegas or Miami or Hollywood.

Whatever changes may develop in format or milieu of presentation, popular entertainment is here to stay. Certainly some novelties will appear, but I believe that the performers and performances will remain basically the same in kind as they have been for centuries. There will continue to be the clowns, singers, dancers, jugglers, acrobats, trained animals, magicians, and all the rest, for one thing is certain: people need entertainment and they will always find it somehow. When Moses said, "Man doth not live by bread only," he knew what he was talking about.

NOTES

1. Joe Laurie, Jr., *Vaudeville* (New York: Henry Holt & Co., 1953), p. 8.

2. For a fuller discussion of early colonial recreation and amusements, see Foster Rhea Dulles, *America Learns to Play* (New York and London: D. Appleton-Century Co., 1940), ch. II.

3. T. Harry Williams, Richard N. Current, Frank Freidel, *A History of the United States* (New York: Alfred A. Knopf, 1959), I:79.

4. Quoted in Dulles, p. 46, from John Quincy Adams, *Life in a New England Town* (Boston, 1903).

5. Robert C. Toll, *On with the Show* (New York: Oxford University Press, 1976), p. 341.

6. Ibid., pp. 208, 210.

7. For an excellent account of the medicine show, read Brooks McNamara, *Step Right Up* (Garden City: Doubleday & Co., 1976).

8. John E. DiMeglio, *Vaudeville U.S.A.* (Bowling Green, Ohio: Bowling Green University Popular Press, 1973), p. 11.

9. Marian Spitzer, *The Palace* (New York: Atheneum, 1969), p. 46.

Bill Smith

Vaudeville: Entertainment of the Masses————————

My interest in vaudeville began during the last days of World War I. I was growing up in Williamsburg, Brooklyn, New York, where there were many small movie houses, all of which showed serials—one episode a week— like the *Perils of Pauline, Exploits of Elaine,* and similar hair-raisers.

Admission to some of these theatres, for kids, was two for five cents. Getting two cents was tough enough, but getting the other three was still tougher. We would stand around near the movie watching for some kid who had three cents, ready to grab him. You can imagine the competition. Once you had the three-cent partner, the next step was to talk some adult into taking you in, because you had to get around the rule "Children must be accompanied by an adult." Once inside, we would abandon the adult and rush down front.

The flu epidemic that raged at this time became an event of major interest in our lives. We all wore necklaces of camphor, onions, or garlic to ward off "germs." Theatres were ordered not to admit children—and this in the midst of our serials! The only theatre in our neighborhood that ignored the order was William Fox's Folly. It showed our serials, plus something called "vaudeville." Admission was high: ten cents, plus a one-cent war tax. The father of one of our group knew the ticket taker at the door, who either passed us in for free or at the two-for-five rate. Years later, one of my vaudeville friends told me that the ticket taker had been William Fox's father.

One day there was an announcement at the theatre that a movie actress, June Caprice, would make a personal appearance at the Folly. To us, she was a beautiful, brave heroine who faced untold dangers in her movies and always came out a winner. On the day of her appearance, we played hookey in order to get to the theatre early. We were not aware that she was not to appear until the evening. We sat through the movie three times, and finally, there she was. She smiled and said something about how happy she was to greet all her fans. We applauded and screamed enthusiastically as she exited.

Some of us dashed outside to the stage entrance to catch another glimpse of her. Finally she came out, holding a bouquet in one hand, the other hand on the arm of a middle-aged man. (He must have been twenty-five or even thirty years old.) We hated him. They got into a big car and drove off. (Years later in Hollywood, I asked about June Caprice. Nobody knew of her.)

Now we became acquainted with vaudeville. It did not matter to us that the Folly played what I later learned were "small-time" acts. To us, they were all vaudeville. Not too far from us was B. F. Keith's Bushwick where admission was twenty-five cents. I was then in high school and managed to save enough from my lunch money to go there every other week or so. It was at the Bushwick that I saw the top vaudeville acts of the day: Gallagher and Shean, Sophie Tucker, Nora Bayes, Georgie Jessel, and many others. There were the acrobats, the animal acts, dancers, comedians, singers—the whole range of performers. I never dreamed that some day I would meet and talk with many of them, or that they in time would seek me out.

Years later I often went to The Palace in New York. As a working news-paper reported, I occasionally even did an interview with some of the vaude-villians. When I joined *Billboard*, a show business trade weekly, I was assigned to cover vaudeville and night clubs. It was then that I ceased being a "civilian" and was accepted as part of show business. I no longer "saw," but "caught," acts and shows. I also discovered the meaning of "dying" and "flop sweat." I was in an agent's office when somebody said of a certain performer that he had "died in Buffalo." I made sympathetic noises. They looked at me with amazement and added, "He dies a lot of times." How-ever, my knowledge of vaudeville slang backfired. Once when I was told about an act "dying," I laughed, only to be sternly told that it was no joke. The performer had died of a heart attack. "Flop sweat" was a definition I learned from personal experience. It was my first lecture at the New School, and I was frightened. Very quickly I found myself covered with perspiration— and not because of the heat. That, I found out, was the meaning of "flop sweat."

At this time, I also joined the Friars, a social club. Its members were, in the main, in some aspect of show business, and of course many of the mem-bers were vaudevillians. It was there that I met many of the actors of whom I had once stood in awe. I heard their stories—how they had "killed them" at The Palace, even though I knew then that some of them had never really made The Palace. I met agents, bookers, and scores of actors who had played what I learned to call the "small time." I learned, too, that there was not a vaudevillian who had not been a big hit at The Palace when it was the pinnacle of the big time—at least that was the way they remembered it. Friars were not at all reticent in talking about themselves or their fellow performers and of the days when vaudeville was the mass entertainment.

As part of my job, I spent time gathering material at Lindy's, Gus & Andy's, the Gateway, and Hanson's Drug Stores. These were favorite meeting places for performers, bookers, and agents, but like vaudeville, they, too, have all disappeared.

Vaudeville was splintered into small-small time, small time, and big time. Big time meant two shows a day, reserved seats, good theatres, good dressing rooms, large orchestras, and higher salaries for performers. Small time was four to five shows a day, smaller salaries, poor dressing facilities, and less competent musical accompaniment. Living was n.s.g. (not so good). Small-small time meant five or six shows a day, even poorer salaries, and the very real danger of being stranded. Some sharp managers would hire eight acts, use them for one show, and keep only four, cancelling the others. Those dropped were not paid and just as frequently did not have enough money to pay their transportation to their next job, if any, or to maintain themselves until there was another job. Missing train connections; spending nights in unheated railroad stations; traveling in cold uncomfortable coaches for long trips; losing wardrobes, props, and music—these were all part of the apprenticeship most vaudevillians went through. They were always buoyed up by the hope that some day their act would be caught by a big-time booker, and from then on the possibilities were limitless.

Most performers came from working-class families. The head of a family who earned twenty-five dollars a week was considered a fair provider. In the 1910-1920 period, eggs cost about one cent each, bread cost five cents a loaf. Benny Rubin, a headliner in those days, stated that "if a person went into a restaurant and ordered steak, potatoes, rolls, butter, coffee, and apple pie, the bill would be about thirty-five cents. And when I brought home a half a buck won in an amateur contest we didn't go to a restaurant. That money fed our family." The earnings of a small-time actor might be as much as $100 for a week, if he worked a full week, which compared very favorably with what he might have earned as an unskilled worker or even as a skilled craftsman.

In addition, there was the adventure of traveling, living away from home, and, as the Ritz Brothers said, "It was a good way to meet girls." If you met a girl who was also a vaudevillian, you might marry and then form a double act. If there were children, they too might be included in the act. Family acts were not unusual. Some of the better known were: the Four Cohans, out of which came George M.; Red Hopper Revue, out of which came Martha Raye; and the Keaton Family, perhaps best remembered for Buster Keaton, a family member. There were many others. Husband and wife acts, which everyone is familiar with because they persisted through radio and television, were George Burns and Gracie Allen and Jack Benny and Mary Livingston.

Sister acts and brother acts were standard in vaudeville. Among others there were the Gumm Sisters, of whom Judy Garland was one; the Watson Sisters; the Dolly Sisters; and the Three Allen Sisters, one of whom was that same Gracie Allen who later married and teamed up with George Burns. One of the Ponsell Sisters graduated to the Metropolitan Opera Company— Rosa Ponsell—a world-renowned diva famed for her Carmen. Some of the brother acts that come readily to mind are the Marx Brothers, the Stroud Twins, the Ritz Brothers, the Slate Brothers, and Willie and Eugene Howard.

Amateur contests were often the door into vaudeville. Many theatres ran such contests one night a week. Families and friends would come to cheer for their favorites. Agents, always on the lookout for new talent, might offer to place them in other showplaces. That's how many began. If they developed any skills, they might advance from small-small time to the small time, and perhaps some day to the big time.

The big time was the ambition of every vaudevillian. But even if they did not achieve that, there were about 10,000 theaters or other showplaces in the United States where they might work. At its height, big time vaudeville meant The Palace in New York, the Colonial in Boston, the Majestic in Chicago, and the Orpheum in San Francisco, to name a few of the forty to fifty theatres in cities all over the country where big-time acts were to be seen.

Big-time acts traveling from theatre to theatre went first class. They lived in good hotels, ate at good restaurants, and frequently had a route that guaranteed work for three or four years before they returned to base, perhaps New York or some other large metropolitan center. There were numerous circuits, some big-time, some small-time, and some a combination of both. Among these were the Keith, Pantages, Sullivan and Considine, Martin Beck, Gus Sun, and Western Vaudeville Association, not to mention others less well known.

The big-time actor had perhaps only eight to twelve minutes on stage, twice a day. But those few minutes were the distillation of years of small-time and small-small time experience. Every word, every gesture, had been sharpened and pruned to receive the greatest attention. No producer, director, or stage manager told a vaudevillian what to do onstage, and heaven help anyone who tried to interfere.

Some actors achieved big time and then slipped back into small time. However much a blow to the acting ego, it was not a financial tragedy. There was still enough work around. If the working conditions were not on a par with those at The Palace, they were bearable, and earnings would still be in the upper three-figure bracket. It must be remembered that there was then no personal income tax, so life was not too bad.

The typical vaudevillian was not concerned with social or political changes or issues, unless he was a comedian who could use them in his routine. He knew his act as well as his routes, train schedules, the best hotels at the best prices; other matters he left to what he called "civilians"—the non-show biz people. It was not until his own working conditions and earnings were affected that he became aware of some of the social and economic changes that were creating his problems.

The behind-the-scenes rulers of the industry, of whom the public was hardly aware, were B. F. Keith (later joined by his chief aide, E. F. Albee), Percy Williams, John J. Murdock, B. F. Proctor, and Martin Beck. These titans represented big time. Keith-Albee virtually dominated the industry and resented all competition. Acts that accepted bookings outside the Keith-Albee domain would find that good routes and good jobs were seldom available in the Keith-Albee chain unless they were already major box-office attractions. To further assure its control of the vaudeville world, the Keith empire created the United Booking Office (UBO), which issued franchises to favored agents who represented the big stars and many of the standard acts. These franchises enabled agents to book their acts through the UBO, and there was no charge for this service. However, the franchise could be revoked arbitrarily by the UBO. An agent who lost his franchise was virtually out of business. Even theatres that were not part of the Keith empire found it expedient to deal with UBO because it provided a regular supply of talent plus occasional big names, and all this within a budget set by the individual theatre owner.

For the performer, the advantage of a UBO booking was the route. It covered enough theatres all over the country, arranged in a geographical progression, that would keep him busy for as long as three or four years. Most of the bookings were on big time. If some small time was included, the salaries and working conditions were equal to those on the big time; UBO guaranteed the salaries. Such routes were worth thousands of dollars, and banks would even accept them as collateral for loans.

By 1915, UBO controlled some 1,500 theatres in the United States and Canada. Keith's domain had originally extended only to Chicago. From that point to California, control was in the hands of the Western Vaudeville Association, which included Martin Beck's Orpheum chain. Keith-Albee and Martin Beck distrusted one another. However, in the interest of business and profits, they had a loose agreement that permitted UBO acts to be booked from coast to coast.

Martin Beck was an ambitious man. He was not content to stay west of Chicago forever. He had other plans. He bought property in New York City, at 47th Street and Seventh Avenue, and proceeded to build a theatre, which was to be known as The Palace. Keith was furious at this invasion of his territory. There were all sorts of clashes and financial wheelings and dealings. When the dust settled, Keith owned 75 percent of The Palace, leaving Beck with only a 25-percent share. Later, Keith bought the Beck-owned Majestic in Chicago and drove Beck out of that city, too.

Keith's acquisition of The Palace created an ironic situation. Every theatre booked by UBO had exclusive rights to Keith acts in a specifically designated area. This applied especially to large cities like New York, Chicago, and Boston, where there were many big time houses. Hammerstein's Victoria in New York, at 42nd Street and Broadway, had the right to all Keith acts from 39th to 59th Streets. Therefore, Keith could not play his own acts at the new Palace. Hammerstein forced Keith to pay him $200,000 before he would waive the exclusivity clause. The Palace opened in 1913 and within a year was the crown jewel of the Keith empire, the mecca of all vaudeville performers. When Keith died in 1914, E. F. Albee succeeded as ruler, and he ruled with an iron hand.

The first pitched battle with the actors came as the result of the formation of an actors' union, the White Rats. ("Rats" was "star" spelled backwards.) Actors had been complaining about switching of routes, sudden cancellations, and sliced salaries. A strike was called in 1916. Albee retaliated by blacklisting members of the White Rats. The strike collapsed. Albee took over the White Rats clubhouse and renamed it the National Vaudeville Artists Club, where vaudeville actors could live and eat at moderate cost. NVA members now got preferred Albee treatment: good routes, no cancellations, and increased salaries. The cancellation clause was used as a weapon. Under the new Albee plan, a performer would get paid even if cancelled. If a performer displeased Albee, he might find the cancellation clause taken out of his contract.

While the inner circle conflicts were going on, more new theatres were opening. Percy Williams opened the Orpheum in Brooklyn, challenging Albee. B. F. Proctor opened in mid-Manhattan, further enraging Albee. New acts were coming on the scene. There was the Avon Comedy Four, which later became Smith and Dale. Others came to the fore: Frank Tinney, Joe Cook, Nora Bayes, Van & Schenck, Benny Rubin, W. C. Fields, and many more.

It was also during this period—1915-1920—that Marcus Loew and William Fox began opening theatres all over the country. The Shuberts and Marc Klaw and Abe Erlanger, Broadway producers, were also entering the vaudeville field. Agent William Morris, ignoring Albee, arranged to book these new theatres. It was Morris who imported Harry Lauder and played him in the non-Keith houses. Keith promptly hit back; he blacklisted all who played for William Morris. The corporate wars did not prevent Albee from spreading. He bought a half interest in the B. S. Moss chain and acquired the huge Hippodrome on Sixth Avenue, which took in the entire block front from 43rd to 44th streets.

New interests were coming into the entertainment field. Joseph P. Kennedy (father of JFK) moved into the vaudeville business when he acquired enough Keith stock to control the company. By 1927, he arranged a merger of Radio-Keith Orpheum, Pathe, and a small film company, and the new outfit was known as the RKO Theaters.

Radio was moving up very fast as an entertainment medium. Vaudevillians who moved into radio incurred Albee's ire. He ordered that the word "radio" was not to be mentioned on his stages unless in a derogatory sense.

Talking pictures became the big thing in 1927. Many vaudeville performers, when offered a few hundred dollars to make movie shorts of their acts, grabbed the opportunity in the belief that they could use it as part of their exploitation. Warner Brothers, who produced these shorts, rented them to movie theatres at a price, thus forcing talking equipment into the theatre. Such equipment cost huge sums, and, in order to buy the new equipment, theatres cut back sharply on vaudeville or dropped it entirely and used the talking pictures instead.

Some theatres held out, including The Palace. In time, even it had to compromise—three shows instead of two a day. Then it had to drop the big-time policy and show movies and small-time acts. By the 1940s, even The Palace, once practically a synonym for big-time vaudeville, was no more. Thousands of other theatres all over the country also gave up vaudeville. It was the era of talking pictures, and the talkies were seeking actors who could "talk." It was then that Archie Leach left vaudeville to become Cary Grant of the movies. Jack Benny, who had risen to stardom in vaudeville and had made a terrific impact on radio, moved into films, as did Jimmy Cagney, once a vaudeville hoofer.

Vaudeville, as such, disappeared. In its place came what were known as the presentation theatre policy, which called for theatres of very large capacity. They used big bands, perhaps one or two acts, plus a feature movie. In New York, there were the Paramount, the Strand, the Capital, and the Roxy. All these, too, have disappeared, phased out when television, the new entertainment medium, came in.

MINSTREL SHOWS, VAUDEVILLE, AND BURLESQUE

Robert C. Toll

Show Biz in Blackface:
The Evolution of the Minstrel Show
as a Theatrical Form _____

In 1860, Frank Queen, the editor of the New York *Clipper*, the *Variety* of its day, reflected on the development of American show business. Unlike the cultural elite, Queen was neither surprised nor disappointed that the blackface minstrel show was far more popular than serious drama or opera, "the majority of people favoring mirth more than melancholy, and being more ready to laugh over the oddities of a darkie on a Virginia plantation than to weep over the solemnity of a noble Moor." Queen praised the minstrel show as "an institution of the people" that provided "real enjoyment" at "cheap prices." "In this one entertainment," he explained, "you have embodied fun, music, and mirth." "So," he concluded, "give us the Ethiopian Opera with its many pleasing features and its truly democratic associations." In 1860, Queen realized that the American public wanted inexpensive, unpretentious "fun, music, and mirth." He was even more astute in observing that the blackface minstrel show was an "institution of the people" with "truly democratic associations."[1]

Performed by white men in blackface makeup, the minstrel show was the first uniquely American entertainment form. And it was much more than just a show. It was no accident that when slavery and race threatened to tear American apart, white men blacked up their faces and literally acted out images of black people that satisfied great masses of white Americans— especially in the North, where early minstrel shows were most popular. It was also no accident that after the Civil War, when white America made crucial decisions about the rights and status of black people, the blackface minstrel show dominated American show business. There were, then, deepseated racial and sociological reasons for the popularity and longevity of the minstrel show.[2]

But to be as successful as it was for as long as it was, the minstrel show above all had to be a good show. And as a pioneering entertainment form in the infancy of American show business, it set many enduring patterns

and precedents. This paper traces the major stages in the evolution of blackface entertainment in America and notes some of its major innovations and
impacts. It began in the 1820s as little more than an incidental novelty in other
shows. But it proved so popular that in the 1840s it developed into a fledgling
entertainment form that worked out its form, features, and material on stage
through give and take with its rowdy audiences. As times changed, so did
the minstrel show. In the late nineteenth century, it grew more and more
like its new vaudeville and musical comedy competitors. Ultimately, these
other forms absorbed the minstrel show, and blackface entertainment ended
as it began—as just a part of other shows. But in the course of learning to
please the American public for over fifty years, minstrels created a distinctive
entertainment form while they pioneered many of the techniques and features
of American show business.

After 1820, America's first urban population explosion produced masses
of entertainment-hungry working people. When promoters began to cater
to this vast potential audience, show business developed. By the 1840s, the
new audiences of boisterous common people were beginning to get the fun,
music, and mirth they wanted. There were touring one-ring circuses, P. T.
Barnum's American Museum, and popular plays with American common
people as heroes. Between the acts of *every* play, there were short variety
shows of songs, dances, comedy, and novelties.[3] These variety performers
drew heavily on American folklore for material with popular appeal. So, it
is no surprise that the unique culture of black Americans became a regular
feature of these between-act variety shows. The only surprise may be that
the performers were white men wearing burnt-cork makeup. But before the
Civil War, black people were rarely allowed on the popular stage, just as they
were rarely allowed in white hotels, restaurants, courthouses, or cemeteries.[4]

In the 1820s, blackface acts became so popular that some white performers
specialized totally in what they called "Ethiopian delineation." Around 1828,
Thomas D. Rice, a typical blackface performer, saw a crippled black worker,
doing an unusual dance and singing a song with the refrain:

> Weel about, and turn about
> And do jis so;
> Eb-ry time I weel about
> I jump Jim Crow.

Rice learned the black man's song and dance, copied his crippled, hobbled
movements, wrote new verses, bought a black man's shabby clothes, and
tried out his new blackface act. He was an immediate hit and was soon
"Jumping Jim Crow" to a standing-room-only crowd in New York's Bowery
Theatre and creating a sensation in London. The "Jim Crow" song and dance
made Rice the first big blackface star.[5] Spurred on by Rice's phenomenal
success, many white entertainers took to blackface song, dance, and comedy,
which grew in popularity throughout the 1830s. But until the 1840s, black-

face entertainment still remained just one feature in a broad variety format.

In the winter of 1842-1843, four successful Ethiopian delineators found themselves out of work in New York City. In desperation, they staged the first full show of blackface entertainment. They obviously had no idea of founding an entertainment institution. But the Virginia Minstrels, as they billed themselves, caused a popular sensation.[6] When other blackface performers joined together to exploit the new craze, the minstrel show was born. Soon there were minstrel shows almost everywhere, from New Orleans to New England, from the California gold fields to the White House. For decades, the American public could not get enough of this new American entertainment form. But what form did the early minstrel show take?

For nearly a decade after 1843, minstrel shows were in an experimental stage where they were many *different* things. Shows ranged from two to four parts and varied greatly in their features and tone. Some minstrel troupes, like the Ethiopian Serenaders, specialized in musically serious concerts of sentimental, melodic popular music; others, like the Virginia Minstrels, stressed folksy music and earthy comedy; and still others, like the Ethiopian Minstrels, featured popular dance.[7] These early four- to five-man troupes were still little more than makeshift coalitions of individual performers doing their own routines. Few early minstrel troupes expanded their personnel and repertoires to create diverse, balanced shows. There was no need to. To put it in business terms, in the mid-1840s, the demand for popular music, comedy, and dance far exceeded the supply. In the 1850s, then, one of the minstrel show's few certain common denominators was its blackface makeup.

Besides the social meanings of white men blacking up when slavery and race were central public issues, minstrels' burnt-cork makeup was also a powerful theatrical device, one with striking visual impact and with very important theatrical functions. At first, minstrels may well have used the blackface to add realism to their acts, just as they used black people's clothing. But minstrel burnt cork, like clown-white, was basically a theatrical mask. To be certain that their audiences understood that the blackface was an artifice, early minstrels worked hard to establish that they were Caucasians, not Negroes. Many early troupes did the first part of their shows without burnt-cork makeup, and many early sheet music covers and posters contrasted the minstrels in and out of their makeup and costumes.[8] So, at the same time that audiences could believe minstrels' caricatures of blacks, they could also, on another level, understand that the minstrel show was an unthreatening white man's charade. The blackface mask allowed performers, and perhaps also their patrons, to cast off their inhibitions and to play out their fantasies of themselves in their stereotypes of blacks. The use of a seemingly harmless theatrical mask made this possible. It also meant that the blackface mask, which was shaped by whites' psychological needs, would outlive the minstrel show itself.

This early minstrel sheet music made clear to naive audiences that minstrels were white men. Courtesy of Harvard Theatre Collection.

By the early 1850s, with minstrel competition increasing, minstrelsy settled into a basic three-part structure. The Christy Minstrels led the way by combining all of early minstrelsy's appeals, by expanding the size of the troupe to eight to ten members, and by developing new features. The first part of the standard show opened with an exciting upbeat song and dance with the singing, strutting minstrels waving their arms and banging their tambourines. When the dignified man in the middle, the interlocutor, finally ordered "Gentlemen be seated!," the troupe sat down in a semicircle. The interlocutor, who spoke in precise, if pompous, English, was a master-of-ceremonies who introduced each act. He was an onstage director who controlled the pace of the show, while also acting as a straight man for the comedians who sat on the ends of the semicircle. The comic endmen, called Tambo and Bones for the tambourine and the bone rhythm clackers they played, used flashy clothes, extreme makeup, and malaprop-ladden dialects to portray caricatures of ignorant, wisecracking blacks.[9] The contrasting roles of the endmen and the interlocutor were themselves evidence that the minstrel show was becoming a structured entertainment form. In early minstrel shows, any performer might play any part.[10] But as the shows grew more elaborate and complex, the need for a regular emcee and for definite comic roles became obvious, and specialization began.

Interspersed with the comic sparring between the raucous endmen and the dignified interlocutor, the first part of the minstrel show blended handsome tenors singing sentimental ballads and love songs, satiric lectures on topics like women's rights, hit songs like Stephen Foster's "Oh, Susanna!" or "Old Folks at Home," and dances that ranged from the forerunner of the soft shoe to fast-tapping jigs. The minstrel's first part closed as it opened—with a rousing group song and dance, like Foster's "Camptown Races."

After intermission, the curtain rose for the second part, the olio, in which individual acts performed in front of a drop curtain. As actress and lecturer Olive Logan observed, the olio might include "banjoists; men with performing dogs or monkeys; Hottentot overtures; . . . song and dance men; the water-melon man; persons who play upon penny whistles, combs, Jew's-harps, bagpipes, quills, [or] their fingers—individuals, in fact, who do every thing by turns, but nothing long."[11] Included in this fast-paced, diverse variety show was minstrelsy's most distinctive new feature—serious female impersonation—another sign that minstrelsy was a distinctive, innovative entertainment form. As the major purveyors of popular music in the age of romanticism, minstrels performed many songs that expressed tender sentiments and emotions that American culture considered unmanly. By the late 1840s, male minstrels, like George Christy, the greatest star of the Christy Minstrels, regularly donned women's clothing to portray attractive, coquettish young women. These convincing female illusions were so popular that most minstrel troupes featured them. But female impersonation was just one of the many roles played by versatile early minstrels like George Christy, who was also a singer, dancer, comedian, and writer. In their small troupes, early minstrels had to play many parts. But in the 1860s, specialists, like Francis Leon, took over female impersonation and other featured roles when a second generation of professional minstrels emerged.[12] Such accomplished specialists made the olios into truly top-notch blackface variety shows.

The third part of the standard minstrel show was a skit blending songs, dances, and comedy. In early minstrelsy, this was usually a stereotyped plantation scene, replete with banjo tunes, dancing "darkies," and sentimental songs about the joys of life in the land of cotton, the most famous of which was "Dixie." By the mid-1840s, the closing skits were often slapstick parodies of current events or entertainment hits, like Wood's Minstrels' "new serio-comico-tragico-melodramatical negro version of Macbeth."[13]

THE SAN FRANCISCO MINSTRELS, CORNER OF TWENTY-NINTH STREET AND BROADWAY.

This advertisement reveals the growing size and the diverse appeals of a famous minstrel troupe of the 1860s and 1870s. Courtesy of Harvard Theatre Collection.

The standard minstrel format was, then, a varied evening of entertainment that set many enduring precedents. The first part—the part that now seems most distinctively minstrel—was essentially an ensemble musical and comedy show held together by the presence of the entire cast on stage, by the opening and closing group numbers, and by the comic banter between endmen and interlocutor. The interlocutor's role as comic master-of-ceremonies and the endmen's slapstick comedy and rapid-fire verbal humor were later perfected in vaudeville, burlesque, and radio. The second part, the olio, was a variety show that set the pattern for vaudeville, where female impersonation also flourished in the careers of men like Julian Eltinge.[14] The third part, the skit, contained the seeds of burlesque, as parody, not as strip-tease. The closing skit also suggested the blend of plot, comedy, music, and dance that later jelled in musicals. Minstrels, then, learned what the American people liked in popular entertainment, lessons that popular performers and producers have followed ever since. They also learned that they had to change with the times.

After the Civil War, minstrels faced serious new entertainment competition from variety shows, musicals, and burlesque. They were also challenged in their specialty when large numbers of black people first broke into American show business as minstrels. White minstrels responded to these challenges by making many fundamental changes, changes that symbolized the general development of American show business and of American society. To broaden their potential audience and to avoid urban competitors, major minstrel troupes began to travel extensively into the heartland. To enhance their appeal, they continued to increase the size of their companies, to expand their olios, and to stage more lavish production numbers. To avoid black competitors, they moved away from plantation and black material. By the turn of the twentieth century, minstrelsy was almost completely transformed. It went from small troupes concentrating on portrayals of blacks to huge companies staging opulent extravaganzas with little black material, from resident troupes with a Northeastern, urban base to national traveling companies whose strength was in the Midwest and the South.[15]

J. H. Haverly, the greatest minstrel promoter, led this transformation. In 1878, Haverly observed that minstrel shows had changed little, while other entertainment forms were greatly expanding the size and the appeal of their productions. Haverly realized that late-nineteenth-century Americans loved grandeur and opulence. It was in this period that circuses mushroomed from one-ring variety shows into three-ring extravaganzas. It was in this period that lavishly produced musicals emerged with gorgeous sets, incredible special effects, beautiful chorus girls, and huge casts. To meet such threats, Haverly combined four ten-man minstrel troupes into one huge new company that he called "The Biggest and Best in the World." "Forty-40-Count-'Em-40-Forty—Haverly's United Mastodon Minstrels," he ballyhooed.

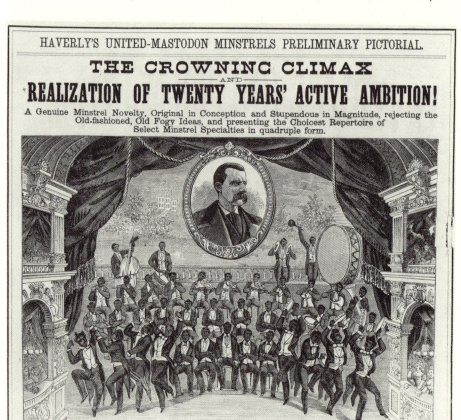

This advertisement shows the inflated size and rhetoric of the Haverly United Mastodon Minstrels. Courtesy of Harvard Theatre Collection.

"Forty is a magical and historical number," boasted one of his ads. "In the time of Noah it rained forty days and nights. The children of Israel wandered forty years in the wilderness. Haverly's famous forty are just as important."[16]

Surprisingly, Haverly's productions almost equaled his rhetoric. The long first part of an 1880 Mastodon show included songs, dances, a skit poking fun at the police, and the comedy of eight endmen. The second part of the show featured a "magnificent scene representing a Turkish Barbaric Palace in Silver and Gold." The production included minstrels dressed as Turkish soldiers, a dance contest in the palace, and a series of tableaux including "The Strong Defending the Weak," "The Dying Athlete," and

The final refinements of the Primrose and West Minstrels removed minstrelsy far from its folk origins. Courtesy of Harvard Theatre Collection.

"Base-Ball." The olio also featured instrumentalists, "Burlesque Amateur Skaters," a comic ventriloquist, and "The Picnic," a parody of a popular musical comedy. And this was not all! The show closed with a burlesque of P. T. Barnum's circus that featured a "glittering Pageant" with "magnificent costumes," "gorgeous effects," bareback riders, tightrope walkers, clowns, gymnasts, and men in elephant costumes.[17] Such productions were certainly a far cry from the early minstrels' small, simple, plantation-oriented shows.

The minstrel troupes led by the song-and-dance team of George Primrose and Billy West took the final step in the evolution of the minstrel show. "We were looking for novelty," recalled George Thatcher of his innovative years with Primrose and West, "and for a change tried white minstrelsy" with the cast in "Shakespearean costumes." One of thei shows, for example, opened with the cast wearing no blackface and dressed in the "court dress of the fops and beaux of the early nineteenth century." The troupe was a hit with such productions and with frothy skits on non-controversial subjects like education, bicycle riding, yacht racing, and lawn parties—just the sorts of things that earlier minstrels would have satirized. But these were not satires. With their formula of inoffensive material, lavish productions, and light-hearted songs and dances, Primrose and West became "The Millionaires of Minstrelsy."[18] But they also brought minstrel shows to a point where they were distinguished from other popular musical and variety shows by little more than name.

Despite these changes, late-nineteenth-century audiences still frequently saw old-fashioned, plantation minstrel shows. But by the mid-1870s these shows were the province of the many black performers who first broke into show business as minstrels.[19] As white minstrels continually moved closer to vaudeville and musical comedy, black minstrels assumed the old, stereo-typed plantation roles—the *only* roles open to them. The great contrast between Haverly's white United Mastodons and Haverly's Colored Minstrels, the greatest black troupe, clearly reveals this basic split in minstrelsy. Instead of the Mastodon's silver and gold Turkish palace and parody of Barnum's circus, the Haverly Colored Minstrels featured "THE DARKY AS HE IS AT HOME, DARKY LIFE IN THE CORNFIELD, CANEBRAKE, BARNYARD, AND ON THE LEVEE AND FLATBOAT."[20] Haverly warned the public not to compare his refined white Mastodons to his untutored Colored Minstrels. "The efforts of these much-abused and uneducated sons and daughters of Ethiopia are," he explained, "but the spontaneous outbursts of nature's gifts . . . presented to show what the negroes do . . . at home on the plantation." The black minstrels were, he claimed, "natural children of bondage" whose stereotyped plantation material he called "truthful to nature."[21] In short, Haverly presented the white Mastodons as the most sophisticated professional entertainers in America, while he presented his black performers, not as entertainers, but as black folks doing what came naturally, as representative plantation blacks put on exhibit—like animals in a zoo.

In the late nineteenth century, major changes in society produced major changes in show business. With the reunification of the North and the South, public interest and concern shifted away from minstrelsy's central topics—from the South and plantations to industrial and urban problems, from blacks to the heavy influx of immigrants from southern and eastern Europe. Black minstrels were locked into portraying blacks, but white minstrels adapted their material to these changes as well as they could. Their black-face makeup obviously limited the effectiveness of their portrayals of immigrants.[22] And they lost their identity as minstrels if they discarded their burnt cork and semicircle. Even though minstrel troupes survived well into the twentieth century, the minstrel show as a popular entertainment form was doomed. Through stars like Al Jolson, Eddie Cantor, and Bert Williams, the blackface act became just one of the many features in vaudeville, musical comedy, and revues.

Show biz in blackface had come full cycle. In the 1820s, it began as just one feature in a broad variety format. A century later, it was in the same position. But in between it had developed into a full-fledged entertainment form that pioneered many of the features and techniques of American show business. Over the years, its form and content changed in response to changes in public interest and taste. When it could no longer adapt, it was absorbed into other, more flexible entertainment forms. But it did not really die. It left many entertainment legacies to other forms of show business, and it left its stereotypes of blacks: the happy, shuffling "darky," the loyal, loving Mammy, Old Uncle, the lazy good-for-nothing, and the flashy city slicker. Like the Cheshire Cat in the topsy-turvy world through the looking glass, the blackface minstrel show, long after it disappeared, left its central image— the grinning black mask—deeply embedded in American popular culture and in American consciousness.

NOTES

1. New York *Clipper*, November 10, 1860 and December 15, 1860.
2. For detailed analyses and interpretations of the minstrel show, early black performers, and the development of American show business, see Robert C. Toll, *Blacking Up: The Minstrel Show in Nineteenth-Century America* (New York, 1974) and *On with the Show: The First Century of Show Business in America* (New York, 1976).
3. Toll, *Blacking Up*, ch. 1 and *On with the Show*, ch. 1.
4. Leon Litwack, *North of Slavery* (Chicago, 1961).
5. For details of Rice's career, see Carl Wittke, *Tambo and Bones* (Durham, N.C., 1930), pp. 20-33; Hans Nathan, *Dan Emmett and the Rise of Early Negro Minstrelsy* (Norman, Okla., 1962), pp. 62-66.
6. Nathan, *Dan Emmett*, pp. 143-58.
7. See programs and playbills for these and other early minstrel troupes in the Harvard Theatre Collection (HTC) and the Theatre Collection, New York Public Library at Lincoln Center (NYLC).
8. "Nigger Minstrelsy," *Living Age* (February 12, 1862), p. 398; representative of such sheet music was "Songs of the Virginia Serenaders," Boston, 1844.
9. For more detail on the features of the standard minstrel show, see Toll, *Blacking Up*, pp. 52-57.
10. Nathan, *Dan Emmett*, p. 129.
11. Olive Logan, "The Ancestry of Brudder Bones," *Harper's*, vol. LVIII (1879), 693.
12. Toll, *Blacking Up*, pp. 139-45, and *On with the Show*, ch. 9.
13. George C. D. Odell, *Annals of the New York Stage*, 15 vols. (New York, 1927-49), VI: 172.
14. Toll, *On with the Show*, pp. 246-53.
15. This transformation is detailed in Toll, *Blacking Up*, chp. 5.

16. Haverly's United Mastodon Minstrels, n.p., 1878, playbill, HTC; New York *Clipper*, Sept. 6, 1879.

17. Haverly's United Mastodon Minstrels, Jersey City, New Jersey, January 3, 1880; and Providence Opera House, March 1880, programs, NYLC.

18. "Interview with George Thatcher," n.p., March 11, 1906, clipping, HTC; Thatcher, Primrose and West Minstrels, programs, NYLC; New York *Clipper*, August 13, 1887; "How Burnt Cork Pays," Boston, 1882, clipping, Boston Public Library.

19. The careers, experiences, and performances of black minstrels are detailed in Toll, *Blacking Up*, chs. 7 and 8.

20. New York *Clipper*, September 6, 1879, and August 7, 1880.

21. *Haverly's Colored Minstrel Libretto* (London, July 1880).

22. Toll, *Blacking Up*, ch. 6.

Paul Antonie Distler

Ethnic Comedy in Vaudeville
and Burlesque —————————————————

Fat, furious, and not a' little foolish, Mike—the little man in the garish,
padded suit with the elk's tooth watchchain spanning his vest—is beside
himself with rage, his stubby goatlike beard quivering with indignation.

"Vhat kindt ov logick iss dot? Idt dondt make no sense, Meyer."

Lean and unctuous, a *schnunbart* also sprouting from his chin, Meyer
prods his rotund victim at arm's length with fingers that would have bruised
the chest but for the cotton batting that comprises most of Mike's prodigious
girth. Verbally, Meyer presses the little man with gutteral suavity and as-
surance.

"Py gollies, idt's as clear as der nose on your face."

To emphasize his point, Meyer twists Mike's nose with a vengeance.
Howling in mock pain, Mike tries to return the favor with a blow or two to
Meyer's midsection, but his shorter arms flail helplessly shy of their mark as
Meyer still holds him firmly at arm's length. Undaunted, Mike rejoins the
argument.

"Idt dondt make no sense. You aindt no politickaler. Der aindt no vay
dot you could know idt dot Harrizon vould beadt Clevelandt in der elecgshion
for prezident!"

Maintaining his physical and mental control over his pudgy adversary,
Meyer continues his assault with more firmness than before.

"Vhat no vay? Ass ve came acrossdt der coundtry, I kebpt dtelling you
dot Harrizon vould vin. Evveryvhere ve schtopped, der vere der panners
zaying Harrizon, Harrizon, Harrizon. Efferyvhere der panners—Harrizon."

Sure now that he has broken through the defense of Meyer, Mike gleams
with the visions of imminent victory within grasp.

"Yah, der vere panners for Harrizon, Meyer; panners vere efferyvhere for
him. Budt, panners dondt vote."

Facing the beaming Mike who senses that, for once, he will get the better
of the argument, Meyer smiles with wicked disdain and delivers the *coup de
grace.*

Joe Weber and Lew Fields in a Mike and Meyer
Double Dutch Act. Courtesy of Theatre
Collection, New York Public Library, Astor,
Lenox, Tilden Foundation.

"Shure, panners dondt vote. Budt, dey shure do show vhich vay der windt
is plowing."

Victory snatched from him, the beleagured Mike wails and tries to strike
a blow for all little men, but this physical assault just opens the door for
Meyer to pummel and jostle him offstage as the audience laughs, applauds,
and waits in anticipation for the final line they know will come when Mike
and Meyer reach the wings.

"Dondt poosh me, Meyer!"

More applause and curtain, the double act of Weber and Fields as Mike
and Meyer is over, and the San Francisco audience of 1888 settles back for
the lyric soprano performing "In One."[1]

A continent away and some four years later, a lanky figure ambles onto
the stage of Tony Pastor's 14th Street Theatre in New York City and eases
himself comfortably into a chair awaiting him in center stage. Although he
often forgoes a special costume in favor of dark, everyday dress, tonight the
figure is garbed in hob-nailed boots, rough trousers, an open shirt, a green

vest, and a soft cap atop a head and face that are adorned with a bristly, red beard that wreathes his face from ear to ear.

The audience is familiar with his work and settles back for another monologue from J. W. Kelly, the Rolling Mill Man.

Now, its aisy enough to get a drink with money, but to get a drink without money—now that's where ye show your superiority over your fellowman. Don't go into a bar-room with a sort of a hope-I-don't-intrude air and say to the bartender: "It's a cold morning this morning," bekase the minute ye go in there with your surething weather tips, he's got your number. Do the way I do. Walk up boldly to the bar and say: "Gimme a little liquor out of that black bottle." Now, back of every bar there are two bottles containing liquor. They're both alike, only one's a little worse than the other. No matter which one he offers ye, don't touch it. Stand back with an injured air and say: "I asked for a little liquor out of that black bottle." Then ye take the bottle and pour out a nice moderate-sized drink. About two fingers. [Here, Kelly would extend his hand with the first and little finger separated.] Now, at the end of every bar there is a receptacle containing cloves and spices. Ye select a clove, and whilst ye stand there munching on your clove and feeling in your pocket for the money, which ye haven't got, ye look out the door and suddenly cry: "Great Hivins, there goes me trolley car," and dash out the door. Always close the door after ye, bekase no sane bartender is going to throw a heavy beer mallet through a plate glass door. And be sure ye catch that car—no matter whether its going uptown or downtown—that's your car.[2]

Had some of the audience who heard J. W. Kelly at Tony Pastor's in 1892 been visiting Chicago some ten years later, they might have encountered a very different sort of monologist—Julian Rose, playing his way east from success on the Orpheum circuit and soon to attempt the jump from variety to legitimate theatre in Al. H. Woods's 1905 comedy-melodrama, *Fast Life in New York*. In contrast to the relaxed, folksy Kelly, Rose is fidgety and nimble as he shuffles his way on stage dressed in oversized shoes, a baggy black coat, a derby pushed down on his head to the top of his ears, and his face featuring a scraggly, unkempt beard and some putty on the nose.

The audience is familiar with this type of comic, and they attune their ears to what they know will be a dialect monologue concerning events among an immigrant group in Lower-East-Side New York. They are not disappointed.

Well, I guess Abe's lucky, now he's married. I'd like to do it, too; but every time I fall in love with a girl, I find she ain't got money. So what can I do? One thing I didn't like about Abe's wedding was right away it said at the top of the invitation: "Your presents is requested." They can't wait to let you know you must help pay the expenses. And down at the bottom was: "Please come in evening dress." Ikey Blatt wore his pajamas.

The groom had it a new suit, made for his brother when the brother got married. When Abe sat down, it stood up. His gift from the bride was a fine watch, Swiss cheese movement.

Inside that little hot room everybody was crying, except big fat Mrs. Bloom. She perspired. Mrs. Bauman was dressed to kill; but no wonder, her husband's a butcher. The four little Wolffs were there, and, oi, how they did eat! Now I know why it is always said keep the wolfs away from the door.

We had so much to eat I was a stuffer. First we had menu, but I didn't get any of that; I guess they ran out of it early. Then was tomato surprise. But it was no surprise to me, I ate 'em before lots of times. Irving Blatt emptied a whole bottle pickled onions in his pockets. He thought they were camphor balls.

I had to go outside, on account I couldn't stand any more. I was under a table so long, almost to suffocation. Outdoors I met my old friend Lepinsky. I invited him to take a little drink, and he said sure, so we went across the street. He put in five cents, I put in five cents, and together we had a good time.

We stepped across the room to the free lunch, and there was a roast chicken just put on the table. Lepinsky grabbed the whole chicken by the neck and brought it to our table.

"Lepinsky," I said, "You can't have that chicken all alone to eat."

"You're right," he says, "I'll go back to the table and get some potatoes to go with it."[3]

Acknowledging the applause as the orchestra plays him off at the end of his turn, Julian Rose shuffles into the wings knowing that another of his Levinsky stories, *Levinsky at the Wedding*, can be added to his repertory.

However brief and incomplete their presentation here, these samples from the work of Weber and Fields, J. W. Kelly, and Julian Rose are representative of a type of humor that was the mainstay of vaudeville and burlesque during the late nineteenth and early twentieth centuries—ethnic comedy. Whether performed with a German, an Irish, or a Yiddish accent (with a sprinkling of other ethnic or national types thrown in for seasoning), ethnic or racial comedy acts reigned supreme for some three decades—roughly, 1875 to 1905—as the dominant comedic force in variety entertainment. No vaudeville bill, no burlesque would have been complete without the inclusion of at least one ethnic comedy turn.[4]

Though the racial comics gradually fell from sight in the early years of this century, a portion of their comedic appeal—the dialect gag—continued on variety stages, in films, and on radio and television, even until the present. But whatever success later dialect comedians may have had working purely with the verbal twists of the foreign accents, they pale in comparison to the fulsome, robust, and three-dimensional character creations of such racial comics as Joe Weber and Lew Fields, John T. Kelly, Sam Bernard, Barney Bernard, Joseph T. Ryan, J. W. Kelly, Maggie Cline, Joseph Kline Emmett, the Russell Brothers, Julian Rose, Ned Harrigan and Tony Hart, Gus Williams, Cliff Gordon, and Dave Warfield.[5]

Central to the comedic appeal of the ethnic comics was their creation of total characters based on the generally accepted prototypes of the millions upon millions of European immigrants who flooded the United States in the middle and later years of the nineteenth century. And it is with these immigrants that we must begin in attempting to understand the unique quality of the ethnic comedy of vaudeville and burlesque.

Politics, potatoes, and pogroms would seem to have little to do with the American variety scene; yet, this unlikely trio was primarily responsible for the massive influx of immigrants to the United States in the Atlantic migration of the 1850s and 1860s and the Slavic migration of the 1890s—the two migrations that brought the dominant immigrant groups of Germans, Irish, and Jews to these shores.[6]

In Ireland, a series of successive potato crop failures in the late 1840s brought about a situation in which famine stalked the populace, killing through starvation and disease. The fortunate Irish who were relatively untouched by the famines were soon deprived of their land and property through laws passed by the British Parliament that were avowedly to aid the ravaged country. Those peasants, laborers, and small landowners who were financially able rushed to emigrate to the utopia across the ocean. Though they sought farmland, most never traveled farther than the point of debarkation and entered the American lifestream as laborers and servant girls.

Germany also suffered from the potato famines of the 1840s, and many of the German immigrants fled the formerly rich farmlands of Bavaria to seek new lands in America. As well, various of the German cantons and duchies were in states of political upheaval, provoked primarily by the intelligentsia—the upper middle class and the university students. Quick to stem the calls for democratic or republican government, the rulers of these palatinates used such repressive measures that a second stream of German immigrants joined the farmers in their flight to America. Most settled in the East and the Midwest.

The third of the prototypes, the immigrant Jews, were the victims of a combination of political pressures and outright pogroms in Russia and neighboring eastern European countries in the 1880s. Primarily small tradesmen and shopkeepers from urban areas, these persons fled their homelands when economic and religious sanctions made life virtually unbearable. Though many found new homes in western Europe, most emigrated to the United States and established themselves in their former trades as shopkeepers and peddlers in the major eastern cities, most notably New York.

So, in these two major waves of immigration that have never been equaled in size or impact, somewhere in the neighborhood of ten million Irish, Germans, and Jews poured into the United States to confront a confounded and slightly overwhelmed native American population. These immigrants were, in a phrase, in prominent high relief, and the comedians of the developing vaudeville and burlesque scenes seized upon them as readily identifiable and as rich raw material with which to mold comic characters.

For some writers on ethnic comedy, the development of the immigrant prototypes into vaudeville and burlesque characters is viewed as archetypal of the comedic impulse to conquer the unknown by assimilating it through laughter. Put rather simplistically, the line of logic is as follows: here are all of these alien people; they speak strangely and dress oddly; I wish they were not here; since they obviously will not leave, I will create a special niche for them in my social sphere; I will transform them into a medium with which I am familiar, the variety stage; thus, I will assimilate them into my culture.

Other ethnic comedy theorists posit that the immigrant burlesques were created in fulfillment of another, though not unrelated, archetypal comedic impulse—that of aggression. Again, simplistically stated: the aliens are here; they will not go away; I will make them funny and make fun of them; if I can laugh at them, then I can conquer them, and they cannot harm me. Still other writers propose other theories, and in all of them, as well as in the two just mentioned, there is probably much validity.[7]

But overriding all comedic theories is the very simple proposition that the primary, the seminal humorous instinct in American culture was, has been, and still is the creation of comedy through exaggeration. All writers of and about the history and current status of American humor agree on this single point, from Mark Twain to Constance Rourke to Art Buchwald.

Exaggeration is a simple method of creating comedy, but it is effective. In his book, *Enjoyment of Laughter,* Max Eastman puts it this way:

> The easiest way to make things laughable is to exaggerate to the point of absurdity their salient traits. It requires no more ingenuity than is possessed by the multiplication table, and it does not matter whether the traits are good or bad. The laughing mirrors show how mathematical this kind of humor can be, and the mocking bird how unintentional.[8]

The ethnic comics utilized any and all of the act and sketch formats standard in vaudeville and burlesque; but at the heart of them all were the fully developed, individualized immigrant figures created through exaggeration of such recognizable traits as mode of dress, style of head and facial hair, usual occupations, generalized qualities of character or demeanor, and, of course, dialect.

One of the greatest of the Dutch comics, Sam Bernard, recounts in a 1920 interview one way in which the ethnic comics viewed and utilized these general traits ascribed to the various immigrant prototypes.

> To me, the funniest thing in New York at that time [late 1870s and early 1880s] was the German-American. He was a pompous, weighty, slow-thinking citi-

zen. Through American influence he had fallen under the spell of a prosperous sign peculiar to that period. It was the spell of the two-pound chain attached to a five-pound watch. The chain stretched like a huge cable across the mountainous expanse of his colored vest. He always preferred the outdoors, and was generally found standing on the rear platform of the streetcar. When spread out he became a bulwark for the passengers wedged near him. He was a joy and inspiration to me.

Riding on a car one day, squeezed into an obscure corner, I saw a man snatch a German's watch and hop off the car. The chain hung down straight. I waited leisurely for the climax of the drama. The German emerged slowly from his usual somnolence. He emitted various gutteral sounds, half-finished sentences, clipped words in an effort to articulate his feelings. Obviously his mind was functioning. Anger and explanations were incumbent, but no one could understand what he was saying. Finally, he looked sadly at the chain and said: "Dis ist der zecondt vatch I haf lost dis veek!"

That night in the joke factory I gave an imitation of this perplexed German, inarticulate, yet outraged. With variations, I have been doing the same ever since.[9]

David Warfield in one of his many Jewish comic characterizations. Courtesy of Theatre Collection, New York Public Library, Astor, Lenox, Tilden Foundation.

For the Russell Brothers, the prototype was transformed into a raucous knockabout act, *The Irish Servant Girls*; for Dave Warfield, a series of Jewish peddlers; for Weber and Fields, the Mike and Meyer Double Dutch Act; for Joseph T. Ryan, the irascible (yet lovable) hod-carrier, Mike Haggerty, in the series of sketches he did with his wife, Mary Richfield; for Joe Welch, the woe-be-gone Jewish merchant who was constantly wheezing— "Und I vished dot I vas dead"; and for Pat Rooney, the singing and clogging Irish laborer.

Whatever the ethnic type chosen, whatever traits of dress, character, occupation, or dialect emphasized, or whatever the degree of exaggeration exacted, the result was always a full-fleshed comic character creation based squarely on the immigrant prototype. And while the ethnic comics reigned, they had no peers in audience popularity.

But all reigns must end, and the ethnic comics faded from vaudeville and burlesque in the early years of the twentieth century, when the immigrants upon whom they patterned so closely their creations either died or became assimilated into the mainstream of American society, when glorified vaude-

Pat Rooney as an archetypal Irish comic.
Courtesy of Theatre Collection, New York
Public Library, Astor, Lenox, Tilden Foundation.

ville and burlesque showed preference to the straight, stand-up comedian, when musical comedy began to develop sophisticated libretti, and when the sons and daughters found the exaggerations of their immigrant parents a form of ridicule.

As indicated earlier, however, some vestiges of this broad and wholesome type of humor did continue in vaudeville and burlesque, in the films, and in the electronic media. Without the immigrant prototype, though, much of the three-dimensional quality and character of the humor was missing, as it had to be.

Every now and again, however, it's nice to slip into a nostalgic mood and imagine, through the mind's eye and ear, that one is at Kostar and Bial's or Minor's Bowery as that feuding twosome, Mike and Meyer, greet each other with their inevitable:

"I'm delightfulness to meedt you."
"Der disguzt ist all mine."

NOTES

1. This routine is extrapolated from the set-up and snapper lines as quoted in Felix Isman, *Weber and Fields* (New York: Boni and Liveright, 1924), p. 148. In addition to charting the major work of Weber and Fields as Dutch comics, Isman's book provides a good account of all the varieties of ethnic comedy that constituted the backbone of the burlesque comedy as purveyed at the Weber and Fields Music Hall—the citadel of ethnic comedy in the late nineteenth and early twentieth centuries.

2. Cited in Robert J. Conkey, *Conkey's One-to-Fill* (Chicago: R. Conkey, 1929), p. 44.

3. This is ony a portion of the full routine as printed in the *Los Angeles Examiner*, October 24, 1915. Rose was blackballed by the Keith-Albee United Booking Office in 1911 and played small-time vaudeville until 1921, when he went to Great Britain. He was an immediate success there and remained a headliner (often playing the Palladium) until his death in 1935.

4. In addition to such standard books as Douglas Gilbert, *American Vaudeville* (New York: Whittlesey House division of McGraw-Hill Co., Inc., 1944) and Joe Laurie, Jr., *Vaudeville* (New York: Henry Holt and Company, 1953), much of the importance of ethnic comedy can be substantiated through the pages of the *New York Dramatic Mirror*, I (January 4, 1879) through LXXXV (April 29, 1922).

5. Joe Weber and Lew Fields have been chronicled in the earlier-mentioned book by Felix Isman, and the work of Ned Harrigan and Tony Hart has been brought to life in E. J. Kahn, Jr., *The Merry Partners* (New York: Random House, 1955). Sketches of the work and lives of these two teams and the other ethnic comics cited are included in the author's doctoral dissertation at the Tulane University Library, New Orleans, Louisiana, or University Microfilms, Ann Arbor, Michigan, 1963.

6. For the best account of this monumental migration, see Marcus Lee Hansen, *The Atlantic Migration* (Cambridge: Harvard University Press, 1940), pp. 243-306. Also, good short summaries of this immigration deluge are found in Arthur Charles Cole, *The Irrepressible Conflict* (New York: The Macmillan Co., 1934), p. 120 ff., and in Maldwyn Allen Jones, *American Immigration* (Chicago: University of Chicago Press, 1960), pp. 109-11.

7. Among many comedic theorists, the following speak persuasively to the concepts of assimilation and aggression: Martin Grotjahn, *Beyond Laughter* (New York: McGraw-Hill Book Co., Inc., 1957) and Albert Rapp, *The Origins of Wit and Humor* (New York: E. P. Dutton and Co., Inc., 1951).

8. Max Eastman, *Enjoyment of Laughter* (New York: Simon and Schuster, 1936), p. 156.

9. Sam Bernard, interview in the *Boston Traveler*, June 18, 1920.

Ralph G. Allen

At My Mother's Knee
(and Other Low Joints)_____

First, a brief autobiographical note. When I first began collecting burlesque material in 1962, someone from the Associated Press interviewed me. I told him, which was true, that my mother first took me to the theatre. In the published story, he reported that my mother first took me to burlesque shows, which was not true, but she received letters from all over the country accusing her of being a corrupting influence on my life. My mother was not amused because as she well knew, and as I now publicly admit, I corrupted myself.

I began going to burlesque shows in the later 1940s, as soon as I was old enough to reach up to the counter and pay my fifty cents (Q: How did you get in here? A: On my brother's ticket. Q: Where's your brother; A: Outside looking for his ticket.) My theatres were the Troc in Philadelphia and the Globe in Atlantic City. And by the time I became a fan, the great days were over. I never saw Columbia Burlesque or Mutual Burlesque, but some of the talented comics were still around when I first became a patron—Billy Hagan and Bert Carr, Bob Ferguson and Billy Foster. I found them irresistible. There were still choruses in burlesque in those days, and while everything seemed a little hand-me-down, there remained at least the memory of a more glorious entertainment.

There were thirty-five shows on the Mutual circuit in 1926, and when I was asked to do a paper about the enthusiasms of my misspent youth, I thought at first that I might try to reconstruct one of those shows for you. Then I had a better idea. Why not create a quintessential burlesque show out of authentic materials?—a show of shows as I have played it so often in the theatre of my mind. After all, in a theatre of the mind nothing ever disappoints. The comedians are always brilliant and witty, and the girls are beautiful—which was sometimes not the case in the Majestic, Wilkes Barre or the Garrick, St. Louis or the Mayfair, Dayton.

I propose to call our entertainment *The New Bowery Follies and Lyceum*

Gardens Revue. Mutual burlesque shows had titles like *The Broadway Belles* or *The Moonlight Maids*, but our entertainment, being the essence of all such entertainments, should have a generic name. After Miner's and the London closed, there were no big-time burlesque shows on the Bowery, but there should have been. So we will let the word "Bowery" represent in our title all the tenderloins in all the cities where burlesque flourished, from Boston to Des Moines. Bowery means Eighth and Race streets in Philadelphia, where the Bijou stood for many years. It means Scollay Square in Boston, where the Casino and the Old Howard flourished during the Depression. It means Ninth and Chester streets in Cleveland, and Liberty Avenue in Pittsburgh, and Washington and Bradford streets in Newark, and South Main Street in Buffalo—all those shabby thoroughfares that were brightened by a Palace or an Athenaeum or a Lyceum Garden of Delights.

Outside the theatre is a poster:

BILLY "CHEESE AND CRACKERS" HAGAN
[or] BERT CARR
[or] BOB FERGUSON
[or] HARCOURT and FOSTER in

That Peppery Burlesque Extravaganza

THE NEW BOWERY FOLLIES
AND LYCEUM GARDENS REVUE

With a Jolly Company of High Steppers and
Merry Twirlers

Including that Powder Puff of Melody ANNA TOEBE
[or] HINDA WASSU
[or] ROSITA ROYCE and her Dance of the Doves

And of course Those Tempting Toe-Tappers

THE BELLES OF THE LYCEUM

Every GIRL a STAR in her own RIGHT!!!

Inside the lobby are posters for coming attractions. (Next Week "The Dimpled Darlings of 1927" or "Jack Reid's Record Breakers" or "The Speed Girls of 1926.") Also, there is a refreshment stand, not to mention a second ticket booth where exchanges can be made for seats in the first three rows.

The theatre itself is freshly painted, but the curtain has seen better days. There is no runway. This is pre-Minsky, and the Minsky brothers were the first impresarios in burlesque to experiment with a thrust stage.

Opening

The overture is brief. A few bars of "Ain't She Sweet," perhaps, played by Merrick Valenote and his Merry Notes or Harry "Lips" Ross and his Gayety Syncopaters.

The curtain is raised to reveal eight girls dressed in historical costumes—that is to say, wide paniers and Marie Antoinette wigs. A few simple conventions suffice in burlesque. Any historical period, except ancient Greece and Rome, is represented by wide paniers and Marie Antoinette wigs. To our surprise, the girls seem to be what the press agents used to call "a demure vision of loveliness" in their pink satin frocks. The Merry Notes begin a very chaste rendition of "Humoresque," to which the girls sing the following words:

> We are girls of some allure, sir,
> Dainty damsels and demure, sir,
> We are modesty personified.
>
> Other follies to be sure, sir,
> Have some girls who aren't so pure, sir,
> Girls who show what decency should hide.
>
> And gentlemen who crave sensation
> Sometimes yield to Base Temptation
> Praising what, in fact, they should deride.
>
> But you, as men of cultivation,
> Always greet with approbation
> Shows where truth and beauty are allied.

During the break-strain, an elegant gavotte is performed—or what passes for a gavotte. The girls never play in profile, but always keep their smiling faces fixed at some point in the center of the house.

> Truth and Beauty
> Are enshrined here.
> You'll never find here
> Tasteless display.
>
> Art and Culture
> In full measure,
> Innocent pleasure,
> Nothing risqué.

Is this a ballet or a burlesque show? Step right toe, step left toe, left heel, kick. Step right toe, buree backward five times, skirts up, skirts down. On it goes: arabesque three times, arms in first, arms in second, arms in third. Back to the first theme.

We have made some brief excursions
To competitive diversions;
Virtue blushed, then hung her head and cried.

Though far from us to cast aspersions,
Sure as there are Greeks and Persians,
We couldn't be suggestive if we tried.

All the girls walk straight toward the audience.

We couldn't be suggestive if we tried. *(bump)*
We couldn't be suggestive if we tried. *(turn around)*

Lo and behold! The demure costumes have no backs. The girls are wearing only a red heart pasted rakishly to an exquisitely bare buttock. Blackout.

Flirtation Scene in One

A few bars of a signature tune, perhaps "The World Is Waiting for the Sunrise." Lights up on a street drop. No *Bibiena scena per angolo* here. Rigid, one-point perspective. City landscape with ice wagon and parked cars.

The appearance of the street drop signals to the audience that it is about to witness a "flirtation scene," a short, single-joke situation played in one by the second comic, the straight man, and a talking woman or two. (The first comic never appears in the opening scene of the first act.)

In a typical flirtation scene, the straight man (an immaculately dressed authority figure) has a secret method for succeeding with women. He may own a manual of seduction *(The Love Book)* or a magic peanut which emits stimulating vapors ("The Tweeter or King Tut's Nut"). Or he may simply be such a smooth talker that women find him irresistible ("The Ukulele Scene"). He promises to teach his technique to the comic whose approaches to the opposite sex have not been notably successful.

Comic: Do you smoke?
Girl: I don't know.   I never get that hot.
           ("Poppy Poppy" as played by Billy Fields)

Comic: I beg your pardon.
Girl: What the hell are you begging for? You're old enough to ask for it.
           ("The Ukulele" as played by Billy Hagan)

Habitués and (as the candy butcher might say) sons of habitués know these jokes, but knowledge in no way diminishes enjoyment. Bergson notwithstanding, surprise is not one of the essentials of burlesque humor. Patrons enjoyed knowing that no new ground would be broken. Like Aristotle, they preferred irony to suspense.

In most flirtation scenes, the comic eventually blunders into some kind of dubious success. Burlesque comedy, you see, is seldom pathetic, and clowns like Hagan and Foster and Ferguson never belonged to the tearful school of Chaplin. Elsewhere I describe the stock character of the baggy-pants comic as follows:

In most bits he [the comic] is represented as a child of nature—the slave of stimulus and response. A girl with obvious attractions appears. He is obviously attracted. The straight man, in attempting to demonstrate lovemaking techniques to the comic, starts massaging the latter's stomach, and the comic forgets about the girl and kisses the straight man. The Burlesque show tramp represents man stripped of his inhibitions, stripped of restraints of all kinds, free of moral pretense, innocent of education, and, above all, lazy and selfish. . . . We root for the comic . . . but [our] emotions are definitely not engaged. We want him to win because all of us (with part of our minds, at least) are anxious to see authority toppled. The burlesque show appeals to our inner passion for anarchy.[1]

But why is anarchy never threatening in the great burlesque scenes, as it is, say, in Jarry or Ionesco? I can offer one explanation. In burlesque, as distinct from other forms of absurdist humor, the celebration of disorder is contained in an orderly, indeed, a highly conventional structure. No answer to a question is unpredictable. We love the jokes we know. They reassure us, and therefore the earth does not yawn at our feet.

Back to *The New Bowery Follies*. Each aficionado has his favorite. Mine is "The St. James Infirmary." Why? Well, consider this classic exchange, which occurs at the beginning of the scene, between the comic and a lubricious widow who happens to cross his path.

(enter SOUBRETTE dressed in black, from left proscenium)

Girl: Boo hoo, boo hoo.
Comic: What's the matter, dear?
Girl: My husband just died. My husband just died.
Comic: Well, you're a beautiful girl. You'll get a new husband tomorrow.
Girl: But what am I going to do tonight?
Comic (taken aback, but recovering quickly): Well, I'm a husband out of work. What did your husband die of?
Girl (grinding): He died of in - flu - enza.
Comic: I'm a little hard of hearing. Would you mind saying that again.
Girl (grinding): He died of in - flu - enza.
Comic: Your husband didn't die of influenza.
Girl: Oh, no?
Comic: You bumped him off. And while you're at it, bury him again.
                                                          (version of Maxie Furman)

And on goes the scene to a predictable conclusion.

Tough Number

Blackout. Lights up on yet another cityscape, this one a night scene with a lamppost center stage. The audience immediately recognizes that it is about to see the "tough number." It is not surprised when the chorus appears, swinging pocketbooks, and the soubrette, accompanied by The Merry Notes, sings "Louisville Lou." ("What lips, some pips, and no more conscience than a snake has hips.")

A dance by the soubrette follows—one that is calculated to curl the ticket of the most jaded habitué.

Body Scene

A few bars of the signature tune again. Lights up. It is time for the first of several "body scenes," the name given by burlesque people to bits that use a full stage set, special costumes and properties, and a cast that includes at least two comedians, a straight man, a character man, perhaps a juvenile (who does fag comedy), and several talking women.

We have a wide variety of body scenes to choose from. "Julius Squeezer," which features "Cleopatra and her Snapping Asp," is always reliable. And there are hotel scenes, courtroom scenes, restaurant scenes, schoolroom scenes—to mention just a few of the more familiar types.

The origin of these stock scenes is obscure. Many of them are based on what burlesquers called "nigger acts," that is to say, minstrel show afterpieces. They are like the *sogetti* of the *commedia dell'arte*—an outline of the action into which each comic put his own personality, his own business, his own jokes. Of course, there were standard *lazzi* to draw upon and *concetti*, too.

In hotel scenes, the following lines were sure to occur:

Comic: Give me a room.
Straight (as room clerk): Do you want a three-dollar room or a five-dollar room?
Comic: What's the difference?
Straight: The three-dollar room has a rat trap. The five-dollar room has a rat trap with cheese.
Comic: Give me the three-dollar room. I'm not hungry.
Woman (entering in an agitated manner): Clerk, clerk, I gotta leak in my bathtub.
Straight: Well, lady, you paid for the room.
            (a noise next door)
Comic: What's that?
Straight: Oh, upstairs they're holding an Elks ball.
Comic: No wonder the damn thing is screaming.

A restaurant scene might include the following exchange:

Straight (a customer, ordering from menu): I'd like chicken soup.
Comic (as waiter, calling to kitchen): One chicken soup.
Chef (offstage, from kitchen): One chicken soup coming up.
Straight: On second thought I think I'd like pea soup instead.
Comic (calling to kitchen): Hold that chicken and make it pea.

Many scenes have street vendors—either ice cream salesmen or balloon hawkers or candy butchers.

Straight (to Comic selling candy): Do you have nuts?
Comic: No.
Straight: Do you have dates?
Comic: If I had nuts, I'd have dates.

Domestic disagreements are common in burlesque:

Wife: You only married me for one thing.
Comic: And I soon got tired of that.
Wife: When you married me, you said you worshipped the ground I walk on.
Comic: Well, I thought your father owned that piece of property. Anyway, you can't cook.
Wife: What's the matter with my cooking?
Comic: You can't make coffee.
Wife: What's wrong with my coffee?
Comic: Your coffee tastes like water.
Wife: I'll have you know when I make coffee, I make coffee; and when I make water, I make water.
Comic: Next time, don't make them in the same pot.*

Courtroom bits are, of course, the most humorous of all the body scenes. There are at least fifteen basic ones, all deriving, according to Billy Hagan, from an old minstrel show afterpiece called "Irish Justice." In most of the scenes the judge is the comic. He is invariably addressed again and again by the straight man (a district attorney) as "Your horseship," until finally in exasperation he snaps, "That will be enough horseship out of you."
My favorite judge scene is "The Westfall Murder Case," in which a beautiful society woman is accused of shooting her husband at the breakfast table. The finish of this scene is inspired:

Comic (Judge): Tell me, Mrs. Breastfall, just where did you shoot your husband?
Mrs. Westfall: I shot him between the buttered toast and the cream pitcher.
Comic: It could have been worse.
Straight (D.A.): It could?

*As you may recall, this time-honored joke appears in slightly altered form in the first chapter of James Joyce's *Ulysses.*

Comic: Yes, if she'd shot him two inches lower . . .
Straight: Yes?
Comic: She'd have caught him right in the percolator.

Justice is blind in these scenes and sometimes also has other infirmities:

Straight (D.A.): Stand on your dignity, judge.
Comic: It won't reach down that far.

Other Numbers in the First Act; Also Specialties and Added Attractions

  After the first body scene, there is another chorus number, perhaps in front of a Hawaiian drop, with the girls in grass skirts and coconut shell bras.

  Chorus numbers usually alternated with scenes, and the numbers sometimes led to specialties by the prima donna or the soubrette. A fan dance is a sine qua non of nearly all 1920s burlesque shows, and *The Bowery Follies* would not be complete without one. We must also have two legitimate vaudeville acts (perhaps a dance team or tumblers, but never adagio dancers). There should also be an "Extra Added Attraction," perhaps a boxer who challenges the audience to survive three rounds with him "inside the squared circle." Jack Johnson toured for a season on the Mutual Wheel, but I doubt if we could persuade Muhammad Ali to do likewise.

The Finale of the First Act

  After the final body scene of the first act, the orchestra plays a fanfare, and the straight man now dressed in a tuxedo appears in front of the first traveler:

Ladies and gentlemen, before the Lyceum Belles return for the finale of the first act, let me remind you of the attractions which are scheduled for this theatre in the coming year. On January 18, Harry Gallagher will return with his peppy revue Speed Girls of 1929. Mr. Gallagher promises that his show this year is tasteful and amusing. He assures us that the problems of last season are past and forgotten.

Now ladies and gentlemen, here is your favorite tenor, Bod Ridley, supported by the distaff members of our cast, in a horticultural display that celebrates at once the beauties of the American garden and the glories of the American girl.

  Enter the tenor (the juvenile), also dressed in a tuxedo. He sings the chorus of that celebrated ballad, "The Garden of Girls." ("All the world is just a beautiful garden/ Each pretty girl is a flower blooming there . . .") The first traveler opens to reveal the prima donna dressed as a butterfly. She dances on point in front of the second traveler, which soon parts to reveal four Lyceum Belles dressed as blossoms of variegated hue. Their heads are hidden by outsized petals.

The tenor serenades each flower in turn. First, to the rose he sings, "Marta, Rambling Rose of the Wildwood." The straight man then presents her to the audience with an appropriate literary allusion. Perhaps he says something like this:

Straight: No garden is a garden without a rose, and our own blushing rose, Miss Lisa Feather, by any other name would smell as sweet.

At the mention of her name, the petals part, and the girl within the flower accepts her applause.

The tenor next serenades the tulip ("Tulip Time"), and the straight man counters with an even more recondite allusion, one perhaps invented for the occasion.

Straight: When the great Catullus told a gentle youth to press the blushing tulips to his maytime bosom, could he, by any chance, have meant the two lips of our own Miss Andrea Delight.

The iris is next ("Iris, I'm kneeling at your feet"), and the straight man seems not quite sure what kind of iris is meant:

Straight: The great poet Tennyson once said: "In the spring a lively iris changes on the burnished dove,
In the spring a young man's fancy lightly turns to thoughts of love."
The poet must have been referring to our own lively iris, Miss Pepper Ross.

The morning glory ("Fairest of flowers, sweetest on the vine") is introduced and saluted with some poignant lines:

Straight: When John Keats wrote, "The blue bared its eternal bosom and made the morning precious," he could have been describing our own precious glory of the morning, Miss Mitzi Malone.

The word "bosom," needless to say, receives the heaviest emphasis.

Only the daisy remains. The tenor sings, "Daisies won't tell." Surprise! this final flower is no chorus girl at all, but the thick-stemmed character man. He is suddenly surrounded by the ponies in the chorus dressed as bees. The bees and the daisy sing a duet ("Be My Little Baby Bumblebee"); a parade of insects and flowers follows. The curtain falls on a tableau, and the straight man reminds the audience that this is "not the end of the show, simply a brief pause for refreshments."

The Candy Butcher

The interval is graced by the presence of a familiar figure in shows of this sort—the candy butcher, whose *spiel*, like everything else in burlesque, follows time-honored conventions.

It begins with the description of a big combination offer:

Candy Butcher: Ladies and gentlemen, may I have your attention please? You have approximately seven minutes before we continue our big burlesque revue. You won't want to miss the first number in the second act, which is called the "Dance of the Virgins," performed by our lovely Lyceum Belles, strictly from memory.

Now to while away the time during the brief pause in the entertainment, you may feel the need of some nourishment, something to munch on, something to provide refreshment. I have here a box of chewy, delicious chocolates, manufactured especially for the patrons of this theatre by the Lofty Candy Company of St. Louis. Now, a box of chocolates such as this would cost a dollar in any confectionary establishment—and you would consider those chocolates cheap at the price.

We're not charging a dollar, ladies and gentlemen. Not fifty cents. A quarter is our price, and that quarter entitles you to more than candy. You buy the chewy delicious chocolates, and you receive absolutely free all the items in our big combination offer.

He takes from his tray a magazine and waves it in front of the audience. His hand hides the title at the top of the page.

Candy Butcher: Part one of our big combination offer is a little booklet entitled *The Gentleman's Home Companion and Theatrical Digest*. This little booklet has been banned on all newsstands, but the authorities, realizing that an audience attending a theatre of this type is apt to be a bit more broad-minded than the average audience, have given us permission not to sell it, but to give it away as part one of our big combination offer.

Let me call your attention to page four of this little booklet. On page four you will find a story entitled "Love Below the Border." This story is about a girl named Mexico Rita who lives in a town just south of the Rio Grande—a town which promises more than its share of exotic amusements and foreign delights. One of those foreign delights is Mexico Rita herself. People from all over come to watch her play with her castanets. The hair-raising adventures of this provocative lady are sure to arouse and stimulate the interest of the most jaded reader of unusual fiction.

Now he puts the magazine back in his tray and holds up a small black pasteboard square.

Candy Butcher: Now part two of our big combination offer is this little novelty item
imported directly from Paris, France.

I have in my hands what appears to be an ordinary square of black paper.
But this is no ordinary square of black paper. You take this paper home,
you soak it in vinegar, you hold it up to the light, and you will see sights
that will amaze and astound you.

What you will see, of course, is soggy black paper. The candy butcher
has assistants who work the aisles, hawking the merchandise while he keeps
up a running patter from the stage. After a few minutes, he calls his salesmen
down front.

Candy Butcher: Stop the sales, boys. Stop the sales. I don't know what's the matter
with me tonight. I must be getting forgetful in my old age. I forgot the
most important part of our big combination offer.

Concealed in some of the boxes of chewy delicious chocolates is a selection of big bonus gifts. You buy the candy and may receive either a twenty-
dollar bill, the key to a Ford automobile, a season pass to this theatre, a
lady's alligator-style wallet, a gold-plated pen and pencil set, or a deluxe
smoking article.

They start selling again. After a few minutes of purposeful confusion, the
candy butcher again signals for silence.

Candy Butcher: Stop the sales, boys! Stop the sales! Well, ladies and gentlemen,
you've been very generous and to show my gratitude, I'm going to do
something very unusual, something that I've never done before. Tell me,
Harry, are the managers in the house? No? Good! To tell the truth, ladies
and gentlemen, the producers of this show aren't always as generous as I
would—well, enough of that. Let me just say that what I'm doing now could
get me in trouble. *(Sizes them up.)* You all look pretty discreet to me, so I'm
going to risk it. Now, I want all my salesmen to put aside the boxes which
do *not* contain one of the big bonus gifts. *(One of the salesmen protests.)*
No, Harry, I'm going to do it, and nothing you can say will change my
mind. Is it done, boys? Have you put to one side everything except the
bonus boxes? Good!

Now, ladies and gentlemen, the boys will make one more pass among
you. You buy the chewy delicious chocolates for one quarter, and you get
not only the booklet and the novelty items from Paris, France, but you
must also receive either a twenty-dollar bill, a season pass to this theatre,
the key to a Ford automobile, a lady's alligator-style wallet, a gold-plated
pen and pencil set, or a deluxe brand new smoking article. And thank you
for your attention.

He exits. Suddenly the lights dim; the orchestra begins a brief second-act overture, and the asbestos curtain is raised. A quick escape for the candy butcher before his customers have a chance to examine their newly acquired alligator-style wallets and/or smoking articles.

Numbers and Scenes in the Second Act

As you can see from the examples I have cited, burlesque eschewed novelty. Every patron of long-standing knew that when the straight man asked, "Are you getting a little on the side," that the comic would reply, "I didn't know they moved it." Nor was there any doubt that when the comic said, "I took my girl fishing," and the straight man asked, "Did you catch anything?" the comic would reply, "I certainly hope not."

In an uncertain world, burlesque gave to airy nothing a local habitation and a name:

Straight: Did you know that in Venice the streets are filled with water?
Comic: You should see some of the alleys in Youngstown [or Camden or Dayton or Baltimore or wherever the comic happened to be]!

No surprises here. Nor in the chorus number that begins the second act: an "audience number" hoary with tradition.

The girls sing "Put Your Arms Around Me, Honey" or any song with a similar invitation. The soubrette stays on the stage, reflecting light on the heads of the older patrons, while the chorus runs energetically into the house. There, the girls sit on appropriate laps and eventually return to the stage after much ad-lib adjusting of bras and squeals of simulated embarrassment.

The second act of a burlesque show is very short, only half an hour or so. Therefore there is room for two scenes only, one more chorus number (perhaps a harem dance), a specialty number by the prima donna, and the finale.

One of the scenes might well be "The School Room," which was much favored as a second-act opener by Mutual Wheel comedians. In the schoolroom, the talking woman is a tough teacher who administers pedagogical justice by hitting her five charges (the two comics, the character man, the ingenue, and the soubrette) with a rolled up newspaper. The scene concludes with a notable English lesson:

Teacher: Tell me, Jimmy, what's the difference between prose and poetry?
Comic: Gee, I don't know, teach.
Teacher: Poetry rhymes and prose doesn't.
Comic: Is that so?
Teacher: Yes. If I were to say:
      The girl went round the mulberry bush

        And I went round to meet her,
        That little girl will never know
        How glad I was to greet her.
Comic: What's that?
Teacher: That's poetry, because it rhymes.
Comic: Meet her—greet her. I see.
Teacher: But if I were to say:
        The girl went round the mulberry bush
        And I went round to meet her,
        That little girl will never know
        How glad I was that day.
Comic: What's that?
Teacher: That's prose. Because it doesn't rhyme.
Comic: I could do that.
Teacher: You could?
Comic: Hell, yes.
        The girl went round the mulberry bush
        And I went round to meet her
        She pulled up her petticoat
        And I pulled out my. . . .
        Now, what do you want? Prose or poetry?

An Interruption Scene

The blackout is followed by the prima donna's bubble dance, after which the straight man makes the following announcement:

Straight: Ladies and gentlemen, as you know, *The New Bowery Follies* is no ordinary palace of vulgar entertainment. We spare no expense to bring to you, our cultured patrons, distinguished and distinctive entertainment. And in keeping with the policy, we are proud to present that basso profundo of the Metropolitan Opera, Ricardo Antonio Galuppi.

The traveler parts to reveal the character man disguised as a legitimate opera star. With him is a mousey, female accompanist who sits at the piano behind him.

An arpeggio. The character man, Galuppi, begins an aria. The second comic enters dressed as a stagehand. As Galuppi sings, the comic begins to hammer on the floor.

Character: What are you doing?
2d Comic: I'm hammering.
Character: Whose idea is that?
2d Comic: That's my idea.
Character: Well, you can't hammer here. I'm singing.
2d Comic: I think they'd rather hear me hammer.

Character: If you don't stop, I'm going to get the manager to take you out.
2d Comic: I don't go out with managers.
Character: Mr. Engel, Mr. Engel.

(2d Comic exits while Character is not looking.)

Straight: What's the matter, Signior Galuppi?
Character: That man is hammering while I'm trying to sing.
Straight: Oh, yes. What man? I don't see any man. My, it's hot in here. You must be hallucinating. *(The accompanist takes off her hat and cape.)* Maybe the heat is affecting your sense of proportion. Miss King, give him an arpeggio. Pray continue, Signior Galuppi.

(He exits. 2d Comic appears in audience, hammering.)

Character: What are you doing out there?
2d Comic: I'm hammering.
Character: I told you not to hammer.
2d Comic: You told me not to hammer up there. Well, I'm hammering out here. I'm fixing seats. Does any lady want her seat fixed?

This is the beginning of "The Hammer Scene," one of the most famous of the so-called interruption scenes of burlesque. The key figure is the opera singer who will be driven mad by the entire cast before twelve minutes have elapsed. The straight man plays the manager of the theatre—sane at first, but gradually yielding to very peculiar impulses. A recurring line ("My, it's hot in here") triggers a reaction from the accompanist. She removes an article of clothing each time the heat is mentioned.

Straight: What is it now Signior Galuppi?
Character: That man is hammering again.
Straight: Really? My, it's hot in here. What man? Really, Signior Galuppi, your imagination is running away with you. *(Off comes the dress of the accompanist.)* Pray, Signior Galuppi, compose yourself, and share your magnificent voice with our discerning patrons.

(He exits.)

Character: Perhaps I'd better try another song. Miss King, "I Love Life," if you please.

(Sings "I Love Life and I Want to Live")

1st Comic (sitting in the audience): Hey fella, if you want to live, you'd better stop singing.
Character: How dare you, I'm the star of this show. Didn't you see my name up in lights?
1st Comic: Yeah, I did.
Character: What did it say?
1st Comic: Exit.
Character: Mr. Engel. Mr. Engel!

Straight (enters): My it's hot in here. *(Off comes the slip of the accompanist.)* What's the matter, now, Signior Galuppi?

Character: That man out there is insulting me.

Straight: Nonsense, we have the best behaved audience in the world.

At this point in the scene begins a series of what are called crossovers:

2d Comic (entering): Oh, why did he die? Why did he die?

Character (dazzled, he stops singing): Why did who die?

2d Comic: My wife's first husband. Why did he die? *(exits)*

Soubrette (enters): Hey, fellow, hey fellow, do you know the difference between mashed potatoes and pea soup?

Character: No.

Soubrette: Anyone can mash potatoes. *(exits)*

Prima Donna (enters, crying): I had to shoot my dog last night.

Character: Was he mad?

Prima Donna: Well, he certainly didn't enjoy it.

    (She exits.)

Juvenile (enters): Hey, fella, don't send any more letters to Washington.

Character: Why not?

Juvenile: He's dead, you know. *(exits)*

    (Arpeggio. Character sings. Ingenue enters cartwheeling.)

Character: What are you doing?

Ingenue: I'm going to stand on my head or bust.

1st Comic (enters): You'll get a better balance on your head.

Ingenue: Do you really think so? *(goes into split)*

1st Comic: Hey, don't stretch a good thing too far.

    (They exit.)

2d Comic (enters): Wait a minute. Wait a minute. Don't anyone move.

Character: What's the matter?

2d Comic: I lost my wallet?

Character: Where did you lose it?

2d Comic: Over there.

Character: Then why are you looking for it over here?

2d Comic: There's more light over here.

The scene continues in the same vein for several minutes until Galuppi again calls the manager. This time the straight man enters mincing, and to the basso profundo's surprise, he pinches Galuppi's cheek.

Straight: What is it, my dear fellow?

    (pinches cheek again)

Character: I'm nearing the end of my endurance. The most bizarre things keep happening.

Straight: Don't worry, Signior Galuppi. I've sent for a nurse. I expect her any
             moment. She'll see that you don't hurt yourself.
Nurse (enters): Here I am, Mr. Engel. I came here straight from the Sanit—I mean
             the hospital. Where is the patient?
Character: I'm no patient. I'm a singer.
Straight: You just continue to think that, Signior Galuppi. But never mind, you're
             in capable hands. This is a very clever nurse. I'll prove it to you. Oh,
             nurse.
Nurse: Yes, Mr. Engel.
Straight: How do you cure a man with erysipelas?
Nurse: You cut off his ear.
Straight: How do you cure a man with ptomaine poisoning?
Nurse: You cut off his toe.
Straight: How do you cure a man with prickly heat?
Nurse: How do you think?

By now the character man is thoroughly disconcerted. More crossovers
follow until, upon the fourth entrance of the manager, the singer notices
that his accompanist is almost naked.

Character (shocked): Mr. Engel, Mr. Engel.
Straight (entering): Here I am again, Signior Galuppi. Always at your beck and call.
             (pinches rump)
Character (shocked): Mr. Engel. Miss King, Miss King. *(noticing)* That girl is naked.
Straight (mincing more): Nonsense, Mr. Galuppi. Look at that magnificent gold
             lamé gown she's wearing. I wish I had a gown like that. Now come to
             my office, Miss King, and take off that gown. I want to wear it to the
             party tonight.

   (They exit.)

In a minute the straight man reenters to the accompaniment of the full
orchestra. He has a white rose in his mouth and he is dancing the Baltimore
strut.

Character (furious): What do you call that?
Straight: That's a new dance step. I call it "The Birth of a Rose."

   (Character pulls out gun, shoots him.)

Juvenile: What do you call that?
Character: The death of a pansy.

The Shimmy Contest

We are ready for the finale, which is announced with appropriate fanfare
by the juvenile.

Juvenile: Ladies and gentlemen, Monday [or whatever day] is chorus girl oppor-
              tunity night at the *New Bowery Follies.* Five of our delightful Lyceum
              Belles will compete for your applause, the winner to receive a year's
              contract as a featured dancer in the theatres of the Mutual Burlesque
              Association. You are the judges, ladies and gentlemen, so reserve your
              most enthusiastic approval for the girl of your choice. So, here it is, the
              first annual shimmy contest of *The New Bowery Follies and Lyceum
              Gardens Revue.*

There are six contestants, each introduced by an appropriate announcement:

Juvenile: The first of our Lyceum Belles, Miss Mizi Malone, possesses a lyric soprano
              voice of magnificent compass and clarity, having been educated for the
              grand opera. While performing her shimmy, ladies and gentlemen, Miss
              Malone will scale the heights. . . . Our second Lyceum Belle is our
              premiere danseuse, Miss April May. Miss May studied with the great-
              grand-nephew of Nijinsky, practiced her pirouettes at the Paris Opera
              and brings to the mysteries of the shimmy a rare sense of classical dignity
              and style. . . . Our third Lyceum Belle is our saucy sergeant major,
              Miss Marianne Lamour. Miss Lamour is the step-daughter of a general
              in the French Foreign Legion. She brings to her shimmy the sense of
              military precision that she learned while on maneuvers behind her
              father's parade ground.

And so it goes until the sixth girl has been introduced. This last contestant
has a wild look in her eye and, although stripping is forbidden, she is suf-
ficiently imbued with the spirit of competition to rip off her bra at the climax
of her dance, making sure, of course, that thereafter she faces demurely
upstage. Her daring awakens the spirit of emulation among her fellow contestants, and soon chaos reigns, while the straight man and juvenile rush
about in mock rage and horror as if they were desperate to restore order.
Finally, the asbestos curtain is dropped, and the straight man, wiping his
brow, silences the orchestra:

Straight: I must apologize, ladies and gentlemen, there is no question that Girl No. 6
              exceeded the bounds of decency and good taste. You will be happy to learn
              that she has been disqualified from the contest, and her applause will be
              redistributed equally among the other contestants. You have been so
              generous in your appreciation of the other girls, ladies and gentlemen,
              that we have decided to continue this contest during the remaining per-
              formances of this engagement. Cumulative applause totals will be kept,
              and the winner will be announced on the evening of December 18th [or
              whatever]. You are, of course, free to return again and again to swell the
              applause and improve the chances of the dancer of your choice. And
              here, once again, ladies and gentlemen, is the entire cast of *The New
              Bowery Follies and Lyceum Gardens Revue.*

Back the cast comes, and soon the bows are taken, and the performance is over.

Final Thoughts

In my imagination, of course, all performances are perfect; but in life, disappointments abound. I was often bored at the Gayety, Baltimore and at the Casino, Pittsburgh. But just as often I was amused, delighted, and charmed, especially when one of the great mutual comics was on the bill.

Why did I haunt those old theatres in the tenderloins? What were the virtues that I saw in this robust but vulgar style? Burlesque, or so it seems to me, charts a course between the shoals of sentiment and the rocks of cynicism and despair. Most comedy in our century is beached on the one or battered by the other. If it is not *The Goodbye Girl*, then it is likely to be *King Ubu*. If you don't want to be Mary Tyler Moore, you risk becoming one of the heroines of Megan Terry.

Personally, I'd rather be Billy "Cheese and Crackers" Hagan. I began this talk with an autobiographical note. Let me conclude with one. He was the first burlesque comic I ever saw and perhaps the best. That was thirty-years ago. He is ninety-two now, having acted until he was eighty-five.

The cunning tramp that Billy created in scenes like "Lady Lamar" and "The Dying Gladiators" and "Meet Me Round the Corner" was naive but never innocent, hard-headed but never despairing or brutal. I shall never forget him as the bewildered plumber in "The Doctor Shop," mistaken for Dr. Plummer, the eccentric heart specialist. Tools in hand, he has come to repair a leaky valve in the bathroom. Instead, he is invited to scrutinize a beautiful, nearly naked patient to see if she has a leaky heart valve. "What a break for a plumber," he says, masking his delight from the straight man, but letting all the rest of us share it.

I can still hear Billy's squeaky voice when he said that line, and the little smile that hinted at profound delight. Billy's tramp gave the rest of us hope, as did the rogues and vagabonds that Billy Foster played, and Bert Carr and Maxie Furman and the rest. Perhaps we, too, will be mistaken for a Dr. Plummer or draw five aces in a poker game, or win the favors of a luscious lady by waving a magic poppy underneath her nose. Not all our aspirations are heroic, and we should not despise those shabby comforts that sometimes lead to (threadbare) joy.

NOTE

1. "Our Native Theatre: Honky-Tonk, Minstrel Show, Burlesque," in *The American Theatre: A Sum of Its Parts*, edited by Henry B. Williams (New York: Samuel French, Inc., 1971), pp. 282-83.

Morton Minsky, Joey Faye, Judi Faye, Eleonore Treiber

Modern Burlesque [Discussions and Skits] _____

Morton Minsky, the last survivor of the Minskys, here reminisces about the Minsky burlesque empire and its ultimate demise. With his wife Judi, Joey Faye, one of its luminaries, then samples some of the famous burlesque comic routines, and Eleonore Treiber briefly illustrates the striptease, burlesque's most famous feature. This part of the program concludes with the participants answering questions by members of the Conference audience.

I am grateful to Joe Papp for having introduced a number, "What I Did for Love," in his *Chorus Line* hit. And I'm here today because I'm doing this for love, and so are the other people who are accompanying me: Joey Faye, Judi Faye, Eleonore Treiber, and our music "Professor," Dennis Buck.

When I meet people for the first time, I note the glint in their eyes while they conjure up all kinds of erotic associations that burlesque suggests, and I wonder whether they will be brave enough to ask the usual question, "Are you one of the Minskys?" Well, yes, I am one of the Minskys and this afternoon I would like to share with you some recollections of what the Minsky brothers contributed to a unique American art form, which became a cult for many of the intelligentsia of the 1920s.

The Minskys became the darlings of the columnists, writers, and artists, among whom were H. L. Mencken, Edmund Wilson, Hart Crane, Reginald Marsh, Jean Cocteau, and many others. At one time, the Minskys controlled the burlesque industry in America, shaping and influencing various theatrical forms. Today, the name is part of our country's legend.

There were four Minsky brothers. Abe, who was the oldest, could have been my dad. He was the playboy of the family, who kept going to Paris to the Folies-Bergère and coming back with ideas about such things as the belly dancer and the illuminated runway. Billy was the shrewd showman who had developed a great deal of experience working as a journalist for Mr. Pulitzer of *The World.* H. K., or Herbert, was the brother who was particularly interested in art, with his Columbia College and Columbia Law School background. He was a great lover of opera, and this led to the introduction of snatchings from opera into the Minsky shows, usually completely out of context. I, Morton Minsky, joined the trio in the early 1930s. I was publicity-minded and introduced Minsky's burlesque to varied media such as the *New Yorker* magazine, where we started a sophisticated advertising campaign, using the slogan "Not for Your Aunt from Dubuque." In those days, Minsky's was not for your Aunt from Dubuque, but that's not so today.

I am in a position where I can tell you a little bit about what made up the Minsky show in the early days. Girls, of course, beautiful girls—you saw the Reginald Marsh painting out there in the Exhibit Hall, and I believe I have a slide that we will show you. These were lovely show girls who knew their position—knew their place in the chorus. There were the mediums and there were the ponies, who were the dancers. And the dancers in the Minsky shows were *dancers*—in most other burlesque shows, the dancers had two left legs.

The comics were extremely important, and we had a very, very good ethnic mix. We had the Irish and the Dutch, the Italian, the hobo, the Yiddish, and, of course, there were the straight men who played foils for them. I'm going back many, many years. These were the comics who were responsible for the creation and development of double entendre, although a spade was often called a spade. The intellectuals of the day, Hart Crane, H. L. Mencken, Edmund Wilson, the famous columnist Bob Garland of the *Baltimore Sun,* and others, loved it. They all took on the Minskys because of this special art form that had been created.

And I must tell you also about the outlandish features of Minsky's that made up this great appeal. If Mr. Ziegfeld, across the street, were doing a tableau with an elephant, with a gal sitting on this elephant, with her tresses flowing, with her bosoms exposed, we, at the Republic Theatre on 42nd Street, used a horse on a treadmill with *two* girls on the horse, one at the back and one at the front, to impress upon the people that we were completely up to date and modern in our approach. The show titles were extremely important. There were weekly conferences at which titles were developed, and these appeared in the newspaper advertising and on the theatre marquees. Some examples: *From Bed to Worse, Anatomy and Cleopatra, Julius Teaser, Panties Inferno, Mind over Mattress, Sway of All Flesh.*

I am going to call on the booth now to project a few slides. Our time is rather limited, and we have so much coming up in this wonderful little unit today that I don't want to deprive any of these people of the fun. This was the typical interior of the Minsky Theatre with the plushes, the gilt on the boxes, and bald heads up front. No. 2, please. We copied and stole where we could. You recognize the author? No. 3. The gal had layers and this—oh, this precedes Minsky—layers of clothing over a union suit: very, very

National Winter Garden Lobby

demure. The next, please. A typical chorus, 1917 at Minsky's National Winter Garden, and you see that the setting is a hotel lobby, and there are the keys—and what would you do in a hotel in those days? Next, please. This is a young lady who found it very, very difficult to smile, but she managed somehow: rather modest. Next, please. Rose Gordon, one of the famous beauties, who at times did a bit of the choreography. Next, please. This is Curls Mason, really a very serious-minded young lady, who played with dolls. Next, please. We move a little further forward in time, and that is one of the beauties who was in the chorus for the Republic Theatre. Next, please.

Curls Mason, 1926

Another beauty with the French motif, and she used French perfume. Next, please. This is a typical three-part strip; the stage manager had instructions to cancel the contract immediately and pay the ladies in full if they took off any more than that. Next, please. Typical of the Minsky tableau, where the costuming was extremely important. Next, please. This is a comedy scene; the usual routine: the comic and the policeman and the gal who is being bothered. Next, please. Backstage—(this is by Vanveen). You notice the panties on the girls: they never disrobed completely. Next, please. These are typical rules: no spitting on stage, no relatives, no dogs, and no ad-libbed dialogues without permission. (That's a warning that Joey Faye is coming on soon.) Next, please. The Minskys actually originated the "twofers," and here you see a season pass signed courtesy H. K. Minsky, on a copy of a racetrack pass. These were sent to doctors with a personal perfumed note signed "Lily." The doctors' wives kept calling, asking, "Who is Lily?" Next, please. This is a typical Minsky program, and, as you see, it's tantalizing. Next, please. *Swing Baby Swing,* that's a show with Phil Silvers and many others now famous. Next, please. This was the demise, a slide taken from the movie *The Night They Raided Minsky's.* This was a sad day for the intellectuals and the hoi polloi.

Panel Discussion and Skits

JOEY FAYE, JUDI FAYE, and ELEONORE TREIBER;
MORTON MINSKY, *Moderator*

(Girl): Oh, Mr. Minsky. You are Mr. Minsky, aren't you? This is Mr. Minsky? *(Minsky):* What is it you want? *(Girl):* Oh, Mr. Minsky, I've heard about your love-making. *(Minsky):* Oh, it's nothing. *(Girl):* That's what I've heard.

(Minsky): Judi, Judi, will you come on please? Come on, Judi. This is Judi Faye, our very talented young lady, who happens to be fortunate enough to be married to Joey Faye. Judi, would you please sit down over there? The next thing I must talk about. . . . I have to keep watching that clock. It's twelve minutes to one, and we're racing against time. I hope that we can finish by 1:30 because one of our performers has to leave at about 1:10. What's going to happen next? Anyway, "Professor," will you give us just a little interlude? *(piano music)*

(Joey enters, holding a mirror.): Oh, no, no, no! It can't be! No, no, this is terrible! This is terrible, this is awful! I can't stand it! Oh, this is the worst, oh, this is terrible! *(Minsky):* What's the matter? *(Joey):* What's the matter? Look in that mirror. *(holding it up to Mr. Minsky)* What do you see? *(Minsky):* I see me. *(Joey):* Oh, thank God, I thought it was me. *(Minsky):* I'm turning the stage over to Joey, and if you don't mind, Dennis, will you help us move this lectern a bit? We have to act as our own stage hands. *(Joey):* Oh, by the way, I was going to be funny for a few minutes, but Mr. Allen used all my jokes, so I might as well leave *(as he moves the lectern, which is heavy)*. Oh God, I think I hurt myself! All right. Now.

Joey Faye

I'm not gonna tell you a lot of jokes, you'll only laugh at them. I don't know where to start. First of all, I started with the Minskys in burlesque. I was a kid. My mother used to bring me into the theatre. My father, when he heard I wanted to go into burlesque, started to holler. "A gentleman of the theatre," he said, "if you want to go into the theatre, go into the legitimate, go into opera, go into something dignified, not burlesque. In fact, don't even walk into a burlesque show. You're liable to see something you shouldn't see." Well, being a kid, naturally this aroused my curiosity. So, the next day I snuck into a burlesque theatre and I found out my father was right. I saw something I shouldn't see. I saw my father seated right in front of me.

My mother, a little Italian woman, when she heard that, she became hysterical. She wanted a doctor, a lawyer. She heard I was going to be an actor in burlesque. She took me into the living room—and it wasn't even a funeral or a wedding!—and said, "Oh, my poor son, he's gonna go into burlesque. My son, with the dirty parties and the orgies and the drinking and the chorus girls. My son!" And my father in the back, saying: "Take me!! Take me!"

First of all, I have collected, before it became popular, a lot of sketches. I also wrote quite a number of sketches. You may remember "The Barretts of Flugel Street" or one of the big shows that Mr. Minsky left out, "Tillie Pipik from Peru," one of the shows I was in. Billy Minsky, Morton's brother, hired me for $25 a week as fifth banana—I used to stand outside the burley house and watch the dogs nibble at my billing—and he also gave me a couple of extra dollars because I was a thief. Let me explain. I used to go to all the shows, the revues, the *First Little Show*, the *Second Little Show*, and all the vaudeville shows, and I would *steal!* You know, I had a great memory, I'd steal complete sketches. And I'd take these sketches and do them up in the Catskills—the borscht circuit.

Now I had all these sketches, and when I came to the Minskys, Billy says, "Have you a sketch you can. . . ?" I say, "How about this?" He says, "Oh, that's great. We'll put that in." I said, "But that's from the *First Little Show*." He said, "Shhhh, don't tell me!" So I got some extra money for putting on. . . . Let me explain about the Minskys. They were really honorable men. We'd put on a new scene on Friday. Now somebody from the Shuberts, from George White, anybody, would come in and they see it—it's their scene. Now, they'd sue! But by the time the Minskys got the summons, it was Monday or Tuesday. Billy says, "Don't worry, because by Thursday the scene is out anyway. New show every week."

It was a theatrical concentration camp. Every comic had to do four, five scenes every week. Now, to put on those four, five scenes, you had to suggest two hundred scenes. Now, let's say the top comic is Red Marshall. The producer, who was also the choreographer, he's gonna save Red Marshall, his first banana—he's not going to let a fifth banana put on a classic scene. He wants to save the best scenes for Red Marshall. Now, if Red does a court-room scene, and you're a newcomer coming in, you're never gonna get a top routine on, because you say, "Hey, how about doing *Under the Bed?*" "Oh no," he says, "We did that two months ago." "Well how about doing. . . ?" He still says "no." Before you know it, you have to suggest about two hundred scenes. You wind up like a new comic.

You always do a flirtation scene, like this (Hey Judi—Help me "flirt"):

My oh my! Here comes a pretty girl now. Oh boy! Hey! Honey, would you like to go to the park with me and watch the squirrels bury their nuts? *(Girl):* Oh, I think I'm in love with you. Yes, I am—take my eyes. Take my arms. Take my lips. *(Joey):* Sure, the best parts you keep for yourself. *(Girl, with rhythmic chant):* Well, you can meet me around the corner in half an hour. Meet me around the corner in half an hour. Meet me around the corner in half an hour. *(Turns to Comic, grind and bump to slow rhythmic beat)* M-e-e-t m-e a-r-o-u-n-d t-h-e c-o-r-n-e-r i-n a h-a-l-f a-n h-o-u-r. *(She bumps; Comic's hat flies off although he's fifty feet away from her. As she exits, Comic says):* Wind that up and set it for six o'clock.

We're here to show you sketches. Instead of just talking about them, let's do a sketch. Get me a phone. We'll go into the sketch in a minute. This is all unrehearsed.

(Voice over loudspeaker interrupts): Joey Faye, call Circle 7-8300. *(Joey):* Circle 7-8300. It must be important for them to call me here. Where's the phone? Oh, here's the phone. Excuse me, Miss, but do you mind if I use the phone? *(Judi):* Not at all. *(Joey):* Thank you. *(Judi):* After I get through with it. *(Joey, to himself):* Circle 7-8300, I got to remember that. Circle 7-8300. It must be important, they wouldn't call. I better remember the number—If I had a pencil I could write the number down. What's the number again, now? Pencil, pencil—Pennsylvania 7-8300. *(Judi):* I tried to call you *before.* *(Joey): Four,* Pennsylvania 4-8300. *(Judi):* Well, I know I said I'd call you before, but I had to see grandma, see grandma. *(Joey):* Gramercy 4-8300. *(Judi):* This guy was gorgeous, woof-woof! bark-bark! *(Joey):* Barkely 4-8300. *(Judi):* We danced. For a while I thought he was mine. *(Joey):* Nine. Barkley 9-4300. Hurry up. *(Judi):* Then my escort and I cut one out. *(Joey):* Endicott 9-4300. We went to about seven or eight places and got lit up like a Christmas tree. *(Joey):* 7-8300. Will you hurry up, Lady? Endicott 7-8300. *(Judi):* I got to hang up now, some nut wants to use the phone. *(Joey):* Nutley 7-8300. *(Judi):* Bye Barbara. *(Joey grabs phone):* Nutley 7-8300. *(Judi):* What's the matter, Buddy, they got you running around in circles? *(Joey):* Yah, Circle 7-8300.

That is a skit, a sketch, whatever you want to call it. Actually, no sketch should run over eight minutes because the audience loses interest. Let me tell you about sketches. In the theatre, nothing ever dies. We stole from everybody. I'm speaking about burlesque. Mr. Minsky always had a prima donna, a tenor, a lot of girls, and beautiful dancers that he stole from the ballet, from all the arts, but we also stole from the ethnic groups. Well, how do you classify a belly dancer? Exotic? An exotic, yah. A belly dancer would cost you $3, and an exotic was still thirty-five cents admission. We have a young lady who is going to do an exotic for us. Miss Eleonore Treiber will show you a belly dance.

(Miss Treiber does the belly dance.)

Dancers would dance on stage; blood pressures (among other things) would rise, and the boys in the front row would try to go backstage. But no go. We had our own security, a tough doorman—which means: nobody came backstage—so all the history of the burley backstage never went past the people in the shows. So whatever we burley people say about burley has to be accepted as the truth. Who is going to say *no*? The evolution of burlesque comedy is the same as the evolution of *all* comedy. Comedy can never be defined. It's like a great, giant tree: the trunk is one plateau of comedy, the branches another, the twigs another, the leaves another. Let's take maybe one branch—malaprops. Let's start with the concept. I worked with a fellow who is a genius. He's a professor of journalism. His name is Joe Lesser, Professor Joe Lesser. He and I have been trying to write a book or a paper on the evolution of comedy. Don't look at me for big words; the only big word I know is delicatessen. We've gone through a number of things, but we found out that comedy always endures. Through the ages it's always the same. It's always against the constabulary, the in-laws, money, landlords. The things never change. You always make fun and even the sense, the nucleus of comedy, is always the same.

Let's go back to Shakespeare. *Midsummer Night's Dream*, Bottom, with the malaprops, with the language; then we go to Dogberry, and then we go to Sheridan's *The Rivals*, with Mrs. Malaprop herself; and then we come to the turn of the century, with Weber and Fields as Mike and Meyer. Well, they did the malaprops. They did the German dialect. Maybe my Judi will help me, and we'll do a little piece and you'll see where all this came from. Here's a little bit of Mike and Meyer.

(Joey): Oh, I'm so happy to see you. What are you doing downtown here? *(Judi):* Well, I work here. *(Joey):* You work around here? *(Judi):* Yes, I do. *(Joey):* Oh, that's wonderful because you are the only one that doesn't make me nervous. Why don't you have lunch with me sometime? *(Judi):* I'd love to. *(Joey):* I'll tell you what I'll do. If you tell me the name of the street where you are, I'll come down in my car and I'll pick you up and we'll have lunch together. *(Judi):* Sure. *(Joey):* Well, tell me the name of the street you work at. *(Judi):* Sure, Watt Street. *(Joey):* All right, tell me the name of the street you're working on. *(Judi):* Watt Street. *(Joey):* Yah, that's what I mean, tell me the name of the street you're working on. *(Judi):* Watt Street. *(Joey): I'm* asking you. Don't *you* ask me. Now, tell me the street. You don't understand. I'm asking you the name. Everything has a name. The street has a name. The city has a name. You have a name. I can't tell you what the name is, there are nice people out there. Now what is the name of the street you work on? *(Judi):* Watt. I'll spell it for you, okay? Watt. W-a-t-t, Watt Street, see? *(Joey):* Oh! Watt? I though you were making fun of me. *(Judi):* Oh, come on, would I make fun of you? *(Joey):* I'm sorry, will you still have lunch with me? *(Judi):* Of course. *(Joey):* So, you work on Watt Street. You must have a good job? *(Judi):* Yes, I do. *(Joey):* What are you doing on Watt Street? *(Judi):* I'm dyeing. *(Joey):* You look good. *(Judi):* I feel good. *(Joey):* Then why are you dying? *(Judi):* I'm dyeing to live. *(Joey):* You're starting again. *(Judi):* . . . and if I can't dye I can't live. See? *(Joey):* Look, let me give you a for instance. *(Judi):* All right. *(Joey):* Eight o'clock, I'm sick. Nine o'clock, I die. *(Judi):* Oh, you can't dye. *(Joey):* I can't dye? Why not? *(Judi):* You don't belong to the union. *(Joey):* I have to belong to a union to die? *(Judi):* Oh, you want to dye as a scrub? Go ahead, dye, but we won't recognize you. *(Joey):* If I die, you'll recognize me.

And now we show you where Weber and Fields went (or at least their material). Fifty years later, Kate Smith said on her program, "And now we present two of the funniest men in America." Millions of people heard Kate Smith, they believed it. But were these men funny? Everyone thought they were funny. They weren't exactly funny per se. It was just that they had great *timing*! The material wasn't that good. Now let's update the Weber and Fields material. We have to apologize to the Professor, Mr. Louis. His son loaned us the hat and the bat, and we lost the hat. Here's the metamorphosis of Watt Street.

(Joey): Oh, excuse me. Miss, I'm a stranger hereabouts. Do you know all the people around here? I was looking for the manager. *(Judi):* Oh, I'm the manager of the team. *(Joey):* A lady manager? *(Judi):* Sure, woman's lib, right? *(Joey):* Well, tell me the names of the players so I can say hello to them. *(Judi):* Well, they all have nicknames. *(Joey):* The players have nicknames? *(Judi):* That's right. *(Joey):* Oh, you mean like Dizzy, Daffy? I have a nickname, too. *(Judi):* Oh, really, what is it? *(Joey):* Dopey. You know the names of all the players. Tell me the names of the players. *(Judi):* Okay, Who's on first, What's on second, third base I Don't Know. *(Joey):* You know the names of the players, right? All right. *(Judi):* Who's on first. What's on second, third base I Don't Know. *(Joey):* You know the players, right? Maybe you don't hear too good. You know the players, right? All right. We'll take one player at a time. You got a first baseman. All right, tell me the name of the first baseman. *(Judi):* Who. *(Joey):* The man who plays first base. *(Judi):* Who. *(Joey):* The guy on first base. *(Judi):* Who. *(Joey):* I'm asking you, don't you ask me. I want to know what's the man's name. *(Judi):* No, What's on second. *(Joey):* I'm not asking who's on second. I don't know. *(Judi):* Third base. *(Joey):* How did we get to third base? *(Judi):* Well, you just happened to mention his name. *(Joey):* Well, if I happen to mention his name, who's . . . *(Judi):* No, Who's on first. *(Joey):* I don't care what the man's name is. Who's on second? *(Judi):* Who's on first. *(Joey):* I don't know. *(Judi):* He's on third. *(Joey):* We're back to third base again. You got a first baseman? Are you the manager? You paying the salary? When the first baseman comes up to your office, who gets the money? *(Judi):* Every penny of it. *(Joey):* If you say Who, I'm gonna hit you right on the head now. I want to know the man's name on . . . *(Judi):* Wait a second. Who's on first. *(Joey):* I don't know. Third baseman. You gotta pitcher? *(Judi):* That's right. *(Joey):* Tell me the pitcher's name. *(Judi):* Tomorrow! *(Joey):* Let's get this straight once and for all. I'm a pretty good catcher too, right? All right, I'm the catcher. Now, suppose some guy hits the ball . . . bunts the ball. I'm gonna throw him out at first base. All right. I pick up the ball and throw it to who? *(Judi):* That's the first right thing you said. *(Joey):* I don't even know what the hell I'm doing anymore. And the hell with you, too.

(Aside): You know, I'm sorry. I'll tell you, if you want to leave, just raise your hand, I'll let you out. I'm only gonna be a few more minutes. You

know what I'd like to do, if it's all right with everyone? I'd like to save the last few minutes for questions and answers, because how can you tell about this subject . . . *(Mr. Minsky):* Joey, you're stealing my stuff. *(Joey):* The place is haunted. I'll tell you what we did. We did a burlesque show, but we stole it! We had to steal. We couldn't buy stuff, so we stole, but also we got away with the innuendos—is that the word? What am I asking you for? The thing is, we could change the meaning of a whole thing. Minsky spoke about Fiorello La Guardia. A very nice Italian. I happen to be Italian. *(Mr. Minsky):* Joey, to be continued. We're running against time, please. Please, Joey, introduce the next star. *(Joey):* As long as Eleonore Treiber is here, we asked her to do a strip. So if you'll dim the light, we'll bring her out again. Let's have a little applause for Miss Eleonore Treiber. *(Music plays)* *(Audience):* Take if off! Take it off! *(Girl):* I can't take it off, I'll catch cold.

Ann Corio was ill, and Mr. Minsky asked Eleonore to please come down, and in fifteen minutes, she did the whole thing. She never did a strip in her life, except at home. *(Eleonore):* But I told him I wouldn't take it off.

(Joey): Hey, you know what's funny, she's a soloist for the ballet company. *(Minsky):* Back to La Guardia. *(Joey):* Back to La Guardia and the comedy sketches. I wrote a scene called "The Barretts of Flugel Street," during the Depression. My partner was a fellow called Jack Diamond; he was the short fellow in the *Kiss Me Kate* Broadway production. *(Pause.)* Yes, that's right. He was the short fellow. I can't think in the morning, you know. The operator said this morning, "Seven o'clock, Friday morning." I looked out; it was still Thursday night. I don't get up this early. What do I know? Jack Diamond was in vaudeville and then burlesque, an acrobat, and we became a comedy team. Minsky would always say to me, "Joey, do the first scene with a straight man," and then we would do our scenes together. Diamond says, "Let me do a scene alone with the straight man."

So we put on a scene which we stole from a vaudeville act called "Moss and Frye." The actors were two black boys, and the routine was: One says, "You know nothing; you don't know a thing. I'll show you how dumb you are. Suppose you were standing on the corner with a handful of nickels, how much money have you got? You see, you don't know! You just stand there with the money in your hand, don't even bother to count it! Suppose you go to a railroad station, you buy a ticket, where are you going?" He says, "I don't know." Then he says, "What's the idea of getting on the train? You don't even know where you're going. Suppose you're at a ball park, right? The ninth inning, the score is tied, who's playing?" He says, "I don't know." He says, "What's the idea of going to a ball game? You sit through nine hot innings, you don't even know who's playing! See how dumb you are?" Later on, Abbott and Costello used this routine very successfully. But anyway, we stole from that act, and that category was called lecturing on a guy's skull. The straight man would do all the talking, the comic would just do "But . . . but . . ." Well, this opening skit ran seventeen minutes.

So Minsky says, "Joey, get in there and change the scene." So I gave this sketch a "reason" and I changed it. At that time, the big thing was getting the job. That was in depression days. I had the man come on with some straw hats; he has to get to the Pascunyak Hat Company on Flugel Street in five minutes to get the job, so naturally he's lost. So who's he gonna ask? He don't know. He knows Flugel Street's around there, somewhere, so he asks a cop. "Excuse me, sir, officer, do you know where Flugel Street is?" He says, "Do I? Of course, I know every street around here. What do I look like, a moron? What am I, a somnambulist, walking around in my sleep or something?" The Comic says, I don't care how you got here. *(Straight man cop):* Listen. My father ran for mayor. *(Comic):* Hurray for the mayor! And all this, and he never tells him how to get there, see?

Now I came on as a comic stutterer. I say, Oh the fa . . . the first thing you do . . . *(He says):* is get away from you. *(I say):* Hey, hipatippy, hipatippy. *(He says):* Hipatippy. *(I say):* Hey H . . . hello. *(He says):* Hello. *(I say):* Now ha . . . Hello. *(He says):* Hello. *(I say):* No hello. Hello. How long have you been stuttering? *(He says):* Me? Ever since I met you. *(I say):* Well, if you s . . . . . . stutter that bad, why didn't you see do . . . Dr. Lesser? *(He says):* Why? Is he good? *(I say):* Geebeegeep. *(He says):* Geebeegeep. *(I say):* Good. He cured *me*. *(He says):* He did a helluva job here. *(I say):* Oh, I used to stutter worse than you. I stuttered with both hands. He taught me how to say, P. . . Peter Piper picked a peck of pickled peppers. *(He says):* Hey, that's pretty good. *(I say):* Yah, but it seldom comes up in conversation. Now this was frustration. This category was frustration. He tried to get away from me, he couldn't get away from me. And the finish was, we broke the straw hats.

In burlesque, the semblance of elegance or having money was always a straw hat. A straight man would come in, give the waiter the hat. He says, "Hang this up." And the waiter would put it right through a hook, you know—that type of thing. Break the hat. Now we needed a woman in the sketch. You have to have a woman. Minsky says, "What is this, four men? Get some sex in there." Now where are we gonna get the woman? Well, from St. James Infirmary that the gentleman mentioned. Well, that was a vaudeville act. Jans and Whalen did it. They were doing jokes to the audience, and a woman would come out in widow's weeds. She would say, "Oh, my husband just died." They say, "Oh, tell us about it." Then she sings:

> I went down to St. James Infirmary,
> I saw my baby there,
> He was laid out on a cold white table,
> So cold, so white, so bare,

(This last line is done rhythmically and finishes off with a bump.) The two boys, Jans and Whalen, would run into the audience shouting, "French postcards! Get 'em here!" Then one would turn to the other and say, "Hey, Harry, how does she look from there?" His partner says, "Great, but I'd like to see it again." They turn to the widow and say, "Would you mind burying your husband again? Yeah, throw a little more dirt in his face, please!"

Well, anyway, we took that widow character from this vaudeville act, stole it, put into "Flugel Street," and when the guy leaves the cop, the comic says, "I'll ask this lady."

(Comic): I beg your pardon, Madam.

(Lady, fast talk): Oh a beggar! Well, I always carry coins for a beggar. I always . . .

(Comic): I'm not a beggar. Do you know where Flugel Street is?

(Lady, hysterical): Flugel Street—Why do you say Flugel Street? Don't you know my husband died on Flugel Street? He was so good—so kind and now *(beginning the bump)* he's dead. *(Bump!!!)*

(Comic): He didn't die a natural death: *You* bumped him off!! Is that a Pascunyak hat? Here we go again. Here. Give me. Take that, that, that. Here, have that cleaned and blocked.

(Lady): Oh, my poor husband. *(She exits.)*

(Comic): You're gonna hurt yourself doing that.

Then we had an original sketch. Original? As we say, comedy endures. Moss Hart, rest his soul, was my social director at a camp. And who do you think my writers were? Allen Boretz, who wrote *Room Service*, and a fellow called Herman Wouk. I don't know what the hell ever happened to *him*; I think he went with my partner Jack Albertson—nobody has ever heard of either one again. But they were the writers, and all they did was copy down the jokes. Allen Boretz says, "I have a play called *Room Service*. If I ever do it, I'm taking all your jokes." I said, "They're not my jokes, they're vaudeville jokes." He said, "I know I'm taking them from you. If I ever do the play *Room Service*, you're in it." And sure enough, I was in it. I wasn't in the original, because George Abbott wouldn't break up the company of *Three Men on a Horse*, but I was in the national company, and I left a $300-a-week job with them to go for $100.

Moss Hart used to say to me at Camp Copock, "Tell my father about your uncle." And the joke was, with the straight man, I say, "Listen, I'm gonna go out and get a drink, I'm thirsty." He says, "Drink? What are you gonna drink?" I say, "Whiskey." He says, "Why?" I say, "I'm thirsty." He says, "You're thirsty? If you're thirsty, drink milk. Milk makes blood." I say, "I'm not blood thirsty." He says, "Look at me—I'm in fine physical condition. Thirty-nine years old, never drank a drop of whiskey in my life. How do I look?" And I say, "Listen, I had an Uncle Max who drank a quart of whiskey every day of his life. Lived to be 83. Three days after he died, we dug him up and he still looked a whole lot better than you do right now!"

A year later, Moss Hart put me in *The Man Who Came to Dinner*. I was in Chicago for three years with Clifton Webb. Clifton onstage is eating candy, and the nurse comes in and says, "Mr. Whiteside, you shouldn't eat that candy, you're a sick man." He says, "Listen Miss Bedpan, my Aunt Matilda ate a box of candy every day of her life and lived to be 83. Three days after she died we dug her up and she still looked a whole lot better than you do right now." Everybody steals.

(Mr. Minsky): Thank you, Joey. We're ready for questions. Are there any questions? Just stand up please and let us have your name.

(Question): What about La Guardia? My name is Al Goldin. What about La Guardia? *(Mr. Minsky, to Joey):* You take one, and I'll take the next.

(Joey): Well, I knew Mr. La Guardia when he was a congressman. He and my father were very friendly. La Guardia came from an Italian family and he was really into politics. He really believed that we were corrupting the young soldiers, the young 18-year-old soldiers, during the war and just before the war. He wanted us off the street, and he tried every which way. He did one thing in which the Minskys could have fought him. He said, "You can't use the Minsky name because it's synonymous with burlesque," and that's ridiculous. You can't take away a man's name, you know. But they took away the name. There was nothing in the shows that was dirty or that they could be arrested for. They took off the name and they put up "Follies" instead. But the other men—the Wilners—who owned the Apollo next door to Minsky's, they put up "Ann Corio," who was synonymous with burlesque, even more so maybe than Minsky, she being a strip woman. And they got away with it, and there was a continual fight, but I don't think they should have kept it.

(Minsky): The famous Little Flower read comics to the children on Sunday morning. Chased the fire engines to fires. He was a juvenile at heart—a man who thought he was the most efficient mayor that New York ever had. He was not the debonair, brilliant Jimmie Walker. La Guardia used this as a ploy to be reelected. Mrs. La Guardia is still alive. I happen to run into one of the La Guardia judges every now and then on the bus, and he still swears that La Guardia was the greatest mayor of all and will continue to think that, despite the fact that the Minskys suffered a traumatic experience. They were put out of business and had to create new lives for themselves. However, it is fortunate that we did contribute an art form, and quite recently I was honored by doing an eight-and-a-half-hour tape for the Weiner Oral History Library, sponsored by the American Jewish Committee. So Minsky is in good company, with Sulzberger, Arthur Miller, Richard Rodgers, Horowitz, Rubinstein, and possibly forty or fifty other greats of our community. Thank you very much. Are there any other questions?

(Question): Joey, how did the blacks fit or not fit into our burlesque?
(Joey): Well, the Minskys integrated a few blacks who were great comedians—one in particular. *(Minsky):* Hamtree Harrington, Pigmeat Markham.
(Joey): And they did all the sketches at a time when a black man wasn't allowed to get his head on the same stage with a white girl. *(Minsky):* "Here Comes The Judge" was developed at the Minsky 125th Street Apollo Theatre.
(Question): How many Minsky brothers are there still left?
(Minsky): I'm the sole survivor of the four brothers.
(Question): Are you the youngest?
(Minsky): Yes.
(Joey): May I inject one moment, just trying to build up the Minsky name. Minsky took all the great comics. At that time, I happened to be in that category, maybe because we were a good team, Jack Diamond and I. But he took Red Marshall. He took us to California. He was very magnanimous. Let me put it this way. He says, "Here's a hundred bucks. Get to California." So we all bought tickets and went to California. We put on a show called *Life Begins at Minskys* that was a sensation in California. Tickets were supposed to be $5 each, but they were selling for $150 a pair. Charlie Chaplin and Mary Pickford (at that time, in the late 1930s) couldn't get into the orchestra. They had to sit in the mezzanine. That's how popular it was, and, of course, somebody was conniving with the tickets—not the Minskys. We put on a great show and were sold out for nine months. While the show was at its height, unfortunately for the Minskys and some of us in burlesque, the burlesque troupe went out on strike here in New York. We went out in sympathy and that was the end of it. But we got booked to work in vaudeville theatres. They wouldn't allow Mr. Minsky to use his name as a vaudeville presentation. They said, *"Life Begins at Minskys* is synonymous with burlesque. We can't bring it into a family theatre. The name of Minsky, that's all." The show was absolutely clean. Well, Ken Murray, three months later, took over the same type of show, blackouts, and stayed in the theatre for seven years. Just a little note.
(Minsky): Any other questions?
(Question): When did the strips begin and why?
(Minsky): Well, I can give you that. The strip was supposed to have been created or originated in Kansas City during the early Pendergast regime, and worked east and worked west from Kansas City. I happened to be out there about twenty years ago and I met with an executive of one of the fine department stores. Over lunch, we were talking about the origin of the strip, and he said, "Do you know that we had a very famous restaurant here about the same time, where the waitresses served in the nude?" I said, "What?" He said, "Well, it was copied from Paris." I said, "How was the food?" He said, "Great."

(Joey): Excuse me, I don't know how true this is, but I think Hinda Wassau, as a chorus girl, was the first stripper. What happened was that she was in the line and her husband was the manager. She let her brassiere strap fall, and out flashed one. Well, it was so great they kept it in. Oh, I'm sorry, they kept them both in.

(Minsky): Are there any other questions?

(Question): Has the step and choreography of the strip always remained the same?

(Treiber): There's a basic dance step, but each one does it according to her own personality, you know; it's whatever the girl feels. There's the walk and then the dip, and then the grind and then the bump; but then, you know, the stripper would elaborate on it. Some people used furs, some used animals, some had a chair. The thing is, it's the tease. It's not so much taking it off, it's teasing, which is really the most important thing. So you take a lot of time, because once you're undressed, that's it.

(Joey): May I add something? Gypsy Rose Lee, who was the most famous stripper, was the third strip when she first worked for Minsky. She wasn't the star. But Gypsy was a great saleswoman. She had a body like a boy—she had nothing. But what a saleswoman! And she ended off with a laugh. She would start to take off the G-string and she had her dresser, a woman, in the audience go "ahhhh . . . ." Big scream, and she'd get off that way, if you remember. But Carrie Fennell, the second stripper, had bosoms that were very well trained. She could make them bump with the music, and they would both come up or jiggle, or one would come out. They also had the tassel twirlers—the ones whose rear ends worked better—so they'd turn around and they'd shimmy and shake. Everybody developed her own style. But you had your walk, and you could have the lights set dim and music very slow and very sexy. Then there were the ones that chewed gum, very fast, to get it over with. They're all different.

(Joey): One more question.

(Question): What was the origin of the runway?

(Minsky): As I mentioned earlier, my brother Abe experienced this wonderful idea in Paris, the illuminated runway at the Folies-Bergère, and my brothers immediately picked that up, and it was installed at the National Winter Garden on Houston Street. The runway extended back about twelve rows. It was illuminated. There were special effects, with spots hitting the girls as they were on the runway. The girls created a sort of personal relationship with the members of the audience sitting alongside the runway. Otto Kahn's favorite seat was in Row C, right alongside the runway, and Horace Liveright used to sit next to him. Their Minerva was downstairs, and after the show there would be two girls who accompanied them uptown to the garage.

Helen Armstead-Johnson

Blacks in Vaudeville: Broadway and Beyond_____

A proper consideration of blacks in vaudeville at once becomes a much broader subject than it appears to be. It forces accent upon transition and continuity from minstrelsy, upon both general and specific influences—especially those identifiable as one-to-one—and it requires illumination of the pioneering presence of black performers who literally spread throughout the world. In addition, the importance of black vaudevillians in black theatres must be brought into focus. These theatres involve considerably more than a discussion of the Howard in Washington, the Lafayette in New York, and later, of course, the Apollo. To all of them, whites went regularly to enjoy, study, and steal. Within the framework of these considerations, key people—and some not so key—will be set in place. Entertainers, as referred to in this paper, include producers, composers, and writers as well. In 1969, with historical perspective, former choral conductor Leonard De Paur observed on the *New York Times* radio series "Music Makers" that "the black man's contribution of music, dancing, and humor were basic to the very creation of the modern musical theatre" ("Black Musicals on the Great White Way"). In fact, he continued, "if there had not been black man's music, there could not have been an indigenous American theatre." Let us follow, then, the black performer as he entered the bloodstream of the American theatre and provided transfusions for others beyond these shores.

Although there were free blacks performing long before emancipation, when large numbers of them sought to become professional entertainers, they were faced with a mélange of problems such as the duplicity of white managers and theatre owners, the jealousy of white performers—which often included outright refusal to work with them—stagehands who refused to set for them, to say nothing of being able to eat, sleep, and bathe properly. One cause of the high death rate among blackface comedians, for instance, was systemic poisoning from makeup that could not be removed adequately, given the lack of hot water. A victim of many such problems herself, Florence Mills, the musical comedy star who was practically born in vaudeville, made her first appearance at the age of four, singing "Don't Cry, My Little Piccanninny." She died at thirty-one in 1927, when she was an international sensation. Yet, she once wrote, "Always there was the bogy of my color barring the way. That I was able to win through at all was due to sheer determination to rise superior to prejudice." Miss Mills spoke for the whole body of headliners. We are all aware of the stresses of achievement in the theatre, but when one has added unto them the color problem too, those of us who make the assessments must respect the character traits as well as the talents of black achievers.

It is a very rare thing to find more than one black act on a white vaudeville bill. The very existence of a name, however, always signals the same message to me: "He had to be darn good." The trouble was that some of these people were so good that nobody wanted to follow them, especially the headliners. As Noble Sissle, once a vaudevillian, explained, many black acts were moved up next to closing because the animal acts that followed could not complain. Even so, the money did not change.

What we need to understand more about, however, is *why* they were so good. One of the reasons, apart from basic talent, is that most of the early performers in vaudeville were experienced ones whose proving grounds had been the medicine wagon, the side show, the circus, *Uncle Tom's Cabin*, and the minstrel olio. They were seasoned performers, and their material was original. Vaudeville demanded freshness. One who offered it was Archie Jones from Louisiana, who wrote all of his own material. After he was already a professional, he sent for his brother, who was known as Bodiddly, and they formed an act. In one sketch, Bodiddly had stolen a watch. Archie says: "You stole the watch and don't know what time it is. What time is it?" Bodiddly is indignant: "Who don't know what time it is? There it is!" As he thrusts the watch at Archie who can't tell time either, Archie looks at it and says, "Um hum—sho is." Ulysses S. Thompson, a veteran minstrel man who knew the brothers well, said, "Low as it was, it was original." It isn't very funny now, of course, because we have seen it so many times. The Jones Brothers never reached the very top because too few people understood what they were actually saying. When Lew Leslie took them to England, he had to drop them after the first week because the English never did find out what they were talking about.

Although U. S. Thompson was the husband of Florence Mills, he was a star in his own right—an acrobatic dancer, singer, and comedian. He represents transition, seasoning, and continuity better than anyone I know. He started out with a "doctor" show on a medicine wagon. In 1904, when he was sixteen—he is now eighty-nine—he worked in Louisiana with the Mighty Hagg Circus in its winter quarters. The list of his employment, even with omissions, is staggering: Patterson's World Carnival, Heger and Hopper stock shows, other street medicine shows, stock shows in Kansas City, Sells-Floto Circus, Gentry Brothers Dog and Pony Show, Hagenback and

Ulysses S. Thompson (front, left-hand side) with P. J. Lowery's Circus Band, a sideshow attraction with Hagenback and Wallace Circus (1912-1914). Courtesy of The Armstead-Johnson Foundation for Theater Research.

Wallace Circus, and Ringling Brothers' Circus. At the end of the 1915 Ringling season, Thompson joined Ralph Dunbar's Tennessee Ten on the Keith-Proctor circuit. After spending 1918 in France with an army band, he returned to the Tennessee Ten on the Keith Proctor circuit for five more seasons, doing forty weeks a year.

In 1922, Thompson went into *Shuffle Along* shortly after his wife joined it, and then to the Plantation Club for Lew Leslie in *Plantation Revue*, which starred Florence Mills. With the *Plantation Revue*, he went to London for C. B. Cochran's *From Dover Street to Dixie*, which was a satire of *Beggar's Opera* in the first half, with Odette Myrtil and Stanley Lupino, and Leslie's *Revue* in the second half. From London, Thompson and Mills went to Paris in *Dixie to Paris*, and then back to New York in *Dixie to Broadway* (1924-1925). In 1926, Thompson went back to Paris with Leslie's *Blackbirds of 1926*, in which Mills was also the star, and he was one of the featured players. After Mills died in November 1927, Thompson wanted to prove that he was an independent talent, so from then until 1939, his taps echoed in such distant places as Sydney, Auckland, Wellington, Bucharest, Budapest, Berlin, Bombay, Manila, Shanghai, and Hong Kong. Billed everywhere as "Fleet of Feet," he was also booked into Hawaii, Cuba, and the Canal Zone.

Florence Mills in *Blackbirds of 1926*. Courtesy of The
Armstead-Johnson Foundation for Theater Research.

During the 1930s, Thompson made three tours of Australia under the
management of George Sorlie, with whom he still corresponds. As recently
as this past year, Australian dancer Jimmy Haines, while being interviewed
about a television appearance, mentioned having studied with U. S. Thompson, the first of his black dance teachers. Ulysses S. Thompson is unquestionably a brilliant example of transition and continuity, although he is by
no means an isolated case.

One of the places Thompson did not reach until 1977, when he vaca-
tioned there, was Russia. There were, however, many Negro performers
there before the turn of the century and until World War I. A very large
number of blacks had gone to Europe with minstrel shows, *Uncle Tom*
shows, and in 1903, with Bert Williams and George Walker's *In Dahomey*,
among others. Many of these performers developed speciality acts and
stayed abroad. Some returned as late as the outbreak of World War II;
others never did return.

An examination of a number of "antique" pre-1915 performer postcards
reveals that most of them were made in Germany, France, England, and
Russia. A few of them were actually mailed between performers in Odessa
and Moscow. Although all of these people have not been identified, there is
little doubt that those of very dark skin and thick features—especially the
women—had played plantation and African roles, for the most part. Those

of very light skin were, in all likelihood, former members of creole choruses, which were very popular. Some, of course, had been with *In Dahomey*. No matter what they had been, all of these performers had established reputations before going abroad. If they had not been good, they would not have been taken there in the first place. Many good reputations grew even better in Europe, but some of their owners stayed away too long. The distance between 1900 and 1939 was too great to bridge, and some of the top performers came back home and worked as maids and taxi drivers. Creighton Thompson, a singer, was so reluctant to return that when a former partner cabled him to come home, he cabled back a cryptic message that said, "When they build a bridge." The government, uneasy about the impending war, thought it a coded message, and it is quite true that Thompson had one hell of a time explaining.

One of the most popular entertainers in Russia was Ollie Burgoyne, whose partner was Usher Watts. They were billed as The Duo Eclatant. Ollie stayed for ten years and was the successful owner of a large lingerie shop, as well as an entertainer. When she returned to the States, she taught Russian dances to others, and they began appearing in a number of vaudeville acts. Her Russian influence was even seen in *Shuffle Along*. Another dancer was Ida Forcyne from Chicago. When Pete and Laura Bowman, the Darktown Entertainers, arrived in Moscow for a theatre engagement, Ida was working at the Bal Tabarin. In Miss Bowman's autobiography, *Achievement*, she describes Ida, known as Topsy, as one of the most sensational Russian dancers. On the Bowmans' second night in Moscow, Tolstoy was expected at the Bal Tabarin, where the Bowmans and their partners were the guests of their manager. When Tolstoy learned the Darktowners were a quartet, he sent for them to sing "Simple Simon" at his table—a song that nobody knew. He offered them one hundred rubles to sing it just once. For thirty minutes they sang everything they knew, but he was not satisfied. Miss Bowman, in desperation, did a single comedy number, but that did not satisfy him either. Finally, however, he paid the rubles, giving Miss Bowman an extra ten, and announced that he would be back the next night to hear "Simple Simon." Miss Bowman found the experience degrading, but Russian entertainers were expected to entertain private parties—even, as in this case, when the entertainers themselves were guests.

What we are talking about here is the experience of early black vaudevillians. It was these people who spread throughout Europe and Asia, and left their black influences there. They, in turn, were influenced to a lesser degree by their new environments. Back in the States, many performers tried to use songs in other languages in their new acts, but, for the most part, Americans did not want to hear them.

Let us return briefly to an earlier period to examine the influence of the dancer William Henry Lane, who was known as Juba. He had the rare distinction of receiving top billing in this country with a white troupe

Bill "Bojangles" Robinson, former partner of U. S.
Thompson. Courtesy of The Armstead-Johnson
Foundation for Theater Research.

during slavery. He, however, was a free black. In a 1947 article on "Juba
and American Minstrelsy," Marian Hannah Winter called Juba "the most
influential single performer of nineteenth-century dance, a prodigy of our
entire history." That Negro historians apotheosized Ira Aldridge and
ignored Juba is, according to Miss Winter, like writing a twentieth-century
theatrical history mentioning Paul Robeson and ignoring Bojangles. "The
repertoire of any current tap dancer," she asserts, "contains elements which
were established theatrically by him. Since Juba was born in 1825, his influence was not only pervasive but permanent. By 1845 it was flatly stated
by members of the profession that Juba was beyond question the very
greatest of all dancers." In 1848, Juba joined Pell's Ethiopian Serenaders in
London at Vauxhall Gardens. There was a curious transference, Miss Winter says, of Juba's characteristics to English clowns, who were influenced
not only by Juba's dance but by his appearance, and so they applied black
makeup. Touring British circuses influenced French and Belgian ones. All of
this was before 1852, the year of Juba's death in London.

It is very clear that the precedents for Negro entertainers abroad were established very early. To talk about blacks in vaudeville on Broadway is impossible without discussing the beyond. Yet even though black entertainers went to Europe in droves, they left others behind, and they left their influences. One aspect of this is that whites in show business lifted Negro material from the stage bodily. Imitation can be flattering, but theft never is. When Miller and Lyles returned from England, they were told by their manager that they could no longer do the vaudeville act they took over there, which included their famous boxing sketch. The reason given was that Moran and Mack, the Two Black Crows, were doing their act. When Ted Lewis popularized "Is everybody happy?" he was using Ernest Hogan's material. Hogan had a song by that name, and the *Columbus Evening Dispatch* of October 5, 1906, tells us more. "Is Everybody Happy? sung Ernest Hogan, the Unbleached American . . . and the large company of colored singers and performers arrayed about the stage chimed in. From the gallery gods echoed the reply of scores of voices. 'Yes, everybody's happy.' Then there was a stampede because the inimitable colored comedian refused to sing another dozen choruses. But he was tired of working and responded with a witty curtain address."

In dance, at one point, John Bubbles was teaching Fred Astaire intricate steps, which Astaire had trouble learning. He also taught Eleanor Powell when she was a young girl. At Billy Pierce's studio, Buddy Bradley taught Adele Astaire. When Artie Hall became a popular coon shouter, she was indebted to Nathan Bivins who took "Bill Bailey" out of the morgue for her and taught her how to sing it. Sophie Tucker's "Some of These Days" was written for her by Shelton Brooks. Fannie Brice's "Lovie Joe" was written for her by Joe Jordan, who was not allowed in the theatre the night she introduced it in brown face. The experience was so bitter that he is said to have left the country for several years. When Gertrude Lawrence arrived from England, her first hit was "You Were Meant for Me," written by Sissle and Blake.

In addition to these one-to-one connections, Ziegfeld had his own. One of his most successful scenes in the *Follies* was purchased from J. Leubrie Hill's *Darktown Follies*. People are still living who know this. What is more, Ziegfeld used a black arranger and a black musical director, Will Vodery and Ford Dabney. When *Shuffle Along* was such a success in 1921 with its dancing, rather than prancing, girls, Ziegfeld hired black choreographer Lawrence Deas to teach his girls how to dance. Bert Williams taught Eddie Cantor a great deal about comedy when Cantor worked in blackface as Williams' son in the *Follies*. Fats Waller sold many a tune to Irving Berlin, and Harold Arlen was said to have bought "Stormy Weather" for twenty-five dollars—and we all know what Ethel Waters did with that. Clayton, Jackson, and Durante were taught dancing by Garfield Dawson and his

wife, Elida Webb, the black choreographer for Miller and Lyles' *Runnin'*
Wild on Broadway in 1923, as well as for the chorus lines at Reisenweber's
and the Cotton Club. Over in Paris, Louis Douglas created Maurice
Chevalier's style, which was a takeoff on the minstrel dandy. From 1900 to
1903, the most popular songwriting team in the country was that of Cole
and Johnson—Bob Cole, Rosamond Johnson, and his brother, James
Weldon. Some of their successes accounted, in part, for those of Ziegfeld's
wife, Anna Held, who sang "The Maiden with the Dreamy Eyes" in *The Lit-*
tle Duchess; for May Irwin in *The Belle of Bridgeport*, and for the Klaw and
Erlanger production of Drury Lane Pantomimes, *The Sleeping Beauty and*
the Beast. For this they wrote three specialty numbers: "Tell Me, Dusky
Maiden," "Come Out, Dinah, on the Green," and "Nobody's Lookin' but
the Owl and the Moon." Week after week, Cole and Johnson were cited in
the *New York Clipper* for the number of their songs appearing in vaudeville
acts.

To discuss blacks in vaudeville, then, is to deal not only with their own
acts, but with their influence on the development of popular theatre. When
Shuffle Along taught Broadway about hoofing and rhythm, it created a
demand for Negro entertaiment abroad as well as at home. In most cases,
the successful acts were drawing top dollar, and they did not know what the
Depression really was. Actors did, but not entertainers. When Mills and
Thompson left London in 1927, they cabled thirty thousand dollars ahead
of them. Among those who literally formed a colony in Europe were
Creamer and Layton. At one time, they were bigger than any English act of
the kind. The colony also included Browning and Starr, who had been in
vaudeville since 1915; Adelaide Hall, who is still singing in England; Elliot
Carpenter and his Red Devils; Scott and Whaley; The Three Eddies; Paul
Robeson; George Dewey Washington of "Chloe" fame; and, of course,
Mabel Mercer, Bricktop, and Josephine Baker. The social lion was female
impersonator John Payne, who was indulged by a rich patron, Lady Cook.
Payne performed as Black Patti, who was Sisieretta Jones, a trained concert
singer who pioneered with her own company, Black Patti's Troubadours, in
the 1890s. It carried a distinguished group of people, including Bob Cole,
who put the first production together, and Ada Reed, who later became the
wife of George Walker, the partner of Bert Williams.

The performers mentioned above are representative, but not exhaustive,
examples of vaudeville acts whose American successes literally pushed them
out of the country. They wanted to reach the top as performers, not as
Negro performers, a distinctly limiting identification. Even Irving Berlin
sent a telegram to Florence Mills as "the greatest of all colored performers."
The policy of one Negro act to a bill in the major houses would certainly not
meet the needs of so many talented people. Moreover, there was so much
hostility from white performers. Ziegfeld people threatened to quit if Bert

Sisieretta Jones, BLACK PATTI, of Black Patti's
Troubadours at the turn of the century. Cour-
tesy of The Armstead-Johnson Foundation for
Theater Research.

Williams were hired. He was, and they didn't; but he did not work on stage
with the girls. At one time, the Shuberts needed a top act to beef up a weak
show and successfully attracted Florence Mills, who doubled for two weeks.
She quit the show because of the gross hostility of the white performers and
because she had no dressing room. Yet she was important enough to be im-
personated in the 1925 *Grand Street Follies.* Such are the eccentricities of
fame, especially when it is boxed in by color.

Our final turn is toward black performers in black theatres. In the days of
the Lafayette in Harlem, there were essentially two circuits. The smaller one
was made up of independent theatres, which included the Lafayette, the
Howard, the Royal in Baltimore, and the Standard in Philadelphia.
(Perhaps it should be pointed out here that the Apollo was white until
1935.) The much larger circuit was the TOBA (Theatre Owners Booking
Association). TOBA was translated, however, as "Tough on Black Actors."
It was so because the owners' mutual agreements made it difficult to
bargain, and thus the performers were rather poorly paid. *The Colored
Theater Directory* of 1928 lists forty-five of these theatres, but there were
more. They were in widely separated areas throughout the South and
Southwest, but Pennsylvania, Ohio, and Illinois were also listed. Cer-

tainly one of the positive aspects of these theatres is that they provided a proving ground for black performers.

Tab shows were frequently a part of the vaudeville presentation. Thus these theatres gave writers a chance to see their works performed. Composers who would never get to Broadway could hear their music in production. Stage managers, advance men, and other essential people were able to develop new careers. An assessment of black talent by black people, unfortunately, has never been enough to get black performers where the money is. Many blues singers, for instance, were grossly restricted until the Beatles absorbed Chuck Berry and until Tom Jones lifted James Brown's undressing act.

The late Moms Mabley is another case in point. Black folks had loved her for years. When whites discovered her, she was an old and sick woman. During the war years in Washington, D.C., climbing the stairs to Jean Clore's small club to hear Moms Mabley was a compulsive ritual. Male impersonator Gladys Bentley is of the same time and condition. When George Craft came to town, missing him was more sinful than for his Catholic devotees to miss confession. (As a matter of fact, two of them who consistently tried to make mass as inebriated celebrants were finally asked by the priest to stay home.) In the early 1940s and the insanity of the war years, people threw dollar bills on the stage at Craft, which he draped around his fingers like extended pieces of jewelry hanging from each one. Snake Hips Tucker was another black favorite, a model for scores of imitators.

When the Apollo opened in 1935, *everybody* played there. Before they hit big time—which is white time—Glenn and Jenkins performed there as the hilarious Two Railroad Porters. Later they washed the cork from their faces and kept on doing the same thing. One of the best imitators of Bert Williams was Hamtree Harrington, who nearly lost his wife because he spent all his free time in museums copying great paintings. In her early days, Ethel Waters was not the fat domestic type. She was billed as Sweet Mama Stringbean and later as one of The Two Ethels—the other being Ethel Williams. Langston Hughes once wrote that Negroes have such a good time when nobody's looking. This was certainly true in the theatre. Negroes could even use racial material that would have been offensive in the mouths of whites. *Entre nous*, it was the ability to laugh at oneself. Nevertheless, white folks came and laughed with us and at us as they carried our materials away. There is an irony, therefore, in the way some of the influence was fed into the bloodstream of the American stage. There is an irony, too, in that so many of the whites who worked so hard to keep blacks out of the theatre are so deeply indebted to them. Al Jolson even boasted that Negroes were not intelligent enough to get out on the runway and do what he did.

In conclusion, however, there can be no lessening of the importance of blacks in vaudeville on Broadway and beyond, regardless of the variety of ways—good and evil—in which this importance developed.

Nahma Sandrow

"A Little Letter to Mamma": Traditions in Yiddish Vaudeville___

In the last years of the nineteenth century, Yiddish variety entertainment started appearing in saloons on the Lower East Side of New York. Often the stage was only a little platform in the back room. If you bought a ten-cent glass of beer, you got to see the show. Soon the institution caught on, and there were music hall saloons on Clinton Street, Suffolk Street, Houston Street, Rivington Street, Cannon Street, Grand Street, the Bowery—all over the Lower East Side, as well as in equivalent Jewish immigrant neighborhoods in other American cities. Next, the saloons began selling tickets for entrance to the entertainment, even in those establishments where waiters trotted constantly among the patrons, and food and drink competed with the actors for attention. Finally, not long into the twentieth century, vaudeville bills moved into handsome theatres for the regular season from fall to spring, and even filled extra houses in the summer, when legitimate Yiddish theatres closed or went on the road.

From the continuous shows of the early days, the normal vaudeville bill eased off to three to five shows a day, often on weekends only. By the 1930s, acts often alternated with films. (Usually, these were Yiddish feature films, made in this country or in Poland. Other vaudeville programs included Yiddish short films, made especially for that purpose; "American" movies in English; or, most recently, Israeli feature films.)

Yiddish vaudeville became so substantial that Yiddish variety entertainers organized their own union. The industry employed gag writers, sketch writers, composers, and lyricists. Publishers printed sheet music with photos of the Yiddish stars who had popularized the songs. Yiddish radio shows nourished the Yiddish record industry, and vice versa. Stars like Herman Yablokoff—billed as "Der Payats" ("The Clown")—had their own radio shows, which in turn publicized their vaudeville acts. All this activity peaked in the 1930s. But it continued to be healthy through the 1950s, and, in fact, there was regular Yiddish vaudeville in Miami Beach until 1976. All in all, then, we are talking about a popular art with many American practitioners and many, many American fans.

Yiddish vaudeville is an American art form. It flowered here, rather than in the Jewish communities of Europe or Israel. In fact, it had a great deal in common with English-speaking American vaudeville. The sentimental tenor single turn, the comic sketch in which a policeman hits someone over the the head with a nightstick, the half-hour drama of love and murder—these were as familiar on the Yiddish vaudeville stage as on the "American." A soprano might sing a Puccini aria in Yiddish. A wrestler, a rhumba duo, a chorus on roller skates all made appearances on the Yiddish vaudeville stage. And, of course, acts from outside, such as Step'n Fetchit, visited Yiddish vaudeville, just as individual Yiddish acts played on American bills.

What interests us at the moment, though, is not how Yiddish vaudeville was typical, but rather how it was special. It had to be special. After all, Yiddish-speaking audiences had the option of going to English-speaking vaudeville, and many of them did go. From Yiddish vaudeville they wanted pleasures they could not get elsewhere: the Yiddish language itself, of course, and distinctively Yiddish musical modes. Above all, they were drawn by Jewishness (a matter of religion and common history) and Yiddishness (a cultural, social, linguistic matter). Specifically, Jewish and Yiddish elements remained traditional and constant in Yiddish vaudeville, from its beginnings up to the 1970s, giving Yiddish vaudeville its continuity and its vitality.

What exactly were those special elements? First, religion. Second, memories of the old country. Third, the audience's own experiences of immigration and of Jewish life in America.

The most obvious representative of religion on the Yiddish vaudeville stage has always been the cantor. Moishe Oysher and Yossele Rosenblatt were two of the most famous of a long list of cantors who performed in theatres, sometimes while holding synagogue positions as well. Most of them did not perform on the Sabbath (from Friday sundown to Saturday sundown). Onstage they sang liturgical chants, as well as operatic arias, folk songs, and more popular songs.

Yiddish culture has a tradition of songs and comedic numbers about cantors, some of which found their way onto the vaudeville stage. One monologue, which was already being performed in the sixteenth century, portrays three cantors auditioning for the same synagogue position and contrasts their distinctive styles. Another version shows synagogue members reacting to a cantor's singing in various ways. Moishe Oysher played a cantor as romantic lead in several Yiddish feature films; Al Jolson followed his lead in *The Jazz Singer*. Singers who were not cantors also sang cantorial music onstage. A special group of these were women, such as "The

Hungarian *Khazente"* ("Female Cantor") and the most famous was Fraydele Oysher.

Other religious figures appeared on the vaudeville stage. Old-country rabbis were characters in playlets, wearing beards and earlocks and giving godly advice. More commonly, the pious were treated as figures of fun: silly *Hasidim* (members of ecstatic cults) and mischievous *yeshive* (Talmudical academy) boys. Such prankish schoolboys made piquant roles for Molly Picon, Nellie Casman, and other soubrettes.

Prayers and rituals from daily life were comfortably adopted as vaudeville material. Onstage, women drew lace shawls over their heads to bless the Sabbath candles; families gathered around the table for Passover *seder* ceremonies. The actors recited the prayers accurately except for the name of God, for which other syllables are ritually substituted. As audiences assimilated into American life and began to skip traditional practices in their own homes, they found ever-greater satisfaction in celebrating and maintaining them vicariously, through the performer, in a communal situation.

Just as all American vaudeville, including the Yiddish variety, marked the Fourth of July with patriotic pageantry, so the Yiddish stage celebrated its particular holidays with special numbers. Passover, for example, often brought scenes of the exodus from Egypt; Hannuka brought reenactments of the Maccabean rebellion against the Romans in ancient Jerusalem. Similarly, King Saul, King David, and other biblical figures made appearances, as did scenes of other periods of Jewish history.

All this make-believe can be defined as genuinely religious, in its way. Through cantors and other religious figures, through prayers and holidays and biblical history, vaudeville was serving the synagogue. For many of the twentieth-century Americans in the audience, it was even replacing the synagogue. Also, it was using the synagogue, infusing vaudeville with the emotional vibrations that come out of religious associations, and thus heightening the experience beyond simple entertainment.

Memories of the old country were also very important in Yiddish vaudeville. The stage was often colorful with embroidered peasant blouses, high boots and ribbons, balalaikas, and gypsy guitars. The entertainer Vera Rosanko, for example, billed herself as "Di Yidishe Shikse" ("The Jewish Gentile"); her specialty was singing Russian peasant songs in the characteristically high and raucous Russian voice. Songs about the world these immigrants had left behind included "Rumania, Rumania," "Mayn Shtetele Belz" ("My Little Hometown Belz"), "Odessa," "Bessarabia"—each claiming that back home the wine was redder, the cafés livelier, the girls prettier. Old country weddings made a popular scene, providing an opportunity for singing and dancing as well as for religious ceremonial and comic byplay.

Situations characteristic of old-country life were the raw material of many vaudeville sketches. A Cossack, speaking only Russian, flirts with a Jewish girl, speaking only Yiddish, for example. Comic encounters on the train—that staple of central European jokes—also provided the setting for many sketches.

Regional peculiarities from the old country seemed an inexhaustible well of comedy, especially the antipathy between Litvak (Jew from Lithuania) and Galitsianer (Jew from Polish Galicia). In their accents, their cuisines, and so on, the Litvak and the Galitsianer provided a contrast as dramatic as that between, say, farmers from Maine and from Georgia. One routine that milked this contrast for laughs was based on an old joke about a cantor. When the new cantor arrives in town, several Jews compete in praising his marvelous voice. The Litvak, speaking with his strong distinctive accent, compares the cantor's voice to herring and potatoes and to borscht; the Galitsianer, in his own very different accent, compares the cantor's voice to meat cooked with marrowbones and a flask of wine.

That old-world institution, the matchmaker, was another comedic gold mine. Take, for example, the chestnut about the matchmaker whose business was doing so well that he hired an apprentice. On the first day, they set off for the home of a young prospective groom to try to arrange a match. The matchmaker gave instructions: "Whatever I say about the bride, you back me up."

When they arrived at the young man's house, the matchmaker settled down with the parents and, after some preliminary small talk, he began praising the bride.

"Do I have a girl for you! A pretty, a very pretty girl."

"Pretty!" chimed in the apprentice on cue. "She's a beauty. A Queen Esther!"

"She's intelligent," continued the matchmaker.

"Intelligent!" the apprentice echoed indignantly. "She went to the university. She knows six languages."

"She's from a good family," said the matchmaker.

"A good family! Her father and grandfather were rabbis, her great-grandfather was a famous scholar."

"She'll bring a nice dowry."

"A nice dowry! Her uncle is Rothschild!"

"There's just one thing, though," acknowledged the matchmaker, in a somewhat quieter voice. "The bride does have a sort of a little hump."

"A hump!" cried the enthusiastic apprentice. "A regular Mount Sinai!"

The matchmaker was a familiar figure in comedy sketches, often equipped with his conventional umbrella and bandanna handkerchief, and perhaps a flask of schnapps in his pocket to be ready at all times to celebrate a betrothal.

The Litvak and Galitsianer jokes ring changes on differences a continent away, in another world. The matchmaker, too, is essentially an old-world character. Yet, the jokes were told to the third and fourth American-born generations. Furthermore, the plays condensed for vaudeville were often set in the old country. One popular one was *Mirele Efros* by Jacob Gordin, an adaptation of the King Lear story in which a pious, old-fashioned, proud matriarch is estranged from her sons and daughter-in-law but is finally reconciled. Such plays—classics in the Yiddish literary theatre—became traditions in their own right. Seeing them on the stage was as much a cultural tradition as watching the enactment of religious or social rituals.

Besides religion, and besides an evocation of what they left behind them in the old country, audiences came to Yiddish vaudeville for a reflection of their own ongoing lives. Thus, one important recurrent strain is the pain of homesickness and separation. The song "A Little Letter to Mamma," a paradigm of the type, describes the mother far away, all alone and longing for word of her dear child. Similar songs were "A Mamma's Tears" and "Her Mamma's Wedding Dress." Mamma herself was a popular figure on the stage; an actress named Esther Field actually billed herself as "The Yiddishe Mamma" and specialized in suitably sentimental songs. Elderly parents separated from children, lovers separated, husbands and wives separated— their suffering was basic to immigration and therefore part of the vaudeville scene.

Henrietta Jacobson and Julius Adler in vaudeville film *Catskill Honeymoon*. Reprinted with the permission of Henrietta Jacobson and Julius Adler.

In the early days of vaudeville, the actual experience of crossing the ocean was still vivid to most of the audience. Thus, the actress Henrietta Jacobson recalls making her vaudeville debut at the age of three, in a sack. Her mother was playing a woman just off the boat, burdened with boxes and bundles and trunks, mattresses and feather pillows—and twelve children. But she had left Russia with thirteen children! The comic sketch consisted of searching for the baby through the boxes and bundles, until they discovered Henrietta in the sack.

Songs about "greenhorns" (newly arrived immigrants) were standard in Yiddish vaudeville. Greenhorn newsboys, tailors, peddlers, and other Lower East Side characters populated the sketches. One such type was the boarder who took a room in a tenement apartment while saving up to bring over his family and, according to folklore, gave his landlady more than just the rent.

Another Lower-East-Side type was the landlord. Predictably, there were skits in which the landlord demanded his rent. In some cases, he remained hardhearted despite tears and pleas. In others, the tenant was female and flirtatious, and he was not so hardhearted after all. The landlord also appeared in comic songs like "Steam Steam Steam." Verse after verse curses the landlord and his rotten building. The chorus runs: "Steam, steam, steam/ *Di* pipes *zenen* [are] *gerusted*/ And *der* boiler is *gebusted*/ *Gib mir* [Give me] steam, steam, steam." (Later, by the way, comes a verse about the girl who married an old man and on her disappointing wedding night turned to him in bed and complained," . . . *Di* Pipes *zenen gerusted*/ And *der* boiler is *gebusted*/ *Gib mir* steam, steam, steam.")

Early Yiddish vaudeville reflected the immigrant's growing acquaintance with his fellow Americans. One vaudeville song concerns a henpecked husband who ran away from home. His wife finally tracked him down in Chinatown, which was after all only a few blocks from the Lower East Side; he had grown a pigtail and was working in a Chinese restaurant. References to other cultures also included songs about the "Galitsianer Caballero" (the "Galitsianer Cowboy"). One vaudeville sketch, produced by Dr. Mark Slobin at Wesleyan University in 1977, portrayed the misadventures of a Jewish peddler out west, trying to sell suits to the Indians; he even attempts to outfit a totem pole.

As vaudeville assimilated all the new influences affecting the audience's lives outside the theatre, traditional cantor jokes expanded. Thus, in the routine in which Jews react to a cantor's singing by comparing it to characteristic foods, a typical American is added to the typical Litvak (herring and borscht) and typical Galitsianer (meat and wine). In this new version, the "American" declares that the cantor prayed "sweet like sugar, like chop suey and chow mein, . . . like ham and eggs, like hot dogs *mit* mustard."

Hymie Jacobson and Fannie Lubritsky as Mexicans in *The American Rebitsin* by William Segal, an example of escapist entertainment.

Indeed, the adjustment itself, the very effort to assimilate, is part of Yiddish vaudeville's special material. A typical comic song, whose chorus asks rhetorically "What can you *makh* [do], *es is* [it's] America," contrasts the way Jews are supposed to behave in the old country and the new. (This mixture of Yiddish and English is common in the choruses of comic songs.) In the old country, complains the singer, you knew which was the man and which the woman; but here in America, the man has no beard, and furthermore the earlocks and even the pants are worn by women. In the old country, first came the wedding and then, a year later, the circumcision; in America, couples have the baby first and then get around to getting married. But—the chorus keeps repeating ruefully—might as well get used to the new ways: *"es is* America."

As life in America went on, vaudeville accumulated material, so the body of tradition grew by accretion. Miami Beach retirement hotels and fancy suburban bar mitzvah parties joined the Catskill bungalow resorts as subjects that always got a laugh. For Yiddish vaudeville audiences of the 1940s, the Lower East Side had begun to seem as far away as the old country and evoked the same sort of sentimental nostalgia. Audiences savored medleys of old show tunes and references to stars of what, in retrospect, came to be perceived as the golden age, now past, of Yiddish theatre.

Although Zionism was always part of the material of Yiddish vaudeville because it was part of Jewish culture, it became more important onstage with the establishment of the state of Israel in 1948. There were patriotic songs, Israeli folk dances with Middle Eastern motifs, jokes about Golda Meir, Brezhnev, and Nasser. Young Israeli performers joined the bill, singing Israeli hit tunes in Hebrew and in Yiddish translation. Besides Israel, another pressing concern of American Jewry has been assimilation, in particular the growing rate of intermarriage. So it was only natural that songs like "A Yiddish *Meydl* [Girl] Needs a Yiddish Boy" should have become popular, and stayed popular.

Abraham and Rose Rabinovitch, Tillie Rabinovitch (fourth person, unidentified), an example of portrayal of homesickness scenes.

Not only is much of the substance of Yiddish vaudeville traditional—the religious figures, the memories of roots, the experiences of immigration and Americanization—even some of the very forms of Yiddish variety entertainment are traditional. The stand-up comic, for example, is a Yiddish tradition. Since the middle ages, the *badkhen* (jester, or wedding bard) has entertained at festivities. His specialty is to deliver a long witty, rhyming speech—a sermon with laughs, or a comic routine that plays with serious ideas. He improvises the speech, at least in part, to suit each individual occasion.

A related Yiddish entertainment form is *kleynkunst* (miniature revue). *Kleynkunst* is variety, but it is more refined than vaudeville. Its material is playlets by the classical writers, as well as recitations of poems and monologues. Its music is usually art and folk songs. Its language is pure Yiddish, unmixed with English, as opposed to vaudeville's cheerfully vulgar linguistic jumble—what intellectuals call "potato Yiddish." The performers themselves—those who are still around—have come to seem like part of the cultural tradition. Jacob Jacobs just died in 1977. Among those who appeared primarily or even occasionally on the Yiddish vaudeville stage, we still have Nellie Casman, Vera Rosanko, Pesach Burstein, Lillian Lux, Herman Yablokoff, Seymour Rexite, Miriam Kressyn. They rarely perform, but when they do, their powers are clear.

As late as the 1970s, even the audiences are still traditional. They feel they are among their own. They recognize the actors, greet them, and comment on the stage action. They join in the choruses and loudly anticipate the punch lines. When the actors speak too much English, people call out *"Redt Yiddish!"* ("Speak Yiddish!"). Actors sometimes speak directly to the audience. One popular routine is to plant a heckler in the house, then bring him onstage to continue the bantering dialogue. For this warm interplay between stage and house, this intimacy and rough fellowship, television can provide no substitutes.

I have seen American Yiddish vaudeville on the Lower East Side and in Brooklyn; in midtown New York at Town Hall and on Broadway; at Lincoln Center (for several benefits); and in Miami Beach, where Leon Shachter and Gitl Stern produced a full season of daily continuous vaudeville turns for many years, until Mr. Schachter's death in 1975. Also, the *kleynkunst* company of Ben Bonus and Mina Bern still tours American cities with large Jewish populations.

In the last half century—most dramatically, in the last decade—Yiddish vaudeville has been drastically diminished. Physically, most vaudeville shows got shabby and old, as did many of the houses in which they appear. The last glitzy production was a decade ago. Performers have streamed steadily out of the Yiddish into the larger, English-speaking, entertainment world. The fate of Yiddish vaudeville is a pessimist's microcosm—violently speeded-up and exaggerated—of the fate of the Yiddish culture as a whole and of the Yiddish language itself. It is difficult to know which tense to use in describing Yiddish vaudeville: the present or the past.

Nevertheless, on those occasions when Yiddish vaudeville can still be seen, the constants remain: traditional motifs and references; traditional material for jokes, and often the traditional jokes themselves; traditional songs, with new songs gradually entering the tradition; traditional performers and performance styles; traditional sense of community. These traditions remain the heart of Yiddish vaudeville. They are what have made it a truly popular entertainment—of and for its own people.

Laurence Senelick

George L. Fox and Bowery Pantomime*_____

A pantomime may have been the first original play staged in New York. When the "New Pantomime Entertainment in Grotesque Characters, called the Adventures of Harlequin and Scaramouch, or the Spaniard Trick'd" played on February 12, 1738-1739, at Henry Holt's Long Room east of Broadway, it initiated a style of comic spectacle that came to stay.[1]

By the middle of the eighteenth century, the Hallams and other troupes had added pantomimes as welcome leavening to heavier bills. These were in the manner of the so-called mythological pantos popularized in London by John Rich, with their murky neoclassical opening scenes and mute, mimic harlequinades to follow. For the most part, the American version clove closely to the English, with the same scripts and the same performers appearing on both sides of the Atlantic. That some attempt was made to acclimate the form is apparent from such titles as *Harlequin Traveller and the Temple of the Sun* (1800) and *Harlequin Panattahah or the Genii of the Algonquins* (1810),[2] fanciful counterparts to Sheridan's *Pizarro* and Rogers's *Ponteach*.

In shape and content, however, the pantomime remained a foreign transplant, suitable for rounding off an evening or celebrating the holiday season. Grimaldi's style of pantomime—a full evening of song and slapstick on a fairy tale base—was never very popular in the early republic,[3] although his London hits were exported. The prestigious Park Theatre, declining in its fortunes, stooped to attempt full-length pantomime under the tutelage of Joe Grimaldi Wells, but even there the experiment failed.[4] When the English clown E. J. Parsloe sailed to New York at Christmas 1831 to repeat at the Bowery Theatre his successes in *Mother Goose*, he was so

---

*Professor Senelick wishes it to be understood that this essay is a drastic abridgement of a longer, more reflective study of Fox.

dismayed by the audience's silence, "broken only by the cracking of peanuts," that on the fourth night of the run, during his transformation from
Squire Bugle to Clown, he burst into tears.[5]

Greater enthusiasm was shown to the French *ballet-pantomime* perfected
by Mazurier when it was introduced to New York by the Ravels, whose
name for thirty years stood for pantomime. Mazurier's most famous
creation—Jocko the Brazilian Ape—had appeared at the Bowery, in an interpretation by Gouffe, the same season as Parsloe's *Mother Goose*, and it
proved so successful that he played it in a number of variations, such as *The
Island Ape* and *Pitcairn's Island*.[6] The Ravels, who arrived the next year
(1832), offered more sophisticated versions of Jocko and of other Mazurier
scenarios, loading the originally low-key and delicate work of Mazurier
with elaborate tricks of transformation and full-scale ballets to cover the
more difficult scene changes. Heightening these balletic *féeries* with rope-
dancing, acrobatics, and spectacular leaps, the Ravels made a smash at
Niblo's Garden in the summer months, and so came to popularize what was
known erroneously as "the Italian style" of pantomime, which used no
dialogue. The pathos was considerable, and tears flowed freely at the death
of the ape in *Jocko* and *Pongo*. With this emphasis on gymnastics, scenic
display, and refined feeling, the Ravels were halfway to *The Black Crook*,
and, as Hannah Winter has noted, "what the Ravels began, the Kiralfys
would finish"[7] in the direction of spectacle and extravaganza.

But between the Ravels and the Kiralfys appeared one performer who
imitated the former and imported the latter, and meanwhile brought pantomime to a pitch of success it was never again to enjoy in America. George
Washington Lafayette Fox (1825-1877), though heralded in his day as "the
American Grimaldi" and "the Talma of pantomime," remembered for a
generation afterwards as the funniest man of his time, has remained as
mute in histories as he was in his pantos. So well known was his *vis comica*,
so well attended were his best productions, that critics and chroniclers
thought it supererogatory to go into detail. Yet his earliest attempts at launching pantomimes at various theatres in the Bowery were, for the most
part, ignored by newspapers uninterested in recommending such sordid fare
to their family readership.

Fox came to pantomime early and casually. He had first seen the Ravels
at the Tremont Theatre in Boston in November 1832, four months after
their arrival in the States. He was then seven years old, but was already a
stage veteran of two years' standing.[8] As it happened, his first successes
were made as comic Yankees and burlesque heroes; and it was not until he
had moved from Boston to the Bowery that he tried his hand at a pantomime.

James Purdy, the manager of the National Theatre in Chatham Street,
began enhancing his pantos to compete with the Ravels at Niblo's Garden,
and attempted to imitate their *Mazulem the Night Owl*, in which he cast a

Frenchman as clown and Fox as harlequin, chiefly because Fox was a good dancer who could take high leaps through the flats and pratfalls on the floor. When the clown left after a quarrel, Fox succeeded to his role.[9] His first "official" appearance in pantomime was on December 24, 1850, in *The Golden Axe*, as Farmer Gubbins, the sort of yokel part he had mastered in his Providence and Boston apprenticeship.[10] In fact, *The Golden Axe* had been produced at the Boston Museum three years earlier, billed as a "pantomimic fairy play"—its finale described in the programme as "Stars and Stripes, American Colors, *warranted not to run*, Bunker Hill, and Buena Vista! Lots of Patriotism!"[11] The combination of chauvinism and slapstick proved irresistible, and Fox was to prescribe the mixture as before in heavier and heavier doses.

But for all the flag-waving, Fox might never have developed pantomime beyond an afterpiece had it not been for the influence of foreigners. He attended Ravel matinees assiduously, studying Gabriel's finesse and acrobatic grace with great concentration.[12] In 1855, he staged *The Green Monster*, a blatant copy of a Ravel original,[13] and for Christmas 1856, he imitated an English pantomime by Pereth entitled *Planche, or the Lively Fairies* "with extensive additions and new inventions" by Fox, who had undertaken the entire *mise-en-scène* at Purdy's insistence. It proved to be a huge success.[14] "The people's theatre is filled to overflowing every night to witness the fairy spectacle of 'Planche'," proclaimed *The Spirit of the Times*. "The spectators spend the evening here in admiration of the tricks, transformations &c. in the piece. Some of the tricks are rather 'broad,' rather indelicate, but they were heartily laughed at by the masculines, while the ladies tittered and hid their faces."[15] It is likely that the bawdy latitude, not in the English original, had been provided to suit the taste of "the people's theatre."

Success, as it tends to do in America, led to the belief that bigger is better. Purdy laid on a scene designer and a special machinist to enable Fox to produce *Boreas, the Spirit of Air* in 1857 "in a style of brilliancy and splendor never before witnessed on the stage . . . at a cost of over three thousand dollars."[16] By the time Fox and his partner James Lingard assumed the management of the Old Bowery Theatre in 1858, his public had expressed its preference for seeing him whenever possible in pantomime, and there he was to stage brilliant and striking productions, remarkable for stage tricks of his own devising. In essence, the stories remained the standard fairy tales of English panto: *Aladdin, Mother Goose, Jack the Giant Killer*; but they were infused with local references, hearty vulgarity, and Fox's inimitable comic inventions. When he reentered the Bowery Theatre in 1862 as sole lessee, pantomime had become the principal industry of that establishment.

"The New York audiences," Olive Logan assured her readers, "are, for the most part, extremely sedate, decorous, and, save at the Bowery, seem devoid of the decidedly plebeian element."[17] Her one exception is classic in its understatement. When Fox first began acting in New York in 1850, the area around Purdy's National was already a byword for roughnecks and rowdies. It was infested with the notorious "Bowery B'hoys" or "Dead Rabbits" who, when not interfering in municipal elections, spent their time chasing fire engines and indulging in rock fights with aficionados of rival engine companies. A local conflagration could result in a neighborhood war that went on for days, with skirmishing moving from street to street, like a lethal version of a floating crap game.[18]

This was the audience that Fox wooed and won. The motley crowds of butcher boys, bootblacks, prostitutes, and harnessmakers of Chatham Square and the Five Points were not easy to please; any entertainer had first to overcome the noise produced by the crowd before he could proceed. Punching their neighbors in the side or mashing down hats in their enthusiasm, Bowery audiences could be vociferous in their approval, but highly exacting in their appraisal. Continuous devouring of pigs' feet and peanuts during the performance inspired the journalist's nickname for the "gods," "the peanut gallery."

As at the transpontine playhouses of London or the theatres of the Boulevard du Crime in Paris, the public called for blood-and-thunder, wanting to feed fat on horrors. The criminous and the sulphurous were its favorite elements, and its most popular hero was Richard III in a writhing, ranting interpretation, striking sparks off his sword blade. "They don't affect anything humorous on the stage unless it be in the shape of burnt cork or comic song," commented one observer.[19] Consequently, the only kind of comedy that could capture the attention or slake the thirst for sensation would depend more on buffoonery than on wit, more on pantomime than on verbal humor; yet these mobs soon learned to greet Fox's entrance on stage with roars of welcome and howls of laughter. Clown, in his portrayal, with his ruthless disregard for the safety of his fellowman, his pursuit of his own selfish ends, and his constant recourse to violence, appealed as a species of albino Gloster, the sword exchanged for a billy club pilfered from the constabulary. Onstage, his power over the mobility was complete. "A word from Fox would still a tumult, and at his command the shrill strains of the 'Bowery pit' would instantly cease."[20]

The loyal audience at the National had followed him when he moved to the Old Bowery (or "Old Drury," as he preferred to call it), a large house that sat nearly three thousand in its benched pit and its four semicircular galleries, the topmost reserved for blacks.[21] And the same crowds traveled with Fox when he took over the lease of the New Bowery in 1859, remodeling it to suit a more fashionable clientele that was being lured downtown by his reputation for hilarity. The pit was removed, a more elegant "parquette" installed, and the Bowery boy relegated to the gallery.[22] Before the renovation, the pit had been packed with newsboys, kept in order by a policeman wielding a rattan, but incapable of stifling their shouts of "Hi! hi!" after a star-spangled tableau.[23]

If, by these alterations, Fox hoped to cater to an audience with more decorum than gusto, he still responded zealously to the demand for horse-play. All but the rough outlines of a Ravel barbershop sketch disappeared in Fox's translation with its whitewash brushes, buckets of lather, and cleavers stropped in place of razors.[24] He was never above a bit of crudeness or in-decency if it got a laugh, a habit that would tar his good name when he transferred to Broadway. It was his fondness for "crude" material, com-bined with the sweaty proletarianism of his admirers, that kept his name out of the papers until his successes were too great to be ignored. However funny his performances, families could not safely be recommended to ven-ture their children or their reputations into the Bowery.

This may explain why the best description we have of a Fox pantomime of that vintage comes from an Englishwoman, the wife of the music hall singer Sam Cowell, who was making a financially disastrous tour of the States in the first years of the Civil War. The Cowells attended the New Bowery on March 28, 1861, where they saw the pantomime *Raoul* as an af-terpiece. Cowell's praise[25] calls to our attention a number of striking fea-tures in Fox's performance. There is the silence, the seriousness with which the absurdities are carried out, possibly a legacy from the laconic down-easterners Fox had incarnated in his early career. It seems to be a charac-teristically American way of playing comedy, later honed to a fine edge by Buster Keaton.[26] Unlike the antics of Grimaldi, Fox's boisterousness is tem-pered by sobriety of execution. Then there is the familiar delinquency of defacing a feminine image with a moustache, a piece of mischief congenial to every newsboy in the house. Bowery children were old before their time—"street-wise" in the modern phrase. No wonder Mrs. Cowell could not con-ceive of these "gags" amusing Victorian parlor-bred juveniles. Fox's rascality was homegrown, never so extravagant that it lost the correlative of every-day life, even in surrealistic pieces of business worthy of Deburau. One of his most popular *lazzi* at the Bowery was to be shot out of a gun, flattened up against a wall, and be peeled off like a piece of paper.[27]

Mrs. Cowell also makes the comparison to the Ravels, whose example Fox had not yet discarded. Disastrously, in December of the same year that he won the Cowells' kudos, Fox leased the Academy of Music to present a pantomime. The New York *Tribune* was dismissive; it referred to the piece plainly as "one of Ravel's pantomimes," and pronounced "the imitation of their style not . . . very successful."[28] Fox took a long time learning his lesson. The next year he toured his company to New England with the billing "Fox's Ravel Troupe,"[29] although two years earlier he had patriotically

advertised the same company as the Fox Troupe of American Pantomimists.[30] At the same time, he hired Tony Denier as his assistant and
understudy. Originally a circus clown, Denier had been given copies of the
Ravels' pantomimes by the French mimes themselves, and had just returned
to America after years of training in London and Manchester.[31]

When Fox appeared at Barnum's New American Museum in 1866 with
The Frisky Cobbler and *The Golden Axe*, the *Tribune* considered it point-
less to describe "pieces so thoroughly familiar to persons who have seen the
Ravels—and who hasn't"; and although the paper granted that Fox amused
uncritical children, it also hinted that he had better abandon indelicacy.[32]
He must have taken these criticisms to heart, for soon afterward he launched
a style of pantomime that owed much less to his French masters. As the new
audiences of middle-class children and parents whom he had delighted at
Barnum's began to drift toward the Bowery, he commenced a series of successes that brought American pantomime to a height of perfection it was
never to scale again.

It was while appearing at Barnum's that Fox was seen by John Oxenford
of the London *Times*, who proclaimed him "the Grimaldi of America."[33]
The justice of the title is worth examination. One admirer of Fox believed
that, had the chronology been otherwise, Grimaldi might have been described
as the Fox of England.[34] Another, who, when a boy, had seen Grimaldi,
recalled that "the G. was saturnine, F. is mellow, like its note in music. G.
was not so unctuous. He was more mobile in his face, but not so irresistibly
comic as Fox is when he strikes an attitude, or lets his brow go up and his
jaws come down, as if struck by opposite currents of electricity."[35] More
important, while Grimaldi was renowned for his catch-phrases and chorus
songs, Fox seldom spoke, following the principle of the French Pierrot. Fox
was more a comic actor than a gymnast; his absurdity resided especially in
his wide range of facial expressions, from a Fanny Brice smirk of smugness
to a Stan Laurel grimace of tears. His costume was that of the Joey, elaborately
spangled satin, ornate with frills; but the makeup was that of the Pierrot,
white face and egg-bald pate, touches of color only in the outlined lips, and
three apostrophes between his eyebrows. This *tabula rasa* was the best surface for the face-making, which delineated the character. And it was the
character of Clown, behaving like a flour-smeared Bowery b'hoy—feisty,
pugnacious, bullying, and showing off, yet cowardly, greedy, and expedient—
that enlivened the Bowery pantos and distinguished them from the elegant,
but less earthy, mimes of the Ravels. Some historians, taking a leap of faith
from Fox's early impersonation of New Englanders, claim that he turned
Clown into a Yankee;[36] but this cannot be demonstrated. The Yankee character was defined by its pithy and aphoristic speech, its phlegmatic temper,
and its native cunning and common sense; whereas Clown was not only

dumb (in both senses), he was manic, sensual, high-spirited, brutal, and enterprising, and exhibited all his emotions on his countenance. Fox turned Clown not into a Yankee, but into a New Yorker.

That a full evening of pantomime could be highly profitable as well as audience-pleasing was finally proven to Fox by the welcome response that greeted *Jack and the Beanstalk*, which had three runs in 1863 alone—a very uncommon phenomenon. He had never been shrewd at managing money, but he soon realized that the cash laid out for spectacular effects and clever tricks would pay off. *Jack and the Beanstalk* initiated a series of six increasingly popular spectacles, including *Jack the Giant Killer* and *The House that Jack Built*, that culminated in Fox's removal to Broadway. By 1865, reviewers were noting that the general public was enticed downtown by rumors of Fox's skill and the promise of amusing entertainment; and as the confluence swelled, so did pantomime's prominence on the bills, growing from a colorful afterpiece to the be-all and end-all of the evening's entertainment.[37]

Jack & Gill Went up the Hill, the offering for 1866, outdid its predecessors and packed the Bowery to the rafters for what was to be an unprecedented run of nine weeks (February 19 to May 5) twice extended, with a five-week revival in 1867. It drew in a "better class of spectator than was wont to throng to 'Old Drury,'" prompting the *Tribune* to hope that Fox would thereby be stimulated to improve the quality of Bowery amusements in general.[38] *The Spirit of the Times* deemed it "the most profitable play of the season. . . . It is, of course, to a certain extent, founded of the French models," the paper pointed out, "—this is inevitable—but though in its construction it has a foreign smack, in the acting it is thoroughly American. The Clown of Mr. Fox is neither English in broad, ungainly, stupid heaviness, nor French in pure trickery and sporting gymnastics, but while partaking somewhat of the characteristics of the two, it has still a peculiarly American humor of its own."[39]

The American twang was apparent in the name of Fox's clown, Jackadaw Jaculation; and in such local types as P. O. Bummer, a beggar; Freedman Bureau Bill, a black boy; Levy Stickemall, a merchant offering "two segars for five cents"; the Irishman Mike O'Rafferty; a Yankee peddler; and a lady shoplifter. The play opened with a grand tableau of "The Frozen Regions" near the North Pole, the site for a contest between the Ice King and the Sun Spirit. These "illuminated pictures" offered three Visions, whose relation to one another was tenuous. The first, which displayed Sir John Franklin and Doctor Kane, the great explorers, had some topical importance, since the American Captain Hall had for three years been trying to trace the remnant of Franklin's party that had perished in the Arctic wastes. It would be even more relevant in the 1867 revival, after America had annexed Seward's

Folly. Vision Two presented Washington crossing the Delaware, and Vision Three was "Our Country's Glory, General Grant!"[40] By beginning rather than ending with a patriotic tableau, Fox secured the audience's sympathy straightway and cleared the stage for more serious buffoonery. The scene shifted, not to an English farm, but to a plantation. The harlequinade unfolded in a series of familiar locales, including a tobacco and wine store that featured Jim Crow; a hotel dining room with a peripatetic stuffed turkey, who turned the tables on the diners by attacking them with a carving knife; and a dry goods and variety store. Among Clown's disguises was that of an Italian organ-grinder with his monkey.

On September 9, 1867, Fox abandoned the Bowery and moved uptown to Mrs. John Wood's Olympic Theatre, east of Broadway above Houston Street, where he contributed to American mythology by staging and starring in *Humpty Dumpty*. But *Humpty Dumpty* was the culmination of all that had led to the sophistication, if that is the word, of pantomime in the United States; the move uptown was symbolic. It meant that a popular entertainment, hitherto regarded as ancillary and low, had gained social and commercial respectability. The year before *Humpty* opened, the New York *Clipper* had dismissed one pantomime by remarking, "Now that the dramatic season is over, this sort of entertainment, combined with a variety of curiosities, helps to fill out the dull season."[41] But there were no seasons to *Humpty Dumpty:* it ran on and on, breaking the record set by *The Black Crook* and garnering $,1,406,000 in its first version. Whenever Fox or his managers needed a box-office draw, it was revived with alterations, until Fox had compiled an exhausting 1,168 appearances in the title role in New York alone.[42] It inspired imitators galore; toured the country in miniaturized adaptations; spawned cigarstore effigies of Fox in costume and dozens of advertising handouts, gimcracks, and household items with Clown's bald countenance and Fox's name emblazoned on them. Significantly, the Olympic Theatre, by running a pantomime, became the most fashionable amusement spot in the city, its "patrons being those who used to visit Wallack's,"[43] which house took to pantomime in self-defense.

The times were absolutely ripe for this brand of elemental humor, embellished with the most gorgeous accessories money could buy; and *Humpty Dumpty*'s combination of coarseness and luxury was typical of the age. This period of social transition—when the United States was transferring its attention from political issues to business; when the North was anxious to efface its memories of the recent carnage by frantic moneymaking; when a canny trickster who sidestepped the law in his financial transactions and wound up unjailed was deemed "smart"—could appreciate the downright slipperiness of Fox's Clown as much as it did the opulent decor against which he was posed.

Humpty Dumpty, in its *Ur*-form, was pure New York. Thomas Nast composed caricatures for it, and the prologue was contributed by no less a celebrity than the mayor of the city—"Elegant" Oakey Hall. His prologue was larded with topical allusions to New Jersey and Erie Railroad stock that were greeted with knowing laughter. There followed a New Year's offering to young America, in which the four continents marched on, with Alaska and St. Thomas—the latest adjuncts to the Union—prominently featured.[44] Topicality, novelty, patriotism: a surefire, well-tested preliminary to the mélange of ballet and slapstick that was to follow.

The violence of the slapstick was extreme, involving pistols, hot flatirons, billy clubs, snowballs, and any handy missile. But this, too, corresponded to life in a city so crime-ridden that vigilante committees to protect pedestrians and safeguard property were being formed in 1869. Of this knockabout, one clown recollected that "as played by Fox, it was art of the most convincing kind. It was all action—action—action."[45]

The most classic sequence depended upon the bricks from this wall. The Fop, a Gothamite equivalent of the Dandy in Regency pantomime, comes on singing:

> My Jane, my Jane, my dearest Jane,
> Oh, never, never look so shy.

As he says "shy," HUMPTY fires a stuffed brick from the wall and hits him bang on the head. FOP stops singing, runs down to footlights, takes off his hat, and feels his head with his hand—looks at his hand—don't see any blood—shakes his fist, and expresses "he will sing it or die"—goes down in front of cottage and commences again—

> "Oh, let me like a soldier fall."

As he says "fall," HUMPTY throws a second stuffed brick, which hits him in the head, and he does a sort of half-forward somersault, and lands sitting. He gets up quick, looks towards pig-pen, sees HUMPTY laughing, and shakes his fist at him. HUMPTY fires third stuffed brick. FOP dodges it and runs off 5 E.L., just as OLD ONE TWO [the Pantaloon] comes out of cottage and catches brick in the face, which knocks him down flat on his back in front of cottage. HUMPTY laughs, and ONE TWO gets up apparently stunned—picks up brick, looks at it, rubs his head, studies a moment, puts finger aside his nose, and walks with a circling motion, the brick in his hand, to front of the pig-pen and looks behind it, supposing someone to be there hiding, when HUMPTY takes all the bricks and lets them fall on ONE TWO, who falls flat on his face from the weight of the bricks—he gets up, takes three bricks, and circles around stage very cautiously to R. corner. HUMPTY jumps down, takes three bricks and follows very cautiously—when ONE TWO gets to extreme R. he turns quickly and meets HUMPTY face to face. They both stand still in a picture, each with a brick raised to throw. *(Music chord)* HUMPTY makes three big steps backward to L. corner—ONE TWO follows, but makes big steps forward in time with HUMPTY— at end of third step picture as before. Repeat back to first position. HUMPTY fires brick at ONE TWO who dodges—ONE TWO fires brick at HUMPTY, who dodges in turn. This is repeated until each has thrown three bricks, when HUMPTY hits ONE TWO with a fourth brick in the head.[46]

Witnesses of this scene vividly recalled the accelerating pace of the choreography, until the air was thick with brickbats, a favored Bowery weapon; members of the audience were moved to call out, at the height of battle, "Who threw the last?" This ballet of assault, if it might be so termed, enters the folklore of American comedy and is eventually transmuted into poetry by George Herriman in the sadomasochistic courtship of Krazy Kat by Ignatz the Mouse. Just as Fox's bald and leering physiognomy recurs in the grinning inanity of the Yellow Kid, so his epic war of projectiles—bricks or loaves of bread, as in *Hiccory Diccory Dock*—lives again in the circus ring, the Keystone comedies, and the strip cartoon.

But the apotheosis to which Fox brought pantomime in America was also the start of its degeneration. The successors to *Humpty Dumpty* merely tried to imitate a good thing, and although audiences were loyal to Fox personally, they could not help pursuing more novel entertainments. E. E. Rice's *Evangeline* in 1874 gave fresh impetus to the burlesque, which began to rival pantomime in every sphere but that of the comic dumbshow.[47] Fox's pantos became cluttered with specialty acts, no longer maintaining even a pretense that they were connected to the plot. In 1872, a rumor ran that the Olympic was to be converted to a variety theatre; it might as well have been. The revival of *Humpty Dumpty* there the next year devoted its entire second act to special attractions, such as yodellers, wirewalkers, Bedouins, champion hat-spinners, and players of "musical rocks," the harlequinade not resuming until Act III. This tripartite structure, segregating Fox's antics from the olio of specialties, definitively replaced the original organic sequence of Prologue-Opening-Transformation-Harlequinade in ten scenes, and was retained in all further editions of *Humpty*. Cultural features that the Bowery boys would never have tolerated swamped the comedy. The final edition of the pantomime, *Humpty Dumpty in Every Clime,* included an aria from *Il Trovatore* performed on an oboe, and concluded with an extended multiphased set of tableaux to celebrate the upcoming Centennial of the United States. Patriotism was elbowing out comedy once again. Hidden behind all the variety acts and balletic extravaganzas, Fox ceased to be the prime feature and became a passive make-weight to the spectacle. While inferior imitators, with their *Humpy Dumpy* and *Dumpty Humpty,* cheapened and debased the original in the hinterlands, the brief flowering of pantomime in New York succumbed to the growing taste for miscellaneous diversions and lavish musical spectacle. The audience had changed: the old Bowery boy was a relict of the past, and his successors wanted diversity and splendor in place of the evening unified by one man's hilarity.

Fox, who had single-handedly glorified pantomime, now overworked by one-night stands and driven to exhaustion at having to contrive newer and better tricks and transformations, slipped into a dementia that made his grimaces hideous to those in the know and his relapses into blatant indecency frequent. In the 1875 revival of *Humpty Dumpty in Every Clime*, his dresser had to be kept in the wings in a monkey suit to rush out and belabor Fox whenever he began to get obscene, and to redirect his energies to the stunt at hand. So Mazurier's Jocko, having passed through various avatars with the Ravels at Niblo's Garden and with Denier at the Bowery, descended to a madman's attendant. One night, after an outburst of violence in the first act, Fox was persuaded into a closed carriage and transported to the insane asylum in Somerville, Massachusetts. Humpty Dumpty was too badly cracked to be mended.

NOTES

1. G. C. D. Odell, *Annals of the New York Stage* (New York, 1931) I:21-22; O. S. Coad and E. Mims, Jr., *The American Stage* (New Haven, 1929), p. 15.

2. Odell, II:91, 313.

3. Antoine Denier, *Tony Denier's Parlor Pantomimes . . .* (New York, [1864?]), Series 2, p. 2.

4. Paul Preston, "Pantomime Ancient and Modern," New York *Clipper* (May 8, 1869), p. 36.

5. M. Willson Disher, *Clowns and Pantomimes* (London, 1925), p. 143. I have been unable to verify this story from original sources.

6. Odell, III:569.

7. M. H. Winter, *Le Théâtre du Merveilleux* (Paris, 1962), p. 143.

8. W. W. Clapp, Jr., *A Record of the Boston Stage* (Boston, 1853), p. 299.

9. "Old Time Stage Favorites," unidentified clipping in the Lincoln Center Library for the Performing Arts. Another version says that the two Frenchmen engaged to play Clown and Pantaloon at the old Bowery were found "suicided" in their beds and so the Fox brothers volunteered for their roles. ("Humpty Dumpty Interviewed— What He Said and How He Said It!" *Spirit of the Times*, January 31, 1874). The dates are very incorrect here, but neither version carries much conviction.

10. Odell, VI:38-39.

11. Cecil Smith, *Musical Comedy in America* (New York, 1950), p. 8.

12. E. B. Marks, *They All Had Glamour from the Swedish Nightingale to the Naked Lady* (New York, 1944), p. 79.

13. Odell, VI:238.

14. *Spirit of the Times* (December 27, 1856), p. 552.

15. Ibid. (January 10, 1857), p. 576.

16. Ibid. (December 19, 1857), p. 540.

17. Olive Logan, *Before the Footlights and Behind the Scenes . . .* (Philadelphia, 1870), p. 385.

18. Barnaby, "Theatrical Reminiscence. G. L. Fox," New York *Herald*, undated clipping at Lincoln Center Library.

19. J. H. Browne, *The Great Metropolis: A Mirror of New York* (Hartford, Conn., 1869), p. 430. On Bowery audiences, also see New York *Clipper* (October 16, 1869), p. 222; Gustav Lening, *Die Nachtseiten von New York und dessen Verbrecherwelt von der Fünften Avenue bis zu den Five Points* (New York, 1873), pp. 582-86; and J. D. McCabe, Jr., *Lights and Shadows of New York Life* (Philadelphia, 1872), pp. 477-83. McCabe claims that the peanut-eating produced one "low unbroken growl" throughout the performances.

20. Barnaby, "Theatrical Reminiscence . . ."

21. *Spirit of the Times* (May 6, 1858), p. 264.

22. *Spirit of the Times* (October 26, 1861), p. 128.

23. Emilie Cowell, *The Cowells in America being the Diary of Mrs. Sam Cowell . . . 1860-1861*, ed. M. Willson Disher (London, 1934), p. 279.

24. Herbert S. Renton, "Humpty Dumpty [sic] and Others," New York *Sun* (April 19, 1929).

25. Emilie Cowell, pp. 279-80.

26. Keaton, curiously, attributed this trait to the English. "I made a thorough study of how English comedians, whom I consider the most accomplished, attained their results, and gradually I penetrated their secret. It lies simply in the fact that the English comedian is always a little more serious than life itself. On the basis of this knowledge I set myself the task of remaining completely serious in any situation." (Rene Fülop-Miller, *The Motion Picture in America, A History in the Making* [New York, 1938], p. 129.)

27. "The Great Pantomimist," 1874, unidentified clipping in the Harvard Theatre Collection.

28. New York *Tribune* (December 20, 1861), p. 1.

29. *Spirit of the Times* (August 2, 1862), p. 341.

30. Odell, VII:331.

31. Denier later bought the touring rights for *Humpty Dumpty* and continued to play it in a cut-down version for decades after Fox's death. See Sylvester Bleeker, "Antoine Denier," in *Denier's Parlor Pantomimes . . .* (New York [1864?]), No. 1, pp. 3-4; New York *Clipper* (February 5, 1876), p. 351; and "Humpty Dumpty Falls to His Death," New York *Sun* (March 11, 1917).

32. New York *Tribune* (August 24, 1866), p. 17.

33. T. Allston Brown, *A History of the New York Stage from the First Performance in 1732 to 1901* (New York, 1903), III:117.

34. "The Great Pantomimist," Harvard Theatre Collection.

35. Joe Jorum. "Our Dramatic Letter," unidentified clipping in Harvard Theatre Collection.

36. For instance, Barnard Hewitt, *Theatre U.S.A. 1665 to 1957* (New York, 1959), p. 208.

37. New York *Tribune* (October 21, 1865), p. 6; (December 7, 1865), p. 12.

38. New York *Tribune* (March 19, 1866), p. 8; Odell, VIII:171.

39. *Spirit of the Times* (May 5, 1866), p. 160; (March 24, 1866), p. 64.

40. G. C. Howard, *Jack & Gill Went up the Hill, the new, original, dazzling, and gorgeous comic pantomime by G. L. Fox* (New York, 1866).

41. New York *Clipper* (July 28, 1866), p. 126.

42. Odell, X:9; Brown, II:159.

43. New York *Clipper* (March 28, 1868), p. 406. A guidebook to New York in 1872 noted the exclusivity of pantomime at the Olympic: "It is devoted to pantomime, and is famous as the headquarters of the erratic genius who calls himself Humpty Dumpty." McCabe, *Lights and Shadows of New York Life*, p. 477.

44. John Denier, *Humpty Dumpty, a pantomime in a prologue and one act . . . as originally played by George L. Fox . . .* (New York, n.d.), p. 2. New York *Clipper* (March 21, 1868), p. 398. New York *Tribune* (March 11, 1868), p. 4. Fox was shortly to marry the young lady who played Alaska.

45. "Bob Fraser on the Pantomimic Art," unidentified clipping in the Harvard Theatre Collection.

46. John Denier, *Humpty Dumpty*, p. 17.

47. Smith, *Musical Comedy in America*, p. 23.

Max Morath

The Vocal and Theatrical Music of Bert Williams and His Associates _____

Mr. Morath's remarks delivered at the Conference were largely extemporaneous, interspersed with vocal performance of certain songs dealt with in the text, to his own accompaniment at the piano. The following transcript of this section of the proceedings has been edited by Mr. Morath for publication.

These songs were written by a very interesting group of composer-performers at the turn of the century, primarily here in New York. Now, I am essentially an entertainer; that's what I consider myself. I do not attempt deep scholarship into these subjects, as many of you folks do. (I draw upon your writing and on your knowledge quite frequently, I might say.)

The thing that fascinates me about theatrical and popular music and popular acts of the past, generally, is whether they are still usable. I believe that most popular music is almost totally a manifestation of fashion, that it should go out of fashion and should disappear. I don't think we should try to save everything. But in each generation of popular music there are artists whose work will last. My criterion for such work—and it will be the criterion that will govern every number that I do this afternoon—is: can I perform this successfully for a contemporary audience that has no scholarly or historical interest in the song? Is it performable material?—that is, is it repeatable?—and, therefore, not simply fashion, but quality material?

With one or two exceptions, these songs may be considered special material written for performers by professionals. They were not necessarily big hits in the popular market, but were the mainstays of certain vaudeville or theatrical acts.

So this is Bert Williams. It is Bert Williams in 1903 in the famous *In Dahomey* musical, a song written by Williams and Alex Rogers—one of the groups that worked with him. As I do the song for you, I'd like to say that

I'm not trying to *imitate* Bert Williams—I wouldn't do it if I could. It would be demeaning both to him and to me. I'm doing this song as if it were written for me yesterday.

> MY HARD LUCK STARTED WHEN I WAS BORN/
> AT LEAST SO THE OLD FOLKS SAY/
> THAT SAME HARD LUCK, BEEN MY BEST FRIEND/
> RIGHT UNTIL THIS VERY DAY/
> WHEN I WAS BORN MY MOMMA'S FRIENDS/
> TO FIND A NAME, THEY TRIED/
> NAMED ME AFTER MY PAPA, AND THE NEXT DAY MY PAPA DIED/
> I'M JONAH MAN, JUST A JONAH MAN/
> MY FAMILY FOR MANY YEARS/
> LOOKED DOWN ON ME AND THEN SHED TEARS/
> WHY AM I JONAH? I DON'T UNDERSTAND/
> BUT I'M A GOOD SUBSTANTIAL FULL-FLEDGED, REAL/
> FIRST CLASS JONAH MAN. FIRST CLASS JONAH MAN/
>
> A FRIEND OF MINE ONCE GAVE TO ME HIS MEAL TICKET, ONE DAY/
> HE SAID, "YOU MIGHT AS WELL HAVE THIS. I'VE GOT TO GO AWAY."/
> I THANKED HIM AS MY HEART WITH GRATITUDE AND JOY DID BOUND/
> AND THEN WHEN I REACHED THAT RESTAURANT, THE PLACE HAD JUST BURNED DOWN. SO I SAY I'M A JONAH MAN. I'M A JONAH MAN/
> JUST LIKE IN THAT OLD, OLD TALE,/
> BUT YOU KNOW SOMETIMES, WISHED I WAS THE WHALE/
> WHY AM I JONAH? I DON'T UNDERSTAND?/
> BUT I'M A GOOD SUBSTANTIAL FULL-FLEDGED, REAL/
> FIRST CLASS JONAH MAN, FIRST CLASS JONAH MAN.

Bert Williams was writing with a man whom he was to be associated with for several years, Alex Rogers. Now, of course, you've got to remember that this song from 1903 came right at the height of the coon song craze.

The coon song was an extremely popular form of vocal that lasted for a number of years, changed as it went along, and right now resides exactly where it should—on the back shelves of the pop museum collecting dust. It's a sociological curiosity and nothing more. The fascination to me about Bert Williams and this small group of men who worked here in New York with him is that, while in many cases they were forced to work inside that coon-song stereotype, they never really compromised with it. Perhaps even without the knowledge of the white audiences or even the black audiences to whom they played, they *transcended* it; they wrote around it.

I would like to assure you that of the songs I'm going to do this afternoon there is only one word (and I think most of you will not even pick it up) that could be considered a tasteless, stereotype reference. In other words, these men—many of whom, of course, worked in blackface even though they were

Max Morath

black—worked past that stereotype and wrote songs that a person like me or any performer today can do without changing, simply as material that becomes universal. "I'm a Jonah Man," as far as I'm concerned, is universal. Bert Williams wrote and sang about hard times and bad luck, and many of us have experienced those, so the "Jonah Man" fits a lot of us.

Another thing I would like to inject, for those of you who are listening to the harmonies: these are not my harmonies; they are in the original score (with one or two exceptions, of course, I can't help but lend my own piano style to it). But I'm not modernizing the chords in any way. That chord progression in the verse of "Jonah Man"—if you know much about what they were doing in 1903 with vocal scoring, you'll agree that it's a rather rich and unusual chord progression for a popular song.

I don't think "Jonah Man" was a big popular success, but it was certainly a theatrical success—not necessarily in vaudeville, by the way. Most of the songs that I'm doing here are not from Bert's vaudeville days as much as they are from his legit days, from the black musicals *Abyssinia*, *In Dahomey*, and the *Ziegfeld Follies*.

Bert Williams was born in 1874 somewhere in the West Indies. I've heard Nassau, I've heard other places. He probably spoke Spanish until he was about eight years old, and no English. Nobody knows (I believe I'm right) what his real name was. His father became a railroad man, and they moved to Riverside, California, where he grew up. He went to Stanford and took some classes and then he got into show business in the San Francisco Bay area, which is where he met his partner, George Walker. Williams and Walker became one of the great theatrical teams, until Walker's death at a very early age, around 1910. Williams then went on as a single and reached the height of the theatre world—that is, the *Ziegfeld Follies.* He died in 1922. So that's a brief summary of the brief career of Bert Williams, who worked almost all his life in cork, and from behind that mask gave us these songs.

There was a group of writers who worked with him; many of them of course worked with other performers too. They were thorough-going professionals, but you find their names over and over on Bert's songs.

This next one is also from around 1903. It was written by Williams and Walker; by this time the partnership was thriving. The words were added-to or revised by James Weldon Johnson and I'm sorry that I can't tell you exactly when. But here again is a song that was essentially written and performed in 1903. I'm not changing the chords and, except for the change of an "am" to an "is," I'm not changing the words. If you've ever been broke, I think this song will say as much to you as any song ever written about being broke.

MONEY IS THE ROOT OF ALL EVIL. NO MATTER WHERE YOU HAPPEN TO GO/
BUT NOBODY HAS ANY OBJECTIONS TO THAT ROOT. NOW AIN'T THAT SO?/
YOU KNOW HOW IT IS WITH MONEY? HOW IT MAKES YOU FEEL AT EASE/
WORLD PUTS ON A GREAT BIG SMILE AND YOUR FRIENDS ARE AS THICK AS BEES/
BUT WHEN YOUR MONEY'S RUNNING LOW, AND YOU'RE STUCK WITH A SOLITARY DIME/
YOUR CREDITORS ARE MANY, AND YOUR FRIENDS ARE FEW/
THAT'S AN AWFUL TIME/

THAT'S A TIME, THAT IS THE TIME/
WHEN IT'S ALL GOING OUT AND NOTHING COMIN' IN/
THAT'S THE TIME WHEN TROUBLES BEGIN/
YOUR MONEY'S RUNNING LOW. PEOPLE SAY I TOLD YOU SO/
YOU CAN'T BORROW A DOLLAR FROM YOU KIN/
WHEN IT'S ALL GOING OUT, NOTHING COMIN' IN./

WHEN IT'S ALL GOING OUT, NOTHING COMIN' IN, THAT'S WHEN
YOUR TROUBLES BEGIN/
YOUR MONEY'S RUNNING LOW AND PEOPLE SAY I TOLD YOU SO/
YOU CAN'T BORROW A DOLLAR FROM YOUR KIN/
WELL IT'S ALL GOING OUT, NOTHIN COMIN' IN

So there again is Bert Williams around 1903. Actually, it's Bert and these writers again working very closely, apparently, with one another. I don't suppose we will ever know exactly what kind of fraternity that was, but you see these names turning up. There was a professional society called the Frogs that they all belonged to. They had meetings—a regular structured kind of club—but so much of that has disappeared. Their names include, in addition to Bert Williams and his partner George Walker, both James Weldon Johnson and his brother, Rosamond Johnson. They include very prominently Bob Cole, who was introduced to you by Helen Armstead-Johnson as not only a songwriter but also as a performer and an entrepreneur; Ernest Hogan is included, I think to a lesser degree. And then there are other composers whose names are very remote today: Tim Brymn, James Burris, and Chris Smith, whose *music* is not remote. Chris Smith wrote "Ballin' the Jack," among other very popular hits; but he also wrote some of this special material, and I'll get to one of his tunes. James Reese Europe was part of that group. Europe, the great conductor, met a very untimely death right after World War I, or he would have, I'm sure, made a tremendous mark on theatre. So that's essentially this group of Negro men working together, Bert Williams being the star for whom much material was written and to whom it gravitated.

Now I'm sure many of you wonder: Where does ragtime fit in with this? After all, those years we're talking about—1900, 1903, 1906—that's right smack in the middle of the emergence of ragtime, with the "Maple Leaf Rag" coming out of Missouri in 1899. The answer is, of course, ragtime did come into many of these songs: in the underpinnings, in the structure of these songs. I'll tell you something; I have a feeling that a good many more years from now, when the books are finally written, they will declare that ragtime influenced the words of our songs and the conceits of our songs more than it did our dances and piano music. Because the more I look into this, the more I find that as soon as ragtime surfaced—that free, syncopating, vital idea— song *lyrics* changed completely. Structure, Victorian sentences disappeared, and slang appeared. Real people populated rather than artificial types, and one of the first songs to do that was one that was quite popular and I'm sure it's familiar to practically all of you: "Under the Bamboo Tree," written by Bob Cole and the Johnson brothers. It was interpolated in a Broadway show called *Sally in Our Alley* and was introduced by Marie Cahill, a white woman.

I brought the music along, because I want to be sure that I play exactly, from the sheet music, the syncopations that lie in the left and right hands. I think that without those you won't realize how they influence the lyric. This may sound like a dialect lyric; I've never thought it was. The work "like" is spelled "Lak-a." That's not a typical dialect form. I think there is another reason that extra syllables were being put in there and I'll get to it in a minute, but here is "Under the Bamboo Tree," with the piano almost as it was written and published in 1902.

IF YOU LAK-A ME, LAK-A I LAK-A YOU/
AND WE LAK-A BOTH THE SAME/
I LAK-A SAY THIS VERY DAY/
I LAK-A CHANGE YOUR NAME/
CAUSE I LAK-A YOU AND LOVE-A YOU TRUE/
AND IF YOU A-LAK-A ME/
ONE LIVES AS TWO, TWO LIVE AS ONE UNDER THE BAMBOO TREE/

Those extra syllables seem to have been used in early ragtime songs to fill the spaces, so the singer had a sound to put in those syncopated gaps. Very soon, singers and instrumentalists learned to allow the gap itself to do the syncopating.

This leads me to a song I would like to do quickly for you. I think it amplifies that idea of ragtime's influence on words of songs. The composer of this song was not a part of the group that I'm discussing here, but he was certainly in New York singing, playing, and writing. Ben Harney came out of Louisville, Kentucky, in 1896 with his ragtime piano. He opened at Keith's Union Square Theatre on January 26, 1896, with this song, three years before the "Maple Leaf Rag" was published. So Ben Harney kicked off the twentieth century four years early. There are a lot of extra syllables in this song, too, and that's the point. It's ragtime in words. At the time—this is 1896—think of what else was popular. America was singing "Casey Would Waltz with the Strawberry Blonde," "The Bicycle Built for Two," "The Picture That Was Turned Against the Wall," and "She Is More to Be Pitied than Censured." This is Harney. Now I'm certainly not performing it as he did it, but I'm sticking fairly close to the sheet music (which was published by Witmark that year) in the accompaniments and in the lyric.

OTHER EVENING EVERYTHING WAS STILL, OH BABE/
THE MOON WAS A CLIMBIN' DOWN BEHIND THE HILL, A-OH- BABE/
I THOUGHT EVERYBODY WAS A-FASTA-SLEEP/
BUT OLD MAN JOHNSON WAS ON HIS BEAT, A-OH BABE/
NOW I WENT DOWN TO A (FLOATIN') CRAP GAME/
WHERE THE BOYS WERE A-GAMBLIN' WITH MIGHT AND MAIN/

THOUGHT I'D BE A SPORT AND BE DEAD GAME,/
I GAMBLED ALL MY MONEY, BUT I WASN' TO BLAME/
ONE FELLA'S POINT WAS-A-LITTLE JOE/
BET SIX BITS A-QUARTER THAT HE'D MAKE THE FOUR/
HE MADE THE POINT, BUT HE MADE NO MORE/
JUST THEN JOHNSON CAME THROUGH THE DOOR/
OH, MISTER JOHNSON TURN ME LOOSE/
I GOT NO MONEY BUT A GOOD EXCUSE/
OH, MR. JOHNSON, I'LL BE GOOD/
OH, MR. JOHNSON TURN ME LOOSE. DON'T TAKE ME TO THE
CALABOOSE/
OH, MR. JOHNSON I'LL BE GOOD/

I must tell you, that song, as opposed to these other songs that were written by the New York group, *was* a coon song. The "floating" crap game was a "nigger" crap game. The second verse is about the stealing of chickens, and "Mr. Johnson," of course, was a Negro expression for the law. "Mr. Johnson, Turn Me Loose" was a coon song. But it's an exciting song because of the ragtime in it, and because of the slang. So I do it in performance, but I change it. I've rewritten the second verse. I like the song. I don't like some of the words, but it's good program material because Ben Harney was there with it in 1896.

I'll tell you a funny thing about Ben Harney, and I don't suppose anybody's ever going to know the answer to this. It relates to one of my pet theories about what we're doing here in these four days. All that activity back there; all that popular music theatre business; all the things that have happened in the arts in this country are in a state of absolute chaos and we're never going to know what really happened. Everytime you think you've got a handle on the absolute, you find out you're wrong.

Ben Harney played Keith's Union Square and he played Tony Pastor's. That means by definition he was *white*. He was published by Witmark, he toured, he was called Mr. Ragtime. He was a star, Ben Harney. When I first met Eubie Blake back in the early 1960s, we were talking about Harney and one thing and another, and Eubie said, "Well, you knew he was *black* didn't you?" I said, "No, Eubie, I didn't." I did know, by the way, that Ben Harney died in the 1930s in a black neighborhood in Philadelphia. "Well," Eubie said, "of course he was." He meant Harney was "passing," obviously, because he worked white, but he was black. That's a theory and it might be true. It might explain Harney's command of ragtime at such an early point in time. Eubie didn't know him well, but he certainly knew of him and had seen him work.

Another very interesting theory has been advanced on this by William Shafer. I'm sure many of you know him as the author of the book *The Art of Ragtime*, with Johannes Reidel. He's an English professor down at Berea, and he's a very sensitive and scholarly guy, and he's working in Kentucky, which is the home of Ben Harney. William Shafer's idea, which he has never put in print but which I'm sure he would not mind my quoting, is that Ben Harney was white, passing as black; that he preferred to live in a black neighborhood and die in a black neighborhood of Philadelphia. So there's one of those little scenarios. We're never going to know the answer to that. How can we? So there you are: Ben Harney, peripheral to these other performers, except that he was one who injected ragtime into the words and into the theatre and, therefore, influenced other men.

Now we come to a ragtime song which is later—1909—and this introduces some other writers. Tim Brymn, James Burris, and Chris Smith wrote this song, I'm not sure whether for any *particular* performer, but it was in a show called *His Honor the Barber*, in 1909, as an interpolation. This is my performing version in a way, but this type of song was usually talked, with the chorus sung, and it definitely had a strong ragtime base.

> OLE JASPER GREEN, THE DEACON OF THE CHURCH DOWN
> SOUTH CAROLINE/
> HAD A HABIT OF CALLIN' ON FOLKS ALONG ABOUT
> EATIN TIME/
> THE OTHER DAY OUT ON THE STREET MET MY AUNT,
> MANDY LOU/
> HE SAID "SOMETIME TOMORROW I THINK I'LL CALL ON YOU"/
> SHE SAID, "COME 'ROUND ANYTIME, MAKES NO DIFFERENCE/
> BUT THESE FEW WORDS I'VE GOT TO SAY RIGHT HERE IN
> SELF-DEFENSE/
>
> YOU GOTTA COME AFTER BREAKFAST, BRING YOUR OWN LUNCH,
> AND LEAVE BEFORE SUPPERTIME/
> YOU DO THAT I FEEL POSITIVE WE'RE GONNA GET ALONG FINE/
> EVERYBODY'S WELCOME OVER AT MY HOUSE, WHETHER IT'S RAIN
> OR SHINE/
> IF THEY COME AFTER BREAKFAST, AND THEY BRING ALONG THEIR
> LUNCH AND THEY LEAVE BEFORE SUPPERTIME."*

To go to a Bert Williams song now, by essentially the same songwriting team: Chris Smith (who was also a performer) and James Burris. About Burris I can tell you very little, except that he was definitely a member of this group and had a large output of songs for a good ten- to twenty-year period. This song was one of Bert Williams's hallmarks. The lyrics simply defy the fact that it was at one time considered (because of the context in which it must have been presented in the theatre) racist. It's, again, a song about trouble. If the words came from a blackface in tramp clothes to an audience in 1910, one would see another shuffling coon. But I think it's a beautiful song, and I've recorded it, and I've used it. It has that universal quality I spoke of earlier. This is "Constantly," by Chris Smith, James Burris, and Bert Williams. I really want to do these chords very much the way they were written because I think they're remarkable for their time.

GOOD LUCK HAUNTS ME, TAUNTS ME, FLAUNTS ME CONSTANTLY/
BAD LUCK MEETS ME, GREETS ME, SEEKS ME, CONSTANTLY/
SOMETIMES I FEEL LIKE A BIRD IN A TREE/
FLYING ROUND SO GRACEFUL AND FREE/
BUT IT SEEMS HARD LUCK CLIPS MY WINGS FOR ME, CONSTANTLY/
I USED TO BE A LUCKY SMOKE, SPENDING MONEY WAS A JOKE/
BUT NOW IT SEEMS THAT I STAY BROKE, CONSTANTLY/
I NEVER HAD TO WORRY ABOUT MONEY BEFORE/
I HAD GOOD TIMES AND FRIENDS GALORE/
BUT NOW TROUBLE'S HANGING AROUND MY DOOR, CONSTANTLY/

GOOD LUCK HAUNTS ME, TAUNTS ME, FLAUNTS ME, CONSTANTLY/
SOMETIMES I FEEL LIKE A BIRD IN THE TREE/
FLYING AROUND SO GAYLY AND FREE/
BUT IT SEEMS HARD LUCK CLIPS MY WINGS FOR ME. CONSTANTLY/*

That song, I think, will be sung as the years go by simply because it's a great song. It's got everything a song's supposed to have. It's got a good melody that you can remember. It's got a nice chord progression that goes about where you expect it to go, but fools you once in a while. And it can be sung by anybody of any color at any time—*constantly.*

Now, here's what your Conference has done for me. I went to the reception last night, which was delightful, and through my good friend, Helen Armstead-Johnson, I met Garfield Dawson. I had never met Garfield before. Here I was, planning to come in and tell you knowledgeably about Williams and Walker, and *he was there!* This man was George Walker's apprentice: he was taught the strut; he was taught the ropes in show business by George Walker in the last few years of George's life; and when Garfield went on to his own career, he was known professionally as George Walker, Jr. He told me some of the things we don't necessarily want to hear about Bert: that he could be very uncommunicative; that he was not often helpful to this fellow performers (whatever their race); that he was somewhat isolated from the rest of the black community. Then we were talking about some of Bert's songs, and Garfield said, "You know what the big hit was, don't you?" I said, "You mean, 'Nobody.'" "No," he said, "not 'Nobody'; sure, but it wasn't a hit. The one from Abyssinia, in 1906." And he started to sing it, and I realized that I used to do it. I recorded it back in 1969 on an RCA album. Garfield proceeded to do the second verse, which is *not* in the sheet music. That's when I wished I'd brought my cassette. And he told me of the scenario into which the song fits, and I had never known it. You might say it's an "existential" song; it's about minding your own damn business and getting out of trouble. Again, a thing that in blackface must have seemed racially stereotyped. But the scene was set in Africa, and Bert was playing the stupid member of the duo, Walker was playing the dapper one. Bert steals some minor trinket and, of course, he's brought into this Moslem court and told that he's going to have his hand chopped off. Sounds kind of grim, but I'm sure they played it for a lot of laughs, and he sang this song. According to Garfield Dawson, this was Bert's greatest hit. That's probably open to contest, but anyway, it's one of those fine songs, again, with the original words and the original chord progression. *[Plays "Let It Alone"]*

Joe Smith

Dr. Kronkhite Revisited_____

*Joe Smith and Charlie Dale's "Dr. Kronkhite"
sketch is a vaudeville classic. They performed it,
with very slight changes from performance to
performance, from about 1906 until some years
before Dale's death in 1971—and Mr. Smith,
though long retired, continued to perform it
every now and then—as he did, in his mid-
nineties, on November 18, 1977, at Lincoln
Center. The transcript of that performance can
merely suggest the comic effect of the gestures,
tone, and accents: the Patient's (Mr. Smith's)
New Yorkese and Dr. Kronkhite's (Jerry
McGrath's) German accent (the Nurse was played
by Janice Pelham).*

*In his talk, which follows, Joe Smith tells about
his partnership with Dale. (Neil Simon's recent
film* The Sunshine Boys, *starring George Burns
and Walter Matthau, is said to be loosely based
on this partnership.) Mr. Smith also reminisces
about their association with the Avon Comedy
Four, the illustrious comic act that, as Bill Smith
notes in his* The Vaudevillians, *played before
Bowery audiences and American presidents.*

Patient enters
Nurse: How do you do, sir.
Patient: Is this the office of Dr. Kronkhite?
Nurse: Yes. I'm his nurse.
Patient: His nurse? The doctor sick too?
Nurse: I'm a trained nurse.
Patient: Trained nurse. Oh, you do tricks, eh? What's the doctor's office hours?
Nurse: Well, they're from 9 to 12, and 12 to 3, 3 to 6 and 6 to 9, and 9 to 12.

Patient: He gives good odds, he must be a horse doctor.

Nurse: Well, those are his hours.

Patient: The doctor in now?

Nurse: Yes, but he's busy with a patient.

Patient: Okay, I'll wait.

Nurse: Here, have a chair. Take a chair.

Patient: Thank you, I'll take it on my way out.

Nurse: No, I mean sit down.

Patient: I'll fix that up, you wouldn't know. I'll put a needlepoint seat on it. It'll look sharp. I'll kick it a little bit and make Chickendale. Any questions?

Nurse: No.

Patient: No, no questions. All right. I'll wait. Is the doctor good?

Nurse: Yes, very good.

Patient: Thank you.

Nurse: And the doctor will be here very shortly.

Patient: Thank you. *(Watching Nurse's back as she goes out.)* She got a nice face. All of a sudden I have some trouble with my throat. When I had the flu, I took so much medicine during my illness that I was sick for a long time after I got well. Now I think I got hardening of the artilleries, or something. I don't feel so good.

Voice (offstage): Doctor, don't hurt me, please! Please, doctor! Don't, don't hurt me, doctor! Oh, you butcher!

Patient: Well, I'm cured. I'm going.

Nurse (enters): Where're you going? Here, here, where're you going?

Patient: I'm going home. I forgot something.

Nurse: What did you forget?

Patient: I forgot to stay home.

Nurse: Oh, calm yourself!

Patient: Look, I remember where I left my umbrella.

Nurse: Calm yourself!

Patient: What are they doing, hanging a convict there?

Nurse: No, that was only a small boy.

Patient: Small boy! *(Patient starts walking away.)*

Nurse: Yes. Running out on the doctor?

Patient: Better than being carried out.

Nurse: Here comes the doctor now. *(Doctor enters.)*

Patient: Are you a doctor?

Doctor: I'm a doctor.

Patient: I'm dubious.

Doctor: How do you do, Mr. Dubious. It's good to meet you.

Patient: I'm still dubious.

Doctor: I know. Tell me, what seems to be the trouble?

Patient: I don't know. Before I saw you, I saw another doctor. He said I had snoo in my blood.

Doctor: Snoo? What's snoo?

Patient: Nothing, what's new with you.

Doctor: I mean, what ails you?

Patient: I don't know. I'm as sick as a dog.

Doctor: Well, you came to the right place, I'm also a veterinarian. You know, I treat all kinds of animals—monkeys, baboons, rhinoceroses, all kinds of animals.

Patient: Do you treat ducks?

Doctor: Yah.

Patient: Well, you're a quack.

Doctor: What seems to be the trouble?

Patient: I don't know. Every time I eat a heavy meal, I don't seem to be hungry after that. I don't know.

Doctor: That's your problem, eh?

Patient: Yes, doctor.

Doctor: Maybe you don't eat the right kind of vitaminyenyen . . .

Patient: What's your problem?

Doctor: What kind of dishes do you eat?

Patient: Dishes? What am I, a crocodile?

Doctor: No, no. I mean, what is your favorite dish?

Patient: My favorite dish? Aluminum.

Doctor: You don't get me.

Patient: What?

Doctor: You don't get me.

Patient: I don't want you.

Doctor: What I am trying to say is, what kind of meat do you eat?

Patient: Meat? Veal I eat.

Doctor: Look, I don't ask you *vill* you eat, I ask you *what* you eat?

Patient: What did I ask you?

Doctor: You tell me vill, vhat, who, when. Oh for piety's sake, don't argue with me, I'm losing my patience.

Patient: You're losing your patients? I should'nt of been here either. Man alive! I'm telling you what I'm eating. I eat wheel. *(spells)* Wee-hee-ay-el, wheel.

Doctor: But the way you shpoke, I couldn't tell. You see, you make the "v" with the "we," instead of a "woo."

Patient: I should eat veal or wool.

Doctor: No, no, no. You should make v, v.

Patient: Make v, v? I don't have to.

Doctor: And when you eat the veal, how do you like it done, medium?

Patient: No, I like my veal well to do on one side, the side optional.

Doctor: Und when you eat the veal, do you chew?

Patient: Do I chew? No.

Doctor: Oh, you don't chew?

Patient: I smoke.

Doctor: You smoke?

Patient: I smoke soy beans. I smoke Pittsburgh soy beans.

Doctor: Soy beans? Is that fish?

Patient: Cigars. My brother-in-law smokes fish. Last year his net income was bigger than his gross. Figure that out?

Doctor: The hell with your brother-in-law.

Smith and Dale in their Dr. Kronkhite act at the Keith-Albee Hippodrome, February 1917. Courtesy of New York Public Library at Lincoln Center.

Patient: The hell with you, Doctor. Where do you come in to insult my brother-in-law? He is a philanthropist and a rich man.
Doctor: I could buy him and sell him.
Patient: He can buy you and keep you. He don't have to sell you. And as to my mother-in-law . . .
Doctor: The hell with her, too.
Patient: Well you got something there.
Doctor: A case history. You must be married.
Patient: I am, but I wish I wasn't.
Doctor: Oh.
Patient: I am my wife's step-husband.
Doctor: Step-husband?
Patient: He stepped out, and I stepped in.
Doctor: Und, do you have any children, by chance?
Patient: By *me*. What am I, a proxy? I have three beautiful children. A boy and a girl.
Doctor: Three. A boy and a . . . what's the other one?
Patient: So young, who can tell?
Doctor: Do you have any insurance?
Patient: I ain't got one nickel insurance.
Doctor: If you die, what will your wife bury you with?
Patient: With pleasure.
Doctor: Okay, now come over here, please. I would like you to sit down, please.
Patient: What are you gonna do, Doc?
Doctor: I want to Diogenes the case.
Patient: Diogones the case? All right. Don't burn me with the lantern.
Doctor: I want you to relax.
Patient: What?
Doctor: Relax.
Patient: Relax?
Doctor: Loose yourself, loose yourself.
Patient: I did.
Doctor: I know. Don't die here.
Patient: Don't encourage me. I'm sick. Don't take advantage of me because I'm sick.
Doctor: Look, you got sick. I didn't send for you. Now look me in the face.
Patient: What?
Doctor: Look me in the face.
Patient: I got my own troubles.
Doctor: Now, please, open the mouth. Nice and vide now. I just want to look in, I don't want to walk in, now. Steady. Steady.
Patient: Do you take pictures, too?
Doctor: Steady. *(Doctor starts singing.)*
Patient: Do you do the hucklebuck?
Doctor: Just be quiet please, all right, please? *(Taps his knee; Patient jumps.)* Well, the reflexes is okay. Now, how do you sleep?
Patient: How do I sleep? Well sometimes like this, like this. *(Closes his eyes.)*
Doctor: I mean how do you sleep at night?
Patient: I can't sleep at night. I walk up and down all night.

Doctor: Oh, you're a somnambulist?

Patient: No, I'm a nightwatchman.

Doctor: All right now. Let me see, please. Come on, open the mouth. Look back there, open the mouth, let me see . . . oh, that's interesting.

Patient: Boy, I'm glad you don't wear binoculars. Doctor, you hurt me.

Doctor: I wouldn't hurt a flea. I'm painless.

Patient: You're painless, but I ain't.

Doctor: What do you drink?

Patient: What do you got?

Doctor: No, I mean what do you drink, when you drink, *(sings)* when you drink, when you're drinking.

Patient: Wait a minute. Hold it. Don't speak so fluidly. When you talk, you sing "April Showers."

Doctor: Look, what kind of beverages do you drink?

Patient: You mean like coffee or milk or chocolate?

Doctor: Yah.

Patient: I drink tea.

Doctor: Oh.

Patient: And strong tea is my weakness.

Doctor: Oh, you drink sealion tea?

Patient: No, Orange Pekinnease.

Doctor: I see. How much tea do you drink in a day?

Patient: A whole day? About twelve glasses full.

Doctor: It's a lot a' tea.

Patient: Salada tea? I drink Salada tea, too. I don't know, I just got a crick in my neck, Doctor. I don't know this I can do.

Doctor: Yah.

Patient: You see this?

Doctor: Yah.

Patient: Can't do it. Look at this, Doctor. Look.

Doctor: You had that before?

Patient: Yes.

Doctor: Well, you got it again.

Patient: And I got rheumatism on the back of my neck. Bad place to have rheumatism on the back of my neck.

Doctor: What's a better place to have rheumatism?

Patient: On the back of *your* neck.

Doctor: Now, Mount Plemis is a good place for rheumatism.

Patient: What?

Doctor: Mount Plemis is a good place for rheumatism.

Patient: How do you know?

Doctor: Because that's where I got mine.

Patient: Doctor, I got a corn on the bottom of my foot. That's a bad place, to have a corn on the bottom of my foot.

Doctor: That's a good place for a corn.

Patient: Why?

Doctor: Because you're the only one who could step on it. All right, now take the coat off, please *(singing)*. Take off the coat, my boy, take off the coat, take the coat off, take off, take off t-h-e coat. *(As he sings, he rubs his stethoscope with his handkerchief.)*

Patient: What are you doing, Doc?

Doctor: I'm sterilizing the instruments.

Patient: I'm glad there ain't a scalpel. Tomorrow I'll bring you bubble gum.

Doctor: Just keep quiet, please. *(singing)*

Patient: Are you holding an organ recital?

Doctor; Be quiet, please. *(singing)*

Patient: Doctor, can't you get the station?

Doctor: All right. Stick out your tongue. More. More.

Patient: I can't, it's tied on the back here.

Doctor: Stick out your tongue, please. I've seen better tongues hanging in the butcher shop.

Patient: I've seen better doctors practicing without a diploma.

Doctor: I want you to know I practiced in Cairo.

Patient: You're a Cairo-practicer.

Doctor: Just open your mouth und say, FISH.

Patient: Herring. Well, that's a fish.

Doctor: Just be still. Inhale. Inhale I would like to see you.

Patient: Inhale you would like to see me? Inhale I would like to see *you.*

Doctor: All right. Enough. Enough. Enough. Now let's get over here.

Patient: Doctor, were you ever in the army?

Doctor: I'm no army doctor.

Patient: Then you must be a navel doctor.

Doctor: Okay. Put on the coat my boy. *(singing)* Put on the coat my boy. Put on, put on Onnnnnnnnnn the coat.

Patient: Thank you, Doctor, for the concert. I would like to see you sometime in Carnegie Hell. Now you understand the whole case?

Doctor: I understand the whole case. The problem with you is you need new eye-glasses.

Patient: My eyes are all right. It's only my mind. I got women on the mind. When I see beautiful women walking down the street, I lose my mind.

Doctor: Having women on the mind could affect your hearing.

Patient: Is that so?

Doctor: What did you say?

Patient: What do I owe you?

Doctor: You owe me $10 for my advice.

Patient: Ten dollars for your advice? Well, Doctor, here's $2, take it, that's *my* advice.

Doctor: Why, you cheap skate! You schnorrer, you low life, you raccoon, you baboon!

Patient: One more word from you, you'll only get $1.

Doctor: You . . .

Patient: That's the word! Here's a dollar.

Charlie Dale and I ran into each other on bicycles, and that was our first meeting. It was in 1898, on the East Side. We started to argue with each other about who was to blame, and finally I took the bicycle to the place where I had hired it from.

As I'm walking up the street, Dale is behind me. So I turned around and said, "Who are you following?" He said, "I'm not following you, you're walking in front of me." It sounded pretty good. When we got to the place, the store's owner heard us arguing. He said, "Wait a minute, fellas. You remind me of Weber and Fields." (They were great comedians; they argued all the time.) He said, "You fellas got something in common; do you know each other?" I said, "No, I don't want to know him." He said, "Well Joe, this is Charlie Marks, and Charlie, this is Joe Sultzer; I'll give you a tandem, and you keep driving around for an hour and get acquainted." And that's how we got acquainted.

Charlie told me he liked to sing and dance, and I said I did too. So he said, "Well, let's team up." I said, "Okay." Now I was fourteen and he was a little over sixteen. So we practiced buck-dancing, which is tap dancing, in a cellar of a shoeshine parlor. In about six months, we finally got a routine together, and pretty good dancing. Then we went to Tony Pastor's theatre to see the show, and we saw Montgomery and Stone. They did an act, and we said, "That's the kind of act we want to do." And we finally did that kind of an act.

The first job we got was at the Palace Theatre on 13th Street. It was a beer hall. Two shows a night. And when we got there, we saw a sign outside that said, "Smith and Dale, blackface singing and dancing comedian." So I said to Charlie, "Who's Smith and Dale?" He said, "I don't know." I said, "Maybe we're not here; well, let's go in and find out." So when I went inside, I saw my brother Mike talking to the manager, whom he knew. So I called him aside and said, "Mike, who's Smith and Dale?" He said, "You." I said, "Us? What do you mean?" He said, "Well, I went around the corner to the printers to get cards for you, and the printer said he had one hundred cards that said 'Smith and Dale, blackface singing and dancing comedian'—he sold them to me for a quarter: so that's your name, Smith and Dale."

Now we felt that instead of working—I was assistant shipping clerk, and Charlie was in some kind of a business of printing or something—we ought to give up our jobs and see what we could do. In order to keep going, we worked in Childs' Restaurant on 130 Broadway near Wall Street, just from 12 to 3. After that, we could go up to agents and find out about jobs. While we worked at Childs' for about three weeks, we couldn't get anything. We got a letter from people up in the Catskills. It said, "Join us, we're the Imperial Vaudeville and Comedy Company."

So just about two weeks before Christmas, in 1901, we got up there and we found that the Imperial Vaudeville and Comedy Company was four fellows: one was a piano player, one was an electrician, the other two were a singer and a comedian. So we got together and we framed a couple of acts. We did a school act, and Charlie and I did blackface, and then we did "Do and Dutch." It was in the winter time, and we hired a sleigh and went around playing Riftin, New Paltz, and Woodstock, and these places around the Catskills.

After about seven weeks, one of the boys' mother was ill and his brother got in trouble and they left. The piano player got a job in Kingston and the electrician was keeping company with a girl whose father had a general store. So we went back to New York. When we got back to New York, we were told that these two fellas were singing waiters on 116th Street in a café. We went up to see them, and we said, "Now look, fellas, we think that the school act that we did up there in the mountains was pretty good; let's do that and form a quartet." They said, "Okay." As we walked out of this café I said, "Charlie, Imperial Vaudeville and Comedy Company is a long name. We ought to get a short name. What's the name of this café?" It was Avon. So I said, "That's it, the Avon Comedy Four."

We got a job at the garden on the Bowery. (I'm trying to think of the name. At my age I'm forgetting a lot of names, but I'll think of it later.) Anyway, there was a colored act on there and there was a man booking them by the name of Al Mayer. Al Mayer came to us and said, "You fellas look like you got a good act; who's your agent?" I said, "We have no agent." So he says, "I'm your agent."

This was about a Tuesday, and then he came back on Friday with a whole route. We left New York. Now we're talking about popular entertainment, and vaudeville, in those days, was popular. (It could be popular today if there were any theatres open.) We left New York and went first to the Atlantic Gardens—that's the name of the garden on the Bowery whose name I was trying to remember. We went from the Atlantic Gardens to Keith's Union Square on 14th Street: from the Bowery right to Broadway, practically. Now, we were out for pretty near a whole year, playing the different cities from New York all the way up to Canada, Vancouver, San Francisco, Los Angeles, back all the way around from Canada, and around to Texas and New Orleans and all those places. Right back to New York. In those days you could work sixty weeks a year. You'd have to double, and many a time we doubled from one theatre.

I didn't know that we'd do the "Dr. Kronkhite" sketch first on this program today. I thought that I'd talk first about this, but I think it's better this way. Now I'm telling you that Proctor's and the Keith Orpheum Circus—this is vaudeville. This is when we started. And this is the route that our agent, Al Mayer, gave us: New York, Albany, Binghamton, Syracuse, Rochester, Buffalo, Toronto, Montreal, Detroit, Chicago, Milwaukee, St. Paul, Winnipeg, Calgary, Vancouver, Seattle, Portland, San Francisco, Oakland, Los Angeles, Salt Lake City, Denver, Dallas, Fort Worth, Austin, San Antonio, Houston, Little Rock, New Orleans, Birmingham, Memphis, St. Louis,

Kansas City, Indianapolis, Cincinnati, Columbus, Norfolk, Richmond, Pittsburgh, Harrisburg, Altoona, Springfield, Providence, Boston, Worcester, Portland, Hartford, Washington, D.C., Baltimore, Philadelphia, Wilmington, New York City. Now that's fifty-two weeks.

I'll never forget Portland, Maine. Every act on the bill didn't go—nothing! Now we had a school act: we sang, we danced, we did comedy—a real knockabout act. Something should have gone. Nothing! Nobody on the bill went, but the property man had a ledger that had autographs in it and he wanted all of us on the bill to sign, you know, our autograph. So we put in "Avon Comedy Four." This was in 1903, and there was an act on the bill—Sidney Grant—so he wrote, "Sidney Grant, born in New York 1875, died in Portland 1903."

We played in Hartford, Connecticut, and then we went to a Hungarian restaurant. The lady who waited on us was Sophie Tucker. In the summer, we would play in New York and in parks all over the country. You could be away from New York for almost two years and come back and do your act over again. We started out in 1903 and did the school act from 1903 to 1914. Every year we played at The Palace and all the other theatres, and all we would do is probably put another joke in and another song. We worked and did the school act for about twelve years. And then we wrote an act called the "Hungarian Rhapsody." That was a scene in the kitchen.

The first time we were in England was 1909, where we played the Morson Stall Circus. In 1914, we went over there again and played also in Ireland, Scotland, and Wales. While we were in Dublin, we got a telegram to headline the first all-American bill in London. We were the Avon Comedy Four in those days. We started out as Smith and Dale, blackface singing and dancing comedians; then we formed the Avon Comedy Four; and then in 1919 went back to Smith and Dale, because the movies came in. We had this Hungarian restaurant sketch; I was the chef and Dale was the boss, and we had two waiters, singing waiters, and I would get sick and they would send me around to the doctor. And that's how two acts were formed, "Hungarian Rhapsody" and "Doctor Kronkhite"—two acts in one, with singing and dancing. We did an oldtime song and dance.

Next to The Palace Theatre was a saloon. We went in that saloon and we were talking to the editor of *Variety*, Sime Silverman. We told him we were going to do a new act, but weren't decided whether to set it in a saloon or in a restaurant. He said, "Do it in a Hungarian restaurant, because it never has been done." So that's how we did the Hungarian restaurant. In 1929, we went to London to the Paladium, where we headlined as "Joe Smith and Charlie Dale and their Avon Comedy Four in the Hungarian Rhapsody," with Mario and Lazeron. We were there for two weeks and we were a big hit. In fact, we did thirty-five minutes. I told the manager, "Look, we're doing a long act; don't you think it's too long?" He says, "No; you're the headliners here and you're doing good and they're coming to see you."

Now, that is the history of Smith and Dale and their Avon Comedy Four. We had seven fellas singing with us, but in 1919, when we joined the Shuberts' Fashion Show of 1919, he was going to go into vaudeville and he said, "I don't want the Avon Comedy Four, I just want Smith and Dale; and anytime you do anything, you can do singing, you can have the boys with you." Well, anyway, they had the billing there as Avon Comedy Four, and I said, "We want the billing as just Smith and Dale, because we had that in the contract and they didn't put it on." So we left them and went with Keith for about fifteen weeks; when we came back, we were handed a subpoena to appear in court. So it was Shubert against Smith and Dale. They won. They put us on with a unit and they billed it as Smith and Dale.

That is the story and that is how we got the idea of just using the name of Smith and Dale. Charlie died in 1971, and we were together all the time until he died. We never separated once. We always used to finish.

I will now finish this way. Over seventy years together. It's a great age we've lived in—from the horsecart to the jetplane, from Strauss to Irving Berlin. Over seventy years together, but it seems like yesterday from the old Atlantic Gardens on the Bowery to The Palace on Broadway.

> We shared each other's sorrows, and we shared each other's joys,
> In all pages of show business since we were a couple of boys,
> Over seventy years together as close as two peas in a pod,
> And the only one who could separate us was God.

TENT REPERTOIRE SHOWS

Clifford Ashby

Trouping Through Texas:
Harley Sadler and His Own Show___

Harley Sadler, who was to bill himself as owner of "the largest and most successful repertoire show in the world,"[1] was born near Pleasant Plains, Arkansas, the fourth of six children. Little did the parents of this westward-drifting family realize how different this middle child was to become. "I have had," Harley confessed to a reporter later in life, "from my earliest childhood an unexplainable desire to get into show business."[2] After learning to play trombone with the town band of Stamford, Texas, he ran away from home at seventeen and joined the Parker Brothers Carnival. Returning after a few months, he organized a vaudeville company with two Stamford friends. "We were," he laughingly recalled,

without experience but we had plenty of nerve and we barnstormed our way to Kansas City. Our show, which consisted of seven acts of vaudeville and included medicine show sketches, was a financial success but physically dangerous. Our audience usually left before we completed seven acts.[3]

When the company broke up, the young comedian toured the West Coast as "advance man" (probably a euphemism for bill-poster) for a one-night-stand company playing *The Girl of the Golden West*. Next, he worked with the North Brothers Stock Company for a few weeks in Fort Worth, playing small parts and walk-ons; then he got his big break in Waco with the Richard Mandell Company. "It was," Harley told an interviewer later in life, "my first time to play responsible parts and I played the rest of the season—without pay. I was afraid to ask for salary for fear I would get fired."[4]

From the end of 1912, when he closed with Mandell, until Christmas of 1914, there follows a series of names and places, not all of which are verifiable. It is fairly certain that in 1913 he played twenty-six weeks under canvas with Renfrow's Jolly Pathfinders, entertaining troops in Texas City who were waiting to repel the anticipated invasion of Pancho Villa. In

1914, the young actor became principal comedian with the Tarbett and White Stock Company, in Brownwood, and then moved to the Billy House Musical Stock Company, a "tab show"[5] playing the Alamo theatre in Waco. He may also have been with the Glide Stock Company, Fairchild's Stock Company, and Rucker's Comedians (a tent-medicine show owned by Dr. H. B. Rucker). One season was spent on a showboat, Cooley and Pell's Floating Wonderland: a surviving program shows that Sadler played the silly kid role in *The Call of the Woods,* a comedy-drama about the Canadian wilderness.[6]

Some time during this period, the fledgling actor tried out a vaudeville act in Chicago—and failed utterly. This was to be his one brush with the world outside provincial theatre, although opportunities from both film and stage were later to come his way.

In 1914, at the age of twenty-two, he became second comedian with the Roy E. Fox Popular Players, called by *Billboard* "without doubt one of the most thoroughly equipped tent shows travelling."[7] Fox, known by Belasco's title of "Governor," carried a company of forty in three railroad cars and, in 1920, added his own private Pullman. His 65-by-135-foot tent seated 2,000 people.

"I'm a Fox by name and nature,"[8] he used to boast, and Harley could offer ample testimony to his shrewdness. Even after the young actor became principal comedian with the company, his salary never exceeded fifteen dollars a week—even though he also did comedy monologues and played alto horn in the street band.

Harley never acquired the Governor's closeness with a penny, but he did learn something about public relations, a term that had not yet been invented. Fox was simultaneously a Knight of Pythias, an Odd Fellow, a 32nd degree Mason, a Shriner, a Knight Templer, a Moose, and an honorary life member of the Benevolent and Protective Order of Elks—as well as numerous show business clubs and affiliations.[9] There were very few towns the show visited where Fox could not call at least one group of men his brothers. The company was expected to be as friendly and outgoing as its genial manager. Actors routinely provided free entertainment for civic programs, visited ranches, went on fishing parties and bear hunts, attended dinners and picnics. The isolation of the strolling player from the community vanished under Fox's management.

However, public relations and an unusual (for the time) amount of publicity were only part of the Fox formula for success: he also maintained a very salable product. Writing of his own accomplishments in 1917, Fox recorded with typical immodesty that

I have spent years in study of seating arrangements and stage equipment so that my patrons may be as comfortable and feel as secure as in their own home playhouse, while my performers can feel as much at home on my stage as if they were on the largest theatre stage. I have spared neither time nor money in making each performance a complete scenic production. Instead of "tie-on" diamond dye stuff I find well-painted flat scenery just as practical and much more effective. A properly lighted stage with all the necessary offstage strips, spots, and floods, is just as easily operated as a couple of half-filled borders. With my "A" frame stage rigging I am given height enough to properly dress any scene and at the same time remove all poles from the stage front, giving each seat a clear proscenium opening with no poles as obstructions. I find that a well-lighted portable theatre lobby is just as practical as the old marquee and much more attractive. I find it just as easy to heat a tent—if properly constructed heating plants are installed—as it is to heat a theatre, and, in a great many cases, more so. I have established a record of seventeen years without closing. During the winter months I play where local conditions will warrant good business regardless of the weather, and have yet to hear a serious complaint from either patron or performer that the tent is not comfortably warm at all times. . . .

I find the difference in the expense of carrying a good band and orchestra, and the expense of a mediocre one so small that is would be foolish to think of the saving. I try at all times to have absolutely the best band and orchestra in the repertoire game.

A full cast of capable dramatic artists and absolutely feature vaudeville are just as essential as the poles which hold up the top. I have never lied to or fooled my patrons, but try to give them exactly what I promise.[10]

In 1917, as evidence of his continuing prosperity, Fox ordered a still-larger tent, one seating three thousand. But Sadler, now married to a small-town Texas girl and stigmatized in the pages of *Billboard* as a "non-professional,"[11] sought greener pastures. He joined the Brunks, a Kansas-based partnership of three brothers and an uncle, an organization that had as many as nine tent shows touring simultaneously. He became not only principal comedian with the number one company, but also stage director and center fielder with the company baseball team. He and his new bride also were given the "banner concession," sharing equally with the management in the proceeds from the hastily painted local advertisements that surrounded the proscenium.[12]

The Brunks did not perform all year under canvas as did Fox. That winter, after the tent had been carefully dried and folded away with liberal doses of black pepper to discourage mice and moths, the Sadlers toured the Oklahoma opera house circuit with Wil-Bucks Comedians.[13] From this engagement comes the first preserved picture of the young actor in stage costume. Although the name was not to be invented for several years, his "Cowboy" is obviously a Toby: tousled wig—presumably red; huge freckles; blacked-out teeth; pistol unconsciously strapped in phallic position; and boots worn as much off the feet as on.

The following season, when Glen Brunk was drafted and sent to France, Harley became manager of the company. The role apparently suited him, for when Glen returned from France, he realized that Harley would no longer be content as a mere employee. The Brunks agreed to finance an outfit for him on a sharing basis. Brunk's Number Three was an instant success. "I really believe that Sadler would do business on the Sahara Desert," a

Harley Sadler as "The Cowboy," with Wil-
Bucks Comedians in 1917-1918. Courtesy of
Dr. Jere C. Mickel and the Southwest Collection
of Texas Tech University.

visting actor wrote to *Billboard.* "With cotton a cent and a half a pound in
the field and costing two cents to pick it, people are in no mood for amusements or letting go a nickel unless absolutely necessary."[14] In 1921, an advance agent for Honest Bill's Circus caught the Sadler show at a Texas Pan-
handle town, and sent the following account to *Billboard:*

On July 23 I was booking Tulia, Texas, where Brunk's #3 was playing a return date.
Wish to state that the public demanded Harley Sadler, manager, to give two night
performances, and both houses were packed to capacity. Mr. Sadler is a real fellow,
well met, and an entertainer both on and off stage. He is surrounded with a company far above average. Business has been wonderful, and the show deserves it, for
it is giving the public a real show.[15]

In 1922, when Harley had fulfilled his contract with the Brunks, he bought
out their interest in the show. Billie, his wife, quickly learned to act as well
as take care of the bookkeeping. Their daughter, Gloria, who was born in
1922, became the performing child—an indispensible ingredient of tent
show vaudeville. Tent shows tend to be family affairs, and the Sadler show

was no exception. Harley's mother-in-law worked backstage, his brother-in-law was a canvasman, his brother, Ferd, served as advance man, and Ferd's wife ran the box office. During the summer, nieces and nephews spent their vacations working on the show.

"Why were the actors of the Italian comedy so popular with the audience?" Yevgeny Vakhtangov asked rhetorically while preparing his *commedia* production of *Turandot*. "Because they were no different from the spectators, from whom they were separated only by a rope stretched across the square," he replied.[16]

Each performance begins with you and your public getting to know one another. Everyone has the right to greet you, to ask how you feel and even about your romance, if he has seen you with some charming girl the day before. . . . You can't imagine how interested the spectator is in an actor's private life. Don't blame him for his curiosity. He likes you and wants to know everything about the person he likes. That's why it's important to be not only a hero on the stage, but also an honest citizen in real life.[17]

Sadler's troupe was composed of honest citizens. Throughout the sixty communities of West Texas and eastern New Mexico which the show played year after year, the members of the very stable company were regarded as part of the community. Townspeople greeted the performers as old friends each new season when the show came to town. The same clerk would hand an actor the key to the same room in the same hotel where he had stayed the previous year. The actor would buy a meal ticket at the same restaurant and, if he was single, he would call up the same girls to see if they were still dating. With rare exceptions, these were not college or academy trained actors; they were West Texas people who "went with" the show. Many children grew up dreaming of the day when they would be old enough to "join up" with Harley's troupe.

The tent season began in March. (During the winter months, a smaller company played a "circle stock" engagement of one-night stands in theatres around a "wheel" of six communities.) After a week devoted to painting, repairs, scenery construction, and the rehearsal of six plays with accompanying vaudeville, the tour began. Routes were roughed out, but were often changed on short notice: a crop failure, a railroad washout, or an unforeseen "day-and-date" conflict with a circus or wandering evangelist might cause an abrupt change of direction.

In the good times, before the Depression of the late twenties, Ferd Sadler, the advance man, would step off the train at the little wooden depot about four days before the show was to arrive.[18] Bearing an unmistakable resemblance to his famous brother, he would howdy and shake his way to the center of town, leaving window cards at every place of business and proffering free passes for Monday night to all passersby. He would check at the barber shop to learn the local news—and especially to find out what new

During the winter and early spring, a reduced company played the regular theatres of Texas and New Mexico. Courtesy of Southwest Collection.

skulduggery the moving-picture man was up to in his perennial effort to harass the tent show. He paid a call on the president of the local sponsor, typically the American Legion, Shriners, VFW, Lions, Rotary, or volunteer fire department, making certain that the three "L's" would be provided. These were: lot, license (if any), and 'lectricity, which were to be supplied in exchange for 10 percent of the gross ticket sales.

Along his route, Ferd would pick up several requests for free entertainment: a noon Rotary luncheon, a church social, a fund-raiser for the hospital. These were honored, if at all possible. There was also a Saturday afternoon baseball game to be scheduled between the Sadler team and the local champions. Baseball was one of Harley's passions, and he played to win, sometimes hiring company members as much for their performance on the field as on the stage. Ferd also had the responsibility for borrowing a wide collection of properties, for the show travelled with little or no furniture. Chairs, sofas, stoves, and even a baby could be obtained for a pass or two. This method made touring a great deal easier.

Monday morning (no work was done on the Lord's day) saw Harley's gaudily painted baggage and passenger cars arrive on a downtown siding, propelled by a little, smoke-belching switch engine. Local draymen, alerted by Ferd, would be waiting with their wagons to begin moving the masses of equipment to the show lot. From the baggage cars emerged bundles of canvas, a forest of poles, coiled ropes, stakes, marquee, lights, wardrobe, bleachers, reserved seating, scenery, stage platforming—an almost endless amount of equipment to be moved to the lot and set in place for performance that night.

From the passenger car came the performers, self-consciously parading before the townspeople who had come to welcome them. Each actor carried a small suitcase (the hotel trunk would follow later) and possibly a small dog on a leash or a canary in a cage. If the weather was still chilly, a fancifully slip-covered coal-oil heater would also be part of the impediments carried to rooms that were inadequately heated—or not heated at all. The company's first stroll through town was an important event, and performers always chose their spiffiest outfits. "Dress well on and off," was a frequent requirement stated in *Billboard* ads, and actors spent a great deal of time and money on their wardrobes.

By the time Harley arrived, the lot was ringed with small boys desperately hoping for the "Hey you, kid, grab some of them chairs and carry 'em inside" that would mean a free pass for opening night. After a quick check to make certain put-up was proceeding properly, the youthful manager left the lot for a stroll downtown. Everywhere he was regarded as a local boy, and he managed to convey the impression that this particular town was one of his special favorites. His memory for names and faces was incredible and infallible. In place after place, he could stand on a street corner and greet by name almost everyone who passed.

Exterior of the Sadler tent, probably in the early thirties. The "dramatic end" construction eliminated the need for a center pole in front of the proscenium. Courtesy of Southwest Collection.

Late in the afternoon, the young actor-owner would break from the crowd of people surrounding him and journey back to the now-erected tent. There, members of the all-male marching band would be changing into their uniforms. In later years, after the show was motorized, the musicians would ride on a truck, but during the twenties, they marched. Harley had given up the trombone and alto horn in favor of the bass drum, a change that allowed him to greet his friends along the line of march. His exuberant greetings did little, however, for the tempo of the band, which was frequently off beat and out of step. "Harley," a cornet player said plaintively one day, "you gotta either hire somebody to wave at the people or somebody to beat that derned drum: *because you cain't do both!*"[19]

A *Billboard* correspondent described the free concert given by Sadler during the early twenties:

They give a concert uptown on opening day only. Each evening they play in front of the tent where the show is located—never uptown where the drink stores and picture house are. Sadler is a likeable fellow. He has a real man's voice which he uses in a pleasing manner. He talks in a conversational tone, never in the raucous, ponderous style assumed by most spielers. Neither does he assume the patronizing tone nor the broad smile of undue familiarity. Then he steps behind his bass drum, they play another tune and the crowd is his from then on.[20]

By show time that evening, the tent would be crowded with row upon row of grandparents, adults, teenagers, children. The Sadler Show was, above all, a family affair, one that would make a present-day Walt Disney production appear just a little racy. Plays with sexual overtones were avoided, and cuss words were either eliminated or changed to the milder "heck," "dern," or "jimminy." Acts were carefully scrutinized to see that no blue material crept into the "polite vaudeville."

If the weather was chilly, the tent would be double sidewalled, with a "mud flap" buried in the earth to avoid drafts on the feet of the spectators. On hot summer days, the sidewalls were raised, allowing breezes to play over the audience. If the show was a sell-out, a second sidewall would be set up outside the perimeter of the tent, with spectators bringing their own seats: soap boxes, buggy seats, benches, and sometimes rocking chairs from the front porch.

In front of the tent, the brightly painted box office was flanked by sandwich boards displaying pictures of the performers. If the weather appeared threatening, the displays were moved inside to a small lobby which housed the popcorn machine and other concessions. A spectator, once he had passed by the ticket taker at a canvas archway, found himself in the midst of the bleacher seats, still called "blues" from circus usage. As required by the laws of the time, one side was labeled "Colored." In front of what the town boys called the "chicken roost" sat the reserved seats, separated from the cheaper

blues by a low wooden fence. An opening in this divider was manned by
another "ticket-catcher," who collected an additional charge for those wanting a closer view of the stage.

Around the proscenium hung a profusion of advertising banners, an important source of income. Stage right of the proscenium sat the orchestra
platform, a curtained doorway in the canvas wall providing access from
backstage. A sign over the piano player's head stated that "IF THE BABY
CRIES, PLEASE TAKE IT TO THE REAR OF THE TENT."

Six plays were presented during the typical week's run. By the thirties,
Toby had become an artistic liability that totally dominated the bill; but
during the earlier days, a true repertoire was presented. This ranged from
such lachrymose classics as *Ten Nights* and *Uncle Tom*, through "book
plays" like *Lena Rivers* and *St. Elmo*, together with pirated versions of current Broadway hits. A great many still-unpublished scripts were written by
tent-show actors to fit the tastes of the audience and the size of the company. Problems plays, usually concerning the trials of a good man married
to a bad woman, were not uncommon, but comedy was the staple com-
modity of the tent show. If a tear or two could be wrung from the audience
in the course of a succession of belly laughs, that was all to the good. George
Harrison, the "Shakespeare" of the "rag opries," had a firm grasp of the
formula: reviewing *Other People's Business*, the editor of the *Albany (Texas)*

Interior of the Sadler tent in the early thirties, showing the "reserved seat" sections.
Between two and three thousand spectators could be accommodated. Courtesy of
Southwest Collection.

News remarked that the Harrison play offered "rolicking and frolicking farce . . . interspersed with pathos."[21]

The acting of the company was sincere, none of the contrived, over-stated "mellerdrammer" style that is seen so often today when plays of this genre are presented. The actors played sincerely and honestly, caught up in the emotions of the characters they were portraying. One actor recalls that in *Seventh Heaven*, a drama about a little blind girl, "I'd get to crying so hard that I couldn't get my lines out."[22] Harley's playing, even in a comic role, had such a naturalness that the editor of the Albany newspaper had difficulty in perceiving the art beneath the apparent artlessness. He wrote:

You know that it's a great gift to be funny without trying to be funny, just a look, shake of the head or the gesture of the hand, a short, pithy expression, and the multitude goes into a fit of laughter, and the spokesman really wonders what on earth they are laughing about, that's the born humorist, funny and don't know it. That's Harley Sadler, and all of West Texas are wending their way down to his tent to laugh and be glad.[23]

Between the three or four acts of the play, vaudeville specialties would be presented. Sometimes acts such as performing dogs were carried on the show, but usually the actors doubled in vaudeville routines, or specialty performers doubled as actors. Accordianists, hillbilly and one-man bands, tap dancers, performing children, jugglers, and monologuists were popular with Sadler's audiences. On occasion, a very discreet amount of flesh, as in a South Sea Islands production number, would help keep the spectators in their seats during the brief intermissions.

At one of the intermissions, Harley made the candy pitch that was common to all tent shows. Still in costume, he would step around the cur-tain with a vendor's tray slung from his neck. Frankly admitting that the few pieces of dried saltwater taffy were not worth the money, he would point to the stage where a rising curtain revealed a collection of prizes to be redeemed for coupons to be found in the candy boxes. The stage held the usual carnival "flash," but there were also canning kettles, cake dishes, radios, chairs—useful as well as ornamental items—often purchased from local merchants to gain their good will and to demonstrate that the show was not "taking the money out of town." For West Texans, the "bally candy" sale was as exciting as a horse race, and Harley, with several helpers, unloaded trays of candy almost as fast as they could hand out the boxes.

Before the beginning of the last act, Harley would step in front of the curtain for a talk with his audience. If he were wearing his Toby wig, he would remove it, emphasizing that he spoke as himself, not as a stage char-acter. He would always plug the play for the following night, telling some-thing of the plot and mentioning featured actors. Local, often competing, events were publicized; and he even had a kind word for his bitterest rival, the picture show manager. "This man's doing his best to bring you good, wholesome entertainment," Harley would say, "and you need to patronize him."[24] Often he would preach a little sermon—a homily about loving, and helping, and forgiving—one that would have his audience nodding agreement by the conclusion.

The orchestra slipped into place before the final curtain, ready to play the chaser at the final curtain. "Good Night, Sweetheart" was frequently used, but if a second show was to be given, or if it was "getaway night," a quick march was substituted. A "concert," an hour of straight vaudeville which brought in additional revenue, was offered after the closing show on Saturday night. Teardown began as soon as the concert commenced. Marquee and box office were removed; then bleachers were silently disassembled behind the rapt audience; finally, vacant chairs were folded and taken away. Scenery and costumes were packed away as each act finished, so that the final number was performed on a totally bare stage. By the end of the concert, a considerable portion of the show was already bound for the baggage car waiting on a nearby siding.

If it were not a moving night, the actors would drift down to Main Street, entering restaurants where walls would be lined with townspeople who had come to watch the actors eat. These "neighbors" stood silently, seldom speaking, but making note of each little detail, every overheard snatch of conversation. For a rural population, tent-show actors were the embodiment of glamor, and their actions were observed as raptly as a later generation was to study the personal habits of movie stars.[25]

By the late twenties, Harley Sadler was a wealthy man. One surviving set of sponsors' records shows that in 1929 he played the village of Slaton, population 3,876.[26] The smallest audience for the week's stand was Wednesday, the traditional church night, when 944 backsliders forsook the temple for the tent. The second show on Saturday night drew the largest house—1,504. The week's total was 8,094, more than twice the population of the town. Gross ticket sales for the six-night run totaled $2,408.60, with income from concessions, bally candy, and advertising probably bringing the grand total to around $3,500. These figures seem small today, but at that time, advertisements in the nearby Lubbock paper offered men's shoes at $3.95 and "hand-tailored" suits for $18.50 up. Swift's Cloverleaf bacon was thirty-five cents a pound and lettuce was six cents a head. A "fine wheat farm near Clovis" was listed at $15 an acre and a "brand new" five-room brick-veneer house could be had for $3,500.[27]

Like many people who had known only prosperous times, Sadler was not prepared to cope with the Depression. Instead of retrenching and cutting back on payroll and touring expenses, he purchased a larger, grander tent and added many out-of-work actors to his always-large company. He was quickly in trouble. He bought a circus, but was unable to control the leakage of cash from the box office. A Texas Centennial production of *The Siege of the Alamo* proved a total disaster, and the once-prosperous showman found himself flat broke.[28]

Selling all his assets and agreeing to pay his outstanding debts rather than filing bankruptcy, he rented a ragged little tent and, with a small company, played farming villages in the lower Rio Grande Valley. By the end of the season, he had contrived to pay off all his bills, even forgotten ones involving hay for his circus elephants.[29] When introduced at a luncheon as "the first man to make a million dollars in a tent show" he added wryly that he was also "the first man to lose a million dollars in a tent show."[30]

Needing money to sustain his style of living, he became an independent oil operator—a "wildcatter." He stayed off the road for a season, but in 1940 decided to try again. By now, the huge tent and company of fifty was only a memory: talking pictures, the drive-in theatre, and the advent of refrigerated air in movie houses had robbed the tent show of much of its audience. Now, according to *Billboard*, "Manager Sadler presides as boss canvasman, chief electrician, and head truck driver. . . . Billie Sadler sees the family trailer through."[31] The tent was small, and the star doubled on drums in the tiny orchestra.[32]

Harley ran for the state legislature, was elected, and proved to be an honest and compassionate, if somewhat naive, representative in both the house and the senate. In 1943, unable to stay completely away from show business, he took his tent on a war-bond tour, showing *Ravaged Earth*, a propaganda film.[33]

After World War II, Sadler was deep into oil and politics. But there was to be a farewell tour in partnership with Joe McKennon. The season before the partnership, McKennon, primarily a circus and carnival man, and his wife had listened to the arguments of Howard Lindsay, a former tent-show actor turned playwright. "Bring Broadway to Main Street," Lindsay had urged, and the McKennons agreed to try.[34] *Arsenic and Old Lace*, *Kiss and Tell*, and *Over Twenty-One* were put into repertoire—but Main Street was not at all impressed. "We didn't realize," Marian McKennon wrote, that the bill "would sound snooty to people in little towns."[35] Halfway through the season, the Broadway plays were supplemented with old tent show favorites, and eventually the bill became a straight run of Toby plays.

The Sadler-McKennon season was highly successful from an audience standpoint, but there was, as might be expected in a farewell tour, a certain sadness about the shows. The faithful followers turned out in record numbers, but they were older and grayer, and their idol offered a pale imitation of what he once had been. Harley spent his late nights in political caucuses and his days on the oil rigs, leaving very little sparkle for the evening performance. "The heart had gone out of it," one former trouper remarked.[36]

The last season under canvas for Sadler was that of 1947, although he did appear in a few amateur productions of Geoge Harrison's *Saintly Hypocrites and Honest Sinners.* He suffered a fatal heart attack in 1954 while emceeing a benefit for the Boy Scout Troop of Avoca, one of his many hometowns. His grieving widow, shortly after his death, made a memorial funeral pyre of all the records, pictures, and scrapbooks that Harley had assembled for a projected biography.[37] Today, all that remains of the Sadler Show is a large script collection donated to Texas Tech University by Joe McKennon and a few pieces of show equipment mouldering on McKennon's North Carolina farm.

But there is a sequel. In 1976, as part of the Bicentennial, Texas Tech University presented a summer revival of the Harley Sadler Show under canvas. There was an orchestra, a bally candy sale, vaudeville, and plays such as Harrison's *The Awakening of John Slater,* in which John leaves his farm family and sweetheart to become a lawyer, only to fall into the clutches of a scheming city woman. An eighty-seven-year-old Toby, Harve Holland, traded jokes with Euna, his eighty-four-year-old wife, as part of the vaudeville. Response was strong enough to indicate the continued viability of this kind of entertainment, at least among the folk of West Texas.

The tent show represents a brief but important phase of American popular entertainment, one that has received little attention in the histories of American theatre. There were, according to a 1927 advertisement in *Billboard,* "over 400 Dramatic Tent Shows, serving 16,000 communities and playing to over 78,000,000 annually."[38] Even allowing for the probable overstatement of the Tent and Repertoire Managers' Protective Association which placed the ad, the figures remain impressive.

David Belasco, for one, recognized the importance of the tent show. Writing for a projected Sadler broadside in 1928, he stated:

As matters stand nowadays, the tent theater seems to be the drama's only hope in the small town—and the only hope of the small town that wants drama.

While a canvas playhouse is not exactly like a regular theater, it nevertheless can be just as much a temple of art as were the outdoor theaters of ancient Greece, the crude showhouse of Shakespeare's time or the extravagant palaces of contemporary times.

After all the play is really the thing and the audience may enjoy themselves just as wholeheartedly under a tent as under a golden canopy—so long as the illusion is there and the spell is cast upon them.[39]

NOTES

1. Sadler advertisement in *Billboard,* May 24, 1947, p. 80.
2. Howard Barrett, "Actors a Frivolous Lot? Well, Not Sadler," *The Western Weekly,* February 7, 1926.

3. Ibid.

4. Ibid.

5. Tab shows (from "tabloid") were very popular at this time. They featured a chorus line, comedians, singers, and variety acts.

6. Paul Kalmbacher [stage name, Thardo], Papers, 1878-1960, Southwest Collection, Texas Tech University.

7. "Roy E. Fox," *Billboard*, January 8, 1916.

8. Paul Kalmbacher interview, Fort Worth, Texas, April 1975.

9. "Roy E. Fox," *The New York Clipper*, December 25, 1915, p. 13.

10. Roy E. Fox, "The Repertoire Show, Under Canvas," *Billboard*, December 22, 1917, pp. 11-12.

11. "Harley Sadler Weds," *Billboard*, February 24, 1917, p. 18.

12. Henry Brunk interview, Lubbock, Texas, January 1975.

13. "Wil-Bucks Comedians," *Billboard*, December 22, 1917, p. 55. The Buck of Wil-Bucks was J. A. Buckingham, owner and manager while the Sadlers were with the show. Wil was Fred Wilson, credited by many with being the first actor to crystallize the Toby role. Wilson was not with the company at the time that Sadler was playing the "silly kid" roles.

14. "O. A. Peterson Offers Report on 'Rep' Shows Playing Texas," *Billboard*, February 26, 1921, p. 16.

15. "Praises Brunk (No. 3) Show," *Billboard*, August 13, 1921, p. 16.

16. Nicolai Gorchakov, *The Vakhtangov School of Stage Art* (Moscow: Foreign Languages Publishing House, n.d.), p. 114.

17. Ibid., p. 115.

18. This description is based largely upon a series of interviews with Mr. and Mrs. Ferd Sadler, Ruidoso, N. Mex., during 1974 and 1975, and an interview with Mrs. George Sorensen, San Antonio, Texas, June 1974.

19. Gil (Sheep) Lamb interview, Muleshoe, Texas, April 1976.

20. O. A. Peterson, "Harley Sadler Wins Much Favor in Repertoire Field," *Billboard*, April 16, 1921, pp. 17, 217.

21. *The Albany (Texas) News*, undated clipping, Ferd Sadler Papers, 1922-1971, Southwest Collection, Texas Tech University.

22. Bob Siler interview, Lubbock, Texas, June 1974.

23. *The Albany (Texas) News*, undated clipping.

24. Ferd Sadler interview, Ruidoso, N. Mex., July 1974.

25. Erman Gray interview, Mt. Pleasant, Iowa, August 1974.

26. Magnus Klattenhoff Papers, 1929-1930, Southwest Collection, Texas Tech University.

27. *Morning Avalanche* (Lubbock, Texas), October 5, 1929.

28. Ferd Sadler interview, Ruidoso, N. Mex., May 1974.

29. Ibid.

30. Ibid.

31. "Harley Sadler Rep Beats Texas Heat," *Billboard*, July 22, 1944.

32. Flo Darling interview, Lubbock, Texas, November 1975.

33. Advertising postcard in Sweetwater (Texas) County Museum.

34. Marian McKennon interview, Fletcher, N.C., September 1974.

35. Marian McKennon, *Tent Show* (New York: Exposition Press, 1964), p. 39.

36. Rolland Haverstock interview, Lubbock, Texas, February 1976.

37. Ferd Sadler interview, Ruidoso, N. Mex. April 1975.

38. Don Carle Gillette, "The Vast Tent Drama Industry: Facts & Figures About the Little-Known Canvas Playhouses, Which Constitute a Business Bigger Than Broadway," *New York Times* (October 16, 1927), 9:2.

39. Museum of Repertoire Americana, Mt. Pleasant, Iowa. This quote is contained in several pages of typewritten material labeled "HARLEY SADLER, from Broadside, December 15, 1928." No published version of this defense of the tent show has been uncovered.

William L. Slout

Tent Rep: Broadway's
Poor Relation_____

Beginning with the circuses of the 1820s, and continuing through several
varieties of traveling entertainment, canvas theatres and hippodromes by
the hundreds made annual visits to large and small communities, situated
along the railroad lines or off the beaten paths. These varieties included
medicine shows, where frock-coated doctors sold various "kickapoo"
remedies; concert companies, featuring snappy bands and acts of comic and
musical virtuosity; Uncle Tom's Cabin troupes, with their equal comple-
ments of actors and bloodhounds; and dramatic repertoire shows, which
brought a kind of Broadway to rural areas. Their combined yearly performances reached audiences that totaled in the millions. Their entertainment output was too vast to measure.

It is dramatic repertoire under canvas that is of particular interest here.
Although it was as much a product of the nineteenth century as Negro
minstrelsy, burlesque, comic opera and the other various types of house
entertainments that disappeared with the collapse of the "road," and although it was every bit as doomed at that time as those other amusement
forms, it persisted beyond the opera house era. It became the sole vestige of
a strolling tradition on which our American theatrical history is founded;
and, if for no other reason than that, it is worthy of scrutiny. Therefore, as
time permits, I shall plot the rise and decline of tent repertoire as a collective
business, taking note of significant developments as they became an identifiable part of tent show operation. The shows were variously referred to as
rep shows, tent rep, rag opries, and simply tent shows. For the sake of con-
sistency, I shall use the latter.

Tent shows carried with them the paraphernalia for stage presentations
within a portable facility large enough to accommodate several hundred
people. Each company restricted its movements to a limited territory, returning to many of the same locations year after year. They brought replicas
of big city dramas to rural America, with the content fashioned to appeal to

Preparing the canvas theatre for another opening night.

provincial tastes. The repertoire of plays and accompanying vaudeville allowed a nightly change of bills for as long as a week or more. The stock of plays varied from aged melodramas to recent New York successes, as well as comedy-dramas written for the tent show by tent show people. Local color themes were popular with small-town audiences, particularly "rube dramas" portraying Victorian ideals of virtue and a reverence for mother, home, and heaven. At the peak of activity, there were literally hundreds of tent shows traveling throughout the United States. They operated in relative obscurity, remote from the eyes of city editors and drama critics; and, because of this, tent shows, as an entertainment entity, have only recently received serious attention as a significant subject for study.

One of the problems one faces in recording the progress of these shows was their lack of organization as an industry. They functioned independently of each other, often concealing their itineraries for competitive reasons, as well as changing play titles to avoid paying royalties. Because of their nomadic existence, they rarely came in contact with each other. A common link, however, was the well-known entertainment weekly, *Billboard*. This show business periodical began carrying a news column under the heading "Dramatic" around 1904. Ten years later, a full page was devoted to "Repertoire." This page remained one of *Billboard*'s weekly news features for as

long as there was an active tent show industry. It formed the only continuing record we have from which to assess the development of tent shows as a
collective business.

Since there is no way of knowing just which dramatic repertoire group
first used a canvas theatre, we must begin our chronicle of the tent shows
with an arbitrary date. We know that Yankee Robinson completed his first
tenting tour in the fall of 1851. His company performed in the Mississippi
River towns of Iowa and Illinois. Robinson claims to have made a tent with
his own hands the following winter. He then repeated his summer tours
under canvas for three more seasons until, by his own account, "in 1854 I
produced 'Uncle Tom's Cabin' as a feature during the summer, and by this
time I had succeeded in using large tents."[1] With a larger canvas theatre,
Robinson began to include gymnastic feats, balancing acts, clowning, and
so on. Soon, horses were added to the program, and the show was well on
its way to becoming the famous Yankee Robinson Circus.

Tent show information is sketchy prior to 1900. One can find only occasional references in the theatrical trade publications. It can be assumed,
however, that more and more house repertoire troupes began augmenting
their winter seasons by moving under canvas as soon as the weather became
too hot for comfort in the poorly ventilated houses. They performed such
pieces as *East Lynne*, *The Hidden Hand*, *Fanchon the Cricket*, *Kathleen
Mavourneen*, and *Camille*. Their summer touring was carried on in much
the manner of their winter touring, except that they brought along a portable
canvas replica of a small-town opera house, including seats, stage, and
scenic necessities.[2]

Tent show activity is more visible with the beginning of the twentieth
century. By this time, shows were touring in large numbers and were evident
in nearly every part of the country, although the largest concentrations
were in the Midwest and the South. With the new century, audiences were
beginning to tire of the old melodramas; and copyright laws had become
more punitive toward managers and actors who performed plays without
authorization. So tent show people began writing plays for themselves,
using shorter casts and fewer set requirements; and, at once, making the
dramas more relevant to small-town and rural life. The most successful of
these plays were performed by every tent show on the road and repeated
frequently under a variety of titles throughout the remaining tent show era.
Such pieces as Charles Harrison's *Saintly Hypocrites and Honest Sinners*,
George J. Crawley's *The Girl of the Flying X*, and W. C. Herman's *Call of
the Woods* became classics in the repertoire field.[3]

An important development, growing out of the plays performed under
canvas, is the materialization of the stock character Toby. The character
originated in 1911 when Fred Wilson, an actor with Murphy's Comedians,
began using the name of Toby for all the silly kid roles he performed in

repertoire. Wilson's Toby was so popular, and the use of the name so successful, that other companies adopted the device; and Toby, the red-headed,
freckle-faced country boy, soon became a familiar figure and a beloved
symbol to all tent show audiences across the country.[4]

In the early days, large tents were manufactured to meet the functional
needs of the circuses. As circuses reached their most prolific period, the last
quarter of the nineteenth century, the original "round top" was elongated
to accommodate the larger audiences of the time, by additional middle
pieces of canvas. When these were converted to dramatic use, there was
always the problem of one center pole conspicuously standing directly in
front of the stage platform. The vision appears ludicrous to us now; but,
nevertheless, this obstruction remained for many years until a special
dramatic end was architecturally devised to replace the traditional round
one. The United States Tent and Awning Company announced in 1910 the
sale of "something absolutely new in canvas homes for theatrical performance."[5] Thus, it became unnecessary for tent show performers to act around
that pesky pole.

America's involvement in World War I had a significant effect on tent
show development. Before the war, most established tent shows traveled by
rail, utilizing coach, Pullman, and baggage cars—in the manner of the
opera house companies—carrying actors, wardrobe trunks, and equipment
on a single contract. But because of war needs, railroads encountered car
and locomotive shortages by 1917, and all services unrelated to national
defense were curtailed. Tent show managers who owned their own railroad
cars frequently found them sidetracked to make way for military supplies.
And inconsistencies in time schedules, as well as rising passenger and freight
rates, forced many·shows to hire rigs in each town to move the show over-
land. Because tent show managers could no longer depend on the railroads,
some turned to motor vehicles as a solution to their transportation woes.
The changeover to trucks, trailers, and touring cars continued until, eventually, all tent shows were moved by this method.[6]

Show business is traditionally a beneficiary of wartime. The desire to
escape momentarily from the ugly realities of the day is a common motivation for attending the theatre. It was no less the case during World War I. In
all probability, those years were the most prosperous in the history of the
tents. Industry was in full gear and agriculture was finding new markets
abroad; trade with the Allies was increasing sharply. And, important to
rural show business, crop prices were high and going higher. Farmers were
in a spending mood. The number of tent shows increased as more and more
managers entered the field to share in the wartime bonanza.[7] By 1919,
Billboard was reporting a tremendous growth in repertoire, with small
companies enlarging their rosters and with many actors going into business
for themselves.[8] Admission prices were jacked up to as much as $1.00,

Members of an opening night audience, hopeful that their early arrival will result in seating close to the stage.

more than double the previous rates. With this kind of money circulating freely, it is no wonder that Chicago agent A. Milo Bennett could report in the spring of 1920 that "the number of tented attractions will exceed that of any previous season."[9]

The completion of World War I marks the end of the first period of tent show history. By that time, dramatic repertoire under canvas had grown into an active industry, with a set form of operation common to every tent company. Tentmakers were manufacturing special designs for dramatic use. Motorized transportation was an accepted innovation, with many shows already having made the switch from rail to roadway. There was a shared body of comedy-dramas fashioned particularly for tent show presentation. A comic character, Toby, was a recognizable figure within many of these plays. And a period of wartime prosperity had enabled managers to refurbish and replace old equipment, some to enlarge, and others to enter the field for the first time. Tent shows were at their peak as Americans faced a new decade of peace.

The first phase of tent show history, a period of development and growth, ended on a positive note. The second, a period of containment, began with an air of confidence. Tent showman John Lawrence wrote in 1919, "During the past couple of years a 'bloomer' has been a rare occurrence with any of the better repertoire shows through the Middle West."[10] That same year, a *Billboard* editor made the lofty proclamation that the fame of the tent shows "has been spread into the remotest corners of the earth. . . . Education, art, morals, ideas, all improved, giving us greater recognition, which in turn gives us the right to demand a place far at the top of show-dom."[11] Managers reveled in their new prosperity and anticipated more of the same.

But good times did not last long. The wartime economy could not be sustained. For example, when government support of wheat was withdrawn in 1920, wheat prices sank from $2.00 a bushel to an end-of-the-year value of sixty-seven cents. With a sharp slump in the economy, bankruptcies and foreclosures increased sharply. Over 400,000 farmers lost their farms as the nation experienced its greatest agricultural depression. In his book, *Republican Ascendancy*, John D. Hicks summed matters up in this way: "Thus at last the economic consequences of the war caught up with the nation. For industry, the Depression was severe, but soon over; for agriculture, it lasted for two full decades."[12] Tent shows, reliant on rural prosperity, were in for trouble.

Although it was apparent early in 1921 that the number of tent shows forming for the summer surpassed that of any previous year, rural show business proved to be a financial disaster. Potential audiences had little money to spend. Many who had formerly been nightly regulars did not come at all. Others became selective, picking only the feature nights to attend. For week-stand repertoire the loss was painful. That summer in Mansfield, Missouri, Kell's Comedians opened to a night's gross of $19.80, and this after heavy pre-opening advertising.[13] And another company, managed by Billy Terrell, performing in the same Missouri territory, grossed less than $150 on one of its weeks.[14] "Repertoire is on the wane," wrote showman Lawrence Russell. "It is safe to say that not 20 percent of the repertoire shows that have been out the past three years can ever be made paying propositions again."[15] Russell's anticipation was correct, but his pessimism was premature. Repertoire was not on the wane yet. Although tent managers would never relive the prosperity of the previous few years, business conditions slowly improved over the next half-dozen years. The number of companies increased to an overcrowded level, creating problems as damaging as financial depression.

It has been estimated that there were some 400 tent shows traveling throughout the United States by the mid-1920s. Texas alone was said to have 100 companies vying for audiences the better part of each year.[16] And similar congestion prevailed throughout the South, the Midwest, and the West. It is not surprising, then, that competition created problems among the many shows that followed closely on each other's heels within each limited territory at a time when money was none too loose. Complaints of unfair practices were familiar items in the *Billboard* at this time. For example, the great number of shows that formed each year created a demand for experienced performers and canvasmen that exceeded the supply. Consequently, the temptation to steal personnel away from other companies was too much to resist for some managers. Canvasmen, in particular, could be enticed to change jobs for simply a cash advance on future salary. Billing malpractices caused other problems between shows. Advertising paper was sometimes torn down or covered over. "Wait for the big one!" was a frequent plea when posted alongside rival advertising. City show lots in prime locations were much sought after. To insure against a rival company's being first into town, managers sometimes paid high rent for the lots, tying them up weeks in advance. The result was the creation of inflated and unrealistic costs in many of the places.

One of the frequent tactics brought about by business competition was price cutting. Normal admissions at this time ranged from thirty-five cents to fifty cents for adult front-door tickets and from ten cents to twenty-five cents for reserved seats. With good business, this was sufficient for a manager to make a modest profit. In contrast, the cut-rate admission price offered by some companies was ten cents all around—ten cents for the front door, ten cents for reserved seats, ten cents for prize candy, and ten cents for the concert or after show, giving rise to the expression, "They dime you to death!" A cheaper admission often meant a cheaper performance as well. These price and quality disparities made life difficult for many managers. Leslie Kell of Kell's Comedians exemplifies a general dissatisfaction with this remark: "We all have these ten-cent shows to buck at one time or another, and the best repertoire managers will admit that such shows are ruining many a good spot."[17]

Another problem confronting tent show managers in the early years of the 1920s was unionization. Actors' Equity Association was granted a charter with the American Federation of Labor in July of 1919. Three weeks later, there occurred the greatest strike in the annals of the American theatre, with the forces of this new acting organization pitted against the established

Producing Managers' Association. Although many of the actors' demands were not fully resolved at the end of the month-long strike, the position of Actors' Equity Association was secured. At once, Equity set about expanding its membership behind the leadership of its president, Frank Gilmore. A Chicago office was opened under the supervision of Frank Dare; and, shortly, a Kansas City office under W. Frank Delmaine. Both Chicago and Kansas City were repertoire centers, where casting and other organizational activities were carried on before the beginning of each season. It follows, then, that Equity would be interested in unionizing the tent shows and in setting up an Equity shop within each company. One hundred percent Equity was its goal for each tent outfit on the road. But organizing the tents was more difficult than organizing the permanently located theatres that were clustered within metropolitan areas. It was found to be an impossible task. One hundred percent Equity was accomplished on only a minority of the shows out each year. However, the aggressive recruitment of members, often carried to the extreme of signing up misguided canvasmen, created within many managers an antagonism toward Frank Gilmore and his Actors' Equity Association—an antagonism that never went away.

The large number of tent shows on the road for the entire decade of the 1920s, along with the many circuses, carnivals, and other traveling outdoor attractions, was looked on as unwanted competition by the moving picture theatre managers. At this time, moving pictures had emerged as a dominant entertainment form in the cities and towns where previously live theatre was the principal means of amusement. So great was the takeover, that touring companies declined and disappeared, and the theatres and opera houses in which these companies performed were turned into places for moving pictures. The moving picture theatre managers were permanently located businessmen, available the year around to campaign against the intrusion of traveling outdoor attractions that were arriving much too frequently each year. "These tent shows are taking money out of our community" was the persuasive argument of the local managers. The moving picture interests were powerful and well organized at state and national levels; and, consequently, they were able to create favorable legislation to combat the incursion of the tented menace. This came in the form of high state, county, and local license fees.

Early in 1923, manager George Roberson issued the challenge, "Let's organize!" It was in response to a bill introduced in the Texas legislature, calling for a state license fee to be levied on every theatrical company touring through Texas. The amount ranged from $5 a day, when performing in towns under 1,000 population, to $35 a day, for cities above 30,000. In addition, cities and counties were allowed to assess taxes equal to one-half of the state's. The bill included "every theatrical or dramatic presentation and every musical comedy show, and all similar amusements for which pay for admission is demanded or received, that travels from place to place and gives exhibitions, shows or performances."[18]

Actors' Equity Association threw its support behind the Texas tent managers in an attempt to defeat the bill as discriminatory "class legislation." A Southwest Tent Show Managers' Association was formed to present organized opposition to the bill. The final passage of the bill was challenged by a test case which went as far as the Fifth Court of Appeals, Fort Worth. It resulted in the court's ruling that "traveling road shows or theatrical companies, not exhibiting in regular theatres, cannot be compelled to pay the Baldwin Occupation Tax," and that "the law is arbitrary and capricious."[19] What happened in Texas was to be repeated in many states—Missouri, Arkansas, Florida, South Carolina, and Tennessee, among others. Attempts were continually made throughout the decade to prohibit or discourage traveling shows. The constant harassment and expensive legal fees created a necessity for some kind of tent show organization to resist effectively the powerful moving picture managers' associations.

In the summer of 1925, Actors' Equity Association came forward with an offer to do just that. *Billboard* carried the headline, "Equity Preparing to Organize Repertoire and Tent Interests."[20] Equity's purpose was to form an organization of tent and repertoire managers resourceful enough to eliminate unethical practices within the industry, fight the competitive actions of the motion picture lobby, and obtain reduced royalties by contracting for plays as a group. In return, Equity expected each member company to be one hundred percent union. The tent managers responded with indifference.

Still, Frank Gilmore called a meeting for March 1926. The site was Chicago. A tentative organization was formed, called the Tent Repertoire Managers' Protective Association, with George Roberson as its president and secretary-treasurer. Five vice-presidents represented various sections of the country: Elwin Strong, the West; Addison Aulger, the Northwest; Jack Kelly, Michigan; Norma Ginnivan, the East; and Harley Sadler, the South. The temporary nature of the association was to be effective until a fall meeting and a larger membership could implement a permanent constitution.[21]

The fact that Equity was supporting T.R.M.P.A. was enough to frighten many potential members. Their fear persisted throughout the ineffectual life of the association and was, in the end, the major reason for its early demise. The managers from the South and Southwest, where much of the licensing problem was occurring, showed little disposition for joining. Of the thirty registered T.R.M.P.A. members in the fall of 1926, only three were from those areas.[22] Recruitment went so slowly that the proposed fall meeting was postponed until the spring of the following year, at which time some forty owners and managers met in Kansas City. Frank Delmaine hosted the meeting and Frank Gilmore delivered a spirited address. Equity was still prominently in the leadership. Paul English, a southern manager and one who was outspokenly pro-Equity, was elected president. "I'm for Equity strong, and I don't care who knows it," he wrote. "Long live this wonderful organization that has done so much to make a gentleman's game of the show business."[23]

The T.R.M.P.A. never really got off the ground. There were a number of early resignations because of the Equity affiliation, and new members were noticeably few. In the spring of 1928, a decision was made to hold a referendum on the Equity question: should the 100 percent Equity clause be stricken from the bylaws? The T.R.M.P.A. membership determined that it should. In so doing, they eliminated T.R.M.P.A.'s only sustaining force. By January of 1929, secretary Harry Huguenot was accusing tent managers of being narrow-minded, selfish, and subject to personal prejudice.[24] The annual meeting was called off for lack of interest. This was the final straw for Paul English. Within a short time, his resignation was announced in *Billboard*.[25]

Like most of you I have lost interest, not in the fundamental principles of our association, but in the task of trying to interest the average tent show manager in the advisability of a protective organization. So, feeling that I cannot waste my time further, I wish to take this opportunity of making public my resignation as president and treasurer of T.R.M.P.A.

With this, the Tent Repertoire Managers' Protective Association ceased to exist.

To add to the tent showmen's woes, moving pictures took a bold, new step in 1928 with the innovation of sound. At first it was considered a mere novelty. The editor of *Billboard*, for example, predicted that "an overdose of talking pictures looms as a nemesis of this new form of entertainment" and that "thru being overfed the public soon will be saturated and driven to relief."[26] In reality, the public could not get enough. The tent show industry suffered from the competition of "talkies," just as it was suffering from the competition of radio, and would be suffering from the public's attachment to the automobile and their enchantment with television. These were technological monsters that easily overshadowed an outmoded nineteenth-century amusement.

Tent show's failure to organize into a lasting protective group, the advent of sound alongside moving pictures, and the financial disaster of 1929 mark the end of the second period of tent show history. The 1920s began with promise. The 1921 Depression quickly put an end to it. Although unemployment declined the following year, farm prices remained low. The truth is that although conditions improved gradually through 1927, the 1920s never fully recovered from the changeover to a peacetime economy. Each year had financial drawbacks; but the summer of 1929 served the crowning blow. Many managers did not complete their regular season and many more swore they would store their outfits and find other employment. And they did.

The third (and final) period for the tents, a period of mortification, began with the depressive times of the 1930s. Throughout the next several years, financial conditions forced the managers who had remained operative to alter their customary ways of doing business. Some companies went commonwealth, with everyone sharing in the profits. Others tried using split-week stands, with a three-day repertoire in each location. And still others set up their tents in large cities for permanent stock engagements as long as business held up. Then, on to another location. Most of these desperation methods of coping with an impossible situation were fruitless in the end. Times deteriorated. As the 1931 season began, both casting agents and play brokers were complaining about the depressing lack of activity. The show managers that were determined to buck the bad times were quick to regret it. Leslie Kell closed his company in June, claiming that it was hopeless to continue.[27] The Jesse Colton Company, a show of forty years' standing, soon followed. "If they don't come out for the Jesse Colton Company," one of the performers wrote, "the day of the rag opry is over."[28] Perhaps the symbolic end came when on September 1, 1931, Actors' Equity Association closed its office in Kansas City.

There were fewer shows on the road in 1932 than at any time before World War I. As one manager put it, "It's better to starve at home than on the road."[29] With this state of affairs, hundreds of performers were forced to find other means of employment. A few fortunate ones went into radio, which was flourishing in Chicago at that time, or moved to the West Coast for work in the film industry. By the mid-thirties, the Federal Theatre Project, a part of the WPA, absorbed a large number of entertainers. But the majority of repertoire people went into other kinds of work, abandoning the tent show for good and always. Thus, the pool of experienced and versatile actors, knowledgeable of the tent show way of life, disappeared. When repertoire experienced a brief revival during and shortly after World War II, the performers were merely remnants and replicas of a once-large group of professionals.

By following weekly accounts in *Billboard* that continued as late as the mid-1950s, until coin machines and phonograph records became the new trade emphasis, the story of the decline of tent shows can be clearly plotted. Hundreds of companies closed during the Depression years, never to reopen. World War II, with its drain on personnel and its gas and tire rationing, did away with many of the remaining tent troupes. Following the war, a vestige of a dozen or more shows carried on until one by one they disappeared.

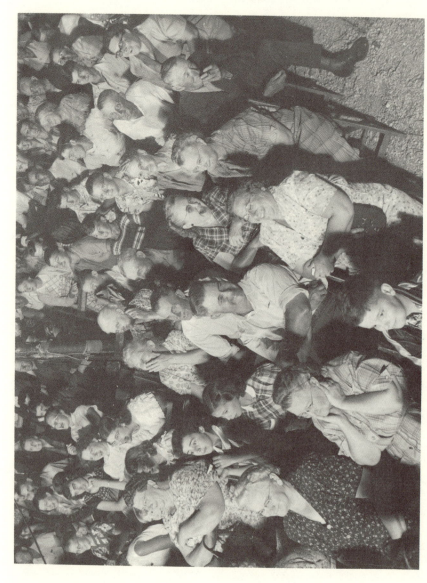

A 1950 tent show audience. This audience is typical in dress and attitude of tent show audiences across the country at the time.

Toby's bucolic comedy succumbed to a conflicting age of H-bombs, jet planes, and massive urban problems—an age apathetic to canvas theatres, down-on-the-farm comedy, and baggy-trousered bumpkins.[30] So, time ran out for the tent show. What was formerly a large and active theatrical industry is now a few scattered museum pieces staffed by college students, and a boneyard of memorabilia in the archives of The National Society for the Preservation of Tent, Folk, and Repertoire Theatre. Oh, Tent Show . . . Broadway's poor relation . . . old timer . . . *ave atque vale!*

NOTES

1. Yankee Robinson, "Dilly Fay, the Clown," New York *Clipper*, February 17, 1872, p. 20.

2. William L. Slout, *Theatre in a Tent* (Bowling Green: Bowling Green University Popular Press, 1972), pp. 71-82.

3. Ibid., pp. 71-72.

4. Ibid., pp. 83-97.

5. *Billboard*, August 27, 1910, p. 18.

6. Slout, pp. 66-70.

7. Ibid., pp. 63, 64.

8. *Billboard*, December 27, 1919, p. 14.

9. *Billboard*, February 14, 1920, p. 22.

10. John Lawrence, "Jesse James vs. East Lynne," *Billboard*, March 22, 1919, p. 33.

11. *Billboard*, December 27, 1919, p. 14.

12. John D. Hicks, *Republican Ascendancy* (New York: Harper & Row, 1963), p. 22.

13. *Billboard*, November 19, 1921, p. 26.

14. *Billboard*, January 14, 1922, p. 26.

15. Lawrence Russell, "The Trouble with 'Rep'," *Billboard*, December 10, 1921, p. 50.

16. *Billboard*, August 25, 1923, p. 5.

17. *Bilboard*, November 22, 1924, p. 28.

18. *Billboard*, July 28, 1923, p. 28.

19. *Billboard*, July 28, 1923, p. 28; August 25, 1923, pp. 23, 139; March 1, 1924, pp. 11, 28.

20. *Billboard*, July 4, 1925, p. 5.

21. *Billboard*, March 20, 1926, pp. 19, 204.

22. *Billboard*, November 6, 1926, p. 30.

23. *Billboard*, June 4, 1927, p. 26.

24. *Billboard*, December 31, 1927, p. 30; March 17, 1928, p. 31; January 12, 1929, p. 29.

25. *Billboard*, March 16, 1929, p. 33.

26. *Billboard*, August 18, 1928, p. 43.

27. *Billboard*, June 27, 1931, p. 22.

28. *Billboard*, July 11, 1931, p. 20.

29. *Billboard*, July 23, 1932, p. 22.

30. Slout, p. 111.

Caroline Schaffner

Trouping with the Schaffners_____

In a way I have go give credit to this museum—Lincoln Center—for the organization that established our little Museum of Repertoire Americana in Mount Pleasant, Iowa. It was here that I first came for encouragement, and it was Paul Myers who encouraged me, and I am grateful.

It was most interesting to watch the Harley Sadler show. Neither Neil nor I ever met Harley Sadler, but we had much correspondence with him because Neil was a prolific writer of plays for the repertoire companies, and Harley Sadler leased and paid for every play that Neil wrote during the time of his trouping. So we had much respect and admiration for Harley Sadler.

I'd like to give you just a brief rundown on the history of Neil Schaffner before we run the film of *Toby and the Tall Corn.* Toby, or Neil Schaffner, started in show business in 1909. He joined the Spedden and Paige Dramatic Company Players, which trouped up through the Dakotas and out west. They even made some of their jumps in a stagecoach. After four years with that company, Neil came back to the Midwest and did a little trouping with some of the rep shows and then became involved in vaudeville. He was with the old Mason & Mason act. It was a German act, and played the Orpheum circuit billed as Mason & Mason. Then later, he was with a burlesque show called the "Whirl of Mirth" on the old Columbia Wheel. He toured one season with that. Then he went back to the Midwest and joined the North Brothers Stock Company in Wichita, Kansas. Later he was with the Princess Stock Company in Des Moines, Iowa. All of this trouping was done B.C.—before Caroline.

I first met Neil in 1924, in Fort Dodge, Iowa. I was a chorus girl in a tab show that was playing in Fort Dodge which was his hometown. Show people in our line of the business always visited other show people when they were in town. So he came backstage, and I was introduced to him. I had, prior to being in the tab show, been in Chautauqua. (I see we do not have anything about Chautauqua at this Conference, so I cordially invite all of you at the next Conference to come to Mount Pleasant, Iowa. We have many memorabilia about the Chautauquas.) I had had dramatic training, being a graduate of the old Horner Institute of Fine Arts in Kansas City, Missouri, and was very desirous of getting with a legitimate company. So Neil hired me for the ingenue in Angel's Comedians.

Mr. Angel was an impresario of the early days of tent repertoire. At one time, Mr. Angel had eight tent companies touring through the country. This particular company was to start rehearsals on April 26, 1925, and I joined them in Murray, Iowa. We got up in six plays in six days. Now that seems very unusual. The rehearsals ran this way: Monday morning you rehearsed one play; Monday afternoon you took another play; Tuesday morning you took another play. You went through the six plays, twice a day a different play for three days. The next three days—Thursday, Friday, and Saturday—you went through the first three you had rehearsed. Then the following week you opened on Monday night.

The repertoire that year included three plays written by Neil. We opened with a play that Neil had written called *The Vulture*, which had a Toby part. We also did another play, *What Every Daughter Learns*, which was our feature heavy dramatic play. Then we did another play called *The Old Grouch*, which Neil had written—and by the way, Harley Sadler played every one of those plays. Many, many repertoire companies played his plays. Angel's Comedians closed in the summer, and Neil and I went to Fort Dodge, where we organized The Schaffner Players.

The Schaffner Players gave their first performance in a theatre on October 10, 1925. Of course, for ten years we operated both winter and summer in the state of Iowa. You played in the tent in the summer; you closed on Saturday night in the tent and moved into theatres or opera houses for repertoire in the fall, and then into a town like Marshalltown, Des Moines, or a larger town for stock until summer, when you could move back into the tent. For ten years we operated that way.

As has been mentioned before, the Depression came along and brought bad times. The Schaffner Players were on the road every summer, never missed a summer. From 1925, The Schaffner Players have continued in operation every year, with the exception of 1961 when Neil had a heart attack and we were not able to tour. However, in 1935, we became involved in radio and wrote an act called "The Bugtussle News." We first did it on a small radio station in Carthage, Illinois. The scene was a small-town newspaper office—Toby was the editor and Suzy was the girlfriend. It was very successful, and so the following winter we went to Chicago to appear on the old NBC "National Barn Dance" with Lulabelle and Scotty, the Hoosier Hotshots, and the people of that era. Perhaps there's someone here in that age bracket (I hope?) who remembers these names. Anyway, the little act went over very well, and two winters we spent in Chicago doing the three-minute skit on the old "National Barn Dance."

Then we were hired to come out to Cedar Rapids, Iowa, to do this same radio skit on a small network of stations, the Midwest Network. And, of course, we had used the title of "Toby's Bugtussle News," but the manager of the station said that there was one very big change we would have to make. We could no longer call it "Toby's Bugtussle News" because our sponsor was The Peter Pan Bread Company (you could not have bugs in association with bread). So we gave it some thought and we came up with the title "Toby's Corntussle News." The sponsor liked that very much. So for eight years, in the winter, Neil and I broadcast this skit in Cedar Rapids, Iowa, on WMT and the Midwest Network, doing "Toby's Corntussle News" with Toby as the editor and Suzy as his girlfriend.

From that radio publicity, which spread out so much farther than the early advertising the Schaffner Players could do, we became associated with the title of Toby, and our company became known as a Toby Tent Show. But I want to try to correct the idea that we were called "Toby Shows." If you were asked to describe a body, you wouldn't call it a leg, you'd call it a body; the leg is part of the body, so that was the way the Toby character was. Many rep companies did no Toby plays at all. And those that did— I will now speak especially of The Schaffner Players—we would only do maybe two plays with a Toby character. The other plays were comedy dramas, and we always closed with farce on Sunday night—we had a variety in our repertoire of plays. So I would appreciate it if you people who are going to write the history of this business that I loved very much would make the distinction, and also remember that for many, many companies, especially in the early days (up through the 1920s), we were in the tents only three months out of the year. The other nine months we were in the theatres and houses and opera houses. So please bear that in mind.

Now we're going to show you the film of *Toby and the Tall Corn.* In our little museum in Mount Pleasant, we have a "Toby Hall of Fame." We are the only museum that has one. And this has pictures of all the men whom we have been able to secure the pictures of—so far—who became identified with the character of Toby in their territory, such as Harley Sadler, Fred Wilson, and many others. Beside our Toby Hall of Fame is a definition or a small explanation that we give of Toby:

Toby has been a show business character for a long time. In Shakespeare's *Twelfth Night,* he bears the title Sir Toby Belch, but Toby, as we know him, is as American as Iowa corn. He is usually portrayed as a freckle-faced yokel with a mop of flaming red hair, wearing rural clothes. Some playwrights endowed Toby with more wisdom or cleverness than did others. Some saw him only as a buffoon. All of them portrayed him as a brash or sly farm hand, as a cowboy, or as the town character, with an uncanny ability to bungle in or out of comic situations. Toby was always a symbol of honesty and clean living. Toby always managed to win out over the bad guys or the villain. Toby is one of the most fascinating characters to come out of the theatre in the last one hundred years.

With that explanation of Toby, we will show you the film of *Toby and the Tall Corn*. Now this play, which you will see only snatches of, is a rewrite of the old book play, *Lena Rivers*, and I hope you will enjoy it. Thank you.

[After the showing of the film, a question-and-answer period followed.]

(Question): When did Mr. Schaffner have time to write these plays?

(Mrs. Schaffner): He was writing constantly, and constantly searching and looking for things to write about. Many people would say to him, "Where do you get your ideas?" We got the ideas for the plays from association with the people in the towns; we knew and understood those people. The most important thing about a play, not only in our era of showbusiness, but also back in the early days of the repertoire companies, was *afterdraft*. That was the most important thing a play must have—afterdraft—meaning that the audience would be so well pleased and entertained that they would come back the next night. When we wrote a play, our only thought in writing the play was: How would the audience be entertained? When we had written a play, Neil constantly watched the audience; if they reacted as we thought they should, if they laughed at the right place or cried at the proper moment, it was all right. If not, we immediately rewrote that scene. I hope that answers your question.

(Question): I wonder if you can tell us a little about the making of the film. How long did they stay there? How did they make that film?

(Mrs. Schaffner): I'd be very glad to tell you. It has an interesting story because a man from New York, Paul Feigay, Director of the Ford Foundation, called via long distance. We were playing in Mount Pleasant, where the museum is now located, in June 1954, and he said to Neil over the phone, "I hear you have a dramatic company out there. People putting on plays in a tent, and people pay to come to see it." And Neil said, "Well, yes, that's true." And Mr. Feigay said, "Well, the world ought to know about that." So he introduced himself and said that the Ford Foundation was making documentaries of different things in our country at that time and that they were interested in making a documentary of *Toby and the Tall Corn*. Neil agreed to it. Paul Feigay, the man whom we had our first conversation with, I understand had been a Broadway director. Then, he and a couple of other men from the Ford Foundation came out to visit the show in the little

town of Delta, Iowa—a town of less than, oh, about seven hundred or eight hundred people, maybe nearer five hundred. We were so very anxious, of course, to put our best foot forward and make a good impression on our visitors from New York City, from Broadway. The cast had been primed on it, and everything was set. The first act had gone over big when the most terrible storm came up. It poured down rain. We had to stop the show. We had to have community singing. It was just . . . oh, it was just terrible. Neil was so discouraged over it, but the snapper to that little joke is that the visitors were so impressed with the way the audience reacted, how the actors reacted, how the people sat and waited for the show to start again, and so forth, that he said to Neil, "When we make the film, if we don't have a storm, we must simulate one." But we didn't have to; the weather, you know, cooperated beautifully. The film crew, with Mr. Russell Lynes, joined us in Shelbina, Missouri, and then traveled with us to Laplatta, Missouri. They were on the show ten days, and I understand the film cost $55,000 to make.

(Question): I would like to know if you were the lady at the piano?

(Mrs. Schaffner): No. No, I was not. I was the mother of the people in the first act.

(Question): And did the action stop when the trains went by?

(Mrs. Schaffner): Depending on how much noise they made, sometimes we had to stop. Quite often, if we had to stop for a long time, Neil would turn to the owner of the place where the play was and say, "Why did you build your house so close to the railroad track?" Good for a laugh!

(Question): You described the Toby character before. Can you tell us what the model for that character was? a prototype? Where did that character come out?

(Mrs. Schaffner): Well, the best explanation is what I read, and I'll be glad to give you a copy of it, and as I said, that's what we have. There are many explanations, and probably every man who played the part of Toby would give you a different explanation. Actually, the early part of it I couldn't answer—I don't know it—and each man's character was, of course, different form the other to a certain extent. For instance, you noticed Harley Sadler blacked out the tooth; Neil never blacked out the tooth. Different ones had different characteristics that they incorporated in the character.

(Question): To go back to the trains. We used to have railroad tracks, too, and my husband would stop and turn around and look in the direction of the train, and he'd say, "Toot, you son of a gun, you can't whistle."

(Mrs. Schaffner): Yes, the people who operated show business in the days that we are speaking of had to meet many, many adverse situations, and you became a master at that. The one thing that I want to say before the program closes is that many of you people will write the history of these

companies. I beg you, please, do research on it and try and be as authentic as possible. If you are writing about a repertoire company, please give dates. Give the date that the company was formed; where it played; how many years it lasted; and so forth—something like you saw on the Harley Sadler show. And please do not think that one description fits all tent or Toby shows or repertoire companies, because every one is different. Sometimes, someone would say to me, "How would you describe a Toby tent show?" I'd say, "That's like saying, 'How would you describe shoes?' What kind of shoes are you talking about? What size shoes?" Because the shows were all sizes: a two-people company, a repertoire company of five people, a family show, ten people, fifty people. There were so many different kinds. As the man told about the tent pole being in front of the stage—that was the W. I. Swain Show, which toured down through Louisiana and Mississippi—of course, the actors all resented the pole that was in the middle of the stage because they had to read their lines on each side. Mr. Swain was very much the manager. I guess I never saw the man, but this was one of the tales told: If an actor complained about the fact that there was a pole, W. I. Swain would turn to him and say, "Huh! where's your tent show?"

(*Question*): Just one small point, the bit about the watch, where he takes it off. Was that really ad-lib?

(*Mrs. Schaffner*): Well, Neil was a master of the ad-lib, and he did a great deal of ad-libbing in his performances. Someone wrote to me once and said, "I understand that the tent shows didn't use scripts, that all the plays were ad-libbed." Well, I immediately answered his letter and said, "If my husband had been alive, he would have called you on the telephone, because he would have been furious over that." While Neil did a great deal of ad-libbing, no one else was allowed to ad-lib. And some people would say, "Oh, he doesn't want anybody else to be funny on the show. I wouldn't work on that Schaffner Show." But it wasn't that he didn't want anybody else to be funny, because if, in the script, you had a line that was supposed to get a good laugh, he would rehearse you over and over and over on that until you had it, until you got the laugh. You see what I mean? And he was always polishing the performance, and if everyone was funny, you see, there was no contrast, the whole thing was lost. And, of course, in the early repertoire companies (which I hope some of you will write about), they were strictly legitimate theatre, the directors were very severe and very demanding. One of the stories that has been told for years in the rep business was about a man named Old Bob Sherman—Robert Sherman—who wrote many plays and also wrote a book on the repertoire companies. And he had several companies out of Chicago. He had written a play called *My Friend from Arkansas*, and Mr. Sherman knew exactly how he wanted each line read. A very young actor joined the company and he had a heavy dramatic scene in which another actor pulled out a gun and shot him, and he was supposed to kind of stagger back and say, "My God, I'm shot." At the first performance, he was very bad. As they fired the gun, he said, in a most amateurish way, "Oh, Heavens! I'm shot." The next night it was not very good, either, and the other actors were getting bored with all this rehearsal and directing and so forth. So one of the old character actors says, "I'll fix him!" The gun was on the prop table, and the character actor had brought a little container of ketchup from a restaurant. So he put this ketchup in the muzzle of the prop gun. Anyway, the play went on; the scene came up; and the man pulled out the gun and fired and splattered ketchup all over the young actor's white shirt. The young actor said, in the same amateurish way, "Oh, Heavens! I'm shot." Then he looked down, saw the ketchup, and, in the most professional way, declared, "MY GOD! I AM SHOT!"

THE CIRCUS,
WILD WEST SHOWS, AND
MEDICINE SHOWS

Marcello Truzzi

Circus and Side Shows_____

The Definitional Problem

Because the circus has undergone great changes throughout its history, and because no exact technical definition exists, many of the basic questions about the circus, such as its origins, its antiquity, and the character of its growth and decline, present semantic problems. This is compounded by the general, public confusion of even the contemporary circus with other outdoor amusements such as the carnival and the fair. This confused image of the circus has, in part, resulted from a number of popular motion pictures (such as *The Wagons Roll at Night* and *The Greatest Show on Earth*) that have portrayed circuses as having carnival games, rides, and gambling in them. The confusion has been present because various historians assigned the circus's beginnings to different epochs. Thus, though most modern historians of the circus would agree that the true circus is only about two centuries old, others have seen it as originating with the early Roman circus of the colliseum or even the early Greek hippodrome. To some, the circus represents a specific variety of entertainments, such as wild animal trainers, jugglers, clowns, and acrobats. In the early days of the American circus, the term "circus" referred merely to a specific building. To others, the circus may mean such things as a tent, elephants, a freak show, and pink lemonade.

All these folk definitions—different ones were central at various times in American history—complicate any serious analysis of this remarkable institution. Rather than attempt any exclusive and exhaustive definition that could not satisfy all concerned, a sociological definition of the circus had best be given as a pure or constructed type, recognizing that rather extreme deviations sometimes occur that some would still label a circus. A circus is thus defined as *a traveling and organized display of animals and skilled performances within one of more circular stages known as "rings" before an audience encircling these activities.*[1] Unlike the carnival, which centers about its audience's participation and which has come to us from the medieval fair, the circus is primarily a spectator activity and is an extension of theatre.

Almost since its beginnings, the circus has had associated with it numerous specialized entertainments that were offered to the public as adjunct or supplemental exhibits and displays, for which the public was usually separately charged a fee and which were normally housed under separate tents. All these were referred to as "sideshows," but the term today has a specialized meaning within the circus. During the history of the American circus, such sideshows have included: collections of wild animals (the circus menagerie); special, unusual animal displays (such as the "blood sweating behemoth" or hippopotamus, or the "sacred white elephant of Burma"); displays of new scientific and mechanical novelties and inventions (including balloons, the power-driven carriage, the electric light, the talking machine, and the airplane); human abnormalities or oddities; and certain specialized types of entertainers.

Many early circuses grew out of such animal displays and menageries, and these early traveling menageries were functionally the equivalent of the later zoos which displaced them. The early displays of new inventions were also important as a means of communicating advances in technological development to the rural population. But in modern times, the term sideshow has come to mean a single, combined tent attraction made up of only the last types of exhibits. This display of unusual people and acts is one of the few entertainments to be found in both circuses and carnivals. In circuses, it is referred to as the sideshow, while in carnivals, it is called the "ten-in-one" (since you see ten or so attractions under one tent for one admission ticket).

Among the human abnormalities that have been displayed in the sideshow, there have been such curiosities as: giants and midgets, fat people, "human skeletons," women with beards or unusually long hair, persons born without arms or legs or both, cases of abnormal twinning, blue people, albinos, exotic persons from strange lands such as the "giraffe-necked Burmese" or the "saucer-lipped Ubangis," "petrified men," "alligator-skinned" women, persons with unusual facial features that resembled those of animals (such as the "dog-faced" boy or the "mule-faced" woman), and persons with a variety of other birth defects. Such human abnormalities were usually valid presentations, but hoaxes were not uncommon and included such things as transvestites posing as hermaphrodites (the half-man half-woman), or a woman who washed her hair with an unusual brew of beer so she could be exhibited as "the woman with seaweed hair." Today, the more grotesque forms of humanity thus exhibited are quite rare. This is due to both the advances in medicine and to changing public taste, much of which would today be offended. From the standpoint of these unfortunate performers, this is often a tragedy; for the sideshow was a place where many of them could live nearly normal lives, be self-sufficient, and be relatively happy.

Among the special types of entertainers one might find in the sideshow, there have commonly been: magicians, ventriloquists, sword swallowers, fire eaters, Punch and Judy and marionette showmen, mind readers, tatooed people, snake charmers, performers on unusual musical instruments such as saws, skilled throwers of knives and tomahawks, Hawaiian musicians, Negro minstrels, strong men and women, and "human pin cushions" (persons who could demonstrate the tolerance of pain). Some of these unusual entertainers have occasionally been presented in the circus itself, but most of these forms have become traditionally associated with the sideshow.

At one time, in 1889, Barnum and Bailey even carried two sideshows, a regular one and a special "black tent," which displayed illusions and automations. Today, the sideshow is a rarity, and Ringling Brothers, Barnum and Bailey, no longer even carries one with it. Circuses with sideshows are becoming quite unusual, and most circus sideshow personnel have moved to carnivals where the ten-in-one still operates more commonly.

Circus History

Although individual circus acts can be traced to antiquity, the first circus as we know it today was founded in 1770 by Philip Astley on the outskirts of London near Westminster Bridge. Astley was a war hero with a cavalry background who demonstrated trick riding and developed an equestrian comedy routine. Similar trick riders worked in America and sometimes combined their exhibitions with other entertainments including a clown and music. On April 3, 1793, John Bill Ricketts presented the first complete circus performance in America in a permanent building he established in Philadelphia. His was a combined riding academy and circus; and the latter included trick riding, a tightrope walker, and a clown. His April 22 performance was attended by George Washington, and Ricketts's show prospered. Ricketts made appearances in New York, Boston, and Albany, along with other cities in the United States and Canada. His later building in Philadelphia was able to accommodate about 1,200 people. In 1799, Ricketts's building in New York burned down and another accidental fire soon afterward destroyed his Philadelphia building. The history of the circus has continually been punctuated by similar conflagrations. Though Ricketts was financially ruined, he managed to earn his passage back to England, but his ship was lost at sea.

New circuses slowly sprouted in both Europe and America, and some of these played on both continents. (The Liaison Circus from France had played across the street from Ricketts's circus in New York as early as 1797.) These

early traveling circuses at first toured the eastern seaboard, moving west-
ward as the nation expanded. While British and French troupes visited the
United States, similar Spanish troupes visited Mexico, where the first full
circus performance, including horsemanship, acrobats, and a clown, was
presented on July 9, 1791. The circus largely developed independently in
Mexico from that in the United States, but the mid-twentieth century saw
many Mexican acts displayed in American circuses.

The growth of traveling animal menageries paralleled the early development of the circus. Beginning around 1824, these two institutions
started to merge. Although an elephant made a brief appearance with a
circus in 1812, Hackaliah Bailey independently toured his elephant, Old
Bet, with great success until 1816. (Circus historians have often mistakenly
associated Old Bet with Nathan Howes's circus.) Also, Howes's partner,
Aaron Turner, has generally been credited with introducing the first full-top
canvas enclosure for a circus around 1824 (previous circuses having employed merely a sidewall of canvas), but new evidence indicates the tent
was probably not introduced until 1826 by J. Purdy Brown. Thus, Howes
and Turner are usually mistakenly credited with two major innovations—
the elephant and the circus tent ("big top"), which became defining elements
of circuses in the public mind.

Experiments were carried on with the railroads as early as 1853, but Dan
Costello's Circus and Menagerie became the first railroad circus to make a
transcontinental tour in 1868. The 1890s and early years of this century saw
many small railroad circuses traveling around the country, usually on two
or three cars, sometimes on a single, long car. The last such small railroad
circus, Cooper Brothers, a two-car show, closed in 1936. Although wagon
shows using mules and horses for motive power continued into the twentieth
century, motorized transportation and the railroad soon displaced it, but
the last show to still use horses to draw some of its wagons—the M. L. Clark
& Son's Circus—was active until 1930. The advent of the combined tractor
and semi-trailer permitted much larger loads than could previously be
carried by truck and they began to be used by circuses widely in the 1920s.
The Tom Mix organization made the first transcontinental tour of the
United States by a motorized circus, from California to Alabama, in 1936.
Though motorized circuses, or "truck shows," have continued into the
present, the great railroad circus, epitomized by the once-massive Ringling
Brothers and Barnum & Bailey Combined Shows—which moved on 108
double-length cars in its 1947 season!—has become part of the general
public image of the circus coming to town.

But possibly the most significant change in the evolution of the American
circus was its expansion from the single-ring European model. Around
1873, W. C. Coup started the tradition of the two-ring circus in the Barnum
show. In 1881, James A. Bailey, again over the objections of Phineas T.

Barnum who earlier had opposed Coup's expansion, opened Barnum & Bailey, Greatest Show on Earth, with three rings. The move to three rings basically changed the character of the American circus because of the new relationship thus created with its audience. Emphasis was now on spectacle and away from intimacy and discrimination of relatively subtle artistic differences. This shift away from the European model of the one-ring show had profound consequences for the development and eventual decline of the American circus, not only for its audience, but also for its internal structure, a topic to be examined in further detail in our discussion of the circus's social hierarchy.

In 1816, John June, Lewis B. Titus, Caleb S. Angevine, and Jeremiah Crane—a group of prominent church members in North Salem, New York—upon seeing the success of Hackaliah Bailey's exhibition of Old Bet, acquired several traveling menageries, later developed into what they grandiloquently called the Zoological Institute. These men were soon joined by others organizing other menageries and, later, circuses. This informal network of shows became the basis for the first circus syndicate—the Flatfoots (so called because they indicated exclusive rights to play the rich upstate New York area by declaring: "We put our foot down flat and shall play New York; so watch out."). The Flatfoots reached its height soon after 1835, when it was joined by about 130 other showmen (many of whose ventures were struck down in the financial panic of 1837), and these interlocking directorates continued to exert effective regional power until around 1880. This first great syndicate in circus history, dominant in its northern territory, was an important phase in American circus history, for its central organization facilitated the modernization and systematization of the whole industry.

The period between 1830 and 1870 saw the emergence of a number of prominent shows including: the George F. Bailey Circus (George was the son of Hackaliah Bailey); the several circuses featuring the name of the "Lion King," Isaac Van Amburgh; the several circuses of Seth B. Howes (brother of Nathan Howes), including his brief association with P. T. Barnum and Barnum's midget attraction, Tom Thumb; the Mable Brothers Circus (playing primarily Wisconsin and the western country); the Yankee (Fayette Ludovic) Robinson Circus (playing mainly in the Mississippi Valley); the John Robinson Circus (playing mainly in the South); the Spalding & Rogers Circus ("The Railroad Circus"); the Dan Costello Circus; the Dan Rice Circus, featuring the name of the great circus clown; and the W. W. Cole Circus. This period saw the beginnings of the free circus parade, and in 1865 Seth B. Howes imported the first ornate wagons carved in England, which soon became a prominent feature of these great caravans' entry into a community. It was also during this period that the circuses, under the direction of Gilbert R. Spalding and Charles Rogers, brought many innovations in equipment and procedures in relation to matters of seating, lighting, and transportation that would modernize the circus industry. These innovations included the perfection of portable bleachers and the intermediate circle of poles which gave circus tents greater size and seating capacity.

In 1871, William Cameron Coup persuaded P. T. Barnum, then sixty-one years old and famous for his museums and hoaxes, to become a partner in the launching of a giant wagon show called P. T. Barnum's Museum, Menagerie & Circus. This event marks the beginning of what has generally been termed the "golden age" of the American circus, a period lasting until about 1917. Barnum lent his name to other shows, which finally resulted in his split from Coup in 1875. Barnum briefly joined the Flatfoots, which was then headed by George F. Bailey. In 1880 Barnum joined James A. Bailey (born James A. McGinnis, he changed his name and was not related to George F. Bailey) and James L. Hutchinson in putting out P. T. Barnum's Greatest Show on Earth & Howes's Great London Circus & Sanger's Royal British Menagerie. James A. Bailey was a master circus manager, and under his control the nearly collapsed Barnum show was transmuted into a powerful success. This partnership lasted until 1885 when Barnum refused Bailey's directions and Bailey sold his interest. But in 1887, after Barnum lost both territory and a Madison Square Garden contract to the rival Adam Forepaugh Circus (resulting in their combined playing of the Garden in 1886), Barnum gave Bailey full control of the show and added his name to what was from then on to be the Barnum & Bailey Greatest Show on Earth. In addition to the Forepaugh Show, other prominent circuses in the first half of the golden age included the Sells Brothers Great European Seven Elephant Railroad Show, the W. H. Harris Nickel Plate Shows, the Walter L. Main Shows, the Great Wallace Circus, the Lemen Brothers Circus, and a number of earlier but still operating shows including the John Robinson Circus and the Van Amburgh Circus. By 1890, there were nearly seventy different circuses operating, and by 1903 there were at least ninety-eight circuses abroad in the land.

In 1884, the five Rungeling brothers from Baraboo, Wisconsin, made arrangements to use the name of the aging Yankee Robinson and they took out on the first tour Yankee Robinson's Great Show, Ringling Brothers' Carnival of Novelties, and DeNar's Museum of Living Wonders, also known as the Yankee Robinson & Ringling Brothers Great Double Shows, Circus and Caravan. Americanizing their German name, the Ringling brothers were soon to become the most famous circus owners in history. Beginning in 1890, the show was called the Ringling Brothers Railroad Show, and the next decade saw its continued expansion and growing reputation as a "Sunday School" (free of crime and gambling) show. In 1907, the Ringlings bought Barnum and Bailey's Greatest Show on Earth, which they ran as a separate circus until 1919, when both shows merged to become Ringling Brothers and Barnum & Bailey Combined Shows. The expansion continued until John Ringling bought the holdings of his main competitor—the American Circus Corporation—in 1929, thereby becoming owner of six major circuses, a number of circus titles, and a winter quarters plant at Peru, Indiana.

John Ringling's reign as circus king of the world was short-lived, for the stock market crashed only a few days later, bringing the great economic depression. By 1933, few other large circuses remained except for the Al G. Barnes and Hagenback-Wallace shows (both owned by Ringling), but small truck shows continued to survive. In 1935, the Cole Brothers & Clyde Beatty Circus was successfully launched, and the next two years showed some signs of growth. But 1938 saw the closing of a number of shows including the Cole Brothers Circus, Downie Brothers Circus, the Hagenback-Wallace Circus, and the Tim McCoy Wild West Show. The Ringling show closed up in midseason and though the Barnes-Sells-Floto and Robbins Brothers shows did complete the 1938 season, they did not go out the following year. The decade of depression brought major changes to the circus as it had been. There would now be few baggage horses, parades, or railroad circuses; and most of the great old names were gone from the scene.

During the war years, Ringling and the Cole Brothers Circus were the only two large railroad shows operating. Several smaller shows developed, including the Clyde Beatty-Wallace Brothers Circus; the Russell Brothers Circus; Mills Brothers Circus; King Brothers Circus; and the notorious Daily Brothers Railroad Circus, more remembered for its thievery and gambling than its performances. Things began to improve for the shows starting around 1943; but 1944 saw the Ringling show engulfed by a fire during its July 6 matinee performance at Hartford, Connecticut, causing the show again to limp home to winter quarters in midseason. But the show went out again the following year, this time with all-metal seating; and the next few years were highly successful, despite the need to pay out substantial sums for the many fire claims.

The postwar years saw the emergence of a few new circuses including the Mills Brothers Circus; the Clyde Beatty Circus; the King Brothers Circus; the Sparks Circus; the Al G. Kelly & Miller Brothers Circus; and the development of the new indoor circuses of Polack, Hamid-Morton, Orrin Davenport, and Tom Packs. In 1946, the Clyde Beatty Circus entered western Canada and found extraordinary success there, and a similar route even farther north to Alaska was followed by the Bailey Brothers and Cristiani Circus in 1954.

The 1956 season proved disastrous for all three of the major tented circuses, as the Clyde Beatty, the King Brothers, and the Ringling shows were forced to close. The following year, Beatty and Ringling resumed business on trucks, but the Ringling show gave up its tent (the big top) and began to play exclusively indoors (playing outdoors was attempted on a few hot-weather occasions but proved unsuccessful). The new indoor operation was successful, and the Ringling show reduced its payroll from about 1,000 to around 225 persons and minimized its transported equipment to the point that it was possible to start moving by special, newly designed railroad cars in 1960. By 1969, a second unit of the Ringling Circus was inaugurated to play many new towns outside the regular route, as well as an extended engagement at the Astrodome in Houston, Texas.

The Clyde Beatty & Cole Brothers Circus continues to operate success-fully under canvas, and a number of small tented shows remain in business. New indoor operations have emerged, notably the Hubert Castle Circus, and new forms continue to evolve. But in terms of size and numbers, the approximate dozen circuses that now travel in the United States are but a shadow of the spectacles that dotted the nation around the turn of this century.

The Causes of Decline

The decrease in size and in number of circuses in America has been at-tributed to several causes, including competing entertainments, particu-larly television. But it is far more likely that the decline has been due most centrally to the increasing urbanization of the modern world.[2] The decline of circuses has been an international pattern in most of the capitalist coun-tries (the communist countries, especially the Soviet Union, have seen a tremendous growth in their state-subsidized circuses), and even the European-style circus might not have survived the social changes in the United States. The grand spectacles of the golden age seem unlikely to return in America.

Despite its lowered size and distribution, the American circus continues to change and evolve, and those few shows now operating are, for the most part, economically successful. More important, the quality of the acts and general performances is remarkably high. Since the history of the circus has been one of cycles of boom and bust, hope still remains that new, adapting circus forms will emerge once more prominently to capture the national mood.

The Structural Organization of the Circus

The changing character of the American circus, especially the move from canvas to indoor performance, has greatly affected its organizational struc-ture. These changes in its structure have been reflected in the circus's social organization[3] and its general culture.[4] Traditionally, the circus system was composed of a number of integrated, functioning subsystems that might number in the dozens. In the 1953 Ringling show, typical of a large show, these subdivisions included management personnel; the concessions;

publicity, including advance men, bill posters, and contracting agents; the ticket department, including sellers, counters, and distributors; many specialized and often quite large departments, including those for canvas, layout, medical treatment, personnel buses, wardrobe, property, ring stock, stables, elephants, menagerie, seats, sideshow canvas, trucks, mechanical repair, lights and electricity, trains, ushers, and the cookhouse (dining tent and kitchen); the circus band; performers; sideshow personnel, including attractions, ticket sellers and takers, and lecturers; and many specialized individuals including twenty-four-hour men (those who went ahead of the show to have everything ready upon arrival), a mail agent, a veterinarian, watchmen, and others. With the reductions in circus size (as when the Ringling show reduced its personnel from around 1,000 to around 225), many of these functions and roles were eliminated. Thus, the 1965 Ringling show listings included only management; performers; the band; departments for concessions, publicity, trucks, the train, wardrobe, labor, tigers, elephants, ringstock, and property; a mail agent; and a personnel bus driver. Surprisingly, very little serious research has been done into most of these circus subdivisions, probably because the jobs are quite unglamorous and have not appealed to those entranced by the romantic elements in circus life. Thus, most of the literature dealing with the circus has dealt with its performers and owners.

Though no complete taxonomy of circus acts is possible, a number of listings have been attempted.[5] Many acts contain a number of techniques simultaneously (as in the case of juggling while standing on a moving horse), and new acts are periodically introduced (as with the recent advent of basketball played on unicycles or the juggling of Ping-Pong balls with only the mouth).

Personnel Origins

In general, performers originate today from families whose members have been in the circus. In recent years, several schools have developed circus performance skills as part of their physical education departments, most notably in Sarasota, Florida, Wenatchee, Washington, at Florida State University, and as part of the theatre program at New York University. Few of these programs have trained professional performers for today's circuses, however, and even some of those who went through these programs came from circus families and had prior training. Since he has a relatively low-status circus role in this country (thus precluding the importing of many from Europe), the circus clown came into short supply.[6] Because of this, the Ringling Brothers Circus started a training center for clowns known as the College of Clowns in 1968 at their winter quarters in Venice, Florida. Many who graduate from this training program obtain employment with that circus.

Most American circus acts have probably been of United States origin, but it was—and remains—fashionable for performers to adopt foreign names to appear "imported" and novel. The same is true in Europe. Thus, many performers with Italian stage names have been German. Many writers have noted that certain national origins seem to be associated with distinct types of acts (for example, East Europeans with acrobatics, the English with horsemanship, wild animal training with Germans and Americans), but this is commonly untrue. If a performer (like the great Italian juggler Rastelli) achieves special fame, those in his line of work have often changed their names to emulate his nationality and thereby suggest that they are performers of the same class of ability. Many circus acts are as represented, however, and the period just before World War II saw a great many circus performers leave Europe seeking refuge in the United States. Following that war, another great influx of performers came into this country. This importation from Europe was followed by an influx of many acts from Mexico during the 1950s, and the 1960s saw many Eastern European acts visiting the United States, as well as a number of acts from the Soviet Union. The circus remains an international set of institutions with many interchanges between continents.

The Circus Today

Despite the near disappearance of the circus's tents, its *total* audience has grown. Around 1932, about 20,000,000 Americans attended the tented shows. In 1969, the two Ringling Brothers Circus units reported record revenues and earnings, with sales reaching $13.25 million. The elaborate Circus Circus, set up among the casinos of Las Vegas in 1968, which has circus acts going on fourteen hours each day, seven days a week, played to over three and one-half million people in 1969. But the largest increase in the circus audience has been the result of television. In addition to an annual presentation of the Ringling Brothers Circus performance on national television—this alone probably doubling the total circus audience of 1932 in one night!—numerous shows centering on circuses and variety shows featuring circus acts have been aired. In addition, many dramatizations of stories using a circus setting, including one regular series, have incorporated circus performances. Television has also shown a number of special documentaries on the American circus, most notable of which is the ten-hour series of films produced by National Educational Television and first broadcast in 1964, which is still rerun on local educational channels and in many schools. Thus, constantly changing and adapting to the modern world, the circus continues to entrance and entertain "children of all ages."

NOTES

1. Marcello Truzzi, "Folksongs of the American Circus," *New York Folklore Quarterly, 24* (1968), 163-75.

2. Marcello Truzzi, "The Decline of the American Circus: The Shrinkage of an Institution," in M. Truzzi, ed., *Sociology and Everyday Life* (Englewood Cliffs, N.J.: Prentice-Hall, 1968), pp. 314-22.

3. Ibid.

4. Marcello Truzzi, "The American Circus as a Source of Folklore: An Introduction," *Southern Folklore Quarterly, 30* (1966), pp. 289-300; and "Folksongs of the American Circus."

5. Hovey Burgess, "The Classification of Circus Techniques," *The Drama Review, 18* (March 1974), pp. 65-70; George L. Chindahl, *A History of the Circus in America* (Caldwell, Ohio: Caxton, 1959); and M. Truzzi, "The American Circus as a Source of Folklore . . ."

6. Earl Shipley, "Old Hand Looks at Clown Alley: Sees Decline of Clowning Art; Few Newcomers Fill Ranks," *Billboard*, November 29, 1952, pp. 79, 111.

Richard W. Flint

The Evolution of the Circus in
Nineteenth-Century America_____

Recalling his early experiences on an Iowa farm in the 1870s, novelist
Hamlin Garland remembered:

> There were always three great public holidays,—the Fourth of July, the circus,
> and the Fair. . . . Of all these, the circus was easily the first of importance. . . .
> No one but a country boy can rightly measure the majesty and allurement of a
> circus. To go from the lonely prairie or the dusty corn-field and come face to face
> with the "amazing aggregation of world-wide wonders" was like enduring the visions
> of the Apocalypse.[1]

In the early nineteenth century, young boys did not fare so well. An
American Sunday-School Union publication of about 1845 told the story of
two young boys who discovered some alluring circus posters. They asked
their father to take them to see the circus. Father explained that there was
cruelty in training the horses, that circus men were idle and drank and
gambled, and, too, that there was danger when little boys tried to imitate
circus riders by standing on the backs of horses.

> 'So, my little boys,' said the father, 'I shall not take you to the circus, but in a short
> time there is to be a show of wild beasts; and then I will take you to see it if we live.'[2]

The story conveniently points out why many early circuses were predomi-
nately menageries—viewing God's creatures was educational, but watching
a circus rider was somehow, for a variety of reasons, immoral.

One of the most popular of the anticircus tracts was *Slim Jack: or, The
History of a Circus Boy*, which was first published in 1847 and is about the
cruel treatment received by an orphan with the circus.[3] When the Springfield, Massachusetts, *Republican* reprinted the story in 1855, an anonymous
member of Welch and Lent's Circus wrote a letter to the editor defending

the circus. The performer first answered the argument which he said was the "main stay of circus-haters, the alleged 'idle lives' of showmen. . . . Anyone who yet clings" to that argument, he suggested, "should travel a week with an exhibition, and his aching bones would convince him of its fallacy."

For those who would consider the circus a waste of money, Welch and Lent's employee pointed to the pleasure given the audience. And as to intemperance among circus folk, it was only as common as in the general population, for the "circus ring is no place for an inebriate." As to the dangerous feats performed on horseback, the veteran performer noted, "an equestrian is as much at home upon the back of his horse as upon the ground" and "is just as careful of his life, and places as high an estimate upon it, as those engaged in any other pursuit." He concluded by noting that apprentices, generally a performer's own child, are eager and ambitious.[4]

Moral issues were continually raised against the circus, but the circus always seemed to prosper. In June 1839, a Cooperstown, New York, lawyer noted in his diary that the town's population grew more than three times—from 1,200 to 4,000—when a menagerie visited. Lawyer Levi Turner described the crowd at the menagerie as "disagreeable" and "vulgar," and when a circus visited Cooperstown three months later, he could only note that it was "less vulgar" than any other circus he had seen. Yet, Turner reveals a certain amount of hypocrisy. He knew that he would find attending the performances a "vulgar" experience for himself yet he went—one time taking his children, another in the company of two ladies.[5]

In the same year—1839—the *Knickerbocker* magazine contained a lengthy and nostalgic story of the circus coming to town—even providing a sentimental description of the old man who has taken the young child to the circus.[6] Moral matters aside, the circus was fast becoming a tradition in rural America.

Other forms of popular entertainment were also emerging to amuse Americans. The first uniquely American form of popular entertainment was the minstrel show. It captured the fascination of the nation in the mid-1840s, and for the following half-century it reflected many of the feelings of middle-class Americans.

In 1856, the New York *Clipper*, a sporting and theatrical journal, published a parody on the mass popularity of minstrelsy and how it was eclipsing the circus:

The circus folks are all at a distance, and we are reminded of the "wheel about" times . . . when "Daddy Rice" might, could, or should have sung:

> The horses soon must cut, and Her-Vio
>   Nano he must go,
> To bide the public taste with Messrs.

> Diamond and Crow,
>> Turn about and wheel about, etc.
> There was a time when standing on
>> The head was all the go,
> But t'other end is righted—we're
>> Again upon the toe.
>>> Turn about and wheel about, etc.[7]

The circus was composed of, or could absorb, many elements of other popular entertainments: dime museum curiosities and minstrels appeared in the side show; vaudeville acts and wild west shows followed the main circus performance for a slight additional charge; and modern burlesque was akin to the hootchy-cootch dancers. The circus is still alive and generally unchanged since the mid-nineteenth century because, in part, it included other popular entertainments and also because of its own immense self-promotion and extravagance.

The circus began as an equestrian exhibition, but by the midnineteenth century it had lost much of its identity as an essentially equestrian performance. Soon after the Civil War and under such showmen as Seth B. Howes and P. T. Barnum, the circus symbolized an age of opulence and splendor such as the imaginations of rural and provincial Americans could hardly conceive. Fantastic beauty, a fairy-like setting, and a sense of heightened sensual excitement pervade the account of a Missouri lad—Huck Finn—who crept under the tent flap and added one more to his string of adventures: "It was a real bully circus. It was the splendidest sight that ever was. . . ."[8] The anticipation of circus day is the key in understanding Hamlin Garland's and Huck Finn's accounts. And the advertising in advance of the circus was a theatrical event akin to a rousing political campaign.

Circuses were the first to use large illustrated advertisements. As early as 1833 a New Hampshire editor noted that the traveling shows were operating "on a new plan . . . in order to excite the curiosity of the people. . . . Large show bills measuring seven or eight feet in length proportionately made with cuts representing the remarkable docility of the lions and the great feats of the monkey" were now to be seen in the towns.[9]

Large presses and the idea of joining several separately printed sheets together enabled printers to produce the first billboard posters in the early 1830s. The posters were composed of several smaller illustrations plus text; the cost and scarcity of large woodblocks cut from either mahogany or boxwood prevented the introduction of large pictures. The style continued until the early 1840s, when Joseph Morse devised a way to cut upon cheap pine, and so began the massive use of pictorial billboard posters.[10]

By 1871, a printing journal was able to report that

One of the most important and valuable branches of the art of printing, as carried on in the United States, is the exclusive business engaged in for the production of colored show-bills. . . . To managers of circuses, menageries, theatres, and exhibitions of all sorts, illuminated show-bills have become an absolute necessity, so much so that the shrewd individual who can show the most elaborate work upon his "bill-board" is sure to draw the largest audiences.[11]

Not until the frequent use of lithography for show posters in the late 1870s was there any change in the technical production. But for any traveling show "to bill it like a circus" meant to use much advertising. A Cooper and Bailey lithographed poster of 1880 indicates that even the circus boasted of its liberal advertising. And perhaps with some justification: for the 1888 season the Barnum and Bailey Circus used 1,480,000 sheets of posters.[12]

One of the great features of the circus that was announced on the posters was the free street parade. Although simple processions had existed earlier (Durang's memoirs note that Lailson's Circus Company regularly paraded in 1797[13]), it was in 1834 that at least five companies simultaneously carried the first known bandwagons.[14] A remarkable poster for the Grand Boston Zoological Exhibition of 1835 provides a view of one of them—a relatively plain affair—as well as a fascinating glimpse inside the show tent.

The bandwagon, however, was not the attention-getter; it was the band itself. Bands were a very popular form of entertainment in the 1830s and 1840s, and almost every town had its military band. They played for militia musters, marched in parades, put on concerts, and were often engaged for political events and dances, and occasionally could also be heard at the theatre. Much of the great popularity for bands can be attributed to the development of the keyed bugle. Without keys, a brass instrument was severely limited in its range, and so bands depended on woodwind instruments for the melody. Keyed bugles changed that and encouraged a number of outstanding and famous soloists, particularly Edward Kendall, who organized the Boston Brass Band in 1835 and appeared almost regularly with circuses.[15] Whether marching on foot or riding in a wagon, it was the band that was the feature until about 1846 when Welch, Mann, and Delavan issued a poster illustrating their "National Circus Band Carriage passing up Broadway" the year before.

No longer was the emphasis on the band; the elegance of the carriage was now important. The change occurred because Van Amburgh and Company had returned from several years of touring Europe and were featuring the first truly ornamental bandwagon with relief carvings to be seen in America. The so-called Roman Chariot, twenty and a half feet long and with a canopy that could be extended to seventeen feet in height, was a close copy of one designed the year before by William F. Wallett for the English showman

Edwin Hughes.[16] The opening parade on April 20, 1846, caused Broadway to be packed with a dense crowd all morning for, as the *New York Tribune* reported, it "completely absorbed public attention . . . and all New York went to see the show." The fifty carriages and 150 horses, said the *Tribune*, "was one of the most splendid pageants ever got up in this Country."[17] A few days later a newspaper reporter visited the show grounds and wrote:

The great Chariot stands within the pavillion, and is quite as much an object of attraction as half a dozen elephants would be. In this Chariot are seated the musicians, twelve in number, composing Mr. Shelton's American Brass Band, and a fine one it is too, who play all their celebrated marches, etc. during the performance of Van Amburgh, and at intervals throughout the exhibition.[18]

The parade of grandeur had begun. The following year—1847—advertisements for Howes and Company promised that their golden chariot was "superior to the one used by Mr. Van Amburgh or any other."[19] The other known, new bandwagon in 1847 was one of what was to be a pair for the two circuses of James Raymond. A twelve-page pamphlet published in Boston in 1847 tells us that the Chrysarma was "a blazing prodigy of crimson, purple, and gold," with "the front of the carriage [resting] upon the backs of two monstrous and grotesque alligators."[20] The pamphlet identified Diana the huntress at the front end of the wagon's left side, and in the center medallion was a painting of a wooded and rocky dell. Above the left hind wheel stood a colossal lion with Cupid astride holding a torch. Over the rear statuary was an arch of branching foliage. On the opposite side was a Herculean archer at the back; in the center medallion, a painting of the Genius of America seated in the Chariot of Neptune heralded by Fame; and at the right front, a full-sized statue of Pan with a couchant tiger. The back of the twenty-one-foot-long car displayed an immense eagle with the stars and stripes. The great chariot and its twin cost $10,000 and were constructed by the firm of John Stephenson at his coach factory on 27th Street, New York City. The carving was the work of the Messrs. Millard.[21]

Other circuses also added ornamental bandwagons: the Great Egyptian Dragon Chariot was with Crane and Company's Great Oriental Circus in 1849 and was a spectacular sight when pulled by ten camels. In about 1850, musical wagons carrying band organs were featured in circus parades, and the famous steam calliope was first played in circus parades in 1858.[22] After touring Europe for several years, Seth B. Howes's Circus returned to America in 1864, bringing with it a number of magnificent European parade wagons.[23] With such elaborate competition, the construction of parade wagons increased in this country as circuses sought to outdo each other with their free street spectacles.[24]

But actually, how spectacular were some of the wagons or the posters, such as one from 1872 for Howes's Great London Circus, complete with an elephant high atop the wagon, or were they largely the fanciful creation of some poster artist? A photograph taken the same year in Vermont shows that this particular wagon was just as advertised. But many are the newspaper accounts describing the grandeur of the free street parade and then noting that the fifty-cent performance was not quite up to satisfaction.

Equestrians, acrobats, trapeze artists, trained animals, and singing clowns were sights to delight anyone who entered the circus tents. In addition to well-known performers, the circus featured exotic animals to entice the public. As early as 1843, a team of elephants with James Raymond's menagerie brought him big business, and Avery Smith, recognizing the powerful attraction of more than one elephant, wrote to his fellow showman Lewis B. Titus that "When your show wants any extra attraction buy a team of elephants it will take."[25] By the late 1870s, circuses placed great emphasis on the number of elephants they featured. In 1878, Sells Brothers published a special musical composition titled "The Seven Elephant March," and Forepaugh increased his herd of pachyderms from seven in 1878 to ten the following year, eleven in 1880, twenty-one in 1882, and a maximum of twenty-five in 1883-1885.[26]

The 1870s also witnessed an important development that would significantly alter the appearance of the American circus and create a show quite different from other circuses around the world. In the 1870s, circuses sometimes added a stage or an extra ring, and in 1881, when James A. Bailey and P. T. Barnum merged their circuses, they featured three rings to indicate that three circuses were combined.[27] The practice of multiple rings was frequent by the end of the century, and often in the twentieth century a circus was not considered worthwhile unless it boasted of three rings.

Two and three rings meant larger tents, extra seating, more performers, and more workingmen. The physical growth of the circus occurred almost simultaneously with the adoption of railroad transportation. Circuses had briefly experimented with rail transportation as early as the 1850s, but success came with the standardization of track gauges, the acceptance of privately owned railroad cars, and the genius of circus manager W. C. Coup in placing the Barnum show on rails in 1872.[28] Twenty-three years after the event, show owner Peter Sells wrote that 1872

was the date of the great evolution in circus business. It was then discovered that greater possibilities were attainable for tented shows than had been dreamed of before. Taking rail . . . came upon the circus fraternity like an avalanche.[29]

With the completion of new transcontinental railroads in the early 1880s, circuses scrambled for exclusive rights over the lines and reaped fortunes for their owners.[30]

When Coup placed the Barnum circus on rails in 1872, it enabled him to skip the smaller, less profitable towns between the large cities. Train transportation permitted circuses to grow to immense size and carry massive amounts of animals and equipment. Suddenly, all circuses seemed small when compared to Barnum's or Forepaugh's, and the little wagon shows that played crossroad villages never seemed quite the same.

The change in moral attitudes toward the circus, the significant development of its self-promotion through posters and parades, the innovation of three rings, and railroad transportation are important aspects in nineteenth-century circus history. But as post-Civil War America became industrialized and urbanized, there was a great burgeoning of other forms of popular entertainment. Hundreds of professional troupes began operation during midcentury to provide a variety of entertainment forms, many of them new, to a population seeking amusement. Increased mechanization in industry and on the farm, coupled with increased affluence, enabled nineteenth-century Americans to find more time for leisure activities. "Circus day" was established in rural America, but by the end of the nineteenth century, America had become urbanized, and circuses had to face the new competition of city-oriented family vaudeville, moving pictures, and amusement parks. In the nineteenth century, circuses competed by extensive promotion and massive growth, for in America bigger supposedly meant better. But as the twentieth century dawned, the circus was still, in the minds of many American youngsters, just what one series of posters said, "The world's largest, grandest, best amusement institution."[31]

NOTES

1. Hamlin Garland, *Boy Life on the Prairie* (Lincoln: University of Nebraska Press, 1961), pp. 231-32.

2. *The Circus* (Philadelphia: American Sunday-School Union, n.d.), p. 14.

3. *Slim Jack: or, the History of a Circus-Boy* (Philadelphia: American Sunday-School Union, ca.1847).

4. *Springfield* (Massachusetts) *Republican*, June 8, 1855, p. 2.

5. Levi Crosby Turner Diary, June 17, and September 21, 1839, New York State Historical Association, Cooperstown, New York (typescript copy).

6. "Circus," *The Knickerbocker* 13 (January 1839), pp. 67-76.

7. New York *Clipper* 4 (November 22, 1856), p. 246.

8. Mark Twain, *The Adventures of Huckleberry Finn* (New York: Charles L. Webster Co., 1885), p. 192.

9. *Newport* (New Hampshire) *Spectator*, August 17, 1833. I am indebted to Stuart Thayer, Ann Arbor, Michigan, for this reference.

10. "Show Bills," *Haddock's Sunshine* 1 (August 14, 1877), pp. 258-59.

11. "How Illuminated Show-Bills Are Printed," *The Mirror of Typography* 3 (Autumn 1871), p. 35.

12. "Big Show Bills" (Wauseon, Ohio), *Northwestern Republican,* April 20, 1888. I am indebted to John Polacsek, Bay City, Michigan, for a photocopy of this article.

13. Alan S. Downer, ed., *The Memoir of John Durang* (Pittsburgh, Pa.: University of Pittsburgh Press, ca.1966), p. 102.

14. Charles Amidon and Stuart Thayer, "Early Parades, Early Bandwagons," *Bandwagon* 21 (November-December 1977), p. 34.

15. Robert E. Eliason, *Keyed Bugles in the United States,* Smithsonian Studies in History and Technology, Number 19 (Washington, D.C.: Smithsonian Institution Press, 1972), pp. 23-28 passim.

16. John Tryon, *An Illustrated History, and Full and Accurate Description of the Wild Beasts, . . . Contained in the Grand Caravan of Van Amburgh & Co. . . . Also a Description of the Gorgeous Roman Chariot, . . .* (New York: Jonas Booth, 1846), pp. 9-10; W. F. Wallett, *The Public Life of . . . ,* 3d ed., edited by John Luntley (London, 1870), p. 69. The iconographic evidence is reproduced in George Speaight's essay elsewhere in this volume; see also "Hughes's Elephant Carriage," *Illustrated London News* 6 (May 3, 1845), p. 285; and "Procession . . . ," *Illustrated London News* 10 (April 3, 1847), pp. 209-210. For an account of Hughes, see Frederick Boase, *Modern English Biography,* 6 vols. (Truro, England: Netherton & Worth, 1892-1921), I:1570-1571 and, on his early career, David Prince Miller, *Life of a Showman,* 2d ed. (London: Lacy, n.d.), pp. 166-67.

17. *New York Tribune,* April 21, 1846, p. 2.

18. *New York Tribune,* April 23, 1846, p. 2.

19. *Newark Daily Advertiser,* April 19, 1847. I am indebted to Gordon Carver of Ocean City, New Jersey, for a photocopy of the advertisement.

20. *Description of the Chrysarma, or Golden Chariot, Connected with Raymond and Waring's Menagerie* (Boston: n.p., 1847), pp. 4, 7.

21. Ibid., passim; for a history of the Stephenson firm, see John H. White, Jr., *Horsecars, Cable Cars and Omnibuses* (New York: Dover, 1974).

22. Fred Dahlinger, Jr., "A Short Analysis of Steam Calliope History Before 1900," *Bandwagon* 16 (November-December 1972), pp. 25-26.

23. Richard E. Conover, "The European Influence on the American Circus Parade," *Bandwagon* 5 (July-August 1961), pp. 4-5.

24. See, for example, Richard E. Conover, *The Fielding Bandchariots* (Xenia, Ohio: the author, 1969).

25. Avery Smith to Lewis B. Titus, June 30, 1843; private collection.

26. Richard E. Conover, *The Great Forepaugh Show* (Xenia, Ohio: the author, 1959), pp. 9-10; Stuart Thayer, *Mudshows and Railers* (Ann Arbor, Michigan: the author, 1971), pp. 39-40.

27. Files of circus newspaper advertisements, Circus World Museum, Baraboo, Wisconsin. Bailey, along with his partners, claimed two circuses in two rings, the International Allied Shows and the Great London. Thus, merged with Barnum's circus, they were three circuses in three rings.

28. For a discussion of railroad gauges, see George Rogers Taylor and Irene D. Neu, *The American Railroad Network 1861-1890* (Cambridge: Harvard University

Press, 1956); the acceptance of private cars is treated in L. D. H. Wild, *Private Freight Cars and American Railways*, Studies in History, Economics, and Public Law, vol. 31, no. 1 (New York: Columbia, 1908). W. C. Coup's posthumous memoirs *Sawdust & Spangles* (Chicago: Herbert S. Stone & Co., 1901), pp. 59-69, reveal his role in the beginnings of the Barnum circus train. Earlier circuses that moved by rail are treated in Copeland MacAllister, "The First Successful Railroad Circus Was in 1866," *Bandwagon* 19 (July-August 1975), pp. 14-16; and George Chindahl, *A History of the Circus in America* (Caldwell, Idaho: Caxton, 1959), pp. 58-59, 88-92, for references about the railroad movements of Spalding (1855-57) and Dan Costello (1868).

29. Peter Sells, "Recollections of a Quarter Century," *Leander Richardson's Dramatic News Circus Special* (1895), p. 6.

30. See, for example: New York *Clipper* 30 (July 1, 1882), p. 246; 32 (May 3, 1884), p. 105; 32 (March 14, 1885), pp. 821, 822; 33 (July 25, 1885), p. 297; 33 (February 13, 1886), p. 256.

31. Used by Barnum and Bailey from approximately 1891-1905.

George Speaight

The Origin of the Circus
Parade Wagon*_____

The circus parade was brought to a pitch of magnificence in America that eclipsed anything achieved elsewhere, providing perhaps the finest free spectacle since the triumphal processions of imperial Rome. These parades originated in the 1830s with the circus band driving round the town in a simple bandwagon to announce the arrival of the circus in the locality; but in the next decade, the parades started to grow more impressive, and the wagons became vastly more elaborate. It is the purpose of this article to note the beginnings of this development and to trace the source from which they sprang.

In 1846, the menagerie of Van Amburgh introduced into its parade a superb vehicle named the Tuba Rhoda and described as a Grecian State Carriage or a Roman Triumphal Car. There is a print of it, published by Currier and Ives in that year, depicting it passing Astor House, New York.

Its carriage was somewhat like that of a pram in shape, and it was marked by certain distinguishing features. An umbrella-like canopy surmounts the high seat of honor; the driver sits at the front between two carved lions, and there is another at the back; the wheels are provided with massive decorated spokes, and the side of the carriage is embellished with a painted cartouche and a shield; the whole is decorated with deeply carved animal figures. Nothing like this had been seen in America before. Where did the idea come from?

To answer this question, we must investigate Isaac Van Amburgh's career. It is known that the cage boy in June, Titus, and Angevine's menagerie had to take over the showing of the big cats after an accident to the trainer in 1833. He made a success of it and caused a sensation. There is a story that his fame went to his head and that he began to acquire ideas above his station, paying court to his boss's daughter. To get him out of the way, Titus sent him to London in 1838.

*This article appeared originally in the November/December 1977 issue of *Bandwagon* and is reprinted with the permission of the publisher.

VAN AMBURGH & CO'S. TRIUMPHAL CAR.

PASSING THE ASTOR HOUSE, APRIL 20TH 1846.

Print by Currier & Ives of Van Amburgh's Parade Wagon, 1846. Circus World Museum, Baraboo, Wisconsin.

In England he achieved an equal success, and in 1843 he teamed up with the American proprietor, Richard Sands, who had brought his circus to England the year before. Together, they put on a show at the Lyceum in London and then toured a combined menagerie and circus for a year or so before splitting up. Van Amburgh was back in America by 1845, and Sands had returned by the next year.

Sands brought the first tented circus to England, and Van Amburgh the first scientific and artistic display of wild animal training. But did they see anything that was new to them while they were there? Well, the most striking circus development of the forties was the touring of Hughes's Mammoth Equestrian Establishment. Edwin Hughes was the son of a steel toy manufacturer in Birmingham who joined Batty's Circus and became the best polander in England, the first, it was said, to succeed in rotating 360 degrees on his head without holding, probably while balancing on the single upright spar of a come-apart ladder. He became Batty's manager in Ireland, and then at the age of thirty formed his own company in 1843. After only five seasons, he retired in 1847 with a handsome fortune.

The chief feature of Hughes's Circus was its impressive parade of fifty horses and richly carved carriages, some in the "gorgeous style of Louis Quatorze," but the most striking feature of the parades was a couple of superb vehicles pulled by elephants and camels. Hughes was said to be the first man to succeed in harnessing these animals.

Firstly, there was a vehicle described as the Rath, or Burmese Imperial Carriage and Throne, which was introduced in 1845. A print shows it entering Gloucester in that year. Its length was 13 ft., 6 ins., and its height to the summit of the Peasath or Royal Canopy was 15 ft. It was pulled by two elephants, whose caparisons were of crimson velvet embroidered with gold. The driver was an East Indian in appropriate costume, and the proprietor of the establishment, similarly attired, occupied the car like an oriental potentate.

There is a poster of Hughes's show at about this date, which incidentally gives a good pictorial impression of the acts to be seen on the show, and there is a fine view of the Rath as it passed the Exchange in London in 1847 on its way to a season at the Theatre Royal, Drury Lane, where the company presented a Grand Oriental Spectacle entitled *The Desert, or the Imaun's Daughter*.

I would draw your attention to the following features: the pramlike carriage shape; the umbrella-like canopy over the high seat of honor; the driver sitting between two lions, with another at the back; the massive, decorated spokes; the cartouche and shield on the side; and the deeply carved animal figures.

The similarities with Van Amburgh's vehicle are too striking to be acci-

Poster for Hughes's Circus in England, c. 1845. The British Library.

Hughes's Burmese Imperial Carriage passing the Guildhall, London, 1847. The Guildhall Library.

dental. Let me remind you of the dates. Hughes had introduced this carriage by May 1845; Van Amburgh was back in New York by December 1845; Van Amburgh had introduced his Tuba Rhoda by April 1847. It was not the same vehicle, for Hughes was still parading it in 1847, but it was a close copy. Whether made in England or America we do not know, but I think it likely that Van Amburgh commissioned a duplicate from Hughes's carriage builder.

Meanwhile, Hughes was extending his fleet of carriages. Let us look again at his 1845 bill. At the bottom, you can see the bandwagon he was then using, which was, I am told, of the same type as was used by American circuses at that time. But in 1847, Hughes came up with something altogether more magnificent. This was what he described as the Egyptian Dragon Chariot or perambulating Temple of Isis and Osiris, drawn by four camels. The print shows the onion-domed roof supported on four pillars, and the carved dragons on either side of the band. The Rath follows behind it.

This was Hughes's last campaigning season, but it was not the end of the Dragon bandwagon. In 1847, Richard Sands, back in the United States, was parading with a serpent band car; but in 1848, he was describing his band-wagon as the Sacred Egyptian Chariot of Isus and Osiris—Hughes's very words. A poster shows what it looked like in 1848. I take it that the engraver misunderstood the artist's drawing or just forgot to put in the four uprights supporting the onion dome; but the dome is there all right, curiously float-ing in the air, and so are the carved dragons on either side of the band. This is either a copy of Hughes's Dragon Chariot or the same vehicle. Once again, the dates fit; the last recorded appearance of Hughes's Dragon Chariot in England was September 23, 1847. The next year what seems to be the same vehicle was in the United States.

In 1849, Sands was not only parading this Dragon Chariot but also an East Indian Car pulled by three elephants. So Sands now had both of the parade vehicles that Hughes had originated. Whether they were the originals or copies, or whether Sands bought Van Amburgh's copy of the elephant chariot, we don't know. My guess is that Sands bought the originals, as we hear no more of Hughes's parade wagons in England after 1847. Here is a little problem that circus historians may manage to solve sometime. But the line of descent of the Van Amburgh triumphal car and the Sands Dragon bandwagon from Hughes's Mammoth Equestrian Establishment is clear.

From that point in time, the style of carved and gilded parade wagons began to spread throughout the United States. In 1847, the American carriage builder, John Stephenson, had built two bandwagons for Raymond and Waring. He called them the Chrysarma, or Golden Chariot. One of them appears in a print of 1848, as pulled by a team of horses driven in hand—I can count eighteen, and there are probably some more round the corner. I believe the first forty-horse hitch was introduced the next year.

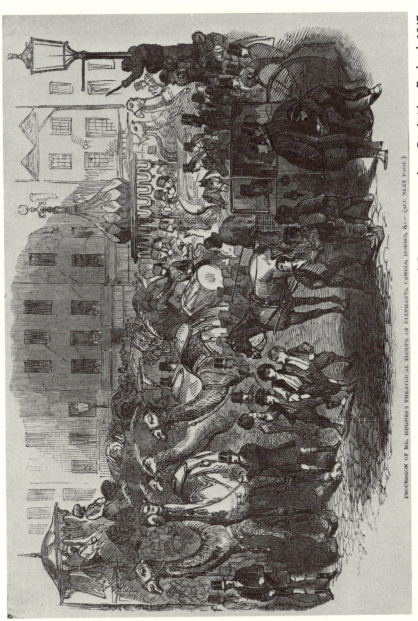

PROCESSION OF MR. HUGHES'S THEATRICAL TROUPE, OF ELEPHANTS, CAMELS, HORSES, &C.—(SEE NEXT PAGE.)

Hughes's Egyptian Dragon Chariot, followed by the Burmese Imperial Carriage, in parade at Cambridge, England, 1847. The Illustrated London News. Copyright The British Library.

Sand's Sacred Dragon Chariot as illustrated on a poster, 1848.

In this same year, 1848, Welch, Delavan, and Nathan were parading with an Imperial Persian Chariot, made after the style of the Imperial Chariots of Cyrus the Great, decorated with eagles and horses in gold and silver; and Howes and Company were parading with their own monster Dragon Chariot, which was drawn by twelve camels of the Syrian breed, imported from the deserts of Arabia, when Crane took the show over the next year. Sumptuously carved parade wagons had now become a feature of the American circus. A proud chapter lay ahead, but that is another story.

Let us now return to the figure of Edwin Hughes in England with whom it all began. Do we know who designed his parade carriages? Yes, it was none other than W. F. Wallett the Shakespearean clown, who once teamed up with Dan Rice in America. In his autobiography, Wallett describes how he was engaged by Van Amburgh in England at a handsome salary, and continues as follows: "I next joined Mr. Edwin Hughes, of the Mammoth Circus, in which I was principally engaged as an artist, I then designed the first and best of all the ornamental carriages that ever travelled with circus tents. The great lion carriage drawn by elephants was my production. The enormous pictorial carriages, with rich carvings and gilding, were my original designs. The noble colossal carriage called the 'Egyptian Dragon Chariot,' which cost 750 pounds in building, and was drawn by camels, and the harness and all the trappings, were also made from my patterns. This carriage was built by Messrs. Holmes, of Derby, coach builders to her Majesty, from my sections and elevations, and under my personal superintendence. Thus I became the humble means of building for the proprietor a colossal fortune." Despite this fortune, Wallett complained that he was poorly rewarded for his work; Hughes presented him with a new suit of clothes to show his appreciation, but Wallett found that he had to pay the bill for them himself.

We now think of Wallett only as a clown, but his early experience had been as a stage scenery painter; he also painted dioramas for peepshows, and once made a large dragon with tremendous jaws, claws and wings, that was worked by a strong man inside it. Moreover, he had studied the technique of marionettes when Maffey's famous Theatre du Petit Lazary had played at the Theatre Royal in Hull in 1828, and later he carved several sets of marionette figures, as he says, "in splendid array and the very perfection of mechanism." He was clearly a versatile, self-taught artist.

But where did he obtain the inspiration for the fantastic carriages he designed for Hughes? Some of it may have come from the fanciful decor of the puppet theatre, but the ultimate source was the triumphal cars of renaissance monarchs. There is a woodcut by Albrecht Dürer of a triumphal chariot for the Emperor Maximillian I, made in 1522, and incidentally one of the largest wood engravings ever cut—the original is seven and one-half feet in length. Note the umbrella-like canopy over the seat of honor; the driver at the front of the vehicle; the massive decorated spokes; and the

The Emperor Maximilian's Triumphal Chariot. Woodcut by Albrecht Dürer, 1522.

deeply carved animal figures on the body of the carriage. We have seen all these before.

In this reconstruction of an episode in the history of the circus on two continents, I must express my thanks to two Americans who have given me much assistance in the American side of the story: Mr. John F. Polacsek, who kindly provided me with a copy of his thesis on the Development of the Circus and Menagerie 1825-1860, submitted to the Graduate School of Bowling Green University; and Mr. Stuart Thayer. President of the Circus Historical Society, who has shared his great knowledge with me with much generosity.

Together, I hope that we have answered the question: What was the origin of the American circus parade wagon? It was introduced by Van Amburgh and Sands; copied or imported from Hughes in England; designed by Wallett, the Shakespearean clown; influenced by the decor of peepshows and puppet theatres; inspired by the triumphal cars of renaissance emperors.

William Brasmer

The Wild West Exhibition:
A Fraudulent Reality

The world is a wearisome desert,
    The life that we live is a bore;
The cheek of the apple is rosy,
    But the canker-worm hides in the core.
Our hearts have a void that is aching.
    That void, then, O hasten to fill
With your mustangs and Injuns and cowboys
    And yourself, O great Buffalo Bill.

Despite all we know about the removal of whole Indian nations from their homelands to the deserts of reservations, and the butchering of four million buffaloes in the half-century history of the settlement of the American West, this piece of poetic doggerel from an 1887 issue of the Manchester newspaper, *Refugee*, does not offend. Rather it delights, for Buffalo Bill on his white horse still canters in our imagination. We see him as a hero of the frontier: a fearless Indian fighter, adventuresome pony express rider, wily buffalo hunter, intrepid scout, fancy marksman, convivial friend of European royalty and Indian chiefs, and colorful show entrepreneur. Several children's books, portraying him as an original American hero, are still in print and continue to sell well. The Cody legend attracts thousands to the warren of museums and tourist spots that make up the Buffalo Bill Historical Center at Cody, Wyoming. In September 1977, Monte Montana, Jr. produced at the Nassau Memorial Colliseum outside of New York City an event publicized as "Buffalo Bill's Wild West and Congress of Rough Riders." The four-day show was puffed as "great, grand and heroic" and filled with "the rugged thrills of America's wild, wild west"—Indian attacks, rescues by the U.S. Cavalry, stagecoach holdups, and pony express races.

It is not enough that the Cody legend has been demythologized by Arthur Kopit in the play *Indians* and in its film adaptation. Popular entertainment historians must make a fresh appraisal of Buffalo Bill's life and work as well. The wild west exhibition needs to be scrutinized: its origin, content, and audience appeal analyzed.

The literature on the wild west exhibition is large—although mostly anecdotal, much of it a refurbishing of publicity handouts and the camp-fire tales spun by W. F. Cody, packaged in books filled with interesting pictures. Cody left few records. His letters are short, chatty, and given over to comments about weather and friends. We have few primary documents; business accounts appear to be missing, as do prompt books and set-up diagrams for the canvas on the show lots. What can be said then of the origins of the wild west exhibition?

W. F. Cody did not originate the idea for the show; nor did Nate Salsbury, the show's early manager, although both often took credit for doing so. The show actually originated in the nineteenth-century custom of exhibiting Indian activities and the outdoor presentation of acts of western life.

Indians and the artifacts of Indian life were exhibited early in the nine-teenth century. In 1827, a group of Iroquois Indians were presented at Peale's Museum in New York, and Barnum first exhibited Indians at his museum in 1841. Even earlier, George Catlin had opened an Indian gallery in Philadel-phia, where he lectured on his Indian paintings and displayed the Indian artifacts he had collected. As early as 1869, bronco-busting and cowboy activities (steer riding and roping) had been promoted at exhibitions in Colorado and Wyoming. For instance, an exhibit called "Cow-Boy Fun" had been given at Deer Trail, Colorado, July 4, 1869, while steers were rid-den in the Fourth of July celebration at Cheyenne in 1872. Santa Fe inaugu-rated its annual outdoor exhibition in 1871: the mélange of events was best illustrated by the program of 1873 which featured lariat throwing; Mlle. Rosetta, the female Blondin, walking the high wire; George Albe, agent for the Winchester Repeating Arms Company, in a shooting demonstration; and Indian ceremonial dancing performed by moonlight.

Enthusiasts for the wild west extravaganza[1] have always held that it originated with an event staged by Cody for the Fourth of July celebration in his home town of North Platte, Nebraska, in 1882. Known as the "Old-Glory Blow Out," this event consisted of a staged buffalo hunt and the exhibition of fancy riding. But it was P. T. Barnum in 1874, just eight years earlier, who had staged the first wild west extravaganza as the concluding "spec" of the circus performance in his new hippodrome. Barnum's enter-tainment was billed as a "thrilling arenic contest" and entitled *Indian Life or a Chance for a Wife*. This pantomimic spectacle included one hundred leading ladies and gentlemen in western equestrian riding acts, a buffalo hunt, and the pursuit of an Indian chief's daughter, performed by Maude

Oswald, in which she "evaded capture with movements of lightning-like rapidity." By November 1874, this hippodrome spectacle was drawing large crowds, while Cody was performing at the Bowery Theatre in *Scouts of the Prairie,* typical of the melodramas called "border dramas" as they dealt with escapades of western heroes and the treachery of Indians in the Border States. We do not know whether Cody saw Barnum's extravaganza, but certainly he was aware of its contents, as Barnum's advertisements in the *New York Times* detailed the program in extravagant wording and over-sized type only a few inches from the one-half inch four-line ad for Cody's dramatic piece at the Bowery.

There is substantial evidence that a Dr. W. F. Carver, a sometime western dentist and crack rifleman, suggested the idea of a traveling exhibition of western life, with many of the ingredients that Barnum had first exhibited in his hippodrome event. Free in the summertime from performing in border dramas, Cody joined with Carver to open on May 18, 1883, at Omaha, Nebraska, "The Wild West, Hon. W. F. Cody and Dr. W. F. Carver's Rocky Mountain and Prairie Exhibition"—a program of shooting acts, roping and riding of horses, a pony express race, and a staged attack by Indians on the Deadwood stagecoach. The Rocky Mountain Exhibition had a shaky life as it moved east from Omaha. By July, the exhibition was playing outside Brooklyn; then it moved to Chicago in October, where Carver contracted out of the partnership. Salsbury helped Cody to take the show to Omaha for a closing stand.

Before the exhibition closed, Cody submitted the minimum requirements for a copyright—a typed title page of the dramatic activity and a single-page outline of its scenario. Historians have ignored this copyright application, but it does provide us with a clear idea of what the exhibition had become under Carver's and Cody's authorship. Dated December 22, 1883, the copyrighted title page reads:

THE WILD WEST
OR LIFE AMONG THE RED MEN AND
ROAD AGENTS ON THE PLAINS
AND PRAIRIES
WILLIAM F. CODY
(Buffalo Bill)
An Equestrian Drama Expositioning on
Grass or Under Canvas
of the Adventures of Frontiersmen
and Cowboys

The incidents in the scenario were briefly listed as sharp shooting marks-manship, trick riding, an Indian attack on a settler's cabin, a buffalo or steer roundup, and an Indian chase. Except for the substitution of a pony express race and an attack on a Deadwood stagecoach, the format of the wild west exhibition was to remain practically the same for the next thirty years. Only for a short period, 1886-1893, did the exhibition pretend to have a coherent dramatic structure.

At that time, 1885, Steele MacKaye, the playwright of spectacle and inventor of stage machinery, was encouraged by Nate Salsbury to envision a series of episodes that would display the settlement of the western fron-tier. MacKaye set down his vision in writing, calling his scenario *The Drama of Civilization*, and planned seven separate episodes (later to be called "epochs") around the pioneer's struggle against the elements and his conflicts "with the ravenous animals of the plains." MacKaye outlined these seven episodes as: the aboriginal savage in his garb of skins and with the weapons used before the white man appeared; the passing of an emigrant train across the prairie; a prairie fire; the stampede of wild cattle; life at a mining camp; frontier life at a western fort; and a realistic presentation of the formation and bursting of a cyclone in the mountains.

For this epic pageant a stage was fitted up in the Old Madison Square Gardens (then located between Fourth and Madison avenues and Twenty-first and Twenty-seventh streets). A grid of support beams was placed on the roof of the building to carry the weight of the panorama drops and the winches that moved them. In addition, a steam line was installed to power exhaust fans to whip the truckload of dried leaves around the arena in front of the stage for the prairie cyclone effect. The lighting system—the largest ever installed—consisted in part of 21 border lights each with 240 gas jets, according to the *New York Times*, November 17, 1886. Prominent among all the trick effects planned by MacKaye and installed by the theatrical wizard, Nels Waldron, were the large panoramic drops, 40 feet by 150 feet, painted by Matthew Somerville Morgan, a former cartoonist for *Frank Leslie's Illustrated Weekly* and recent art director of Strobridge Lithography Company, and his twenty assistants. And Salsbury had added the show-man's touch by quartering the Indians in their tepees in the hall over the entrance to the Gardens and labeling the area "The Indian Encampment," while MacKaye added a narrator (called an "orator") to describe the pantomimic action. When the spectacle opened, production complications arose; machines refused to move the heavy drops, and recalcitrant animals refused to move off stage.

Before the opening on November 23, 1887, Salsbury and Cody wanted to scrap much of MacKaye's ponderous production, for two days after the spectacle opened they copyrighted a simpler version. The typed title page reads:

A DRAMA OF WILD WEST DEEDS AND EXPLOITS
in
FIVE EPOCHS
As Illustrated
By
BUFFALO BILL'S WILD WEST
Originally Invented and
Presented by
WM. F. CODY

The single-page scenario lists: First Epoch—the Primeval Forest of America; the Second Epoch—the Prairie; the Third Epoch—the Cattle Ranch; the Fourth Epoch—the Mining Camp; the Fifth Epoch—the Tragedy of Little Big Horn and the Death of Custer. Although the pantomimed enactment of the Battle of the Little Big Horn was not placed in *The Drama of Civilization* until December, the picturization of a battle scene eventually became the concluding and climactic episode in many wild west productions. When "Custer's Last Stand" no longer thrilled, "The Taking of San Juan Hill" or a similar battle-action scene was easily substituted.

The substance of the wild west exhibition varied little from year to year; the content of the show was determined by the particular skills of the performer and the appetite of the audience for equestrian thrills. It may be difficult to describe exactly what was done in the wild west arena since there are no prompt-books or scripts to study, and *The Drama of Civilization* scenario can only partially be pieced together from newspaper accounts; however, in border dramas we can discover whole scenes which the wild west exhibition duplicated. Two of the border dramas which Cody performed during his eleven years of acting on the stage are extant—both in manuscript. *Life on the Border*, written by an undistinguished actor by the name of J. V. Arlington, has scenes most nearly approximating those in a wild west exhibition. In five acts and fourteen scenes, the play provides Buffalo Bill and his cohorts with escapades with Indians and renegade villains. The climactic end of the first scene sets forth the substance of one of the main wild west exhibition episodes: the burning of a settler's cabin. The stage directions in *Life on the Border* read:

They take faggots behind cabin and set fire to them. Red fire in cabin and work the flash box. Bill fires from rocks. Wolfy is shot. Joe and Indians yell and rush off. Bill rushes on. Fires one or two shots after them. Bill drops his gun and breaks open cabin door. Just as Bill is about to enter, work flash box through door. Bill hesitates . . . crawls on hands and knees. Bill brings out Emma who has fainted. Red Fire. Picture.

The Drama of Civilization was taken to England in May of 1887 and set up near an American trade fair and art exhibit at Earl's Court off the Brompton Road in west London. Open space allowed for a track to be laid out. Covered grandstands were erected and faced along the oval track, while the scenic backgrounds were provided by erecting small hills and by planting trees. Painted canvas sky cloths, the size of carnival advertising banners, further defined the background. Adding the attack on the Deadwood stagecoach in addition to the Battle of the Little Big Horn, the exhibition became the craze of London.

In early winter, Cody took the exhibition north to Birmingham and Manchester, traveling with his personnel in nine railway carriages and two salon cars accompanied by eighteen railway wagons for the animals. At Birmingham, the exhibition failed to draw crowds. At Manchester, the stand was at the Salford Race Track on the outskirts of the city, where a grandstand for approximately 8,000 persons was available. The "orator," Frank Richmond, proved to be more successful in Manchester and, according to local newspapers, caught the imagination of the audience by his apt descriptions of America's earliest settlers and the scenes with Pocahontas and Captain John Smith. The cold in January of 1888, however, cut attendance. Cody held on for weeks, nursing sickness in his company. By May, the company retreated to Hull to sail for the States. Wild west historians describe Cody's first tour of England as a triumphant success. In terms of the publicity gained it was so, but Cody left England in financial distress. In Hull, he found two circuses drawing crowds; therefore, he limited his performances to a single one. Before sailing, he sold most of his animals at public auction. According to the local newspaper, the *Hull Recorder* of May 15, he obtained modest sums. George Sanger bought two American reindeer for forty pounds, the elk went for five pounds apiece to a Mr. Cross of Liverpool, while the bear fetched twenty pounds.

Cody was to return to Europe for another four seasons with the format of *The Drama of Civilization* greatly changed, the scenes with Pocahontas eliminated, and the substitution of many equestrian acts. After 1889, the myth of W. F. Cody as a legendary showman and western hero did not abate, but by the turn of the century Cody became immersed in debt and drink; his wild west exhibition under different managements was a second-rank outdoor amusement attraction. Although several circus proprietors and western stars organized their own exhibitions, often adding rodeo acts and touring with them until the 1930s, the wild west exhibition never developed further than the form it had taken in 1886 in *The Drama of Civilization*, with its style of stage pictorial realism as devised by Steel MacKaye, Nate Salsbury, and Matt Morgan for W. F. Cody.

Who made up the audiences that attended the wild west exhibition? Why did the exhibition appeal? We do not have attendance figures, and firsthand accounts of performances are usually the blatant puffings of publicists for the show or the testimonials requested of noteworthy persons to pad out the forty-page couriers (the souvenir programs sold at the exhibition). However, route schedules do show that Cody's wild west exhibition had nearly two-thirds of its performance time in eastern states. If the exhibition ventured across the Alleghenies, it confined itself to the outskirts of major midwestern cities, such as Chicago or Omaha. The exhibition attracted few rural persons, unlike Chautauqua which played to small-town audiences in the Midwest; essentially, the wild west exhibition was a show for urban cultures, primarily for recent immigrants who had never known the Indian or the West but relished stories and legends about frontier life and the frightfulness of Indian captivity.

Tales of Indian captivity had always dominated the American reading audience. Since the seventeenth century, these reports of capitivity had been America's indigenous form of literature and, through the descriptions of Indian activity, provided the first anthropological descriptions of life on the continent. Originally, these accounts of Indian captivity were set forth as moral or religious tracts. Since the Puritans viewed the Indian as a creation of the Devil, captivity became a time of moral testing by Satan, and the ultimate release was an indication of God's providence. By the nineteenth century, the captivity tales had lost their tone of moral and religious efficacy and had become novelized with imagined acts of sentimentalism and horror.[2] After the Civil War, a new reading public turned from the tales of true captivity to the melodrama of fictitious captivity in the cheap yellow-back novels published by the house of Beadle and Adams. A dozen more publishers brought additional series of novels to the public, until hundreds of "yellow-backs" were in print, romanticizing the West and setting forth the melodramatic actions of frontiersman, Indian, and settler. Nearly one-half of these novels dealt with frontier life. The wild west exhibition fed upon this reading public, and, for the urban immigrant, the written action of the novels could be viewed in the pantomime action of the wild west exhibition as well.

The wild west exhibition presented, in truth, an incorrect picture of western life and dealt with the frontier character as a stereotype melodramatic figure from a border drama or yellow-back novel. The Indian was presented as a freak to be exhibited or as a silent combatant in a shoot-out in which the Indian always lost. The scouts of the plains were devil-may-care scamps with far more prowess with bullet, lariat, and fist than with a knowledge of tracking and hunting. However, it was not until the last major Indian battles—Wagon Box (1867), Beecher Island (1868), and Little Big Horn (1876)—assured the settlement of the West by the white man that the wild west exhibition began to develop as a popular entertainment form. Only with the decimation of the culture of the Plains Indian and the Indian's final subjugation by the Dawes Severalty Act (1890), which motivated the stealing of much of his land, could large audiences be attracted to touring outdoor productions that caricatured life on the frontier. As the Indian became an alien in our culture, his reality was given a fraudulent portrait in the equestrian arena of the wild west exhibition.

NOTES

1. See Don Russell, *The Wild West* (Fort Worth: Amon Carter Museum of Western Art, 1970).

2. Over 200 different published captivity tales in over 400 editions are in the Ayer collection of the Newberry Library, Chicago. For full discussion of the nature of captivity tales, see Richard Van DerBeets, *Held Captive by the Indians. Selected Narratives, 1642-1836* (Knoxville, University of Tennessee Press, 1973).

Mae Noell

Recollections of
Medicine Show Life ————————

Mrs. Noell, one of the last surviving medicine show performers, is also an authority on the whole field of outdoor entertainment. She resides at the show's winter quarters (now known as a "retirement home for aging primates"), Noells' Ark Chimp Farm, Tarpon Springs, Florida. Mrs. Noell displayed a great many slides to illustrate her talk. References to these slides, which are meaningless without the illustrations, have been deleted from this edited transcription.

My family and I performed in many different kinds of entertainments—vaudeville, circus, tent rep, carnival, barnstorming, and, of course, medicine show. My father, Jack Roach, was a ventriloquist, singer, lecturer, and, in "med show" days, a blackface comedian. He was a juvenile or leading man actor in tent rep. My mother's name was Annetta Andt (the "D" in Andt was silent), and it is a family joke that "an Andt married a Roach." She was a talented musician and had mastered piano, vibraharp, xylophone, and the Swiss concert zither, as well as being a gifted dancer who did the (wooden shoe) waltz clog, the buck and wing, and other tap routines, in addition to filling in, in the chorus lines.

My mother was a sainted lady who took unlimited patience with my brother and me by teaching us while my parents were traveling on the vaudeville circuit. She used notebooks—thirty or forty pages thick—and on the top of each page she wrote the lessons for the day. Then my parents would go to the theatre and would work probably five shows a day, and we would be locked in the hotel rooms with instructions on how to open the door if there was an emergency; but we were cautioned not to let anyone in. When they came home, the notebooks had better be filled! And, believe me, we filled them!

One time my brother got out of the hotel room and got lost downtown in Atlanta, Georgia; so we never stayed in the hotel rooms after that, because it was too dangerous a situation. My mother told my dad, in my presence, that every time she went on stage she was thinking about us kids back in the hotel room for fear there might be a fire or something. So, from then on, we sat in the audience while the shows were in progress, or worked on our notebooks in the dressing rooms. The first night we sat in the front row. The leading lady came way down to front stage to do her dancing, and she got all over us for sitting in the front row. "That's 'bald-head-row,'" she said, as she shook her finger at us, "You're not supposed to sit there!" So we sat farther back, and I heard some guy in the row ahead of us remark on what a beautiful girl he saw at the end of the chorus line, and that he was going to the stage door to see if he could date her. I tapped him on the shoulder and said, indignantly, "My mother will not date you!" Until I was practically grown, I didn't know what he was laughing at. He didn't know any of the "girls" were married.

Before we met, my husband called himself "Dakota Bob." (He was never in Dakota in his life.) Because he was a medicine man, he let his hair grow so he could pose as an Indian. But he had to cut his hair because it was curly. When we married, we became a team. It was an easy switch-over for me to work with Bob when he did the blackface routines that were the same as I'd been doing with my father. We really had a lot of fun in those days, and there was no evil intent when we did the old blackface acts; in fact, our black audiences got as much fun out of them as anyone—maybe more. The last time he blacked up was about in 1949. Our kids had always been put to bed at about six o'clock every night and they never got to see the show. (I didn't want the kids to catch the childhood diseases from the crowds.) Then, for some years, we operated a different type of show, and by then (1949), the kids were big enough to help us. One day I said, "Bob, just for the heck of it, let's put on one of the old acts for the sake of the kids; they've never seen us do them." So we did.

In the interim, a lot of things had been happening worldwide, and we didn't realize that we were doing something that was going to hurt anybody's feelings. While we were doing the act and the audience was laughing, I looked down at the kids (then eleven and fifteen), who were lying on the ground screaming with laughter. I nudged Bob and said, "Look at the kids! Look at the kids!" We laughed at them, then looked back at the audience, and with a most horrible, sinking feeling, we watched every black patron walk off the lot. Wild horses could not have brought my husband here, "because," he said, "I'll never put the cork on again." We felt terribly bad about it because we couldn't see how it would hurt anybody's feelings for him to do black when all our lives people had enjoyed so much laughter at the old routines that we had done.

Daytime view of Etling's layout showing canvas removed and cover on piano in case of storm. Also notice living tops in background.

Pan Torch

Some of the medicine shows carried seats under canvas, trapeze acts, and even small orchestras. "Doc" M. E. Etling had raised my husband, and his show was a typical medicine show layout, with "A-top" living tents in the backyard, and with model T trucks to move on. I have made some drawings on posterboards to show some of the details that a lot of people may not know about. (I have given them to the Library Museum here.) One drawing shows one of DeCarlo's "pitch-wagons" on a truck in New York City in the early and mid-twenties. A series of trucks (possibly as many as five or six) were run out from 116th Street to areas where crowds were letting out of theatres or factories. Each truck carried a complete medicine show. My father did his ventriloquism and medicine lectures on one of these trucks for a couple of winters. They pitched the whole line of medications at each performance, parked right at curbside, blocking sidewalks with their "tips" (crowds).

Another of the posters shows an old-time "pan-torch"—some people called them "banjo torches." They were very dangerous, but necessary. They were used in ball fields and at other outdoor functions before the advent of rural electricity. The gasoline was in the pan and was gravity-fed to the burner below. *Very* dangerous, but all we had.

Taken from a photograph made in 1935 at Wrens, Georgia. This was "Doc" Marshall's Sunny South Medicine Show. Notice sales runway that extends into the crowd. "House-cars" were made-over autos or trucks and were the forerunners of the modern, luxurious "motor homes" of today.

One drawing shows Doc Marshall's lot in Georgia in 1935. It shows an early "motor home." The old-timers, tired of the inconvenience of living in tents, were ingenious and remodeled cars *and-or* trucks into living quarters which we all called "house-cars." Doc Marshall's platform and runway was an extraordinarily low stage. It came up to about my short rib, which is very unusual. They were usually at least nose-high for a very good reason. A low runway is almost an invitation for people to sit on it, canceling out its original usefulness, which was to give the lecturer immediate access to the *customer* in the middle of the crowd. With a big crowd packed close around, the "runners" were often unable to penetrate to the center of the crowd. The runway took care of this. Helpers—called "runners"—ran all through the crowd, shouting "Herbs! Herbs! A dollar a box! Herbs! Who wants to buy a box of herbs!" After a convincing lecture, several people running and shouting causes the audience to get "all jived up," and before they knew it, they bought it. Then the runner would yell, "Sold out! Doc! Gimme some more herbs." And the "Doc" would say something like, "And another soul made happy!" And all the excitement would encourage the hesitant to buy.

We all know what "slapstick" is, but I wonder how many modern folk have actually seen a real "honest-to-John" slapstick! Another drawing shows how an authentic slapstick looks. It should be made from two curved staves of a flour barrel. A substitute could be two thin boards about three feet long, with a handle carved at one end, and wrapped to protect the hands that hold it. Then a spacer is placed several inches above the handle so that when something is hit with it, the spaced ends of the boards come together with a "slap" sound that *sounds* brutal, but does no damage. We used the slapstick in several acts.

I also drew several tents to show the different types, but I made a mistake on the "dramatic-end" top. The dramatic-end tent was designed to remove a view-obstructing tent pole from in front of the stage. As was said earlier this evening, most circus tents are round tops, round enough to be used on the merry-go-round. But then, in order to make them longer, you lace in what we call "middle pieces." If you have a fifty-foot round top and two thirty-foot middle pieces, you will have a big top fifty feet wide by one hundred ten feet long.

Another drawing shows a very unusual arrangement for a medicine show. The customer had to pay to go in the topless sidewall to stand and watch the show. But the medicine show was never supposed to cost a thing. Like television, you saw it free, but they expected you to buy something.

Several people asked if I would make a pitch. I've never made a pitch in my life, but I persuaded my father to do my favorite herb pitch on tape. I will read it to you.

After he did his ventriloquist act, he would put the dummy on a chair and say,

Now ladies and gentlemen, in a minute or two I'm going to show you exactly how I make the little fellow talk. You're probably thinking, "Oh, you have to be a ventriloquist to do that." But I'm going to take the head off and have it talk to the little boys and show you exactly how it's done. [Now this is the clincher that holds them. They're going to stay there to see how that's done.] When you saw me come out here this evening, you probably said, "I'll bet that man came here to sell medicine that's supposed to be good for *every*thing under the sun." You never made a greater mistake in your life! And some of you others probably thought, "I'll bet he calls himself a doctor!" I want you to understand to begin with, folks, that I'm not a good enough man to be your doctor. It takes a better man than me to be a doctor. Better physically, mentally, and morally. By that I mean, physically . . . yes, your doctor lives under a great strain. All hours of the day and night he calls on people; he shouldn't have to go at such hours. Mentally? Yes. He's a highly intelligent man if he passes the Board of Medical Examiners. Morally? As far as morality is concerned, how would *you* like to spend the rest of *your* life listening to other people's troubles? That's what your doctor does. I'm not here to take the place of your doctor, nor to promise you that I've got medicine that cures *any*thing under the sun. Medicine doesn't do it. There *are* a few things that will help old Mother Nature. Now I want to get down to facts, I want you to know the best medicines on earth are free. They grow right out of the ground, if you only know where to get them and when. Speaking of herbs [laughter], any legitimate practicing doctor in the United States will tell you that in his practice of medicine he uses cascara sagrada [laughter]. The white man never knew what it was until the "poor old ignorant Indian" showed him what it was—also known as "the sacred bark." Millions of lives have been saved by the use of cinchona bark, the bark of another tree, never known by the white man until the Indians showed him what it was. When we call these "Indian herbs," we don't mean to imply that the Indians planted them and raised them, but the Indians showed the white man the use of different herbs. Now there are herbs for everything that a man can think of, for ordinary, everyday complaints. Medicines have improved a lot. Folks have degenerated so much in their health that there has to be very fancy medicine now to keep some of us alive. And I want you folks to remember this, I'm not trying to pass out anything for sick people tonight. I'm talkin' to you people who *never* take anything until you've *got* to. And when you've *got* to, you find out it's too late. If your doctor told you the truth, when he comes to see you— which he doesn't want to, he wouldn't want to hurt your feelings that way—or you stagger into his office and fall down almost ready to die, and he looks you over and diagnoses your case. Then he tells you he'll do all he can, but it's doubtful he can eliminate the trouble your kidneys are giving you, or your liver's giving you, or some other part of the body. He should ask you the question (and he usually does), "How long have you been feeling this way?" Then, when you tell him you've been feeling bad for the last year or two, your doctor should say, "Well, get on out, I don't want to do anything for you; if you'd come to me when it first started, I might be able to do something." [Laughter.] Now, folks, it doesn't take a doctor, it doesn't take a hospital, it doesn't take anything else to know when you're feeling bad but you yourself. Your *body* tells you. When you were a little baby, your mother tended to your health. You were a baby; didn't know about such things. Now that you're a man, you're too busy thinking about everything under the sun except the most important thing: *the house God gave you to live in.* (Think about it folks. You're laughing, but it's the truth. We *don't* take care of our bodies as well as we should.) If you desecrate and defile that castle, it will be destroyed, no question about that. Everyone knows it's so when you stop to think, but how often do you stop to think? You think about everything else under the sun until you're ready to die, and then you say, "Oh, the Lord's not good to me." It's not the Lord's fault. It's your own fault; you didn't take care of the house He gave you to live in. For you people who don't believe in herbs, I'm going to say just one thing to you tonight: you'll live from the ground, you go back to the ground when you die. [Laughter.] While you're here, you live from that old Mother Earth; Mother Earth produces these herbs. "What you eat is what you are" has been said by big scientific men nowadays. In other words, when you get sick, go back to old Mother Earth to find out what you need, but don't wait until you've got to take drastic minerals and all kinds of mercurial poisons and drugs. Do something the first time you feel sick and get that dizzy little headache. Now, you take the average fellow when he gets a headache. Common sense teaches him that it comes from the stomach, but what does he do? He takes some kind of dope into his stomach. He doesn't take a good laxative to clean out the colon or clean his system out. Now there are herbs that will clean out the stomach, liver, and kidneys, and clean them out good, and help old Mother Nature. When you clean your stomach, liver, and kidneys and get those three organs performing their proper duties, the rest of your body will automatically take care of itself. If you doubt that statement, I'll say to you, your stomach, your liver, your kidneys all have to do with your blood. Blood is made up from the food you eat through these organs. I'm going to say this to you tonight: You give me a man with good blood and good health; let him cut his hand nearly off; reach down on the ground and pick up an old dirty, greasy rag; wrap up his hand; and let him go on. If his blood is good, his hand will heal. But you take that same man and let him get a little scratch on his finger; let him rush in and put on a *barrel* of medicine, fifty yards of antiseptic tapes and gauzes; and if his blood is bad, his hand will rot off. I'll say to you, clean your system twice a year, that's the old-fashioned way to do it. You know, you're still old-fashioned. Whether you believe it or not, you're still very, very much old-fashioned. We make a whole lot better automobiles and have learned how to kill each other on the highways much faster than we ever did before. We fly through the air, but that body we take through the air when we're doing that flying is exactly the same kind of body that man had thousands of years ago. And man, thousands of years ago, lived a healthier, happier, stronger life by taking care of what God had given him to live in. Now the price is of no consequence.

. . . and folks, there's where my tape ran out. My father was so distressed because one of the most important things in making a pitch of any kind is what we call "turning the tip." You say a few little closing words, and the next thing you know, everybody's ready to buy, and . . . I remember a little bit of what he said. I remember snatches like

the price is of no consequence, you think nothing of spending several dollars for a nice meal at a restaurant, $20 for a pair of shoes, or a couple hundred to fancy up your house or car; I'm not going to ask you to buy these herbs at the low and insignificant price of only $5 a box. No, nor even $3. These lifegiving herbs are going tonight for the paltry sum of $1 for the next five minutes and then we will go on with the show.

And then bing, bang, boom, everybody was buying it. Then he would keep his promise and have just the head of the dummy argue with someone in the audience and go on with the show.

When my father joined the DeCarlo outfit it was a blessing because it was winter and during the Depression. When we went to Penna in the Spring of 1928 with our own show, we had a family of San Blas Indians along. They helped in the acts and added color with their beadwork—which they sold—and their beautiful regalia.

We always sold the dollar item first—usually herbs or tonic. The reason? If a man had a couple of dollars in his pocket, you could get one whole dollar, intact, with the first sale. Then let him break the next dollar for the fifty-cent, then the twenty-five-cent items (usually salve or linament at fifty cents and soap or tooth powder at twenty-five cents). Then you could hit him with the ten-cent candy sale, and you'd gotten $1.95 of his $2.00.

The first night you make a short impressive talk on pep pills. (You never say it's an aphrodisiac.) And you talk about them every night, all week. It's a promise or teaser until the night we put on the "double"—a sale that includes the pep pills (vitamins) as one item among several that all sell together as a package deal "for the paltry sum of only a dollar, to get it into the hands of as many as possible as an advertising special." Usually, this is done the last night in town.

The medicine show has been unjustly maligned for many years. As the old-timers die off and cannot defend themselves, it seems to get worse and worse. We sold products that were manufactured in Cincinnati by a big medical company. And that company is still in business. We had it shipped to us with no labels and we put our own labels on the bottles so that the same tonic could be "Apache Jack's" (my father's), or "Dakota Bob's" (my husband's), or "San Blas Indian Tonic" (Doc Etling's). This is still being done today. You can go to any drugstore and get a patent medicine with the store's name on it.

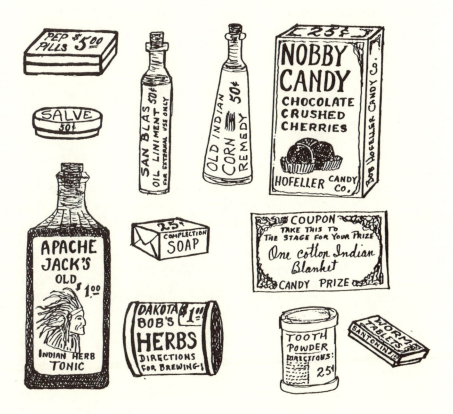

One of the most effective remedies we sold was a worm medicine—not a nice subject, but a very important part of the business. We all know that human beings, as well as all warm-blooded animals, are subject to the infection of intestinal parasites. We don't suffer from them as much today because we have found ways to be free of them. The only thing available back then was a big pink candy wafer, and the ingredients included santonin and rhubarb. The santonin was to kill the worm and the rhubarb was to flush him out. It had to be removed from the market because it was found that santonin caused blindness in some people. This was the accepted remedy for worms in every drugstore throughout the nation. Our family used it. The medicine show people were not to blame for this—we bought it from the same place the doctors and drugstores were buying it. They had found something that worked, but back then they didn't have the Pure Food and Drug Act to enforce extensive testing for side effects.

Dad always sold the worm medicine on the first night for the simple reason that he wanted specimens as quickly as he could get them, and you'd be surprised how tapewormy this nation was! His system was to get three or four samples with name and address as testimonials in exchange for their choice of five dollars' worth of our medications. Then he would say to the audience, "Look! This specimen is from right here in *your town*! Ask Mr. Ichabod about!" My father carried two trunks of all shapes and sizes of alcohol-filled bottles with specimens. He was proud of the good he had done, and there was no worse insult than to accuse him of having bottles with fake specimens.

I heard the candy sale mentioned in an earlier talk, and this was what a lot of shows survived on. We sold ours for ten cents a box. Ours came from the Delight Candy Company and the Bob Hofeller Candy Company, both in Chicago. The last package we sold was "Nobby." Each box contained a Cracker Jack-type prize that was called "slum." But every tenth box contained a coupon redeemable at the stage for a big prize.

This is the way we operated: when we got a shipment of candy in (220 boxes in two cases and two cases of prizes—blankets, pillows, bedspreads, cooking utensils, toys, rugs, bric-a-brac, all kinds of nice stuff—no junk) we would display it all on the stage, then say:

This is the entire shipment. These two cases go with all these prizes. When we have sold all this candy, every prize on the platform will have been taken by someone in the audience. If the prizes are not taken, at the end of the evening we will take a piece of paper, twist it up, and throw it out. Whoever gets the paper gets the prize.

We had one of the most successful candy shows on the road because we were truthful, we never cheated our patrons, and we always did what we said we would do.

We worked in the sideshow on Silver Brothers Circus in 1936-1937. We had the sideshow on Hoxie Tucker's Hoxie Brothers Circus in 1949. Now, *there's* a man who deserves a lot of credit! His show flopped right after we left for the sticks. He went back to Miami—broke. All he owned was his home in Miami. He took a job running a filling station, and every time he ran across an old truck or an old tire that was half-way good, he bought it and painted "Hoxie Brothers Circus" on it. He worked for years—"pulling himself up by his bootstraps"—and now he owns the world's largest round top and has two beautiful circuses on the road.

We were med-show people until about 1940 and have had an animal exhibit from that time on. We have what is probably the largest privately owned collection of anthropoid apes in the world. We have had two orangutan births and forty-five chimpanzee births in our collection. Our show started in 1940 and retired in 1971—had a long run of thirty-one years because it featured audience participation. People out of the audience volunteered to box or wrestle with one of the chimps. You may ask, "How did you get people to do it?" Everybody wanted to get into the act. And I could tell you stories that would keep you here all night. There have been between thirty-five thousand and forty thousand men, women, and children in the arena to box, wrestle, or play with one of our apes.

One last word—don't believe everything you read. It isn't always true. I'm glad to see people like Brooks McNamara and others showing interest in writing about the old timers truthfully.

DANCE

Jenifer P. Winsted

Tripping on the Light Fantastic Toe: Popular Dance of Early Portland, Oregon, 1800-1864

From the beginning of the great move west to Oregon, the traveling pioneers were ambitious and hard working. Their trip was slow and exhausting, but in the evenings many would relax by dancing on the grass near their camps. Jesse Applegate, a minister leading a large wagon train, wrote in his diary of 1843, "It is not yet 8 o'clock when the first watch is to be set; the evening meal is just over. Near the river a violin makes lively music, and some youths improvise a dance. . . . It has been a prosperous day, more than twenty miles have been accomplished."[1]

Most of the early American settlers in the Oregon Territory were migrating farmers who staked claims to large acreages in fertile river valleys of the west or flat expansive prairies of the east. They were miles away from any neighbors, largely because of the size of their individual holdings. Each farm, therefore, was a self-sufficient unit except for recreation. Entertainment was a treasured luxury. One pioneer wrote, "In those days it was the fashion to go to bed with the sun unless there was a dance to go to. Twenty or thirty miles was no great distance to go to attend a dance. You went on horseback, sometimes two on one horse. You arrived about sundown and the fun began immediately, and lasted until daybreak the next day when you had breakfast and started your horseback ride home again."[2]

Many men went out West alone. They were loggers, miners, and adventurers of all types. Far away from their families, life was rough as they worked to survive the wilderness in hopes of finding their fortunes. Apparently they played just as hard, never letting fatigue or the lack of women stop them from dancing. One such traveler, G. E. Cole, wrote in 1850, "We made a jovial night of it by getting up a dance, in which there being but one lady, the wife of our host, three of our party personated ladies by tying a handkerchief on the arm. We had a very enjoyable time, dancing for hours. . ."[3]

Portland began as a land claim split by two men. In 1845, each hoping the name of his former state capital to be the new town's name, they tossed a

Mary Hallock Foote's "Going to the Dance" suggests the ranchers' evening out, when "twenty or thirty miles was no great distance to go to attend a dance." From Lucius Beebe and Charles Clegg. *The American West: The Pictorial Epic of a Continent* (New York: E. P. Dutton and Company, 1955).

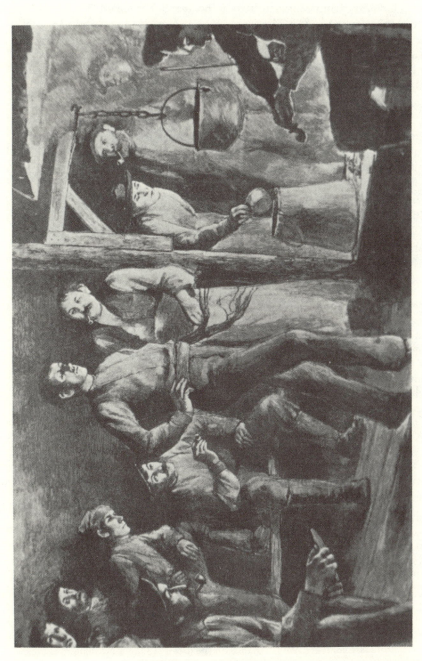

"A Loggers' Camp at Night," drawn by J. MacDonald for *Harper's Weekly*. From Lucius Beebe and Charles Clegg. *The American West: The Pictorial Epic of a Continent* (New York: E. P. Dutton and Company, 1955).

coin. Lovejoy, from Massachusetts, who wanted it called Boston, lost to Pettygrove from Maine.[4] The town remained small for several years since most immigrants continued to live on scattered farms. However, some new residents of Portland and other emerging towns were almost frantic in their attempts to establish the cultural manners they had known in the East. But things were different. Dancing parties—now known as balls—became all-night and all-purpose affairs. After dancing all evening, one pioneer wrote in her diary that "Mrs. Goodwin, and afterwards, Mrs. Riley, served a sumptuous supper at midnight. Before going back to the ballroom, all of the ladies changed their dresses, having saved their prettiest ones for the last half of the night. We had a gay time and danced until morning."[5]

Portland's harbor on the Columbia River was close to Britain's Fort Vancouver. During the boundary disputes, the British sloop H.B.M.S. *Modeste*, with Captain Baillie and crew, arrived to guard Fort Vancouver and the Oregon Territory for England. Captain Baillie took advantage of harbor duty to entertain the settlers with various parties. February 7, 1846, he hosted his first ball at Vancouver. The local newspaper reported proudly:

There was a brilliant assemblage of the fair sex of Oregon and although in the *far west*, yet from the gay display that night we are proud to state that the infant colony can boast of as pretty faces and handsome "figures" as the mother country. Dancing commenced at 8 o'clock, and it was pleasing to see the "tripping on the light fantastic toe" kept up with such spirit. The dresses of the ladies was [sic] a theme of universal admiration, combining neatness, elegance, and ease. Reels, country dances, figures eight, and jigs was [sic] the order of the evening; and if we do not yet come to that fashionable dance, the *Polka*, still we live in hopes of seeing it soon introduced at our city balls. . . .[6]

Before there was regular dramatic entertainment in Portland, pleasure excursions on local steamships were popular along the Columbia, the Willamette, and other rivers. Since most settlers felt more a part of the United States than of Great Britain, the Fourth of July was a particularly favorite occasion for excursions, such as the one on the *Multnomah* in 1856. It was advertised in the *Oregonian* on June 28, to "leave Portland for Astoria . . . July 3d at 8 o'clock A.M. and will return on Saturday July 5th. . . . There will be a Cotillon [sic] Party on the evening of the Fourth in the city of Astoria." The trip itself was also an important part of the festivities, as the July 12 *Oregonian* reported.

The gallant steamer threaded her way down to Green Point, where all again disembarked and were soon enjoying a "dance on the green" to the most delightful music, and upon the most enchanting spot we have ever seen in Oregon or elsewhere. After those who delight to "trip the light fantastic toe" had indulged in that luxury, which seemed more like enchantment than reality, . . . the steamer was off. . . . The music, the dance, the beauty, the smiles, the joyous hilarity, and the most complete order and social bearing was acknowledged to have been seldom if ever equalled at any time or place by everyone present.

It wasn't long before traveling performers began to make stops in Portland. One of the first to arrive was Caroline Chapman. She was called the "leading light" at New York's Olympic Theatre and Niblo's Garden, but eagerly gave up the security of her career for the excitement of traveling west.[7] From 1857 to 1860 she was the first popular dancer actress in Portland. Caroline was missed by her fans when she returned to New York, but was quickly replaced by a new favorite—young Susan Robinson. Portland audiences were not alone in devotion to Susie. As she toured the mines, adoration of her became fanatical. "At that time many Oregon boys had never seen the gay tinsels of a stage costume, never been thrilled by the rich tones of a cultivated voice, or seen a beautiful woman poised on one toe, and she took the frontier heart by storm."[8]

The soldiers at local forts were so infatuated with Susie that at one performance violence resulted. It began with one soldier who continued to cheer her after she had begun, while the rest of the soldiers monopolized the area closest to the stage. This angered the local citizens and "more than fifty shots were fired and the room was filled with smoke. No one was arrested so the theater went on as usual, but Susie never seemed quite the same afterwards. A slight commotion in the audience would attract her attention in the midst of her best song and in her best play she always looked as though she was just a little afraid someone was going to shoot."[9]

Another nationally known performer who was popular in Portland was Lotta Crabtree. She first appeared in gold camps in southern Oregon in 1855, where, as a child, she danced for the miners and was showered with coins and nuggets. In 1861, she visited Portland with her Metropolitan Male and Female Minstrel Show. She was known for her dance portrayals of Topsy, Little Nell, and many others, especially in shows with patriotic themes.

Lotta did find some hostility in the mines during 1862, where the Union was looked on as the opposition. As soon as the curtain went up at one performance, a rebel yell greeted her, and hissing accompanied the singing of Union songs. Jake Wallace, Lotta's manager, advised her against doing her well-known sailor dance with drum, flag, and hornpipe. But she reportedly vowed to go on even if they hanged her. Wallace wrote later that "she won the tribute of neutral response but the troupe moved rapidly out of the village as soon as the performance was over."[10]

Lotta Crabtree. Reprinted by permission of Curtis Brown, Ltd., From *The Triumphs and Trials of Lotta Crabtree* by David Dempsey and Raymond P. Baldwin. Copyright © 1968 by David Dempsey and Raymond P. Baldwin.

Men dancers were also popular, even when their offstage behavior was considered improper. Mike Mitchell was one such jig dancer who was loved openly in Portland. His untimely death shocked the town and his obituary was one of the first to be given a prominent place in the *Oregonian*. On January 14, 1862, it read:

At an early hour yesterday morning, Mike Mitchell, the minstrel and well known as the best jig dancer ever on this coast was found in the yard of a house where he had been lodging—laying [sic] in the snow, and life nearly extinct. A physician was called in, and restoratives applied, but without avail, and he expired shortly after being taken into the house. An inquest was held, and the verdict was that the deceased came to his death by freezing, while under the influence of liquor. It appears that on Saturday night Mitchell, while drunk, abused some of his fellow lodgers and on Sunday night, when he asked admittance, the inmates, thinking that his admission would be followed by still further abuse, denied him and being stupefied with liquor, he sank down on the spot and froze to death. Mitchell was a gentleman when sober, and possessed of many fine qualities, and was well liked by his comrades but his love for strong drink over-came him, and like it does thousands of others—dragged him to an early grave. And thus died the wandering minstrel. It will be a long time before his like is seen again in this country.

Another more widely celebrated performer, William Brady, was not impressed with Portland. He probably was there in the 1870s or 1880s when hurdy-gurdy dance halls had become popular spots for entertainment and recreation. He wrote later in his autobiography:

Perhaps the lowest I sank was playing with the melodrama company at the worst saloon theatre joint in Portland, Oregon. At that period Portland was just two streets on the Columbia River, pretty wide open and tough . . . no place to hold a convention of Sunday School superintendents. . . .

I don't suppose a similar institution ever existed anywhere except on the Pacific Coast in its earlier days. The Old Bowery of blessed memory was the Metropolitan Opera in comparison. The theatre consisted of an orchestra floor, patronized by people who weren't too drunk to have some idea of seeing a show, and a horseshoe of twenty-five or thirty boxes to which came citizens who were so drunk they didn't know whether they were seeing a show or a funeral. . . . Drinks were served everywhere in the house. . . . From eight to midnight, while the house filled up and the noise got going, the stage was occupied with a variety show—a show full of dancing girls, singing girls. . . . At midnight the girls left the stage and came out front to "hustle drinks" in the boxes. They worked on commission. From midnight on the dramatic company . . . played melodrama . . . lots of Indian plays—so long as business held up, which might well mean 5 o'clock in the morning. It didn't matter what we played as long as it was noisy and full of action. . . .

The performance was always being punctuated with uncued revolver shots as some founding father of Oregon whipped out his gun and loosed it off into the top of

"Christmas in the Oregon Mountains—The Backwoodsman's Christmas Frolic," sketched for *Leslie's* by Paul Frenzeny. From Lucius Beebe and Charles Clegg. *The American West: The Pictorial Epic of a Continent* (New York: E. P. Dutton and Company, 1955).

the proscenium arch with appropriate whoops and yells. . . . Night after night it was pandemonium—the toughest audience to play to I ever met yet, and that is saying a great, great deal.[11]

The story of these saloons and other theatres is made even more interesting by the weather—the inevitable Oregon rain. In November 1858, the first theatre opened along with the first winter theatre season. It was a proud moment for Portland and the builder, C. P. Stewart. His Willamette Theatre was 100 feet long, 36 feet wide, and could seat 600.

Beginning with that first season, the weather was used frequently to indicate the strength of a performer's draw. During the first winter, the weather was generally ignored by patrons who went steadily to the theatre, despite conditions reportedly horrendous. For example, an editorial in the *Oregonian*, March 12, 1859, concluded, "The weather continues to incite good pious men to almost swear outright. It is a concoction of rain, hail, snow, wind, mud and sunshine, all mixed together, and must be taken without shaking every hour in twenty-four." During the winter season of 1860-1861, the weather won out. Very few performers could even get to Portland. Hardy dance lovers, however, came to the theatre and used the stage floor as a ballroom.

By 1864, Stewart's Willamette Theatre was rapidly becoming an inadequate facility. It was apparently too small, overused, and taking on water, according to the following letter to the editor of the *Oregonian* on January 18:

Dear Oregonian: I notice that Mr. Holmes advertises the theatre for rent. I would respectfully suggest that if he would expend two or three months rent in improvement in the building it would be money well invested. . . . In the first place the building should be raised two or three feet out of the water; an arched ceiling, with ventilater put in over head, as the present ceiling is much too low; the back seats in the dress circle raised to give a better view of the stage, and then the whole premises should undergo a thorough cleaning with water, white wash and paint.

Portland needs and would support a theatre the year round, without any very extraordinary attraction on the stage, provided the building was made comfortable and pleasant. In its present state the attraction must be very great to induce a person to go there the second time, especially when the water comes up to the front seats in the parquette, and the whole building has, to give it the least offensive name, a musty smell. . . .

It would be several years before solutions were found for these problems. Many performances were given in this seemingly atrocious facility—and most often to full houses.

Meanwhile the saloon dance halls, or hurdy-gurdies, were booming businesses. They were a combination of dancing school, evening club, and saloon, complete with "imported pretty waiter girls" to dance with and for the customers.[12] Women were brought by the shipload to become the wives of new Oregonians *and* to work in the hurdy-gurdy houses. For example, the Republic Steamer passenger list, printed in the *Democratic Standard,* showed that on December 17, 1857, the following ladies arrived from San Francisco: Mrs. LaDa, Miss Alice LaDa, Miss Mary LaDa, Miss Susan LaDa, Miss Sophia LaDa, and Miss Sarah LaDa.

What went on in the hurdy-gurdies? Thomas Dimsdale, an educated and cultured Englishman, came West in 1863 for his health, and his description of the dance houses is one of the most lively.

As soon as the men have left work, these places are opened and dancing commences. . . . On one side is a raised orchestra. The music suddenly strikes up and the summons "Take your partners for the next dance" is promptly answered by some of the male spectators, who paying a dollar in gold for a ticket, approach the ladies bench—and in style polite, or otherwise . . . invite one of the ladies to dance. The parties take their place, as in any other dancing establishment and pause for the introductory notes of the air.[13]

Dimsdale goes on to describe one couple. She is a "first-class dancer":

There she stands at the head of the set. She is of middle height, of rather full and rounded form, her complexion as pure as alabaster, a pair of dangerous looking hazel eyes, a slightly Roman nose, and a small and prettily formed mouth. Her auburn hair is neatly banded and gathered in a tasteful ornamented net, with a roll and gold tassels at the side. How sedate she looks during the first figure, never smiling til the termination of "Promenade eight," when she shows her little white hands in fixing her handsome brooch in its place, and settling her glistening earrings. See how nicely her scarlet dress, with its broad black band round the skirt, and its black edgings sets off her dainty figure. No wonder that a wild mountaineer would be willing to pay—not one dollar, but all that he has in his purse—for a dance and an approving smile from so beautiful a woman.

Her cavalier stands six feet in his boots, which come to the knee and are garnished with a pair of Spanish spurs. His buckskin leggins are fringed at the seams and gathered at the waist with a U.S. belt, from which hangs his loaded revolver and his sheath knife. His neck is bare, muscular, and embrowned by exposure, as is also his bearded face, whose sombre hue is relieved by a pair of piercing dark eyes. His long black hair hangs down beneath his wide felt hat, and in the corner of his mouth is a cigar, which rolls like the lever of an eccentric as he chews the end in his mouth. After an amazing grave salute, "All hands round" is shouted by the prompter, and off bounds the buckskin hero, rising and falling to the rhythm of the dance, with a clumsy agility and a growing enthusiasm testifying his huge delight. His fair partner, with practiced foot and easy grace, keeps time to the music like a clock, and rounds to her place as smoothly and gracefully as a swan. As the dance progresses, he of the buckskin gets excited and nothing but long practice prevents his partner from being swept off her feet, . . . An Irish tune or a hornpipe generally finishes the set, and then the thunder of heel and toe, and some amazing demivoltes are brought to an end by . . . "Promenade to the Bar." . . . The ladies sit down, and with scarcely an interval, a waltz, polka, schottische, mazurka, varsovienne or another quadrille commences. . . .

In the Dance House you can see Judges, the Legislative corps, and everyone but the Minister. He never ventures further than to engage in conversation with a friend at the door, and while intently watching the performance, lectures on the evils of such places with considerable force but his attention is evidently more fixed upon the dancers than on his lecture. Sometimes may be seen gray haired men dancing, their wives sitting at home in blissful ignorance of the proceeding.[14]

In a real-life setting more exciting than most staged dramas, the popular entertainments were by necessity, and by demand, lively. Tastes were not subtly expressed. Performers were loved or thrown out. Dances were exciting, satisfying, or discarded. The love of thrill and appreciation of skill is illustrated by a contemporary preview announcing the appearance of a traveling rope dancer who would "perform the wonderful and dangerous feat of walking a rope head down, from the stage to the top of the dress circle." The reporter, knowing his community well, went on to say: "We suppose that the house will be filled as there is always a crowd, when an opportunity is afforded for people to see a person hazard a chance of breaking his neck."[15]

The more we discover about the lives and entertainments of early Portlanders, the more we find that dance was part of most occasions. It was not limited in setting or style, nor appreciated by only an elitist portion of the community. It was truly part of common experience—for better or worse. This account from the front page of the *Oregonian*, November 8, 1864, typifies the pace, excitement, and spirit of Portland and her dance lovers:

ASSAULT WITH A BOLOGNA SAUSAGE

The new dance house on First Street, in the old Bergman Market, was the scene of much consternation on Saturday night, and the wild cries of "murder" by one of the women inmates, attracted the deputies of the Marshal. . . . It seems that an individual pretty well filled with [liquor] had made his appearance amongst the throng in hilarious state, and was more obnoxious than amenable to the "ladies," when the "boss" of the establishment attempted to put him out. At this juncture of the entertainment the "rough" vigorously "belted" his persecutor over the head with a bologna sausage, which caused the bacon, veal, and pork suet to fly in all directions, and it being mistaken for the brains of the "boss" produced the most intense excitement. When the true state of the case was known quiet was restored, and the joyous dance went on.

NOTES

1. *The Pioneers*, ed., Time-Life (New York, 1974), p. 91.

2. *Reminiscences of Oregon Pioneers*, "Mrs. Ellen Bowman Stover," ed. Pioneer Ladies Club (Pendleton, Oregon, 1937), p. 183.

3. George E. Cole, *Early Oregon Jottings of Personal Recollections of a Pioneer of 1850* (Spokane, n.d.), p. 18.

4. H. H. Bancroft, *History of Oregon* (San Francisco, 1888), pp. 8-9.

5. *Reminiscences*, "Nancy E. DeSpain," p. 39.

6. *The Spectator*, February 19, 1846.

7. George C. D. Odell, *Annals of the New York Stage* (New York, 1931), VI:128.

8. *Oregon Native Son* (May 1900, April 1901), p. 77.

9. Ibid., p. 78.

10. Constance Rourke, *Troupers of the Gold Coast or The Rise of Lotta Crabtree* (New York, 1928), p. 163.

11. William Brady, *Showman* (New York, 1937), pp. 53-55.

12. *Oregonian*, November 11, 1864.

13. Thomas J. Dimsdale, "The Miner's Delight: Hurdy-Gurdy Houses—Circa 1863," *After Dark*, July 1969, p. 48.

14. Ibid., pp. 48, 49.

15. *Oregonian*, December 16, 1864.

Gretchen A. Schneider

Gabriel Ravel and the Martinetti Family: The Popularity of Pantomime in 1855 _____

"Gabriel Ravel, The Martinetti Family, and Their Talented Troupe,"[1] numbering over twenty members in all, arrived to tour California from New York City aboard the steamship *Uncle Sam*, November 3, 1855. Almost five months later, on March 5, 1856, they left San Francisco aboard the *Golden Gate* bound for New Orleans. During that time, they performed a repertoire of over fifty-six pieces that were retitled, shortened, expanded, and otherwise varied to fit into at least eighty-five documented performance dates.[2] This California tour is of special interest as it clearly unites the talent of two theatrical families who performed pantomime at a time shortly after the peak of the Ravels' major contributions to theatre spectacle.

A superficial glance at many of The Ravel Company programs in California would easily lead to the conclusions drawn by too many historians of popular culture—that the company was performing that quaint "motley mixture" which fed an everpresent just for novelty to settle the volatile temperaments of the democratic mob. As historians of popular theatre we must examine statements which contend, on the basis of these advertisements, that "the greatest drama and the grossest novelty were jointly yoked throughout the period (early nineteenth century) to the task of drawing an audience."[3] The nineteenth-century stage might indeed appear to be "decadent and inconsequential, a stage fleeing social and ethical dilemmas and purveying triviality and escapism."[4] It is my thesis that deeper principles of organization operate in these programs, and I extend this thesis to include the acts we "caught" during the last few days of this Conference. It is my purpose to introduce some approaches to this deeper structure of auditory and visual metaphors in order to demonstrate that apparent incongruity of nineteenth-century programs is a misleading point of departure for our critical assessment of their popular appeal.

Although my interest is in the cultural formulae that may have governed the structures of several sorts of popular entertainment in the nineteenth century, the California tour of The Gabriel Ravel Company is the narrower focus for this paper. By way of guiding you through my comments, I shall give you a short outline of what I am going to do. I shall define the tour briefly. I shall describe first a typical program of the tour and then demonstrate how I am using some analytic techniques formulated by circus historian Paul Bouissac, folklorist Alan Dundes, folklorist Vladimir Propp, and anthropologist Claude Levi-Strauss in order to get at structural elements operative in the Ravel and Martinetti repertoires. Lastly, I shall relate whole program structures to their potential for explaining social and cultural meaning and, not incidentally, the popularity of the company. Twelve pages is rather a short space adequately to explain the complexity of my work with the Ravels. I hope that I communicate a direction for theatre research that goes beyond descriptive history.

Pantomime in early nineteenth-century America evolved from a tradition of theatrical entertainment that had gained attention in late seventeenth- and early eighteenth-century Europe. In the United States, dumb show with musical accompaniment, topical innuendos, and commedia dell'arte figures in the capers of the harlequinade had entertained audiences since the 1790s. The work of Alexandre Placide, who staged patriotic pantomime ballets in South Carolina and New Orleans, is exemplary in this mode.

The long-favored Ravel family—rope dancers, ballet dancers, gymnasts, and pantomime artists—first arrived in the United States in 1832 and scheduled regular seasons before finally retiring to Toulouse in 1858.[5] Their "French-style" of pantomime emphasized visual theatre and not language, which was characteristic of more English pantomime players such as we noted with George L. Fox (1825-1877).[6] From the boulevard theatres of Paris and as world travelers, the Ravel brothers—Gabriel, Antoine, Jerome, and François—and their relatives were, in 1832, among the first exponents of the romantic influence in French drama, bringing to the United States romantic ballet, new wonders of physical virtuosity, and scenarios which united these elements (ballet and physical feats) plausibly and with continuity of dramatic action in the pantomime.

The Ravels, advertised as "the best of their line," shared their genre at midcentury in the United States with a host of other foreign and domestic companies,[7] some of whom—like the Martinetti Family—the Ravels brought to the United States from Europe. Some of these "competitors" even performed the same repertoire as the Ravels; but the Ravels had the advantage (which they bequeathed to the Martinettis after their 1858 departure) because they meticulously rehearsed their complicated physical feats with their specially conceived and built stage machinery, they personally controlled all aspects of the production in order to insure flawless illusion, and they cemented their commitment as a company by their "family" relationship.[8]

Broadside of George H. Adams Pantomime Company, ca. 1860s, illustrating the use of physical feats and ballet in pantomime. Courtesy of The New York Historical Society, New York City.

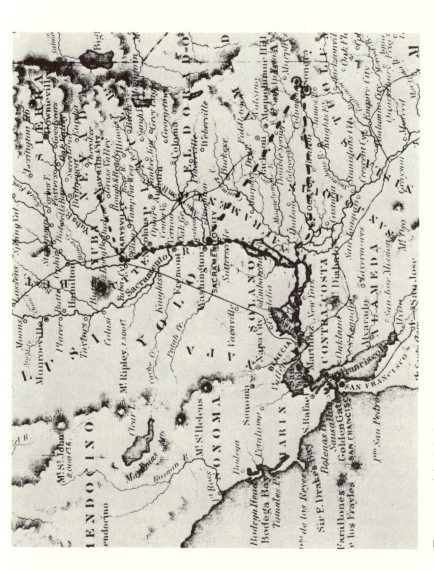

Tour route of the Ravel Company in California, 1855-1856. Courtesy of The Bancroft Library.

The tour of California took for granted the cosmopolitan populace familiar with the company's eastern and European reputations. As set by C. R. Thorne, an American manager familiar with both eastern and California theatres, and Gabriel Ravel, the company's tour schedule allowed no time off. Travel or a "dark theatre," allowing preparation for a particularly mechanical pantomime, are the only nonperformance dates. Three weeks and three days after their San Francisco debut at The American Theatre they made the short, one-day trip by river to Sacramento and took an additional day to set up in the Forrest Theatre. A thirteen-day engagement ended on Saturday; on the following Monday, they opened in Marysville for probably sixteen performances. A possible four-day wagon trip across the Sierra foothills brought them to Nevada City for one week ending January 16. On January 21, they again appeared in Sacramento, this time at the Sacramento Theatre, for twelve nights. During the next two weeks, from February 3 to their last appearances in California in San Francisco (February 18 to March 4), they are reported in the San Francisco newspaper *The Golden Era* as having successful runs in Sonora at The Young America Theatre and at The Columbia Theatre.

If we could take ourselves back to California of 1855, a typical Ravel performance would give us the following impressions.

The evening's program was divided into three major parts: physical feats, ballet, and pantomime. The selection of particular acts, their order on the program, and the length of the various pieces varied. Physical feats—the domain of The Martinetti Family and first grand tightrope performer Blondin—commanded the most attention of the California press. As a matter of fact, at the end of the tour the company was being billed as Gabriel Ravel and The Martinetti Family! These acts consisted of individual skills of balancing (human pyramids and objects), tightrope (dancing, walking, balancing, and acrobatics), exhibitions of military and sporting skills (boxing, wrestling, and combat), and exhibitions of "art" (tableaux and statuary).

The Martinetti Family specialized in a series of posturings and in feats of strength, grace, and agility, which, unlike the company's ballet and panto-mime, had never been excelled in California. *The San Francisco Daily Herald* noted that "the graceful and statuesque posturings of the trio [Julien, Phillippe, and Master Carlo], called forth from the assembled crowd very heavy and unmistakable signs of approval."[9]

[Further,] it was not enough that the exercises consisted merely of balancing, posturing, vaulting, etc. on the frail foundation afforded by a good stout cord, but the actors threw sommersets, danced hornpipes, laid [sic] down, got up, sat in chairs and did all sorts of conceivable and inconceivable things, as leisurely and as safely as though on the floor of the theatre.[10] [Similarly] Gabriel Ravel in his hornpipe, [second

The Martinetti Brothers, Phillippe and Julien, ca. 1855, as "Roman wrestlers." Courtesy of Harvard Theatre Collection.

grand tightrope performer] Mr. Dubouchet in his graceful and airy vaultings and other exercises, '[first grand tightrope performer] Mr. Blondin, the "great and terrific," springs into the air over the heads of two supernumeraries placed on the line, and alighting with his feet on the rope with a steadiness and solidity rather trying to weak nerves—all excited a uniform meed [sic] of approbation.[11]

One particular feat of the Martinetti brothers was the performance of all three together on the same rope at the same time.

While the two eldest balanced themselves adroitly some distance apart, a wooden rod, with a notch at each extremity, and fitting between the necks of the twain, was used to support the third brother—a sprightly, lively lad—who in turn on his elevated perch maintained his dangerous and oscillating position with a steadiness and ease betokening long and arduous study of the art of discovering and, [sic] keeping to a nicety the true center of gravity. This portion of the performances excited the most enthusiastic plaudits, which, when the triad walked off the plane formed by the props to the rope on the stage, and proceeded down the inclination into the parquette and back, redoubled in fervor.[12]

The apex of physical wonder was "The Bedouin Arabs." The act, as recounted by one reviewer, consisted of

a hurried set of tumbling, leaping, vaulting, pitching, flinging and generally frantic feats performed by the troupe, of which the most exciting was the throwing of a summerset, entitled *La Saut de la Bataille*, by Mons. Blondin, over eight muskets, four on a side, with bayonets fixed, and which at the time of the act are simultaneously discharged. It is an uncomfortable performance, and the gazer feels a peculiar sense of relief when the actor, alighting on his feet, shows conclusively that he has neither broken his neck, impaled himself, nor yet had his legs and arms blown off.[13]

The ballets, on the other hand, were "very lightly and gracefully performed." The Ravel Company did ballet because the genre itself assured an audience in the United States and because French pantomime had grown up in the Parisian boulevard theatres where the two disciplines—mime and dance—shared specific elements of gesture, choreography, and themes. The Gabriel Ravel Company was not a ballet company, and their ballets were frequently compared negatively in quality to the Rousset and Monplaisir companies which had first visited California in 1853 and 1854 respectively.

"The Captive," a grand ballet composed by the company's principal dancer and ballet master Monsieur Collet, was the most frequently performed ballet on the California tour. It serves as a good example of what the audience saw. First, the ballet showed off "to considerable advantage the splendid costumes of the Company." It contained a corps de ballet which was well drilled, and it highlighted the dancing of the first danseuse Mademoiselle Celestine Franck and principal danseuse and demi-caractere Mademoiselle Frances, both of whose merits the audience, in romantic fashion, came to adore and debate. Costumes, well-drilled corps, and particularly the artistry of the prima ballerinas were most often singled out for comment by the press. Reviews of the ballet itself support the idea of choreographic structure as a mere vehicle for these three attributes. "The Captive" was reviewed as

devoid of any interest whatever, save that it seems to suggest some pretty Eastern scenes, in which some effective tableaux are formed and some peculiar, though not unpleasing, dancing, credited variously to Asia, Greece, and Turkey, as the waltz, gallop, or fancy dance of those respective regions.[14]

Generally, ballet's "pretty" floor patterns, "graceful groupings," unison movement, static poses, and intertwining bodies, provided a satisfying aesthetic experience of harmony, proportion, line, balance, and delicacy— values underscored in classical ideals of beauty. Pantomime, however, was the distinguishing feature of the company. The terms *ballet* and *pantomime* were frequently confused in the press in California. The confusion illuminates the visual and auditory similarity of the genres. Prior to 1845, pantomimes were of a less spectacular nature and relied on illusion pro-duced by grotesque antics of the body;[15] on the ability to execute various physical skills like stilt-walking; on the ability to delineate particular char-acters such as the ape in *Jocko*; and on the ability to give an illusion of action in movement such as in chases, beatings, and the rest of stock play. The comic pantomime *Godenski*, with its imitation of skaters and skating, con-tained the elements of a less spectacular pantomime. This less scenically involved and thinly narrative work was often termed *ballet*; other companies even produced it as a ballet. Spectacular pantomime, on the other hand, relied more upon the actors' interaction with the scenery and stage machinery. Gabriel Ravel merely disappeared through a hole in the ice (stage floor) at the end of *Godenski*; but, as the White Knight in *The Green Monster*, the most popular and elaborate of the pantomimes brought to California, he was wondrously eaten alive.

The Green Monster enjoyed almost twice as many performances (sixteen) as the other pantomimes in the repertoire. Surviving manuscripts suggest it is a paradigmatic pantomime. For this reason, it seems appropriate to describe it as part of an evening's entainment. Following long tradition, the shorter "opening" part of a pantomime usually gave the pantomime its title. The "opening" drew its subject from legend, classical mythology, literary classics, or exotic locale.[16] *The Green Monster; or The Dream Accomplished* opens with the ominous "Sorcerer's Cave," in which witches and sorceresses sought to maintain their power over the Green Monster, a bottled imp. Obligatory elements of plot and action conspired to create a crisis which

Antoine Ravel as the White Knight in *The Green Monster*, ca. 1850s. Courtesy of Hoblitzelle Theatre Arts Library, Humanities Research Center, University of Texas at Austin.

caused the second part, or "transformation scene." At the expiration of the witches' power at midnight an explosion occurred, and the Green Monster was set free; he vanished into thin air and, in a tableau, hovered over the lovers, whom he was determined to protect.

In the resulting second half of the drama, major characters are eventually "transformed" into "harlequinade" figures. A lovers' plot between Harlequin and Rosalie is set in the first three scenes: Rosalie has constructed her dream man from flowers; when she falls asleep, he comes alive and is determined to answer her dreams. Failing to win her in courtly combat, Harlequin kidnaps Rosalie from her father's choice of husband, then dominates the second half of the drama. In *The Green Monster*, the clown (Gabriel Ravel's traditional role) was a villain, the White Knight.

Harlequin steals Rosalie in her father's throne which has magically turned into a balloon, and the harlequinade proceeds traditionally as a comedy of knockabout pursuit until the next to the last scene, the usual "dark scene," which takes place in a gloomy or macabre setting. Here, the chase threatens to end disastrously. In *The Green Monster*, Scene Eight—a garden, suddenly changes to Scene Nine—a fortress. But reconciliation occurs between the major characters, and all are transported into an apotheosis where a retransformation into their former characters occurs.

Reviews from California do not tell us exactly how *The Green Monster* appeared to a California audience. *The San Francisco Daily Herald* described a

harlequinade, which is of much the same character with all of those performances, commences with demons, witches, etc., and seemingly a very tragic introduction, which runs into the usual routine of the clown, or in this case The White Knight chasing Harlequin and Columbine, otherwise Rosalie, up and down the world, into and out of all sorts and measures of absurd and comical adventures. The shiftings and changes of scenery, slidings of pannels [sic] and traps, the buffoonery and general making up of the pantomime, are very effectively gotten up, and the house was kept in one constant burst of merriment at the ludicrous misfortunes and capital dumb show of Gabriel.[17]

The Daily State Tribune (Sacramento) refers to "a half hundred of the most startling and amusing tricks, which were greeted with round after round of applause and laughter."[18]

As a spectacular pantomime, *The Green Monster* incorporated many of the recent innovative aspects of New York spectacle theatre which were calculated for mass appeal and long runs. Although it is difficult to know exactly why Gabriel chose to bring *The Green Monster* to California, clearly it would have attracted attention on merit of containing the latest elements in theatre spectacle.

So far, we have looked at the tour itself and a typical program. Now I want to ask what means can be used to go below the surface of these program units to the structure of those particular elements that struck responsive cords in the audience. Four contemporary scholars of structural analysis seek to explore the meaning of culture in ways that are particularly adaptable to The Ravel Company repertoire (and I suggest them to you all as inspiring a new direction for theatre investigation). Folklorist Alan Dundes, in his introduction to the second edition of Vladimir Propp's *Morphology of the Folktale* (1968), identifies two distinct types of analysis in folklore. Propp's morphology is one: it describes "the structural or formal organization of a folkloristic text . . . following . . . the linear sequence of elements in the text."[19] The other method of structural analysis, following the work of Claude Levi-Strauss, seeks to describe pattern (usually based upon an *a priori* binary principle of opposition) which allegedly underlies the linear text. Levi-Strauss's pattern is not the same as sequential or diachronic structure. Rather, the elements are taken out of the "given" order and are regrouped in one or more simultaneous or synchronic schema.[20]

To Propp's narrative texts and Levi-Strauss's textual oppositions, circus semanticist Paul Bouissac adds the multidimensional concept of several "texts" operative at once. He asserts that

the concept of *text* cannot be restricted to a type of linguistic performance, either oral or written, because what constitutes a message as a text does not depend on the particular medium or the particular system within a given medium, but rather on formal properties, some of which pertain to the situation or context of the message, some to its constitutive structure.[21]

Bouissac's brilliant article, "Poetics in the Lion's Den: The Circus Act as Text," captures the complexity of acts as they would have occurred in the programs of The Ravel Company. The Ravel acts and program order were elaborately concocted "systems" of formal relationships between characters, their actions, their particular movements, their costumes, lighting, cultural objects and gestures, and scenery. Description of these systems must ultimately depend upon methods that separate formal relationships as (1) narrative texts and as (2) synchronically organized formal properties *whose congruence creates metaphoric meaning*. Bare bones structural elements can then be related (with hopes for new meaning) to social-cultural context. The narrative components of a tightrope act demonstrate the direction of my research with this company.

Imagine again The Martinetti Family on the tightrope—two figures supporting a third on a pole between their shoulders. The event is carried out in linear sequence and is also profoundly multidimensional. Boussac notes that "when an acrobat presents what he calls his 'routine' or 'tricks' for the public, we are confronted with a communicative act that can be analyzed as a complex message inasmuch as it is patterned according to a code and conveys some sort of enjoyable meaning to the public."[22] The "code" concerns itself with formal relationships. Some of these are acrobatics involving the body itself, subject to perceptual and sociocultural filters which must be analyzed. Not only do men act and react on the cord, but parts of their bodies are emphasized in the very nature of the balancing art. The actors' costumes become part of the code, and their demeanor and even their names become significant, identifying heroic qualities in metaphor.

Apart from the technical aspects of a code, the basic narrative text concerns me today. The complete Martinetti tightrope act would have had a cumulative sequence. The simple story of hero encountering danger (the cord) and overcoming danger (maintenance of balance) became progressively more involved. More complex dangers were encountered by the hero(es) as a test; the hero(es) had to use more skill to win and to triumph. Thus, a tightrope performance might start as a single person walking the line. Dancing a hornpipe on the cord or the *corde volante* would have escalated events. The person may have added cultural objects, containing additional meaning, such as a chair, heavy boots, and other appurtenances to the encounter. Gradually, more people are added until the risk is at high pitch as when Blondin, standing on the cord, threw sommersaults over two men, and a whole "family"—the Martinetti trio—demonstrated the double balance. Basic to this Martinetti tightrope act was the narrative text involving a human figure encountering danger and triumphing.

Structural components of the tightrope act were the performers, the cord, and its supports (some cords were anchored onstage with clear limits, while others were anchored out of sight or about the heads of the audience); selection of movements (dance, acrobatics, or walking); accessories; costumes; instructions for musical accompaniment; lighting; and printed programs, posters, and other bills. Selection of these components required their delimitation and control within the skill necessary for balancing. Tightrope acts became art when the skill of balancing could be exploited as drama.

Unlike the tightrope act, *The Green Monster*, as a narrative text, was complicated by the inclusion of several and yet distinct characters. The most important in terms of their spheres of influence were the villain (the White Knight); the hero (Harlequin); the magical agent or helper (The Green Monster); and the heroine (Rosalie). If there were time, I would demonstrate that by using Propp's method, these characters had particular and limited functions to perform in the unfolding of the fairy tale. What is significant is that like the tightrope act, they impose strict limitations on what can happen in the linear development of the text. The characters may have supported social role models, and thus their action in a text illustrates a level of problem solving. The characters' limitations are conventions clearly understood by the audience, which does not tire with their repetition. Delight with the expression occurs when new complications are added to the text which give new recognition to a well-understood threat, villainy.

According to Propp, *all fairy tales* are of one type with regard to their *structure of these functions.* The functions of characters are the constant elements, the number of these functions is limited, and the sequence of functions is identical. Propp notices that a large number of functions is arranged in pairs (prohibition-violation, reconnaissance-delivery, struggle-victory, pursuit-deliverance, and so on). Other functions are arranged in groups relating to the distributions of characters' *spheres of action.* Thus, the hero's sphere is to seek and to wed; the villain, to struggle and pursue; the helper, to fulfill desires and needs, to rescue, to solve difficult tasks, and to transfigure; the heroine, or princess, to wed. In contrast to the constant elements of linear development, the variable qualities—for instance, the characters' attributes of age, sex, status, and external appearance—provide the tale's brilliance, charm, and beauty, as well as the means to complicate the balance of narrative events.

The synchronic, or nonlinear, dimension of *The Green Monster* is analogous to the formal properties of the tightrope act. Quite apart from storyline, *The Green Monster* abounds in binary oppositions. There are (1) black magicians and white magicians (good and evil forces); (2) earth-bound creatures and winged creatures; (3) man of flowers and dreams (ideal or superhuman) and man of flesh and blood (imperfect and stupid); (4) formal procedure (courtly manners and deference) and independent decision (solitary action); (5) escape and capture (freedom and containment); and (6) appearance and disappearance (life and death?). Such oppositions, and their potential for transposition, according to Levi-Strauss, account for the duplication, triplication, or quadruplication of the same sequence in myths. This process of repetition, characteristic of circus acts and less obviously of pantomime, functions to render the structure of the myth apparent and its metaphoric relationship clear. Structured oppositions in pantomime allow the audience to perceive several ideas at once. At this point, I merely indicate that oppositions do occur in the Ravel pantomimes; there is a great deal of work to be done to relate the oppositions to cultural structures and thus to follow some of Levi-Strauss's ideas more closely.

Structural analysis then allows access to the configuration of units of expression and permits us to see how the three larger units that comprised the Ravel programs in California were used to construct program order. Program order appears to have capitalized upon the spectators' expectations of experiencing threat and removal of threat, as the acts themselves moved between simple and more complex metaphors, and from serious to comic. Ballet and physical feats *separately* emphasized the artistry and technical prowess of the performers. The audience was made to believe, to respect, and to be awed by the fine control of the performers over their immediate situation. By itself, ballet underscored lyric form and expressiveness (perhaps "visualized" the musical accompaniment) as opposed to the more static skill and dramatic effect of the physical feats.

Pantomime, however, *disguised* both the physical technology and visual ornamentation of the ballet and feats into a complex storyline.

Thus, as part of the metaphoric system of pantomime, ballet and feats took on different significance. The feats provided the technical means for visual tricks and illusion, such as improbable solutions for escape and rescue. The exotic ballet dances pinpointed the locale of the story; allowed the heroine to be perceived as graceful, romantic, and properly schooled; led to relationships of characters, most obviously in danced love duets; and provided a lyric means to connect pantomimic episodes. Stylized scenes of combat and battle were full of choreographed maneuvers, posturings, and formal illustrations of dueling, wrestling, boxing, and even courtlike tilting.

Quite apart from the pantomime, ballet and physical feats had focused the attention of the audience on the mechanical aspects of execution, individual ability, and expressiveness of the act. The practical-minded American audience was encouraged by the program order (which clearly separated ballet and physical feats) to penetrate the "mechanics" or technology of these units to see how they were done. In the pantomime, however, the physical feats and ballet became illusory and magic devices which were calculated to pique curiosity, accentuate effect, and create mystery about *how* the whole stage illusion was executed. Pantomime thus involved the audience in problem solving, not unlike the contemporary appeal made in other arts by Edgar Allan Poe with his mysteries and P. T. Barnum with his public hoaxes. Involvement with the magic and wonder of pantomime relieved the audience of any thoughts of the reality to which the physical feats related. The old magicians' line, "Now you see it; now you don't," is particularly apt: the audience was led through the program order to see effort and mechanics and then not to see it.

The implication from delineation of texts through diachronic and synchronic analysis is that all the Ravel and Martinetti pantomimes and perhaps their ballets can be eventually "deciphered" and compared. Formulae which underlie their structure can be identified. Such formulae would serve as basic configurations, which might be comparable to other forms of narrative and drama popular at the time. Changes in the fundamental diachronic and synchronic dimensions of the repertoire might relate to cultural and social changes. It might be possible to show that the Ravels maintained their popularity by their sensitive reaction to social changes as well as to particular situations they found as they toured.

Structural analysis can attempt to tell us what the Ravel programs really were, not what the programs meant to their audience. Through structural study of The Gabriel Ravel Company programs, a new level for hypothesizing the meaning of the programs is available. It is, however, a leap from structural components to meaning to an 1855 California audience. It is intriguing to wonder just how conscious performers, audience, and promoters of the company were of narrative texts and program order and, therefore, what latitude and means were available for them to manipulate structure for popular appeal. Certainly, a richness of possibilities for manipulating structure of programs had been either directly stated or alluded to during the last few days at this Conference.

Dundes, for one, believes that much of the meaning of folkloristic fantasy has to be unconscious in order to function as it does. He believes that "folklore provides a socially sanctioned outlet for the expression of what cannot be articulated in the more usual, direct way. It is precisely in jokes, folktales, folksongs, proverbs, children's games, gestures, etc. that anxieties can be vented."[23] The leap, then, from structure to meaning is not easy when the line between consciousness (direct) and unconsciousness (indirect) is not clear. The difficulty is compounded when one is dealing with history and not with an immediate ethnographic situation. The ephemeral nature of dance and gesture arts and the lack of adequate systems of notation and descriptive observations present further problems. Structural analysis does, however, let us arrive at new levels of information about The Gabriel Ravel Company in California. The question of meaning becomes crucial if we are to see in the structured patterns a reason for the company's popularity.

There are several ways to ascribe meaning to structure. I shall look at two—structure as myth and structure as a metaphor of social context. We can understand what The Ravel Company repertoire meant to its audience of 1855 if we view the acts and pantomimes as myths. Human dilemmas are presented and solved. The audience is satisfied because they see explained their everyday lives. Thus, the structure of the performance mediates conflicts in everyday lives. Consistent with this view, the Ravels and Martinettis are lauded many times through their careers for having "fulfilled a mission, as ministers of gaiety and good cheer, driving away from before them all dullness and gloom wherever they have gone." Their success was acknowledged to have been their unique ability to answer a public need—*escape*, from dullness, the anxiety brought about by the unfamiliar urban environment, and the threatened loss of rural self-sufficiency. Newspaper reviewers on the East Coast and in California, describing the company's programs as both "startling and amusing," "absurd and comical," "uncomfortable," and "unsettling to weak nerves," perhaps in their choice of terms were unconsciously drawing an equation between the satisfaction gained from perceiving form in art and the desire for risk, danger, and villainy which motivated the action of the program. The terms that the reviewers chose epitomized the ambiguity of existence at mid-nineteenth century that was intensely felt in California. Paradoxically, the audience sought relief from its anxieties, "tragedy of everyday life," by seeing represented means to control their immediate situation, metaphorically engendered in the balance on the tightrope and in the conventional form of the folktale. However, they also sought "the risk enjoyed" in an everyday life that was becoming increasing ordered, predictable, and dull with the spread of urbanization and the loss of the frontier. They probably came just as often to the theatre to be unsettled and perhaps unconsciously hoping to see Blondin fail in his tightrope antics or to see the stage machinery fail and reveal the pumped-up illusion of the little people on the stage.

More specific meaning emerges from structure when we examine programs to find metaphors of the immediate social context of California. During the visit of the Ravels, California newspapers were remarkable in the number of subjects which paralleled the content of the Ravel performances. One one level, articles on arctic exploration compare to pantomime hero Kim-Ka's arrival by balloon and adventures in China; arguments over the immutability of the species drew spectators to judge the life-likeness of Gabriel Ravel's famous portrayal of the ape Jocko and Phillippe Martinetti's imitation of a bullfrog in *The Magic Pills*. Medicine ads appearing directly next to the Ravel-Martinetti bills (which announce "physical feats") decry "Decay in Man and Woman" and proceed to describe a series of symptoms to be cured by Dr. Jacob Webber's "Invigorating Cordial."[24]

Significantly, newspapers record the second rise of the San Francisco Vigilance Committee parallel to the Ravel tour. Originally directed against pioneer lawlessness, the new San Francisco vigilantism, part of the transition from a rural to an urban America, found its enemies to be ethnic and religious minorities, labor leaders and laborers, and radicals. Under surface pronouncements of ethnic tolerance and good will, political alignments of San Francisco in 1855 and 1856 were representing the ethnic tensions of the most cosmopolitan city of the Western world. Against this background of San Francisco, "a seething cauldron of social, ethnic, religious and political tensions in an era of booming growth,"[25] The Ravel Company appeared with their seemingly trivial programs. On the night of November 15, the audience watched a demonstration by the Martinetti brothers of social antagonism mediated acceptably by boxing and the pantomime *Nicodemus* in which the clown flaunted anarchy with his disrupting actions. An Italian-Catholic gambler named Charles Cora (related to municipal corruption and crime) sat one row behind William Richardson, the U.S. Marshall, in the American Theatre.[26] Two days later, Cora shot Richardson for an alleged insult to his Belle Cora during the Ravel performance, and San Francisco's *Daily Evening Bulletin*, under the editorship of James King of William, fanned the event into an issue of social disorder needing vigilante justice.

Thus, the Ravel performances might be viewed as coming from and articulating a common view of the world in which social order and disorder were major concerns. This interplay of immediate everyday experience and its symbolic expression can be found in other aspects of the popular mind of the period. Parallel social content, whether from newspapers, oral tradition, or other contemporary cultural expressions, lets us view the popularity of The Ravel Company in California as its very efficient exploitation of a cultural network of symbols and metaphors. However, the proof of the vitality of a structural analytic approach to the Ravel repertoire will be when social context and structural system can be much more finely meshed. The implication from comparing the two contents (structural and cultural) is that they may be more related than we would otherwise have suspected. Analytic tools developed and used by anthropologists and folklorists such as Dundes, Propp, Levi-Strauss, and Bouissac will provide us with a means to examine dance and theatre beyond the static model of descriptive history. They will allow historians a perspective on the whole expressive behavior of a society and will force dance and theatre historians into interdisciplinary study. In using the structural analytic approach, our society's arts are not separate and peripheral—novelties, frills, and curiosities—but central pathways of communication and meaning. As theatre historians, we must look for deeper levels of logic that explain the disparity of the acts we have heard about and seen during this Conference. The meaning of these acts as cultural expression will be found when we can bring the act into alignment with the cultural context. We are not, as has been suggested here at one point, on a "nostalgia trip"; we are exploring elemental questions of cultural style and expression and, for the first time, we may have the methodological tools from other disciplines to carry our study forward.

NOTES

1. Ravel Troupe of Artists: Gabriel Ravel, Director and Principal Performer; Henry Wells, First Pantomimist and Dancer; M. Collet, Principal Dancer and Ballet Master; M. Blondin, First Grand Tightrope Performer; M. Dubouchet, Second Grand Tightrope Performer; M. Grossi, First Mime Serieux; M. Gilles, Leader of the Orchestra; M. Phillippe, M. Julien, M. Ignacio, Le Petit Carlo, and Le Petit Louis Martinetti, Tightrope, Acrobatics Feat Performers, and Pantomimists; M. Toledo, First Coryph; M'lle. Celestine Franck, First Danseuse; M'lle. Frances, Principal Danseuse, Demi-Caractere; M'lle. Capel, Second Danseuse, Demi-Caractere; Mlle. Desire; Second Danseuse and Mime; M'me. P. Martinetti, M'me. J. Martinetti, and M'me. Blondin, Mime and Coryphees. (From *The Marysville Herald*, December 12, 1855, p. 2, col. 4).

2. Their repertoire included at least twelve special aerial and balancing acts and demonstrations of physical prowess; eleven ballets; twenty-five pantomimes and various scenes thereof; two tableaux pieces; three special dances; one recitation from *Much Ado About Nothing*; one flagolet solo; and one Grand Divertissement.

3. David Grimsted, *Melodrama Unveiled* (Chicago: The University of Chicago Press, 1968), p. 100.

4. Ibid., p. 1.

5. Since this paper was written, new information has come to my attention

which would indicate that some Ravel family members returned to the United States to perform during the 1860s.

6. "The English harlequinade did not travel well, drawing as it did on London life and locale for its effectiveness, whereas the French used local color and themes from the new land." Bari Rolfe, "Mime in America, A Survey," *Mime Journal*, I (1974), p. 3.

7. Some of these companies were George H. Adams, Maffit and Batholomew, the Foster Brothers, G. E. Locke, the Siegrist Family, the Keller Troupe, the Famous Brothers Byrne, Robert Fraser, and later Tony Denier.

8. The Martinetti Family, whom the Ravels brought to the United States in 1848, had the authority to perform the Ravel repertoire and later used the Ravel name when the two families were not otherwise playing together. The Martinetti Family, unlike the Ravels, established a base in this country and continued pantomime and their various acts until the early twentieth century.

9. *The San Francisco Daily Herald*, November 9, 1855, p. 2, col. 4.

10. Ibid., November 10, 1855, p. 2. col. 2.

11. Ibid.

12. Ibid.

13. Ibid., November 30, 1855, p. 2, col. 2.

14. *The Daily San Francisco Herald*, November 15, 1855, p. 2, col. 1.

15. For instance, Phillippe Martinetti exhibited "turnings and twistings, leapings and grovellings, together with the very palpable gutta percha ribs and limbs that he possesses" as the Red Gnome. *The San Francisco Daily Herald*, November 15, 1855, p. 2, col. 1.

16. David Mayer, *Harlequin in His Element* (Cambridge, Mass.: Harvard University Press, 1969), pp. 19-74.

17. *The San Francisco Daily Herald*, November 21, 1855, p. 2, col. 2.

18. *The Daily State Tribune* (Sacramento), December 11, 1855, p. 2, col. 3.

19. Vladimir Propp, *Morphology of the Folktale* (Austin: University of Texas Press, 1968), p. xi.

20. Ibid.

21. Paul Bouissac, *Circus and Culture, A Semiotic Approach* (Bloomington: Indiana University Press, 1976), p. 90.

22. Ibid., p. 29.

23. Alan Dundes, "Projection in Folklore: A Plea for Psychoanalytic Semiotics," *Modern Language Notes*, 91 (1976), p. 1503.

24. *The San Francisco Daily Herald*, January 15, 1856, p. 1. col. 3.

25. Richard Maxwell Brown, *Strain of Violence* (New York: Oxford University Press, 1975), p. 135.

26. George R. MacMinn, *The Theater of the Golden Era in California* (Caldwell, Idaho: The Caxton Printers, Ltd., 1941), p. 195.

Suzanne Shelton

Ruth St. Denis: Dance
Popularizer with
"High Art" Pretensions_____

In March of 1919, the American dancer Ruth St. Denis paused in midlife and midcareer to assess her own artistry. She was forty years old, with a quarter-century of theatrical experience behind her. From modest beginnings in a dime museum in 1894, she had built a dance career in variety and in vaudeville and on the American and European concert stages. With her husband Ted Shawn she had founded Denishawn, the influential training school and traveling dance troupe that became the seedbed for American modern dance. Now, in 1919, as she looked back on those years of dancing, she wrote a letter of despair to her husband, with this observation: "The 'caviar to the many' is tragedy for the artist . . . and paradoxically my whole art life has been a slow tragedy."[1]

The nature of that tragedy, which became a bitter leitmotif for St. Denis's career, illustrates a deeper tension in American culture between two artistic modes, which I shall call "lowbrow" or popular art, and "highbrow" or fine art. Throughout her career, St. Denis was a popular artist, a genius of lowbrow, whose dance was born in dime museums, in outdoor spectacles, in the Delsarte movement, in variety, and in vaudeville. Yet she longed for the heady world of highbrow art, for the private concerts in wealthy homes, for the esoteric experiments before groups of friends, for the privacy of the rehearsal hall. Torn between the artistic freedom of highbrow and the financial rewards of popular art, she financed her creative experiments through frequent forays into vaudeville. She never enjoyed that schizophrenic existence and periodically announced her retirement from vaudeville, as she did in that letter of March 1919. Yet, from the moment of her 1894 debut, Ruth St. Denis's art was rooted in popular entertainments.

Let me clarify the distinction between highbrow and lowbrow as it evolved in St. Denis's mind. Early in her career, she made the distinction only in terms of externals or context—as we are still prone to do. If the seedy Worth's Museum where St. Denis made her debut was "lowbrow," then the glamorous and gilded Metropolitan Opera House clearly was "highbrow," even if the dancing inside were much the same. For that reason, when St. Denis landed her first job in 1894, her mother wrote her father apologetically that the dime museum catered to "the respectable working classes for there is but one other place and that is the 'Opera House.'"[2] The difference to the Dennises between highbrow and lowbrow was that simple, a difference of social class, of economic and institutional clout. Yet, as Ruth St. Denis matured, and long after she danced at the highbrow Metropolitan, she began to value a broader distinction between popular and fine art—one that it is useful for us to consider.

Popular art is that art which mirrors a culture, reflecting its self-image and confirming its beliefs. Fine art, on the other hand, poses questions for a culture, inverts its formulas or transcends them, offering new self-definitions.[3] If popular art is a cultural mirror, and fine art a cultural weathervane, then theme and form become dominant concerns, and we sometimes find quite experimental art in a popular entertainment context. Particularly this seems true of late nineteenth-century dance, where a good deal of pre-modern dance experimentation seems to have occurred in variety and in vaudeville, as well as in the concert hall. It was this sort of individual, exploratory art that St. Denis longed to create, but ultimately this has not been viewed as her major role in American dance. Unlike her contemporary Isadora Duncan, who revolutionized the vocabulary of movement, St. Denis is remembered as essentially a dance popularizer, and while her art may have had its revolutionary aspects, the themes and structure of her dances were those of popular art. The formula for a St. Denis dance, in essence, was this: Goddess sits on elevated throne, lost in meditation; Goddess descends from throne; dances a dance of sensuality; overcomes that earthly temptation; and reascends to the throne to resume her meditation. For American audiences in the early part of this century, such dances offered all the voyeuristic pleasures of watching this most physical of art forms, with the reassurance that the the dance actually was a spiritual exercise. The double-edged message in St. Denis's art tapped an important need on the part of American audiences—the need for a morale rationale for art.

The cultural roots of the need to legitimize the arts is best outlined in Neil Harris's book, *The Artist in American Society*, where he discusses an American political philosophy which equated art with luxury and privilege, the Puritan suspicion of sensory pleasures and waste, and the geographical isolation that bred conservatism in the arts.[4] Born of these cultural conditions, American art developed an inherent tone of apology, and the popular entertainments that gave rise to Ruth St. Denis's art share the climate of rationalization, as we shall see.

As a countercurrent to the moral rationalization, American art of the transition period in the late nineteenth century also reflected the search for

Delsartean scarf tableaux pictured in *Werner's Magazine*.

new aesthetic forms, the pursuit of art for its own sake. In dance, the search took the form of a quest for a dynamic impetus—a dynamo if you will—for an art form that had become static and pictorial. Late nineteenth-century dance was a collection of images that needed a connecting thread, a movement impulse—and for this reason that period in dance may be likened to the evolution of photography into film. We see the photographic sense in the popular dances of St. Denis's day, but we also see in those popular entertainments the urge to transcend static boundaries, to set dance moving again. Those two concerns—a dynamic for dance and a moral rationale—were important, often conflicting impulses in the popular entertainments that fostered St. Denis's art.

The first of the popular influences on St. Denis's dancing was the Delsarte movement which in the 1880s and 1890s encompassed every aspect of self-expression from elocution to statue posing to gymnastics, hygiene, and dress reform.[5] There was a Delsarte corset on the market and a magazine for devotees called *Werner's,* but what interests us most is the nascent dancing that was disguised as Delsartean hygienic exercise. The Delsarte movement began with the studies of François Delsarte, a French professor of declamation, whose theories were brought to America in 1870 by the actor-playwright Steele MacKaye.[6] Delsarte had analyzed gesture and motivation, and in his cornerstone Law of Correspondences stated that for each bodily gesture there is a corresponding inner emotional state.[7] Steele MacKaye imported the Delsarte system as a training tool for actors, but two of his disciples took Delsartism into the realm of dance and became direct influences on the adolescent Ruthie Dennis. One of these disciples, Aurilla Colcord Poté, maintained a studio in Carnegie Hall, where she taught reading, dramatic art, vocal and physical culture, with "particular attention to the alleviation of nervous trouble."[8] Ruth St. Denis's mother, who was ever plagued by nervous trouble, discovered Madame Poté and passed on her teachings to Ruthie, who studied Delsarte exercises from a manual on her New Jersey farm.[9] Another MacKaye disciple, Genevieve Stebbins, became an even more important influence on Ruthie Dennis through her Delsarte concerts.

Stebbins was but the most polished practitioner of a popular entertainment form based on Delsarte which flourished in late nineteenth-century America. Statue posing and tableaux vivant became a favorite recital form for schoolgirls, who imitated Greek statues or formed Biblical tableaux or presented Delsarte gestures before their school assemblies.[10] Ruthie Dennis probably tried statue posing herself, for on the faculty of Packer's Collegiate Institute, which she attended, was a staunch Delsartist who specialized in such assemblies.[11] A racier version of the schoolgirls' statue posing was the "living statues" of variety, which, in the 1890s, offered models clad in nothing but bronze body powder, assuming vaguely Grecian poses.[12] Another popular variety act, known as "living pictures," arranged models into familiar scenes, such as "Rebecca at the Well," and displayed them onstage inside huge, immobile and ornate frames.[13] These static, pictorial arrangements verge on dance, but it remained for the talented Delsartist Genevieve Stebbins to discover a motivational force by which these statues could come to life.

Stebbins was the foremost Delsarte popularizer, the principal of the New York School of Expression, and author of several Delsarte texts.[14] In one of her books, *Dynamic Breathing and Harmonic Gymnastics,* written in 1893, she discussed the origins of human motion and the importance of the spiral movement form. "There is no such thing as a straight line in the nascent life of nature," Stebbins wrote, "so the spiral motion is the type of

Genevieve Stebbins in the Grecian garb worn in her statue-posing concerts, 1893. From *Werner's Magazine*.

life."[15] She had observed the torsional movement of an Oriental dancer and felt that "her slowly shifting weight coupled with the natural balance of head, arm, and torso, produces the spiral line from every point of view."[16] From that observation, Stebbins explored the spiral form, a three-dimensional movement which contained the seeds of its own evolution, and for this reason the Delsartist may be our earliest "modern dancer." If modernism in the arts means anything, it means the incorporation of time values, and Stebbins's statue posing transcended static nineteenth-century dance and brought dancing into the twentieth century.

Stebbins's yearly Delsarte matinees at Madison Square Theatre were highbrow versions of the statue posing on the variety stage, and during one of those concerts in 1892 Ruthie Dennis was in the audience and witnessed what she later called "the real birth of my art life."[17] During the concert, Stebbins performed a Delsarte pantomime called "Myth of Isis," which re-enacted the cycle of life in ancient Egypt.[18] Ruth St. Denis remembered especially Stebbins's "Dance of Day," in which the Delsartean interpreted the cycle of a single day in pantomime. The curtain rose on a forest scene. Stebbins slept upstage in the pose of a Greek statue. She rose, unfolded from sleep, reached the zenith of noon, began to wilt as the setting sun, then sank back into sleep.[19] This series of linked Delsarte poses became a blueprint for St. Denis's own first dance composition more than a decade later. Her first choreography, "Egypta," was "an epic dance typifying the life of man as revealed by the progress of the Sun in its journey through night and day,"[20] and as the dance evolved it came to include a section also called "Dance of Day."[21] If Stebbins and the Delsarte movement were inspirations for St. Denis's "Egypta," another source may have been a second form of popular entertainment which affected St. Denis's art.

In the summer of 1892, a family friend took the thirteen-year-old Ruthie Dennis to the Eldorado family resort on the Jersey Palisades, where they saw the outdoor spectacle *Egypt Through Centuries.* The succession of colorful tableaux chronicled "110 centuries of Egyptian culture" and opened with a scene in which the gods Osiris and Isis demanded the sacrifice of a virgin in the River Nile.[22] The chosen victim dramatically ascended a sacred altar which loomed above the outdoor stage, and from its heights she indicated the four points of the Universe before flinging herself into the Nile. In the next moment, hundreds of ballerinas filled the stage for the Grand Ballet of the Virgins, and as one critic wrote, "there is a swirl of skirts and 500 agile limbs shoot out and up in unison with the leader. Backward and forward they go, now to one side, then to the other like a piece of animated machinery."[23] While this typically static and mechanized nineteenth-century ballet offered Ruth St. Denis its pictorial qualities and spectacle, she also borrowed its pseudo religiosity, its exoticism, and its heroine's virginal persona.

THE BALLET OF THE VIRGINS.

"The Ballet of the Virgins" from *Egypt Through Centuries*. Courtesy of Hoblitzelle Theatre Arts Library, Humanities Research Center, University of Texas at Austin.

Only a year after Ruthie Dennis saw *Egypt Through Centuries* and the Stebbins concert, she made her own debut at Worth's Museum, a combination curio hall and variety theatre which catered to a family trade. While the Delsartists leaned on the Greek classics for an aura of respectability, and outdoor spectacles presented themselves as history lessons or travelogues, Worth's Museum disguised its popular entertainment as moralizing scholarship. The museum, according to its advertisements, offered "just what the moral and religious portion of the community want, an unobjectionable place of amusement where every one can go and be highly entertained, instructed, and satisfied."[24] "Professor" E. M. Worth had traveled the world gathering his collection of curios, rare coins, historical relics, living curiosities and grotesqueries such as a "human billiard ball." A "lecturer" guided the paying public through the dimly lit displays in the museum into an amusements hall which offered continuous variety acts and a "Grand Sacred Concert" on Sundays. On that stage, during the week of January 29, 1894, the dancer "Ruth," later billed as "The Only Ruth," made her debut on a bill with an equilibrist-juggler, an albino musician, and Lillie the Trick Dog.[25] Ruth's dance consisted of acrobatics—rollovers, skin-the-cats, and splits—the sort of dancing common in variety, dancing which seemed deceptively simple and superficial.

Looking beyond the surface sensationalism, the exoticism, and exhibitionism of this early variety dance, we find experimentation with gravity, with spatial illusion, and with the qualities of light. "Aerial ballets" in 1894 featured dancers suspended from wires on pulleys, their antics bathed in colored lights.[26] With the development of electric stage lighting, Loie Fuller and her imitators pioneered the "serpentine dance," which dominated variety dance during the 1880s and 1890s.[27] In rippling silks, the serpentine dance became a backdrop for the play of moving light, a clever inversion of the vaudevillian's shadowgraph hand tricks which projected animated silhouettes onto a blank screen.[28] One serpentine dancer, Miss Bertha Fisch, performed at Union Square Theatre in 1894 while Ruthie Dennis danced on the nearby Casino stage. Miss Fisch's act took place before a black backdrop with an elliptical aperture through which she danced, illuminated by a backlight.[29] A fancier arrangement belonged to the immensely popular dancer Papinta, who used mirrors to multiply her form, as well as an illuminated glass trap door through which, unfortunately, she fell in 1895, temporarily ending her career.[30] Another variety artist of St. Denis's day, Amatti, perfected a "kaleidoscopic bicycle dance" which attempted to extend her own movement into the fourth dimension.[31] These experiments were the precursors of modern dance, and even as Ruth St. Denis disdained her popular entertainment origins, her art emerged from that milieu.

To St. Denis, vaudeville was lowbrow and antiart, and even though her 1919 retirement was short-lived, she never made her peace with popular

Ruth Dennis ("The Only Ruth") as a skirt dancer, ca. 1896, before she became Ruth St. Denis. Courtesy of Hoblitzelle Theatre Arts Library, Humanities Research Center, University of Texas at Austin.

entertainments. A crisis of sorts occurred in 1927 when St. Denis, her husband, and students joined the traveling company of the Ziegfeld Follies as a featured attraction on a nationwide tour.[32] St. Denis was depressed enough about the grueling lowbrow tour, but during a stop in Sweetwater, Texas, she felt the full force of the tragedy of her career. At issue was her dance "White Jade," perhaps the finest of her solo compositions, a study in stillness, almost non-dance in its meditative abstraction.[33] "White Jade" was an exploration of the lines of Chinese art, and while it had some of the familiar components of St. Denis's popular dances—the pictorial qualities, the explicit hand gestures miming the blossoming of lotuses, the exotic aura—"White Jade" went beyond popular art into the realm of fine art. This dance transcended predictable pattern and drew the viewer into the interface between life and art—that charged stillness—which characterizes much of Oriental art. St. Denis referred to "the held vibrations of the body" at the beginning of the dance and insisted, "I am not just standing there. I am dancing."[34] But the management of the Follies tour thought otherwise and asked her to eliminate "White Jade" from the program. St. Denis was crushed, and while she rationalized her defeat as "casting pearls before swine," she again turned to her husband for an answer to her fine art-popular art dilemma. Ted Shawn's response was that "White Jade" was remote from the common experience of the American public and required on their part "the concentration of aesthetic seeing." The dance, he told her, was too abstract, too purely aesthetic, and it could not survive in a popular entertainment context.[35]

St. Denis may have accepted that explanation, but she never ceased trying to bring the two worlds together, to make the American public tap its own highbrow aesthetic and philosophical potential. Frustrated throughout her long career, which continued almost until her death in 1968, St. Denis found a half-satisfactory solution in later years by performing religious dances in churches, where the freedom to create also carried with it a ready-made audience and moral sanction. Ruth St. Denis was a popular dancer with fine-art aspirations, and in many ways the story of her career is the story of the tensions of American art.

NOTES

1. Letter from Ruth St. Denis to Ted Shawn, March 25, 1919, Ruth St. Denis Correspondence, The Dance Collection, New York Public Library at Lincoln Center, New York (hereafter referred to as NYPL Coll.).

2. Undated letter from Ruth Dennis to "Dear Boy," St. Denis Correspondence, NYPL Coll.

3. Among the many sources which suggest this distinction is William Stott, *Documentary Expression and Thirties America* (New York: Oxford University Press, 1973).

4. Neil Harris, *The Artist in American Society: The Formative Years, 1790-1860,* 1966 (Rpt. New York: Clarion Books, 1970).

5. For an excellent survey of the Delsarte movement, see Nancy Chalfa Ruyter, "American Delsartism: Precursor of an American Dance Art," *Educational Theatre Journal,* vol. 25, no. 4 (December 1973), pp. 421-35.

6. The primary sources for Delsarte theory are Abbé Delaumosne, *The Delsarte System of Oratory,* 1882 (Rpt. New York: Edgar S. Werner, 1893); Genevieve Stebbins, *The Delsarte System of Expression* (New York: Edgar S. Werner, 1885); and Ted Shawn, *Every Little Movement* (Pittsfield, Mass.: The Eagle Printing and Binding Company, 1954). Delsarte himself did not publish a text, though Stebbins includes one of his addresses in her *Delsarte System.* MacKaye never wrote a Delsarte text of his own, but there is valuable information in Percy MacKaye, *Epoch,* 2 vols. (New York: Boni and Liveright, 1927).

7. Stebbins, *Delsarte System of Expression,* p. 67.

8. "Aurilla Colcord Pote," *Werner's Magazine,* vol. 18, no. 12 (December 1896), p. 1185.

9. Interview of Ruth St. Denis by Shirley and Earl Ubell, phonotape 7-56, NYPL Coll.

10. For photographs and notes on such exercises, see *Werner's Magazine* (1879-1902), which covered music, drama, oratory, elocution, expression, the Delsarte system, and various aspects of vocal physiology and hygiene.

11. Notes, *Werner's Magazine,* vol. 17, no. 7 (July 1895), p. 542, identifies Miss Helen K. Alt-Muller as director of the department of elocution.

12. Editorial note on "Living Pictures," *Werner's Magazine,* vol. 17, no. 4 (April 1895), p. 305.

13. "Theatres at Ebb Tide," *New York Sun* (July 4, 1894), 1894 clipbook, Hoblitzelle Theatre Arts Collection, University of Texas at Austin (hereafter referred to as Hob. Coll.).

14. For a broader study of Stebbins, and amplification of other points in this article, see Suzanne Shelton, "The Influence of Genevieve Stebbins on the Early Career of Ruth St. Denis," to be published in *Dance Research Annual* (formerly the *CORD Journal*).

15. Genevieve Stebbins, *Dynamic Breathing and Harmonic Gymnastics* (New York: Edgar S. Werner, 1893), pp. 61-63.

16. Ibid.

17. Ruth St. Denis, *An Unfinished Life* (New York: Harper and Brothers, 1939), p. 16.

18. "Genevieve Stebbins' Recital," *Werner's Magazine,* vol. 17, no. 5 (May 1895), p. 388.

19. Interview with Ruth St. Denis by Walter Terry, phonotape 7-57, 1960, NYPL Coll.

20. Ruth Dennis, *Egypta,* Library of Congress, Washington, D.C.

21. Programme, New Amsterdam Theatre, December 12, 1910; Ruth St. Denis clip file, Reference Room, NYPL.

22. "Egypt Through Centuries" souvenir programme, New Jersey File, Hob. Coll.

23. "New Dance at El Dorado," *New York Herald* (August 2, 1892), 1892 clip book, Hob. Coll.

24. Programme, Worth's Museum, August 29, 1891; Variety Theatre file, Hob. Coll.

25. Stage Notes in *New York Clipper*, vol. 41, no. 48 (February 3, 1894), p. 769.

26. "Amusements," *New York Sun* (September 14, 1894), 1894 clipbook, Hob. Coll.

27. See J. E. Crawford Flitch, "The Serpentine Dance," *Modern Dancing and Dancers* (Philadelphia: J. B. Lippincott Company, 1912), pp. 81-88.

28. Douglas Gilbert, *American Vaudeville: Its Life and Times,* 1940 (Rpt. New York: Dover Books, 1963), p. 173.

29. "The Shows of August," *New York Sun* (August 1, 1894), 1894 clip book, Hob. Coll.

30. "Fell Through a Glass Trap," *New York Dramatic Mirror,* vol. 35, no. 885 (December 14, 1895), p. 13.

31. "Matters of Fact," *New York Dramatic Mirror,* vol. 35, no. 885 (December 14, 1895), p. 17.

32. The "White Jade" episode on the Follies tour is recounted in journals of Ruth St. Denis, October-November 1927, Ruth St. Denis Collection, Research Library, University of California at Los Angeles (hereafter referred to as UCLA Coll.). Also see "Individual versus Institution" discussion in Margerie Lyon, ed., "Denis-Shawn Dialogue," December 12, 1927, Theodore Perceval Gerson Collection, University of California at Los Angeles.

33. See the Philip Baribault film, "White Jade," Film 2-568, NYPL Coll.

34. Ruth St. Denis, "Our Book" journal, December 14, 1935, Box 37, UCLA Coll.

35. Lyon, *Denis-Shawn Dialogue,* p. 3.

ENVIRONMENTAL ENTERTAINMENT (AMUSEMENT PARKS AND THEME PARKS)

James H. Bierman

Disneyland and the "Los Angelization" of the Arts _____

Amusement parks in the United States underwent a thorough revolution in 1955 with the opening of Disneyland in Anaheim, California. In accordance with Walt Disney's intentions, the familiar arrangement of roller coasters, ferris wheels, game arcades, and cotton candy booths were replaced by environments specifically designed to allow their visitors to live out vicariously exotic fantasies of adventurous lives in remote and attractive places. The previously predictable repertoire of thrills offered by amusement parks was expanded infinitely as a result of the example set by Disneyland. It became possible to visit exotic cities, explore haunted mansions, ride through pirate-infested corners of the Caribbean, cruise up dangerous jungle rivers, travel to the moon (later to Mars), or sip a soda in the quaint ice cream parlor of an old midwestern town—all in the space of one afternoon, and without leaving an urban area. After Disneyland came a great variety of parks designed to lead the visitor into one world of fantasy or another: Marineland, Sea World, Africa U.S.A., Six Flags Over Texas, Walt Disney World, Great America, Magic Mountain, and Knott's Berry Farm.

Eighty million people visit these parks annually, exhibiting an appetite for fantasy of such magnitude that other industries have been enticed into the business of theme parks if they have available to them any exotic images that can be marketed. Knott's Berry Farm, the Bush Breweries, Universal Studios, Burbank Studios, NBC, and numerous other businesses opened for tours and geared themselves to provide entertainment for enormous crowds of visitors. At present, three million people annually visit Universal City. Another great attraction among parks is Forest Lawn Memorial Park in Los Angeles. With its talking statuary, its enormous and elaborate monuments and museums, and its variety of daily shows, it has become a Disneyland of the dead, catering to millions of viewers a year.

While theme parks have developed throughout the United States and even abroad, their concentration remains in the sun-belt states of the South and West, with the nexus in the Los Angeles basin. The Orange County area on the southern edge of Los Angeles is so rich in such attractions that visitors often come and establish themselves in a motel for a week or more, visiting one or two major amusement parks a day. As a result, fully appointed places like Magic Mountain in Valencia, California, on the northern side of the city, are presently often wanting for customers, while overflow crowds circulate through the numerous parks along Beach Boulevard forty-five miles to the south. Not only are the parks concentrated in the Los Angeles basin, but within that area they are grouped toward the southern end. For the most part, theme parks are the children of the Los Angeles basin and, like many elements of California life, they are spreading rapidly across the country. In his play *Muzeeka*, John Guare has one of his characters speak of the spread of his Los Angeles-based business as follows: "Our cesspools powered by the sun—spreading out from Los Angeles like an ink blot on an enormous United States-shaped blotter."*

This image of the "Los Angelization" of the United States works equally for the spread of Disneyland-type amusement parks. Many of the characteristics of these parks are particularly related to their place of origin, and, as a result, the culture and aesthetic they spread with them are also part of the greater Los Angelization of America. A look at the design of such places as Disneyland, Knott's Berry Farm, and Forest Lawn Cemetery reveals that the entertainment offered there makes comprehensible several characteristics of the general Los Angeles area which are normally unfathomable because of their scope and scale. These characteristics were particularly unique to Los Angeles when Disneyland opened, but they are now becoming part of the urban environment of almost every major city in the country.

An entire amusement park is an organization of attractions. They may all be grouped into one specialized thematic area in the case of Marineland, or Africa U.S.A., or Universal Studios, where a single dominant fantasy incorporates several subdivisions, or they may be arranged into their own special areas. Disneyland, for example has a main street from which radiates a series of contiguous sub-parks: Frontierland, New Orleans Square, Fantasyland, Bear Country, Tomorrowland, and Adventureland. Knott's Berry Farm is divided into a Shopping Area, the Roaring Twenties, Fiesta Village, and an Old West Ghost Town. Within these areas, rides, shopping, food stands, restaurants, and other attractions all relate to a single dominant theme or fantasy. Together they form a mother environment in which each of the various attractions seems at home. It is intended that there be a specialness to the sub-areas and to the park as a whole that permits experiences which are not common to everyday life.

*John Guare, *Muzeeka*, in *Showcase 1*, ed. John Lahr (New York: Grove Press, 1970), p. 217.

Much is done to assure this specialness: first, through the creation of expectations through media (Walt Disney created the *Mickey Mouse Show* to provide national publicity for Disneyland); and second, through the design of the overall environment. During a day at Disneyland, visitors are always referred to as guests not customers, and they walk through streets and buildings that are scaled down to 5/8 normal size to make them seem more suited to human proportions. Guests entering the Magic Kingdoms are either sold a book of tickets which serve them throughout the day as play money to buy their entry to the various attractions as is the case in Disneyland and Knott's Berry Farm, or they are given blanket passes to all the attractions as is the case at Magic Mountain. In either event, they are spared an entire day of reaching into their pockets to pay out money, once they pass the gates. Every chair, wastepaper basket, sign, and doorway fits the total environment in some unusual way. Transportation is available on double-decker buses, fire engines, horse-drawn carts, submarines, racing cars, monorails, canoes, rafts, paddle boats, and funiculars; but beyond the vast parking lots, nothing is found that resembles an ordinary automobile. This total environment of specialness—inviting people to live as they do not normally live—is more concentrated within many of the attractions themselves.

For the most part, the old thrill rides of the pre-1955 amusement parks have been either replaced by dramatic attractions or have been augmented to include drama. Despite Walt Disney's desire to exclude roller coasters, one has recently opened in Disneyland. Unlike roller coasters elsewhere, Space Mountain provides a carefully designed environment which incorporates the time and space used for standing in line as well as for the ride itself. What is unique about Space Mountain is the environment through which the roller coaster moves. Being entirely enclosed, there is darkness surrounding the ride. The disorientation produced as the car plummets through darkness without any cues to allow the rider to anticipate the sudden curves, banks, or plunges ahead is enhanced by a series of colored lights that whiz past in seemingly abstract patterns and accentuate the feeling of speed. This effect resembles a section of the ride on the "people-mover," in which the rider is surrounded by film projections that were taken from vehicles moving at enormous velocities—an effect designed to create the sensation of speed. At Space Mountain, it is more thrilling because of the basic disorientation of the darkness and because of the abstract "galactic" sounds piped in on top of it.

Most of the major attractions at Disneyland take the form of theatrical events involving some sort of performance. Some, such as *America Sings* and *Country Bear Jamboree*, are musical review. Others, like *The Carousel of Progress*, *Great Moments with Mr. Lincoln*, and *Journey to Mars*, feature realistic performances, while *Pirates of the Caribbean* and *The Haunted*

Mansion are less realistic. All the events are entirely automated, even down to the performers who, for the most part, are automata. These events are designed so that the spectator, in one way or another, becomes a participant in the action of the event. In *Journey to Mars,* for example, the visitors are led in past a space control center where they observe the preparations for a launching. After that, they enter a simulated space ship and take an adventure-filled journey to Mars and back in the space of a few moments. In another attraction, they travel through a microscope which continually reduces their size as they penetrate a drop of water. They are finally reduced to the size of nuclear particles while protons, neutrons, and electrons whirr around them at dizzying speeds. In the *Pirates of the Caribbean,* the audience travels on a series of boats through a particularly raucous and dangerous section of the pirate-infested Caribbean. In addition to riding down pre-cipitous waterfalls, they pass through scenes of pillaging, drunkenness, open warfare, and general rowdiness, as well as observing the macabre spectacles of tarantulas and skeletons guarding old treasures. At one point along this perilous journey, as the audience rides through a burning edifice, one of the beams above seems to break loose and fall on the passenger boat. It is caught at the last instant, before it crushes the spectator, by an un-burnt fragment of a supporting timber.

Other attractions involve the audience in similar manners. While travel-ing through *The Haunted Mansion,* the spectators find themselves sinking through false floors, being attacked by numerous leaping goblins and ghouls, and even picking up an occasional hitchhiking ghost in their carts as they ride past. Even the musical review *America Sings* involves this sort of ride as well as a show, and the audience is moved in their seats through two hundred years of American songs performed by more than one hundred singing animals from various regions of the United States. The same is true at *It's a Small World,* where spectators travel by boat through a world of children's songs, going from country to country. At Disneyland, the effort to involve the audience physically in the action is a part of almost every major recurrent attraction. *America the Beautiful,* for example, offers a filmed journey through a variety of American tourist landmarks. The Disney crews filmed the locations almost entirely from moving vehicles (airplanes, boats, trucks) with nine specially mounted cameras arranged so that the projected picture completely surrounds the audience. This sur-rounding image is so engaging that the spectators at times need metal supports to hold themselves upright as the images are taken from a tilted airplane moving through a Utah canyon.

The effort to involve the audience in the action is not unique to Disney-land. Several of the attractions at Knott's Berry Farm show obvious traces of the Disney model. Even the Los Angeles Wax Museums, in which the performing figures don't move, demonstrate the same emphasis. The figures

are grouped into areas within the museums that correspond to the "kingdoms" of a Disneyland. There is a chamber of horrors, a hall of religion,
and discrete sections for presidents, movie stars, historical figures, and so
on. The wax figures are presented in environments that resemble stage
settings, with entire scenes reenacted but frozen as if caught in a dramatic
moment. It is this insistence on dramatic action frozen in an intense moment
that makes Leonardo da Vinci's *The Last Supper* a favorite subject for wax
museum scenes. To welcome the audience into such scenes, the environment is extended to include not only the figures but also the viewer. Thus
the visitor enters the chamber of horrors through dark stone walls, or
crosses a moat to pass through the castle gates of storyland. It is probably
even part of the design of the San Francisco Wax Museum that the spectator
must travel one flight of stairs heavenward to enter the hall of religions.
Within these environments, the sequence of tableaux are designed to
provide a continuity resembling a three-dimensional cartoon strip. Like the
rapid sequence of still images that form a motion picture, they create action
in their interplay. One unique characteristic of the shows found in such
places as Disneyland is that their design is normally more important than
the writing itself. They are first conceived in terms of the spacial concepts
they embody and then presented as story boards rather than scripts. The
physical manipulation of audience and performers in time and space is more
important than the development of plot and character, partly because the
business of the parks involves routing thousands of people through space,
and largely because of the attitudes created by a larger environment which
is set up to be seen in motion.

Since amusement parks like Disneyland are organized to handle as many
as 40,000 people a day, the basic shows must be repeated often. Some attractions involve portions of action that are repeated as many as twenty times
an hour. These sequences of environmental theatre require no ordinary
actor. In fact, the performers have been replaced by machines much more
capable of meeting the demands placed on them than are human beings.
A rich variety of robot performers impersonate people and animals
throughout Disneyland. Some are extremely lifelike and may be viewed
much as wax museum figures set in motion or Disney's famous animation
carried into three dimensions. So much of Disneyland is automated that
many of the feature attractions are capable of running entirely without
attendants. They are controlled from a central computer bank located in a
vault under Main Street U.S.A. The ushers and usherettes, ticket takers,
and other attendants contribute to the shows like the bits of parsley sitting
on a dinner plate. They are more decorative than functional.

Enormous investments have gone into creating these automated environmental theatres. Each robot show in Disneyland costs approximately six
million dollars, and that sum represents only a fraction of the technological

expenses that made those shows possible. At present, the robots need only be designed and built. After their completion, they can be made to dance and sing by connecting them to an elaborate console that allows control of their movement and records or erases these movements as desired until a progam for their movement can be created and fed into the complex digital control system that governs their performance. At a later stage, the program will also govern all the robots performing simultaneously, as well as the other cues involved, such as lighting and sound. Nothing is subject to the possibility of human error.

It is inevitable that artists would be challenged by the apparently dehumanizing notion of fully automated theatrical performances. Acting is considered to be a particularly human endeavor which involves the expression of deep personal feelings, and it is difficult to imagine how machines could replace people in this function, even if they have the capability of exactly reproducing a person's movements. Robot theatre offers an extreme case of the general threat of automation, in which humans are replaced by computers. It must be remembered, however, that machines will only do what their designers and builders and users have them do and that the final responsibility lies with the artists or workers behind them. Robots are no more responsible for their performances than a typewriter is responsible for the books written on it or a car is responsible for where it is driven. Machines can extend human capabilities; they do not assume responsibility for the way in which those extended capabilities are used.

Certain general characteristics that dominate the environmental design of the Disneyland-style amusement park can easily be seen as a reflection of the region in which they originated. These characteristics reproduce on a comprehensible scale elements that totally permeate the Los Angeles basin but that are so present and so widely spread that they normally go unnoticed. The first of these elements is that of extreme diversity in architectural styles and in the fantasies inherent in these styles. Many of us imagine an immense plane of parallel streets with similar suburban houses, shopping centers, car lots, boulevards, and freeways when we picture Los Angeles. While this image may conform to the reality of the outlying areas, it does not fit for Los Angeles proper. In fact, Los Angeles is not homogeneous in its architectural use, but rather mixes a monumentally extreme diversity of styles and pretenses in its structures. It is almost as if an effort to avoid anonymity, buildings are forced to scream for attention by being outrageous in style and as different as possible from their neighbors. In the Hollywood Hills, for example, one finds a Romanesque, Spanish tile-roof home next to a square modern one, next to a Tudor mansion, next to a Gothic stone structure. Rather than a uniformity of style, diversity is the rule. This is particularly visible when traveling through the section of Los Angeles that has spread to nearly every American city—the strip. Usually located toward the expanding edge of a city, the strip is a wide boulevard of fast-food places, car lots, shopping centers, and often motels. It is practically ubiquitous in Los Angeles. Just looking at the fast-food buildings reveals an enormous diversity of styles with a wide range of fantasies incorporated into them. Taco Bell, Tio Taco, Moby Taco, and so on are neo-Romanesque Mexican hovels with red tiled roofs. Der Wienerschnitzel is a Bavarian chalet with a steeply pitched bright red roof. Jack in the Box is a building constructed to resemble a child's large toy box with a doll figure popping out of the top. McDonald's mixes American and Danish modern functional styles, and so on. The strip is often lined with eating places that resemble railroad stations, windmills, light houses, airplanes, and other familiar structures or objects. These bits of Los Angeles popular architecture are designed for instant iconic recognition from the street. The fantasies implied in them are immediately read, and their demand for attention is unquestionably satisfied. They are built in a variety of styles with no regard for materials because all the materials used are synthetic; therefore, building styles that were previously limited to Mexico, Bavaria, or Normandy because of the indigenous materials available are now easily imitated in southern California. Above all, these buildings are highly visible advertisements for themselves. Rather than be dominated by huge signs, they become their own signs. In sum, a person driving around Los Angeles past Abyssinian palaces, Polynesian tiki houses, Swiss chalets, and Mexican hovels experiences, in diluted form, the environment of a Disneyland.

This experience is heightened by the fact that Los Angeles has no effective central downtown area. It has instead a series of linear centers determined by several major long boulevards, some of them thirty to forty miles long. Along these boulevards are strung like beads most of the city's major buildings, shopping centers, and neighborhoods. A ride down Wilshire Boulevard or Beach Boulevard reveals extreme diversity in neighborhoods and rapid transitions. Two blocks of elegant interior design studios are rapidly followed by three blocks of pornographic movie houses and magazine stores. Although there are some general concentrations of the rich and the poor, this diversity of neighborhoods is also true of residential areas where different racial, ethnic, and income groups rapidly replace each other in a few blocks' space. The enormous diversity of extreme neighborhoods, either commercial or residential, is easily experienced in a concentrated form in Disneyland, where Frontierland, New Orleans Square, Adventureland, Fantasyland, Bear Country, and Tomorrowland are all adjacent to Main Street, U.S.A. In Disneyland, diversity creates the appearance of a richness of options for entertainment.

Essential to the entire structure of the Los Angeles basin is the automobile. The city is spread out over 450 square miles, but transportation provides the links that connect its diverse corners. Freeways and boulevards sew the

A

B

C

Examples of Los Angeles commercial architecture, which embody fantasy in their design. Courtesy of Environmental Communications.

enormous patchwork quilt together. As a result, the environments of the city are designed to be experienced in motion, and such places as the fast-food establishments or motels are forced to take on an identity that is easily recognizable from the street. This is also true of Disneyland. All its main events are designed to be seen in motion. With few exceptions, all the main performance attractions are also rides, so that the audience is insistently moved through its events, both literally and figuratively. Transportation systems are essential to Disneyland, and one of the reasons it has been capable of handling thirty to forty thousand visitors a day is that Walt Disney Productions has found effective ways to move that many people without bottlenecks, long lines, or delays. If there is one area where urban designers could learn from Disneyland, it is in the realm of public transportation. Peoplemovers, trains, submarines, monorails, buses, wagons, carts: all keep large numbers of people moving through a limited space without problems. There are few long lines in Disneyland, and the pleasure of the place begins with leaving your car behind in the enormous parking area and taking a tram to the entrance gate.

Disneyland shares a great amount with the general Los Angeles environment—extreme variety in design styles, an insistence on fantasy in design, environments that are intended to be experienced in motion, and the involvement of people in the action by moving them through the areas in which it takes place. It was originally built on 160 acres of orange-grove land beyond the southern edge of Los Angeles, and within a few years has

Custom-designed car, demonstrating an emphasis on fantasy equal to that embodied in commercial architecture. Courtesy of Environmental Communications.

been surrounded by a sea of spin-off attractions, restaurants, and motels. The directors of WED Enterprises (for Walter Elias Disney), the managers of the magic kingdoms, learned their lesson and built their next establishment, Walt Disney World, considerably larger (forty-three square miles). Now they are expanding further to a resort at Lake Independence, California, and to a new kingdom on Tokyo Bay in Japan.

Amusement parks are big business. Without any reduction in their film earnings over the past twenty-two years, Walt Disney Productions' income from amusement parks has grown to about 75 percent of their total earnings. Large corporations such as Marriott Hotels Inc., M.C.A., and Six Flags Over Texas, Inc., have moved into the business, and the parks are expanding in a way that resembles the urbanization process that dominated Los Angeles' growth for decades. It is obvious that urban sprawl is lasting. Investments in growth are so great that they must produce long-term results to be fully amortized. Not only that, but expansion begets expansion, and it is clearly evident that we are only at the early stages of an era of larger and larger amusement parks of the Disneyland variety.

It is often said that amusement parks achieve their appeal because they offer visitors quick and easy access to the experience of worlds far removed from their own. In reality, the fantasies designed into the parks are little or no more extreme than those embodied in the city's general architecture, and, with the exception of a great difference in scale, their organization is very much the same. From this observation, one can conclude that the appeal of amusement parks is not a function of their strangeness, but rather of the humanization and comprehensible organization of a number of bizarre elements similar to those normally found throughout Los Angeles and elsewhere in the United States.

Denis Gontard

The "Theatre Western" of Marseilles or the French Metamorphosis of an American Popular Myth———————

The word *metamorphosis* indicates a transformation, a change in form. The change need not be progressive or toward something better. It may, as in many of the Greek myths recounted by Ovid in his *Metamorphoses*, be a change for the worse. For example, Arachne is transformed into a spider; Niobe is changed into a weeping rock. In this sense, the beautiful, poetic myth of the Western is hardly recognizable in the caricatural form in which it appears in the *Théâtre Western* of Marseilles. But even a caricature can be interesting. That is my point in this paper.

The myth of the Western is, nowadays, in France extremely vivid. It came to us first through the circus (I'm thinking of Buffalo Bill's circus) and was nourished through children's books of the nineteenth century. More literally, the myth and atmosphere of the far West—with its heroes and their adventures, their loves, their vicissitudes—developed through the movies. Generations of spectators—from silent movies to the talkies—found a strong identity with the myth of the Western, in which fantasy and poetry join forces to keep alive, in our European minds, a period of United States history alas now forever lost.

The myth of the Western is plain, modern, direct. You do not have to know Greek or Latin literature to appreciate it. For some Europeans, it is the myth of the far away, the myth of a dreamland—always remote—opposed to the sad reality of everyday life. It is a kind of Eldorado, a search for a country where everything is possible: a gold rush toward adventure.

The founder of Marseilles's Western Theatre has exploited all these elements of popular myths of the far West in his amusement park, as have others in the United States and Europe for about fifteen years. Following the example of West Germany and Belgium, France now has three western villages: the Red Skin Valley, at Fleurine, near Paris; and the villages of Cuges-les-Pins and Ensuès-la-Redonne, both to the east and to the west of Marseilles.

As in the other western amusement parks, the manager of Ensuès-la-Redonne tried to re-create, in a little pine-covered valley which resembles parts of California, a small western town with its main street, its saloon, its bank, its general store, its prison, and so on. The setup at Ensuès-la-Redonne is unique in that it presents a permanent show every Sunday: the Western Theatre. It is not a mere replica, but a live entertainment. In this sense, the Western Theatre of Marseilles, in my opinion, deserves a place in this Conference on American Popular Entertainment.

The show given each week, with slight variations, tells the story of a man born in Eldorado City (an imaginary town at the American-Mexican border). This main character had left his hometown to live in the North and he returns home to Eldorado City where his troubles begin. Here are two examples of the kind of scenarios used at the Western Theatre in Marseilles: 1. The hero returns to Eldorado City after the Civil War. He finds his father shining shoes in the saloon. The villain of the piece, a Mr. Miranda, has cheated the father of all his property and possessions. The son sets out to revenge his father. 2. A new sheriff is sent to Eldorado City, which is being terrorized by the bandit Cisco. When he confronts Cisco, he recognizes that the bandit is his own brother. In the end, justice triumphs. Obviously, the director of Western Theatre has lifted these simple storylines from American and spaghetti Westerns.

The show takes place in the open every Sunday afternoon from mid-March to mid-November. Since 1972—the year of its inception—the Theatre Western has continued to attract a thousand spectators for each performance. The show takes place on the main street of Eldorado City and may move to other locations in the town, such as the town corral, for the shoot-out, or the mouth of the tunnel, for the attack on the train. The spectators stand for the scenes on Main Street and sit down on the slope around the tunnel. All the sequences are of short duration and they are separated by intervals of fifteen minutes. These intervals allow for costume, make-up, and scene changes, while the spectators move to a new playing area. And, of course, the intermissions make it possible for the spectators to buy refreshments and souvenirs or go for a pony ride—all of which swell the coffers of the Western Theatre.

The owner-director of the Western Theatre acts as interlocutor: not only does he sum up the preceding sequences over a loudspeaker after the intermissions, but he also speaks for the actors during the action since they are often at too great a distance from the spectators to be heard easily. There is also, underscoring the action, the familiar music of American and European Westerns. The actors must content themselves with miming their roles. At present, then, the productions are far from creating the intense atmosphere and poetry of the modern Western. The director dreams of some sort of show in the future in which the voices of the actors can be

Theatre Western near Marseilles, a main street of the village. Photo by Denis Gontard.

heard; he even hopes, perhaps, to attract such stars as Charles Bronson and Alain Delon and have them play the leads.

In spite of its present restrictions and the reduction of the stories to such simple lines that it would seem they are destined for a public of the simpleminded, since 1972 the Western Theatre has continued to attract about one thousand spectators every Sunday afternoon, eight months a year.

The public is made up of children, adults, and even older people, all of whom seem equally involved in the action of the productions. Merely by their numbers and steady attendance, you can detect a certain passive participation in these spectacles; but much more noteworthy to me is the passionate interest of all that public in the hand-to-hand combats, the gun fighting, the falls from roofs, and the blowing up of trains and buildings. There I detect a vicarious but more active participation of the public. It is, as I see it, a vital participation: for example, during the train robbery, the actors appeal directly to the spectators; the train stops abruptly; the gunfire begins; and the bandits sometimes grab the children in the audience away from their parents, taking them as hostages. The parents feign fright and become totally involved in the action. In other words, they identify with the violence of the show. I had the sad impression that the intensity of this audience participation was in direct proportion to the violence of the presentation.

How do we explain the tremendous success of this enterprise? First, the nature of the myth, however much this point may have been worked over by Jungian scholars, would seem to be different from that of classical myth —simpler, more recognizable to ordinary, uneducated people. The identity which the spectators experience here need not be conditioned by a knowledge of the myths of the ancient Greeks—an area probably more accessible to an educated, bourgeois class. Thus, for the most part, classical myth has, quite deplorably, become class myth.

Second, the means which the director employs are simple and forthright— one could speak at length on the intriguing subject of a semiology of the Western (never fear, I shall not!). These means elicit direct and primary emotions from the audience such as hatred, anger, and violence; no intellectual participation is required. They elicit a purely physical one. Since familiarity with the heroes of these western scenarios precludes any intellectual effort on the part of the spectators, the effect is immediate and needs little or none of the kind of transposition which the classical heroes require. This, in my opinion, is a definite limitation, since every effect has been foreseen, every result or consequence has been calculated. I see in the simplistic attitude of these presentations the reflection of that same attitude which, in modern mass societies, seeks to reduce all unforeseen consequences to purely simple, predictable terms.

Third, these spectacles probably owe their popularity to their foreign character. They present to the European imagination something of the myth of the "far-country," a dreamland where everything is simply possible, as opposed to the hard, everyday reality of one's own circumstances where one's possibilities are limited.

Fourth (and intimately contingent upon this preceding point), the success of these shows is readily seen in the immediate and almost unanimous catharsis they produce in their public—a public which, for the most part, has been deprived of its deep sense of identity and culture by mass media.

Marseilles is, by reputation, the toughest town in France—a kind of French Chicago (you all have seen *The French Connection*!). This certainly explains, in a small measure, the acceptability of this kind of violent spectacle to the ordinary inhabitants of Marseilles. This success corresponds somewhat to the success of another American myth: "Things go better with Coca-Cola!"

SUMMATION

Ray B. Browne

Popular Entertainments:
Summing Up———————————————

The papers in this volume—as was the case when they were delivered at the Popular Entertainment Conference—demonstrate how widely the attitude toward these subjects as being proper for scholarly research has changed in the last few years. Whereas a decade ago most scholars felt these topics were not worthy of serious attention, now, at a rate that is almost completely gratifying, more and more academics, more learned societies (like the Modern Language Association, the American Historical Association, the ACLS) and more funding agencies (like the NEH and the NEA) are devoting their resources to finding out about and appreciating the complexity of these forms of American society.

But as comprehensive and insightful as these papers are, they really serve as only the first of the potential fruits to be gathered from studying popular entertainments. More than most scholars have admitted or recognized in the past, popular entertainment has permeated and profoundly affected society throughout history. Nearly all Americans have been active participants or "closet" appreciators of popular entertainments. This attitude is what worried T. S. Eliot when he recognized that the lighter side of amusements does most of the task of perpetuating a culture, and to him the effect was deleterious. "I incline to come to the alarming conclusion," he wrote in *Essays Ancient and Modern*, "that it is just the literature [read 'all kinds of entertainment'] that we read for 'amusement' or 'purely for pleasure' that may have the greatest . . . least suspected . . . earliest and most invidious influence upon us. Hence it is that the influence of popular novelists, and of popular plays of contemporary life, require to be scrutinized."

Russell B. Nye, with none of Eliot's feeling of insecurity, asserts that the works of popular entertainment should be studied for other reasons. "Popular art," he says in *The Unembarrassed Muse*,

confirms the experience of the majority, in contrast to elite, which tends to explore the new. For this reason, popular art has been an unusually sensitive and accurate reflector of the attitudes and concerns of the society for which it is produced. Because it is of lesser quality, aesthetically, than elite art, historians and critics have tended to neglect it as a means of access to an era's—and a society's—values and ideas. The popular artist corroborates (occasionally with great skill and intensity) values and attitudes already familiar to his audience; his aim is less to prove a new experience than to validate an older one. Predictability is important to the effectiveness of popular art; the fulfillment of expectation, the pleasant shock of recognition of the known, verification of an experience already familiar. . . .

There is some disagreement about how popular art corroborates the values of life. Leslie Fiedler, one of America's brilliant critics, perhaps representing a minority opinion, insists that popular culture is subversive and changes the way a nation lives. But he and Nye would agree, with Eliot, that you cannot chart the blood flow of a nation without studying the popular entertainment. And study of the popular arts will have a therapeutic side effect on academia, as the perceptive British critic Richard Hoggart, speaking in a larger context, asserted: "The closer study of mass society may make us have sad hearts at the supermarket, but at the same time it may produce an enhanced and tempered sense of humanity and humility, instead of the sense of superiority and separateness that our traditional training is likely to have encouraged."

If popular entertainments reveal truthfully the attitudes of a society, and if the American scholar would want to understand more fully than we do now the totality of American culture through the past 350 years, then, as a community of scholars, we should seriously turn our attention to new materials for research. For Americans, despite the incorrect generalization about the Puritans being a gloomy and unplayful people, have always been hardworking, hardplaying. This new attitude means, then, a new approach to and a reexamination of the whole area of subjects. Henry Nash Smith once remarked that all criticism of Mark Twain should be suspended until more of the folklore and popular culture in which he lived was uncovered and understood; then fruitful criticism could again be centered on the author's works. Smith also remarked recently that his *Virgin Land*, one of the landmarks in the study of American culture, would have been a stronger book if he had included more aspects of popular culture. Scholarship needs more breadth, more details, and new frames of reference, and the study of popular entertainment offers some of these dimensions.

Let Herman Melville serve as an example. Recognizing that Melville is far too profound and useful a writer to be left to the "pure" literary critics alone, Howard Vincent published fascinating studies of two works—*Moby-Dick* and *White Jacket*—called *The Trying-Out of Moby-Dick* and *The Tailoring of White Jacket*. In both studies, Vincent tried to locate all the books that Melville had drawn from in composing his two works—and there were many—and to excerpt relevant passages to demonstrate how Melville had used these sources. In these two important studies, Vincent throws much useful light on Melville's works, for he fills out many areas about the books and about Melville's methods of working that were unknown. Vincent's work needs to be carried on and expanded. He recognized, for example, that there are many details in his study that are still missing and will eventually be found—details which, in his words, are "interesting in themselves and vital for filling out the record."

Expansion of Vincent's approach will be extraordinarily fruitful. His studies are too narrow, too elite. Vincent isolated and tore out the passages from book that Melville had used. But Melville's debt to these various books and to the whole culture from which they sprang, in which they developed, is far greater than Vincent was able to demonstrate. Vincent left the record incomplete. He needed to broaden the scope of his search—to include *all* the books Melville had read, *all* the magazines, to incorporate the books and magazines that Melville's friends had read and talked with him about, to bring in the folklore and sealore that Melville knew, and all other aspects of life that he experienced. To understand Melville fully—or any other "elite" creator—today's scholar must know as much about every aspect of America in Melville's day as he did. Though this road is long and dusty, it will more than repay the serious traveler.

Serious study of popular entertainment brings two new refreshing and useful attitudes to academia. As the papers in this volume demonstrate, one is that the world of popular entertainment must not be approached with condescension and as though the scholar were slumming. We should study with scholarly detachment, to be sure, but on the same level as the culture itself. We should free ourselves of the conviction that we have to bring our heaviest guns to bear on all aspects of popular entertainment and, where they are weak, pulverize them. Walt Whitman once insisted that to have a great literature you must have great critics. But he did not mean that great critics should be negative and destructive. Rather, the criticism should be positive and constructive. We should not assume that in the democracy of entertainment all works are created equal, but we cannot afford to forget that all works have the right to exist and be heard.

We should disabuse ourselves of the feeling, as A. O. Lovejoy remarked in his book *The Great Chain of Being*, that most scholars are not interested in ideas unless they come dressed in full warpaint. In scholarly and critical work at least, we should scuttle the old Puritanical notion that the arts are meant to improve society (though it may be true) and therefore we should condemn those forms that apparently or obviously have no uplifting quality whatsoever. All forms of entertainment march to different drums, and what is slow progress to one set of feet might be haste to another. Irving Wallace, for example, likes to tell of a conversation he had with James Baldwin while working on his novel *The Man.* Baldwin wanted to know how a white man could presume to write about a black man becoming president of the United States. Wallace responded that he presumed because he knew that he would reach millions of persons with his message of tolerance and understanding who would never read a word Baldwin wrote. If he seeks to know what makes American society operate, the role of the student of popular entertainments is to understand the phenomena.

A second attitude we should keep in mind in approaching the study of popular entertainment is its overwhelming inclusiveness. To paraphrase Lincoln, God must love popular entertainment because he creates (or tolerates) so much of it. And it comes in many forms, both the obvious and in some forms that people might not immediately recognize as a proper area of study. For example, all elements of the stage are obviously popular entertainment, including all forms of ballet, which, thanks to financial support from the National Endowment for the Arts, is becoming one of the more popular forms of stage entertainment. But what about the choreography of professional wrestling? and all forms of folk drama? and music of all kinds, clearly, of the present and the past? What, for instance, was the impact of the Norwegian violinist Ole Bull on America during the last half of the nineteenth century? He was the musician in Longfellow's *Tales of a Wayside Inn.* He established Oleana, a short-lived Norwegian colony in Pennsylvania, and his influence was profound in the Midwest—at least to the author Hamlin Garland, who reported that listening to Bull's haunting violin was enough to transport him completely out of the desperately hard life around him and to keep alive beauty and hope.

The possible list of influences is endless. Let me name only a few: architecture; the fast-food industry; theme parks (especially Disney); fighting (as on the frontier); cockfighting (as seen in the novel *Roots*); storytelling (especially among the folk); the Las Vegas and Hollywood strips, and all Tenderloin districts; popular religious leaders; P. T. Barnum, child actors, giants, and dwarfs; exhibitions, celebrations; sports (including half-time shows); parades; leisure activities; toys; fashions. And on and on.

The places to research these areas of entertainment are in many cases obvious: museums; halls of fame; the Smithsonian Institution; old newspapers, magazines, literary works (both popular and elite); photographs; discarded memorabilia; unpublished diaries, inventories, and wills; interviews with participants now before they die (there should be an active organization dedicated to interviewing people about their engagements in various forms of old entertainment); and various other less obvious forms and places.

A final word might be a spur to activity. Now that scholars realize the importance of popular entertainment in American society and the need for their serious work, we should dedicate ourselves, not only to understanding the various forms of the past and of the present, but also to preserving those of the present so that our counterparts in the future will have more material to work with than we might have now. And in this collecting, we should perhaps remind ourselves that the world of popular entertainments is something like a large orchestra: in order for us to get the full impact, we must listen for all instruments—from the bass to the piccolo.

APPENDIX: BIBLIOGRAPHICAL SURVEY

Don B. Wilmeth

American Popular Entertainment: A Historical Perspective Bibliography_____

A copy of this article constituted part of the material distributed to all who attended the CHAPE meeting.

Introduction

The student and scholar of American popular culture has too frequently assumed that live amusements created by professional showmen for profit and aimed at broad, relatively unsophisticated audiences were unworthy of serious attention—if noted at all. The reasons for this oversight can be traced to the anticommercial bias with which too many scholars have looked at popular entertainment, the apparent unimportance of such areas for investigation, and even the lacking of a strong literary base for most popular entertainment forms, for indeed most of these forms depend more significantly on the performer and the audience than a written text. There are legitimate difficulties in investigating popular entertainments; throughout history popular forms have appeared, merged, mutated, disappeared, and, in some cases, reappeared in new guises, all the while virtually ignored by scholars and historians.

Although many of the better sources on popular entertainment are what one might call "good bad" books—chatty autobiographies and memoirs, undocumented histories, and the like—the attention paid to popular entertainment has changed drastically in recent years. No longer are forms like vaudeville, the circus, burlesque, and popular theatre considered insignificant because they are not abstruse, profound, or complicated. Beyond their primary function, to entertain, as important as that is, social scientists and humanists are discovering other values—the reflection and

Reprinted from CHOICE, October 1977; Volume 14, Number 8. Copyright © 1977 by The American Library Association.

expression of aesthetic and other needs of a large population base, as well as the creation of effective satire or politically motivated comment. Indications of the broader importance can be seen, for example, in American minstrelsy, which spoke for and to huge numbers of common Americans in the nineteenth century and during its heyday provided unique insights into the thoughts, feelings, needs, and desires of the common people who shaped the show in their own image. Vaudeville, which also spoke to a new audience, can be taken seriously as something more than an idle form of mass amusement and can be seen as a manifestation of psychic and social forces at work in American history.

Underscoring the new-found significance of popular entertainment as a legitimate area of study is the attention paid the subject by scholarly journals and organizations. The Center for the Study of Popular Culture at Bowling Green University publishes significant books under the aegis of the Bowling Green University Popular Press and issues the important *Journal of Popular Culture*, which includes, periodically, articles on popular entertainment. In 1971, *Theatre Quarterly* issued a number devoted to "People's Theatre," including essays on melodrama, equestrian drama, British music hall, and American vaudeville. *The Drama Review*, the single best source for essays dealing with the influence of popular entertainment on the avant-garde, published an issue in 1974 focused on "Popular Entertainments," containing articles on popular scenography, commedia dell'arte and the actor, stage magic, and other relevant topics, among them an excellent introduction to the subject by Brooks McNamara which lays out a sensible categorization of forms. The *Educational Theatre Journal* followed in 1975 with an excellent "Popular Theatre" issue featuring articles on the circus, early American musical theatre, burlesque, revue, and pantomime.

This trend has not abated in the scholarly world. In celebration of the American Bicentennial, the American Society for Theatre Research and the Theatre Library Association are jointly sponsoring a Conference on the History of American Popular Entertainment, November 17-20, 1977, at the Library & Museum of the Performing Arts, the New York Public Library at Lincoln Center. This conference will bring together both distinguished scholars in the field and individuals who have worked professionally in such areas as burlesque and vaudeville.

The scope of this essay could be immense, since, despite the mediocre nature of much of the literature, a tremendous amount has been written. In order to contain the subject, I have chosen to deal primarily with major American forms and important predecessors (not necessarily American). The time coverage has been limited to the period from the emergence of a huge market for entertainment in the eighteenth century (paralleling the appearance of a predominantly middle-class civilization in the Western world, which in turn drastically changed the cultural pattern) to the emergence early in the twentieth century of the motion picture, excluding works on the revue and early musical comedy. The focus throughout will be on the best sources available (both recent and standard works in the field). The categories used are, at best, often artificial divisions because of the overlapping nature of the forms. A final section includes significant recent publications in miscellaneous categories.

Reference, Early Forms, and General Sources

Since serious scholarly research is relatively new in the field of popular entertainment, there are no comprehensive bibliographies covering all major forms, although the author is currently compiling a guide to be published by Gale Research. John Towsen's "Sources in Popular Entertainment" is a useful general guide with a very selective bibliography; bibliographies provided in the standard works, indicated elsewhere under specific categories, furnish the researcher with the best bibliographical data currently available. A definitive glossary of popular entertainment terminology is, likewise, unavailable, although *The Language of Show Biz*, edited by Sherman Sergel, is a fair guide to the special language of the circus, vaudeville, burlesque, carnival, and Toby shows. Again, specific works on individual forms tend to be the best guides, many with special glossaries. Maurer's "Carnival Cant," although not definitive, demonstrates the special nature of show biz terminology.

Few attempts have been made to produce a comprehensive history of popular entertainment. The best two sources are McKechnie's *Popular Entertainments Through the Ages* and Toll's *On with the Show*. Although originally published in 1931, McKechnie's book offers a good introduction to major forms (with a focus on Europe), including mimes, minstrels, strolling players, fairs, commedia dell'arte, Punch and Judy, pantomime, music hall, and circus. Toll's recent book is the only attempt to chronicle American forms of popular entertainment and, despite organizational and emphasis problems, this volume is a generally excellent introduction to major American forms. It also contains an excellent bibliographical essay and a comparative chronology showing the parallel between the evolution of American society and American show business.

In order to understand and appreciate the more modern forms of popular entertainment, it is necessary to explore the origins and early forms of entertainment in the European traditions. Three studies on medieval popular entertainment are especially significant: Chambers's *The Medieval Stage*, the oldest of the three, is still an excellent overview of the period; Faral's *Les Jongleurs en France au Moyen Age*, also dated, is a most valuable source; and Nicoll's *Masks, Mimes, and Miracles*, in addition to its superb coverage of popular theatre during the Middle Ages, includes important sections on early mime and pantomime in Greece and Rome and the commedia dell'arte in Italy. Kirby, in his essay "The Shamanistic Origins of Popular Entertainment," attempts to relate and trace many popular entertainments back to the rituals of shamanism.

The role of the fool in history has been dealt with by a number of important scholars. Welsford traces the social history of the fool and relates it to the fool figure in literature; Willeford, a practicing psychotherapist, offers a theoretical study of the fool's appeal; Cox investigates the Feast of Fools and presents an important theological study of the meaning of Christianity in the Middle Ages and modern times; and Swain, though less important than the others, gives a generally useful overview of fools during the Middle Ages and the Renaissance. A good general study on the fool in Shakespeare is Robert Goldsmith's 1955 work.

Any student of popular entertainment should be thoroughly familiar with the commedia dell'arte of the sixteenth and seventeenth centuries, and fortunately the literature on the subject is excellent and varied. Of the published works in English, the following are especially valuable: Ducharte's *The Italian Comedy*, Lea's *Italian Popular Comedy*. Oreglia's *The Commedia dell'arte*, and Nicoll's *Masks, Mimes, and Miracles*. Less valuable are Kennard's *Masks and Marionettes* and Niklaus's *Harlequin*. Nicoll's *The World of Harlequin* is also a good study and includes a useful evaluation of sources available as of 1953. The best collection of scenarios in English offers those of Flaminio Scala translated by Henry Salerno.

Although there is not room in this essay to cover the many studies of popular culture relevant to popular entertainment, a few are too essential for exclusion. Gilbert Seldes's *The Seven Lively Arts* was the first attempt by an American to justify and defend popular entertainment and as such is still stimulating. The work of Constance Rourke is especially important for her analysis of American comic stereotypes in the nineteenth century. Bier's *The Rise and Fall of American Humour* is less significant but still a good study of nineteenth-century American popular culture, as is Bode's *The Anatomy of American Popular Culture, 1840-1861*. Cantor and Werthman's anthology includes a section of reprinted essays on "Popular Entertainments and Recreation" by such authorities as Foster Rhea Dulles, Earl Chapin May, and James H. Young. Dulles's *America Learns to Play* remains the best general introduction to early American popular entertainment and includes much more than show business in its coverage of how Americans made use of their leisure time. Russel Nye's *The Unembarrassed Muse* is also an excellent general introduction to the popular arts and includes a good section on popular theatre.

American popular entertainment depends a great deal on general histories for investigation. Although it is necessary to exclude most of these here, two are essential for the student of popular entertainment: Odell's *Annals of the New York Stage* and Brown's three-volume *History of the New York Stage*. Odell remains the standard history through the 1893-1894 season and is written with charm, accuracy, and impressive scholarship; Brown, a theatrical agent and historian, was a devotee of popular entertainment, and his work contains histories of over four hundred New York theatres, opera houses, music halls, circuses, and other places of entertainment. Brooks Atkinson's *Broadway* is a more up-to-date overview of New York entertainment from 1900 to 1974. Edward Bennett Marks's *They All Had Glamour*, although not limited to popular entertainment, is an amusing source for lesser known theatrical and musical artists and contains a good glossary of "Old-time Colloquialisms." Allen Churchill, the author of numerous theatre studies, offers a survey of Broadway during the revue era and the birth of the modern American musical in *The Theatrical Twenties*. Langston Hughes and Milton Meltzer evolved a major survey of the black performer in American entertainment in their *Black Magic. A Book About the Theatre* gives an interesting perspective on popular entertainments by an important early American theatre historian, Brander Matthews. In *America Takes the Stage*, Richard Moody traces the development of Romanticism in American drama and theatre from 1750 to 1900 and deals prominently with the stage Yankee and Negro minstrelsy. McNamara has written numerous essays of a general nature that are extremely valuable, among them "Popular Sceneography," a survey of the architecture and design of traditional popular entertainment, and "Scavengers of the Amusement World," in which he shows the indebtedness of early cinema to popular entertainment forms. An excellent period source is Jennings's *Theatrical and Circus Life* (1882), a compendium of popular forms. A useful guide to other general sources will be my "The American Stage to World War I," which is forthcoming from Gale Research.

The Circus and Wild West Shows

Sources on the circus, the most universal of all entertainment forms, especially the English and European circus, are numerous and of varying quality. The most indispensable reference is Raymond Toole-Stott's four-volume *Circus and Allied Arts: A World Bibliography* . . . which contains some 15,000 entries drawn from works in thirteen languages. *A Bibliography of Books on the Circus in English from 1773 to 1964*, extracted from the longer work, lists approximately 1,100 books and is equally useful as a guide. Richard Flint's "A Selected Guide to Source Material on the American Circus" is the best single guide on the American circus to date, including data on circus trade journals (the *Clipper, Billboard, White Tops*, and *Bandwagon*). The last, published bimonthly, became the official journal of the Circus Historical Society in 1951 and, although articles vary in quality, is still a major source for essays on the circus and Wild West show. *Amusement Business*, a weekly trade paper which is the *Variety* of the outdoor entertainment industry, lists the current circus and carnival routes. Of the numerous circus journals, *Le Cirque dans l'Univers*, although published in France, deals most specifically with historically oriented topics.

In 1972 the *Journal of Popular Culture* devoted a major section of one issue to "Circuses, Carnivals and Fairs in America," edited by Marcello Truzzi, which presents an excellent overview of current research on the circus. Few successful attempts have been made to write a history of world circus, and the most recent, Croft-Cooke and Cotes's *Circus: A World History*, although containing superb illustrations from all over the world, is less a world history than a survey of highlights, primarily in England and to a lesser extent in the United States. Thétard's *La Merveilleuse Histoire du Cirque*, although thirty years old, is still a comprehensive and authoritative history of world circus up to 1947. Antony Hippisley Coxe's work on the circus is of value to the student of circus history. His *A Seat at the Circus* describes typical circus performances and recounts the history of acts and circus in general; the researcher would find his essay "Historical Research and the Circus" especially invaluable. Of the American authors on the circus, Charles P. Fox, director of the Circus World Museum, is among the most prolific. All of his books are primarily illustrated histories, outstanding among them being *Circus in America*, co-authored by Tom Parkinson. *A Ticket to the Circus, Circus Parades*, and *A Pictorial History of Performing Horses*, though useful, are less detailed and handsomely produced.

There is no one standard history of the American circus, although the following are generally reliable sources: Fox and Parkinson, Earl May's *The Circus from Rome to Ringling* (not to be confused with the less useful book of the same title by Marian Murray). George Chindahl's *History of the Circus in America* (good on nineteenth-century circus), John and Alice Durant's *The Pictorial History of the American Circus*, R. W. G. Vail's *Random Notes on the Early American Circus* (an outline from 1720 to the mid-nineteenth century), and Isaac Greenwood's *The Circus: Its Origin and Growth Prior to 1835* (an undocumented survey with focus on the American circus). The roots of the American circus in England are explored in Saxon's scholarly work *Enter Foot and Horse* and in Disher's *Greatest Show on Earth*, both excellent studies of equestrian drama as well.

The serious student of the American circus should still turn to trade papers and scholarly journals for the better sources and explore the many specialized circus collections, the most comprehensive being the Hertzberg Collection (San Antonio, Texas), Circus World Museum (Baraboo, Wisconsin), Ringling Museum of the Circus (Sarasota, Florida), Illinois State University, Normal, and the Somers (N.Y.) Historical Society. (Robert Sokan's catalog of the Illinois State collection is invaluable.)

Recent scholarly studies on the circus by Saxon, Paul Bouissac, Marcello Truzzi, and Robert C. Sweet, not limited to the American circus, suggest the potential of scholarship on the circus. Fred Powledge's *Mud Show* is a fascinating glimpse of a third-rate traveling circus; Jill Freedman's *Circus Days* offers a visually interesting study of a similar operation; and Gene Plowden's *Those Amazing Ringlings and Their Circus* is the most complete study of this famous circus family. One element of the circus that has received a considerable amount of attention is the clown. Among the important recent studies on popular entertainment is John Towsen's *Clowns*, a survey of all types of clowns throughout history with an exhaustive bibliography and glossary of terms. The works of Tristan Rémy on clowns have long been considered standard sources.

The Wild West show, a purely American phenomenon, too frequently has been treated as part of the history of the circus. As a result, significant studies are just beginning to appear that deal with this form as essentially separate from that of the American circus. To date, only one book, Don Russell's *The Wild West or, a History of the Wild West Shows*, concerns itself solely with the traveling Wild West show of the late nineteenth and early twentieth centuries. Russell's comprehensive work should be consulted for additional bibliographical sources. Rennert's collection of Buffalo Bill Wild West posters is an excellent complement to Russell's history; and Walter Havighurst's books on Buffalo Bill's Wild West show and Annie Oakley, although written for popular consumption, have some merit. Of the many books on William Cody, three contain special insights into his show business career: Croft-Cooke and Meadmore's *Buffalo Bill: The Legend, the Man of Action, the Showman*, Russell's *The Lives and Legends of Buffalo Bill*, and Sell and Weybright's *Buffalo Bill and the Wild West*. The latter is especially recommended. Much information can be found in journals and collections. Useful essays have appeared in *The Ranchman, Western Horseman, Real West, Great West, Frontier Times, The West, Old West,* and *Bandwagon*, among others. The better collections are to be found in the Western History Department of the Denver Public Library, the Buffalo Bill Historical Center (Cody, Wyoming), and the Arizona Pioneers Historical Society.

Variety Forms: Minstrelsy, Vaudeville, and Burlesque

Variety can include all entertainment that depends on a compartmented structure; the three most prominent American examples, minstrel shows, vaudeville, and burlesque, dominated American popular stage entertainment during their heydays. Each grew out of earlier saloon and variety structures and collectively demonstrate the type of mutation that occurred in American popular entertainment. The minstrel show was the first uniquely American show business form and dominated the scene during the last half of the nineteenth century; vaudeville replaced minstrel shows as the most popular form by the end of the century; and burlesque, though incorporating aspects of minstrelsy and vaudeville and paralleling to some extent variety in other parts of the world, was predominantly an indigenous form. Its heyday began in 1905 and ended in the 1930s with the introduction of the striptease.

In-depth study of American variety entertainment still depends a great deal on periodicals of the time and special collections. Of the numerous newspapers of the period, the most valuable are *Billboard* (beginning in 1894), the New York *Clipper* (1900-1918), *Variety* (especially 1905 to 1937), and the New York *Mirror* (1879-1922). Some of the more extensive collections on variety are located in well-known libraries: the Library of Congress, the Harvard Theatre Collection, the Hoblitzelle Theatre Arts Library of the University of Texas, the Library of the Performing Arts at Lincoln Center, and the Boston Public Library. Good minstrel materials are to be found in the Harris Collection, Brown University, and the Buffalo and Erie County Library. Other collections, noted in Young's *American Theatrical Arts*, contain useful holdings of playlets, jokebooks, sheet music, songbooks, and so on.

Robert Toll's *Blacking Up* is the most comprehensive history and analysis of the minstrel show. Toll portrays minstrelsy as an institution that spoke for and to large numbers of common Americans; he also provides a superb bibliography of primary and secondary sources. Wittke's *Tambo and Bones*, though dated, is still a good basic history and explanation of minstrelsy form. Paskman and Spaeth's *"Gentlemen, Be Seated!,"* originally published in 1928, has recently been revised by Paskman and updated to include recent offshoots of minstrelsy. It remains, however, a romanticized history but with examples of music, sample minstrel routines, and good illustrations. For a "how to" book, Haverly's *Negro Minstrels: A Complete Guide* is an interesting outline by a successful minstrel manager. Rice's *Monarchs of Minstrelsy* supplies biographical sketches of minstrel specialists, an index of minstrels, and a list of minstrel organizations up to 1911.

The career of the first blackface comedian, T. D. Rice, is effectively summarized by Molly Ramshaw; Hans Nathan's *Dan Emmett and the Rise of Early Negro Minstrelsy* chronicles the life of this minstrel specialist and the early period of minstrelsy from the point of view of a musicologist. Fletcher places minstrelsy, with a focus on individuals, in the context of black performers over a hundred-year period. The tremendous impact of minstrelsy in Great Britain is adequately told by Harry Reynolds, covering the period 1836 to 1927. Two good specialized essays are Marian Winter's "Juba and American Minstrelsy" and Jules Zanger's "The Minstrel Show as Theater of Misrule." Two dissertations on minstrelsy and songsters (by Davidson and Patterson) add scholarly credibility to the topic.

The definitive history of early variety has yet to be written, although the standard works on vaudeville and one recent study, Zellers's *Tony Pastor: Dean of the Vaudeville Stage*, include some coverage of the early years. Zellers's essay, "The Cradle of Variety: The Concert Saloon," also sheds light on early variety. Myron Matlaw's essay on Pastor's early years, beginning in 1846, is a useful complement to Zellers. Lloyd Morris in his chatty book *Incredible New York* discusses the atmosphere, reputation, and dangers of various concert saloons; Clair Willson gives a good sense of variety in the West; and Eugene Bristow's scholarly study of variety in Memphis during the late nineteenth century provides good social insights.

Of the general histories of vaudeville during its peak period, John DiMeglio's recent book is the best documented and furnishes the most extensive notes and bibliography. Several older histories should be considered essential still: Green and Laurie's *Show Biz from Vaude to Video*, Laurie's *Vaudeville: From the Honky-tonks to the Palace*, and Gilbert's *American Vaudeville: Its Life and Times*. Of more recent investigations, Albert McLean's *American Vaudeville as Ritual* represents the most thorough job of analyzing vaudeville in its social-historical framework and of delving below the surface for greater significance. His more recent article, "U.S. Vaudeville and the Urban Comics," is a natural extension of his book.

A large number of active participants in vaudeville left autobiographies or memoirs. The following early ones are especially informative: M. B. Leavitt's *Fifty Years in Theatrical Management*, Robert Grau's two volumes of memoirs, and Brett Page's insider's view of vaudeville, *Writing for Vaudeville*. Eugene Elliott's study of vaudeville in Seattle, though brief, offers a good look at that northwestern vaudeville capital. Marston and Feller's life of F. F. Proctor, the important vaudeville manager, and Felix Isman's *Weber and Fields* are among the better biographies of vaudeville luminaries. Bernard Sobel's *A Pictorial History of Vaudeville*, recommended for its illustrations, though directed at a popular audience is still an accurate and informative account.

Most recent vaudeville studies are offshoots of the nostalgia craze and vary greatly in content and value. Charles and Louise Samuels's *Once Upon a Stage* is an informal and undocumented history and in no way supersedes earlier histories; Bill Smith's *The Vaudevillians* is a sad and wistful look at daily life on the vaudeville circuit via interviews with thirty-one former headliners (and includes a brief glossary of vaudeville terms); and Marcia Keegan's *We Can Still Hear Them Clapping* is a photographic essay, with limited text, recording the impressions and reminiscences of former vaudevillians still living in the Times Square district. A fair account of the final chapter in vaudeville's history is Spitzer's *The Palace*, which covers this pinnacle of vaudeville from its opening in 1913.

Burlesque has received even less scholarly treatment than other forms of variety and is invariably admixed with the striptease show, which actually spelled the demise of true burlesque. American burlesque, not to be confused with the literary tradition effectively dissected by V. C. Clinton-Baddeley, has only one fairly comprehensive history, Zeidman's *The American Burlesque Show*, and Zeidman, terribly biased in an almost puritanical way, fails to document his investigation. The single best scholarly source, therefore, on the origin and content of burlesque up to the 1930s is Ralph Allen's "Our Native Theatre: Honky-tonk, Minstrel Shows, Burlesque." The standard sources, generally weak on historical fact and the separation of striptease from true burlesque, are Ann Corio's *This Was Burlesque* and Bernard Sobel's *Burleycue* and *A Pictorial History of Burlesque*. The latter contains an informative text along with excellent photographs. Also useful is Sandberg's interview with Steve Mills, a superb old-time burlesque comic, and Mills's version of one of his "bits." Although a fanciful account of burlesque in the 1920s, Rowland Barber's *The Night They Raided Minsky's* provides a sense of the transition from true burlesque to striptease.

Striptease

The subject of striptease is no longer limited to latterday burlesque but more appropriately belongs today to the world of carnivals, fairs, strip-clubs, and striptease cabarets. Nevertheless, as an offshoot of burlesque it deserves inclusion and, surprisingly, the subject has begun to stimulate intriguing sociological and psychological investigations. Few of the numerous memoirs of strippers are worthy of consideration, although two stand apart from the others: Gypsy Rose Lee's memoirs are coherent and offer good backstage atmosphere; Georgia Sothern's *My Life in Burlesque* is the best of its ilk, witty, entertaining, and provocative. Striptease also lacks a comprehensive history, although Wortley's recent pictorial history of striptease makes a somewhat feeble effort. Meiselas's *Carnival Strippers* is a more forthright and honest pictorial essay on the stripper, as is Angier's *A Kind of Life*, which combines pictorial and textual insights into the life of strippers in Boston's "Combat Zone." Investigations into strippers' morality and the sociological-psychological implications of their profession have been undertaken with varying degrees of success by Lipnitski, Skipper and McCaghy, and Salutin.

Fairs, Carnivals, and Amusement Parks

These forms of entertainment are closely akin to variety and the circus but have only recently been examined as entertainment vehicles with theatrical connotaton. They depend on entertainment environments, instead of the conventional theatre, and a mobile audience, as does the dime museum, examined in the next section. Only major sources can be mentioned in this section, but these, in turn, suggest additional materials. The issue of the *Journal of Popular Culture* on "Circuses, Carnivals, and Fairs in America" is an excellent beginning place, especially Easto and Truzzi's essay "Towards an Ethnography of the Carnival Social System," in which they review and evaluate the available literature. As indicated previously, the major primary source on outdoor amusements is the magazine *Amusement Business.*

The fair, carnival, and the amusement park, unlike most forms of popular entertainment, continue to thrive. Their existences stem from old and honored traditions; adequate background material can be found in Frost, Dexter, Morley, and Braithwaite. The best historicals surveys of American outdoor amusements are Mangels's *The Outdoor Amusement Industry* and McKennon's *A Pictorial History of the American Carnival.* The writing of Daniel Mannix, a former carnie, provides insights into carnival performers and life, as do the books by Becker, Boles, Dadswell, and Gresham. Carnival atmosphere is captured by a number of journalistic writers on the subject, despite factual weaknesses (carnies tend to be suspicious of all outsiders and frequently present distorted accounts of carnival life). Good examples are Arthur Lewis's *Carnival*, which makes entertaining reading, and Harry Crews's article "Carny," which reveals more of the seamy side of carnival life. The world of hanky panky and carnival games in general is explored by Dembroski; Drimmer, Carrington, and Thompson focus on sideshow attractions, in particular, human oddities. Finally, unpublished scholarly works worthy of inclusion are Patricia Nathe's historical study of carnivals, fairs, circuses, and amusement parks, and Wittold Krassowski's analysis of the carnival worker.

Dime Museums and Medicine Shows

Two significant areas of popular entertainment that have received surprisingly scant coverage are dime museums and medicine shows. Indeed, little attention has been given the theatrical format of these two American institutions, although both had long and fascinating histories. The medicine show belongs to a tradition of mountebanks, charletans, and quack doctors selling tonics and elixirs mixed with attention-getting free entertainment that dates back to the Middle Ages. The dime museum, from the Civil War to World War I, provided a variety of entertainment to working-class audiences in virtually every city and town in the United States.

Only one major full-length study can be included on the American medicine show, Brooks McNamara's *Step Right Up: An Illustrated History of the American Medicine Show,* which is not only the sole documented history of the phenomenon but an excellent reference for additional sources on patent medicine and related topics, examples of medicine show skits, and a glossary of pitchmen's terms. His essays on the subject, although to a large extent incorporated into the longer work, are also recommended. Graydon Freeman's *The Medicine Showman*, Thomas Kelley's *The Fabulous Kelley*, and Malcolm Webber's fictionalized reminiscences are earlier but less effective attempts to record aspects of the medicine show. In Mae Noell's "Some Memories of a Medicine Show Performer" a med-show artist recalls the best-loved "bits" and life on the rural circuits and provides some additional insights into this American institution. McNamara, however, remains the definitive source.

The dime museum has received even less attention and, again, the major source to date is by McNamara, " 'A Congress of Wonders': The Rise and Fall of the Dime Museum," an excellent survey of the origin and development of this uniquely American brand of popular entertainment. The name most closely associated with the dime museum tradition in this country is Phineas T. Barnum, America's greatest early showman. Although the tendency is to lump him into the American circus tradition, where he indeed did make some contributions, Barnum's major involvement was with his New York American Museum, where he displayed some 600,000 items plus presenting live, popular entertainment and theatre in his "Lecture Room." John Betts in his "P. T. Barnum and the Popularization of Natural History" offers a good critical perspective on Barnum's museum, although the definitive and only documented study of Barnum's career is Neil Harris's *Humbug: The Art of P. T. Barnum*, an excellent analysis of Barnum's contributions in their social, economic, entertainment, and intellectual contexts. Less useful are the other two major, standard biographies of Barnum: M. R. Werner's *Barnum* and Irving Wallace's *The Fabulous Showman*, the latter containing an extensive bibliography. Alice Desmond's *Barnum Presents General Tom Thumb* is a pleasant biography of Barnum's famous attraction, Charles Stratton. Barnum himself authored numerous books and, although their credibility should be questioned, they are still important sources. His *The Humbugs of the World* (1865) and *Struggles and Triumphs* (1869) have both been recently reprinted.

Popular Theatre

Popular theatre encompasses the largest body of sources of any form of popular entertainment, primarily because of its scripted nature and its overlap with mainstream theatre forms. Virtually all American theatre histories deal with various aspects of popular theatre, such as nineteenth-century melodrama, Tom shows, Toby and Suzy shows, hippodrama, tent theatre and touring troupes, mining camp theatre, and other topics that use mainstream theatre structures and techniques. For the sake of this essay, I have chosen to discuss only major sources; additional relevant material can be found in my forthcoming guide, "The American Stage to World War I." A familiarity with the journal *Nineteenth Century Theatre Research* is a must in this area of study, as are the major theatre collections and periodicals of the period.

An excellent overview of popular theatre is included in Toll's *On with the Show*, along with a good selective bibliography. Toll is especially good in his analysis of native themes and characters dealt with in American drama. A. H. Quinn's survey of American drama remains the standard survey of specific plays and playwrights (anthologies of American drama are excluded from this survey but should be consulted as well).

For drama, the most important developments in the late nineteenth century took place in small-town America, where versions of most of the popular plays of the day were presented in town halls, concert halls, opera houses, and ultimately theatre tents. Basic formulas evolved that virtually guaranteed success; drama was geared to reach the common people, reflecting their desires, needs, and tastes. Identifiable, native American characters figure prominently in the evolution of popular theatre. Other than general studies already noted, Francis Hodge's *Yankee Theatre*, Richard Moody's essays on *Uncle Tom's Cabin* and Edward Harrigan (a full-length study, which should be excellent, is projected). Harry Birdoff's *The World's Greatest Hit*, and Willis Turner's study of city low-life in American theatre are especially recommended. Hodge's book is the definitive history of the stage Yankee during its peak period, and Birdoff's is the only full-length study of "Tommers" and derivatives from the original *Uncle Tom's Cabin*.

The story of the "trouper" and the evolution of traveling companies, culminating in repertoire tent shows, is effectively told in William Slout's *Theatre in a Tent*, also an excellent source on operational practices. An excellent introduction to the entertainment business in small-town America, although one of those "good bad" books, is Hoyt's *Town Hall Tonight*. Philip Lewis's *Trouping: How the Show Came to Town* is a pleasant but unreliable history of the same subject. A less successful study is McKennon's *Tent Show*. A more scholarly analysis of touring systems, specifically in California from 1849 to 1859, is McDermott's fine essay in *Theatre Survey*.

Much of the atmosphere and climate for popular theatre is reflected in early western theatre and amusements in the mining frontiers of Oregon, California, and Nevada. This aspect is well covered in studies by Ericson, Ernst, Gaer, Gagey, and Watson. The presence of a popular theatre in New York is revealed with scholarly exactitude in Felheim's study of Augustin Daly and Marker's book on David Belasco. The importance and influence of a strictly American institution, the Chautauqua, which included popular entertainment and theatre under the guise of culture and religion (including a strong tent tradition) is dealt with in detail in Morrison's history of Chautauqua, Horner's *Strike the Tent*, and Harrison's *Culture Under Canvas*, a recounting of the traveling tent shows by the manager of the Redpath Chautauqua.

The American showboat, which included not only floating theatres but circus boats and medicine boats, has been most fully explored by Philip Graham. George Ford's *These Were Actors* is an interesting, if fanciful, account of one of the earliest showboat families.

Of all dramatic formulas, the melodrama was the most enduring in American popular culture and dominated the popular stage during its heyday, 1850 to 1920. A penetrating analysis of the cultural milieu in which melodrama developed and thrived is Grimsted's *Melodrama Unveiled*, a well-documented scholarly work that includes chapters on critics, audiences, stages, and plays, and offers an excellent bibliographical essay on sources. Rahill's *The World of Melodrama* is also an important treatment of the genre, although less perceptive than Grimsted's. There is a close relationship between English and American melodrama; consequently a number of good English sources are recommended, especially those by Booth, Disher, and Reynolds.

One of the last American stock characters to develop, Toby, a redheaded, freckle-faced, country boy, especially popular in the South, Southwest, and Midwest, has been the subject of several scholarly investigations, in particular those of Clark, Snyder, and Mickel. *The Fabulous Toby and Me*, the story of Neil Schaffner, the last of the well-known tent repertoire showmen, is an entertaining and sometimes revealing look at the tag-end of an American tradition.

Recent Sources: Non-American

This final section includes works on a number of topics, some of which could easily be expanded into major categories of their own. The sources indicated here hint at the explosion of literature on popular entertainment during the past few years. As a general rule, these more recent publications are far superior to earlier efforts on the same topics.

English forms have received a great deal of attention recently, in particular music hall and British pantomime (close cousins to several American forms). The first "who's who" of the music hall, by Roy Busby, was just recently published, and David Cheshire has begun to chronicle its history in various works, including *Music Hall in Britain*, the story of the halls told in documents and pictures. George Speaight, an outstanding historian of popular entertainment, has edited a fascinating collection of songs of the "song and supper rooms" in the early nineteenth century. Mander and Mitchenson's revised edition of *British Music Hall* is a superb pictorial history of the halls, and Laurence Senelick, an American scholar, has made significant contributions in recent journal articles, especially his "A Brief Life and Times of the Victorian Music-Hall." The definitive study of British pantomime during its important period was written in 1969 by David Mayer, who continues to contribute to this fascinating study in important journal articles. Mander and Mitchenson's pictorial history of pantomime is recommended also.

The history of puppetry has been covered in great detail by Speaight in his *Punch and Judy* and virtually every topic having to do with puppets is found in Philpott's *Dictionary of Puppetry*. (American puppet theatre is definitively treated in McPharlin's *The Puppet Theatre in America*.) The subject of magic has received extensive treatment through the years and an excellent new guide to the more current sources is Gill's *Magic as a Performing Art*. The first history devoted exclusively to street magic, by Claflin and Sheridan, has just been published. No mention of magic would be complete without the inclusion of Milbourne Christopher's work on magic, especially *The Illustrated History of Magic*, one of the most important magic books of modern times and a superb general reference source. One of the last forms of popular entertainment to develop and establish a significant tradition is the cabaret, a topic that has received virtually no coverage in English. Correcting that omission is Appignanesi's *The Cabaret*, a useful historical survey and analytical account of the cabaret from its Parisian beginnings to its most recent manifestations in London and the United States.

It is increasingly obvious that popular entertainment has always offered the average person a vital and appealing alternative theatre experience that deserves to be studied on its own terms as a significant aspect of popular culture, not derided as a corruption of so-called legitimate theatre. As such, academic libraries must no longer ignore or slight the value of materials relevant to this fascinating area of inquiry.

WORKS CITED

Books and Essays

Allen, Ralph G. "Our Native Theatre." *In* Symposium, The American Theatre—a Cultural Process, Washington, D.C., 1969. *The American Theatre: A Sum of Its Parts.* French, 1971.

Angier, Roswell. *A Kind of Life: Conversations in the Combat Zone.* Addison House, 1976.

Appignanesi, Lisa. *The Cabaret.* Universe Books, 1976.

Atkinson, Justin Brooks. *Broadway.* Rev. ed. Macmillan, 1974.

Barber, Rowland. *The Night They Raided Minsky's.* Simon and Schuster, 1960.

Barnum, Phineas T. *The Humbugs of the World.* Singing Tree a div. of Gale, 1970 (repr. of 1865 ed.).

Barnum, Phineas T. *Struggles and Triumphs: or The Life of P. T. Barnum.* Arno 1970 (repr. of 1869 ed.).

Bawdy Songs of the Early Music Hall, selected, with an intro. by George Speaight. London, David & Charles, 1975.

Becker, Howard S. *Outsiders: Studies in the Sociology of Deviance.* Free Press, 1963.

Betts, John R. "P. T. Barnum and the Popularization of Natural History," *Journal of the History of Ideas* 20 (1959): 353-68.

Bier, Jesse. *The Rise and Fall of American Humor.* Holt, Rinehart, & Winston, 1968.

Birdoff, Harry. *The World's Greatest Bit—Uncle Tom's Cabin.* S. F. Vanni, 1947.

Bode, Carl. *The Anatomy of American Popular Culture, 1840-1861.* California, 1959.

Boles, Don. The Midway Showman. Atlanta, Pinchpenny Press, 1967.

Booth, Michael R. *English Melodrama.* London, H. Jenkins, 1965.

Bouissac, Paul. *Circus and Culture: A Semiotic Approach.* Indiana, 1976.

Braithwaite, David. *Fairground Architecture.* Praeger, 1968.

Bristow, Eugene Kerr. "Look Out for Saturday Night: A Social History of Professional Variety in Memphis, Tennessee, 1859-1880." Ph.D. dissertation, State University of Iowa, 1956.

Brown, Thomas Allston. *History of the New York Stage.* Blom, 1963 (repr. of 1903 ed.).

Busby, Roy. *British Music Hall: An Illustrated Who's Who from 1850 to the Present Day.* Salem, Elek. 1976 (see Performing Arts Section).

Cantor, Norman I. and Michael S. Werthman, eds. *The History of Popular Culture.* Macmillan, 1968.

Carrington, Hereward. *Sideshow and Animal Tricks.* Atlanta, Pinchpenny Press, 1973 (repr. of 1913 ed.).

Chambers, Edmund Kerchever. *The Medieval Stage.* Oxford, 1963 (repr. of 1903 ed.).

Cheshire, David F. "A Chronology of Music Hall," *Theatre Quarterly* 1 (October-December 1971): 41-45.

Cheshire, David F. *Music Hall in Britain.* Fairleigh Dickinson, 1974.

Chindahl, George Leonard. *History of the Circus in America.* Caxton, 1959.

Christopher, Milbourne. *The Illustrated History of Magic.* Crowell, 1973.

Churchill, Allen. *The Theatrical Twenties.* McGraw-Hill, 1975.

Claflin, Edward and Jeff Sheridan. *Street Magic: An Illustrated History of Wandering Magicians and Their Conjuring Arts.* Doubleday, 1977.

Clark, Larry Dale. "Toby Shows: A Form of American Popular Theatre." Ph.D. dissertation, University of Illinois, 1963.

Clinton-Baddeley, Victor Clinton. *The Burlesque Tradition in the English Theatre After 1660.* London, Methuen, 1952 (repr. 1973).

Corio, Ann with Joe DiMona. *This Was Burlesque.* Madison Square Press, 1968.

Cox, Harvey Gallagher. *The Feast of Fools: A Theological Essay on Festivity and Fantasy.* Harvard, 1969.

Coxe, Antony Hippisley. "Historical Research and the Circus." *Theatre Notebook* 21 (Autumn 1966): 40-42.

Coxe, Antony Hippisley. *A Seat at the Circus.* London, Evans Brothers, 1951.

Crews, Harry, "Carny." *Playboy* 23 (September 1976): 96ff.

Croft-Cooke, Rupert and Peter Cotes. *Circus: A World History.* Macmillan, 1976. *Action, the Showman.* London, Sidgwick and Jackson, 1952.

Croft-Cooke, Rupert and Peter Cotes. *Circus: A World History.* Macmillan, 1976.

Dadswell, Jack. *Hey There Sucker.* Boston, B. Humphries, 1946.

Davidson, Frank C. "The Rise, Development, Decline, and Influence of the American Minstrel Show." Ph.D. dissertation, New York University, 1952.

Dembroski, Theodore M. "Hanky Panks and Group Games Versus Alibis and Flats: The Legitimate and Illegitimate of the Carnival's Front End." *Journal of Popular Culture* 6, no. 3 (Winter 1972): 567-582.

Desmond, Alice Curtis. *Barnum Presents General Tom Thumb*, Maxmillan, 1954.

Dexter, Thomas Francis George. *The Pagan Origins of Fairs*. London, C. A. Watts, 1930.

DiMeglio, John E. *Vaudeville U.S.A.* Bowling Green University Popular Press, 1973.

Disher, Maurice Willson. *Blood and Thunder: Mid-Victorian Melodrama and Its Origins*. Haskell House, 1974 (repr. of 1949 ed.).

Disher, Maurice Willson. *Greatest Show on Earth*. Blom, 1971 (repr. of 1937 ed.).

Disher, Maurice Willson. *Melodrama: Plots That Thrilled*. Macmillan, 1954.

Drimmer, Frederick. *Very Special People: The Struggles, Loves and Triumphs of Human Oddities*. Amjon, 1973.

Ducharte, Pierre Louis. *The Italian Comedy*. Dover, 1966 (repr. of 1929 ed.).

Dulles, Foster Rhea. *America Learns to Play*. Appleton-Century, 1940.

Durant, John and Alice Durant. *The Pictorial History of the American Circus*. A. S. Barnes, 1957.

Easto, Patrick C. and Marcello Truzzi. "Towards an Ethnography of the Carnival Social System." *Journal of Popular Culture* 6, no. 3 (Winter 1972): 550-566.

Easto, Patrick C. "Carnivals, Roadshows and Freaks." *Society* 9 (March 1972): 26-34.

Elliott, Eugene Clinton. *A History of Variety-Vaudeville in Seattle*. University of Washington, 1944.

Ericson, Robert Edward. "Touring Entertainment in Nevada During the Peak Years of the Mining Boom." Ph.D. dissertation, University of Oregon, 1970.

Ernst, Alice Henson. *Trouping in the Oregon Country*. Portland, Oregon Historical Society, 1961.

Faral, Edmond. *Les Jongleurs en France au Moyen Age*. Burt Franklin, 1970 (repr. of 1910 ed.).

Felheim, Marvin. *The Theater of Augustin Daly*. Harvard, 1956.

Fletcher, Tom. *100 Years of the Negro in Show Business*. New York, Burdge, 1954.

Flint, Richard W. "A Selected Guide to Source Material on the American Circus." *Journal of Popular Culture* 6, no. 3 (Winter 1972): 615-19.

Ford, George D. *These Were Actors: The Story of the Chapmans and the Drakes*. Library Publishers, 1955.

Fox, Charles Philip and Tom Parkinson. *Circus in America*. Waukesha. Wis., Country Beautiful, 1969.

Fox, Charles Philip. *Circus Parades: A Pictorial History of America's Pageant*. Century House, 1953.

Fox, Charles Philip. *A Pictorial History of Performing Horses*. Seattle, Superior Pub. Co., 1960.

Fox, Charles Philip. *A Ticket to the Circus*. Seattle, Superior Pub. Co., 1959.

Freedman, Jill. *Circus Days*. Harmony Books (dist. by Crown), 1975.

Freeman, Graydon Laverne. *The Medicine Showman*. Century House, 1957.

Frost, Thomas. *The Old Showmen and the Old London Fairs*. Gryphon Books, 1971 (repr. of 1881 ed.).

Gaer, Joseph, ed. *The Theater of the Gold Rush Decade in San Francisco.* Burt Franklin, 1970 (repr. of 1935 ed.).

Gagey, Edmond M. *The San Francisco Stage.* Columbia, 1950.

Gilbert, Douglas. *American Vaudeville: Its Life and Times.* Dover, 1968 (repr. of 1940 ed.).

Gill, Robert. *Magic as a Performing Art: A Bibliography of Conjuring.* Bowker, 1976.

Goldsmith, Robert Hillis. *Wise Fools in Shakespeare.* Michigan State, 1955.

Graham, Philip. *Showboats: The History of an American Institution.* Texas, 1951.

Grau, Robert. *The Business Man in the Amusement World.* J. S. Ozer, 1971 (*repr.* of the 1910 ed.).

Grau, Robert. *Forty Years of Observation of Music and the Drama.* Broadway, 1909.

Green, Abel and Joe Laurie, Jr. *Show Biz from Vaude to Video.* Kennikat, 1972 (repr. of 1951 ed.).

Greenwood, Isaac John. *The Circus: Its Origins and Growth Prior to 1835,* 2d ed. William Abbatt, 1909 (Burt Franklin, 1968, repr. of the 1898 ed.).

Gresham, Wiliam Lindsay. *Monster Midway.* Rinehart, 1953.

Grimsted, David. *Melodrama Unveiled: American Theatre and Culture, 1800-1850.* Chicago, 1968.

Harris, Neil. *Humbug: The Art of P. T. Barnum.* Little, Brown, 1973.

Harrison, Harry P., as told to Karl Detzer. *Culture Under Canvas: The Story of Tent Chautauqua.* Hastings House, 1958.

Haverly, Jack. *Negro Minstrels: A Complete Guide.* Literature House, 1969 (repr. of 1902 ed.).

Havighurst, Walter. *Annie Oakley of the Wild West.* Macmillan, 1954.

Hodge, Francis. *Yankee Theatre: The Image of America on Stage, 1825-1850.* Texas, 1964.

Horner, Charles Francis. *Strike the Tents, the Story of the Chautauqua.* Dorrance, 1964.

Hoyt, Harlowe Randall. *Town Hall Tonight.* Prentice-Hall, 1955.

Hughes, Langston and Milton Meltzer. *Black Magic: A Pictorial History of the Negro in American Entertainment.* Prentice-Hall, 1967.

Isman, Felix. *Weber and Fields: Their Tribulations, Triumphs, and Their Associates.* Boni and Liveright, 1924.

Jennings, John Joseph. *Theatrical and Circus Life; or, Secrets of the Stage, Greenroom and Sawdust Arena.* St. Louis, Herbert & Cole, 1882.

Keegan, Marcia. *We Can Still Hear Them Clapping.* Avon, 1975.

Kelley, Thomas. *The Fabulous Kelley: Canada's King of the Medicine Men.* Rev. ed. Don Mills, Ont., General Pub. Co., 1974.

Kennard, Joseph Spencer. *Masks and Marionettes.* Kennikat, 1967 (repr. of 1935 ed.).

Kirby, E. T. "The Shamanistic Origins of Popular Entertainment." *The Drama Review* 18, no. 1 (T-61, March 1974): 1-9.

Krassowski, Wittold. "Social Structure and Professionalization in the Occupation of the Carnival Worker." Master's thesis, Purdue University, 1954.

The Language of Show Biz, a Dictionary. Dramatic Pub. Co., 1973.

Laurie, Joseph. *Vaudeville: From the Honky-tonks to the Palace.* Kennikat, 1972 (repr. of 1953 ed.).

Lea, Kathleen Marguerite. *Italian Popular Comedy.* Oxford, 1934.

Leavitt, Michel Bennett. *Fifty Years in Theatrical Management, 1859-1909.* Broadway, 1912.

Lee, Gypsy Rose. *Gypsy: A Memoir.* Harper, 1957.

Lewis, Arthur H. *Carnival.* Trident Press, 1970.

Lewis, Philip C. *Trouping: How the Show Came to Town.* Harper and Row, 1973.

Lipnitski, Bernard. "God Save the Queen." *Esquire* 72 (August 1969): 104-7.

McDermott, Douglas. "Touring Patterns on California's Theatrical Frontier, 1849-1859." *Theatre Survey* 15 (May 1974): 18-28.

McKechnie, Samuel. *Popular Entertainments Through the Ages.* Blom, 1969 (repr. of 1931 ed.).

McKennon, Joe. *A Pictorial History of the American Carnival.* Sarasota, Fla., Carnival Publishers of Sarasota (dist. by Bowling Green University Popular Press, 1972).

McKennon, Marian Leigh. *Tent Show.* Exposition, 1964.

McLean, Albert F. *American Vaudeville as Ritual.* Kentucky, 1965.

McLean, Albert F. "U.S. Vaudeville and the Urban Comics." *Theatre Quarterly* 1 (October-December 1971): 50-57.

McNamara, Brooks. "'A Congress of Wonders': The Rise and Fall of the Dime Museum." *Emerson Society Quarterly* 20, no. 3 (1974): 216-32.

McNamara, Brooks. "The Indiana Medicine Show." *Educational Theatre Journal* 23 (December 1971): 431-445.

McNamara, Brooks. "Medicine Shows: American Vaudeville in the Marketplace." *Theatre Quarterly* 4 (May-July 1974): 19-30.

McNamara, Brooks. "Popular Scenography." *The Drama Review* 18 (T-61, March 1974): 16-25.

McNamara, Brooks. "'Scavengers of the Amusement World': Popular Entertainment and the Birth of the Movies." In *American Pastimes.* Brockton, Mass., Brockton Art Center, 1976 (catalog for exhibit).

McNamara, Brooks. *Step Right Up: An Illustrated History of the American Medicine Show.* Doubleday, 1976.

McPharlin, Paul. *The Puppet Theatre in America: A History, 1524-1948.* With a suppl.: *Puppets in America Since 1948,* by Marjorie Batchelor McPharlin. Rev. ed. Plays, 1969.

Mander, Raymond and Joe Mitchenson. *British Music Hall.* Rev. ed. London, Gentry Books, 1974.

Mander, Raymond and Joe Mitchenson. *Pantomime: A Story in Pictures.* Taplinger, 1973.

Mangels, William F. *The Outdoor Amusement Industry, from Earliest Times to the Present.* Vantage Press, 1952.

Mannix, Daniel Pratt. *Step Right Up.* Harper, 1951.

Mannix, Daniel Pratt. *We Who Are Not as Others.* Pocket Books, 1976.

Marker, Lise-Lone. *David Belasco: Naturalism in the American Theatre.* Princeton, 1975.

Marks, Edward Bennett. *They All Had Glamour, from the Swedish Nightingale to the Naked Lady.* Greenwood, 1972 (repr. of 1944 ed.).

Marston, William and John H. Feller. *F. F. Proctor, Vaudeville Pioneer.* New York, R. R. Smith, 1943.

Matlaw, Myron. "Tony the Trouper: Pastor's Early Years." *Theatre Annual* 24 (1968): 70-90.

Matthews, Brander. *A Book About the Theatre.* Scribner, 1916.

Maurer, David W. "Carnival Cant: A Glossary of Circus and Carnival Slang." *American Speech* 6 (1931): 327-337.

May, Earl Chapin. *The Circus from Rome to Ringling.* Dover, 1963 (repr. of 1932 ed.).

Mayer, David, III. *Harlequin in His Element: The English Pantomime, 1806-1836.* Harvard, 1969.

Meiselas, Susan. *Carnival Strippers.* Farrar, Straus, and Giroux, 1976.

Mickel, Jere C. "The Genesis of Toby." *Journal of American Folklore* 80 (October-December 1967): 334-40.

Mills, Steve. "'An Artist's Studio': A Comic Scene from Burlesque." *Educational Theatre Journal* 27 (October 1975): 342-344.

Moody, Richard. *America Takes the Stage.* Kraus Reprint, 1969 (repr. of 1955 ed.).

Moody, Richard. "Uncle Tom. the Theater and Mrs. Stowe." *American Heritage* 6 (October 1955): 29-33, 102-103.

Moody, Richard. "Edward Harrigan." *Modern Drama* 19 (December 1976): 319-325.

Moody, Richard and A. M. Drummond. "The Hit of the Century: *Uncle Tom's Cabin.*" *Educational Theatre Journal* 4 (1952): 315-22.

Morley, Henry. *Memoirs of Bartholomew Fair.* Singing Tree, a div. of Gale, 1968 (repr. of 1880 ed.).

Morris, Lloyd. *Incredible New York.* Arno, 1975 (repr. of 1951 ed.).

Morrison, Theodore. *Chautauqua: A Center for Education, Religion, and the Arts in America.* Chicago, 1974.

Murray, Marian. *Circus! From Rome to Ringling.* Greenwood, 1973 (repr. of 1956 ed.).

Nathan, Hans. *Dan Emmett and the Rise of Early Negro Minstrelsy.* Oklahoma, 1962.

Nathe, Patricia A. "Carnivals, also Fairs, Circuses, and Amusement Parks: A Historical Perspective." Master's thesis, University of California, Berkeley, 1969.

Nicoll, Allardyce. *Masks, Mimes, and Miracles: Studies in the Popular Theatre.* Cooper Square, 1963 (repr. of 1931 ed.).

Nicoll, Allardyce. *The World of Harlequin: A Critical Study of the Commedia dell'arte.* Cambridge, 1963.

Niklaus, Thelma. *Harlequin: or, The Rise and Fall of a Bergamask Rogue.* Braziller, 1956.

Noell, Mae. "Some Memories of a Medicine Show Performer." *Theatre Quarterly* 4 (May-July 1974): 25-30.

Nye, Russel Blaine. *The Unembarrassed Muse: The Popular Arts in America.* Dial, 1970.

Odell, George Clinton Densmore. *Annals of the New York Stage.* AMS, 1970 (repr. of 1927-49 ed.).

Oreglia, Giacomo. *The Commedia dell'arte.* Hill and Wang, 1968.

Page, Brett. *Writing for Vaudeville.* Springfield, Mass., The Home Correspondence School, 1915.

Paskman, Dailey. *"Gentlemen, Be Seated!" A Parade of the American Minstrels.* Rev. ed. C. N. Potter (dist. by Crown), 1976.

Patterson, Cecil L. "A Different Drummer: The Image of the Negro in Nineteenth-Century Popular Song Books." Ph.D. dissertation, University of Penn, 1961.

"People's Theatre." *Theatre Quarterly* 1 (October-December 1971, special issue).

Philpott, Alexis Robert. *Dictionary of Puppetry.* Plays, 1969.

Plowden, Gene. *Those Amazing Ringlings and Their Circus.* Caxton, 1967.

"Popular Entertaiments." *The Drama Review* 18, no. 1 (T-61, March 1974, special issue).

"Popular Theatre." *Educational Theatre Journal* 27, no. 3 (October 1975, special issue).

Powledge, Fred. *Mud Show: A Circus Season.* Harcourt Brace Jovanovich, 1975.

Quinn, Arthur Hobson. *A History of the American Drama from the Beginning to the Civil War.* 2d ed. Appleton-Century-Crofts, 1943.

Quinn, Arthur Hobson. *A History of the American Drama from the Civil War to the Present Day.* Rev. ed. Appleton-Century-Crofts, 1936.

Rahill, Frank. *The World of Melodrama.* Pennsylvania State, 1967.

Ramshaw, Molly N. "Jump, Jim Crow! A Biographical Sketch of Thomas D. Rice." *Theatre Annual* 17 (1960): 36-47.

Remy, Tristan. *Entrées Clownesques.* Paris, l'Arche, 1962.

Remy, Tristan. *Les Clowns.* Paris, B. Grasset, 1945.

Rennert, Jack. *100 Posters of Buffalo Bill's Wild West.* Darien House, 1976.

Reynolds, Ernest Randolph. *Early Victorian Drama, 1830-1870.* Cambridge, Heffer, 1936.

Reynolds, Harry. *Minstrel Memories: The Story of Burnt Cork Minstrelsy in Great Britain from 1836-1927.* London, A. Rivers, 1928.

Rice, Edward LeRoy. *Monarchs of Minstrelsy: From "Daddy" Rice to Date.* Kenny, 1911.

Rourke, Constance. *American Humor: A Study of the National Character.* Harcourt, Brace, 1931.

Rourke, Constance. *The Roots of American Culture.* Harcourt, Brace, 1942.

Russell, Don. *The Lives and Legends of Buffalo Bill.* Oklahoma, 1960.

Russell, Don. *The Wild West: or, A History of the Wild West Shows.* Fort Worth, Texas, Amon Carter Museum of Western Art, 1970.

Salutin, Marilyn. "Stripper Morality." *Transaction* 8, no. 8 (June 1971): 12-22.

Samuels, Charles and Louise Samuels. *Once Upon a Stage: The Merry World of Vaudeville.* Dodd, Mead, 1974.

Sandberg, Trish. "An Interview with Steve Mills." *Educational Theatre Journal* 27 (October 1975): 331-341.

Saxon, A. H. *Enter Foot and Horse: A History of Hippodrama in England and France,* Yale, 1968.

Saxon, A. H. "Shakespeare and Circuses." *Theatre Survey* 7 (1966): 59-79.

Scala, Flaminio. *Scenarios of the Commedia dell'arte,* tr. by Henry F. Salerno. New York University, 1967.

Schaffner, Neil E. with Vance Johnson. *The Fabulous Toby and Me.* Prentice-Hall, 1968.

Seldes, Gilbert Vivian. *The 7 Lively Arts.* Sagamore Press, 1957.

Sell, Henry Blackman and Victor Weybright. *Buffalo Bill and the Wild West.* Oxford, 1955.

Senelick, Laurence. "A Brief Life and Times of the Victorian Music-hall." *Harvard Library Bulletin* 19 (October 1971): 375-398.

Skipper, James K., Jr. and Charles H. McCaghy. "Stripteasers: The Anatomy and Career Contingencies of a Deviant Occupation." *Social Problems* 17 (Winter 1970): 391-405.

Slout, William Lawrence. *Theatre in a Tent: The Development of a Provincial Entertaiment.* Bowling Green University Popular Press, 1972.

Smith, Bill. *The Vaudevillians.* Macmillan, 1976.

Snyder, Sherwood, Ill. "The Toby Shows." Ph.D. dissertation. univ. of Minnesota, 1966.

Sobel, Bernard. *Burleycue: An Underground History of Burlesque Days.* Burt Franklin, 1975 (repr. of 1931 ed.).

Sobel, Bernard. *A Pictorial History of Burlesque.* Putnam, 1956.

Sobel, Bernard. *A Pictorial History of Vaudeville.* Citadel, 1961.

Sokan, Robert. *A Descriptive and Bibliographic Catalog of the Circus & Related Arts Collection at Illinois State University, Normal, Illinois.* Bloomington, Ill., Scarlet Ibis Press (dist. by Rare Book Room, Milner Library, Illinois State University, Normal, Ill., 61761), 1976.

Sothern, Georgia. *Georgia, My Life in Burlesque.* New American Library, 1972.

Speaight, George. *Punch & Judy, a History.* Plays, 1970.

Spitzer, Marian. *The Palace.* Atheneum, 1969.

Swain, Barbara. *Fools and Folly During the Middle Ages and the Renaissance.* Columbia, 1932.

Sweet, Robert C. "The Circus: An Institution in Continuity and Change." Ph.D. dissertation. University of Missouri, 1970.

Sweet, Robert C. and Robert W. Habenstein. "Some Perspectives on the Circus in Transition." *Journal of Popular Culture* 6 (Winter 1972): 583-590.

Thétard, Henry. *La Merveilleuse Histoire du Cirque.* Paris, Prisma, 1947.

Thompson, Charles John Samuel. *The Mystery and Lore of Monsters.* Citadel, 1970 (repr. of 1930 ed.).

Toll, Robert C. *Blacking Up: The Minstrel Show in Nineteenth-Century America.* Oxford, 1974.

Toll, Robert C. *On with the Show!: The First Century of Show Business in America.* Oxford, 1976.

Toole-Stott, Raymond. *A Bibliography of Books on the Circus in English from 1773 to 1964.* Derby, Eng., Harpur, distributors [1964].

Toole-Stott, Raymond. *Circus and Allied Arts: A World Bibliography, 1500-[1970]* based mainly on circus literature in the British Museum, the Library of Congress, the Bibliothèque Nationale, and on his own collection. Derby, Eng., Harpur, distributors [1958-71].

Towsen, John H. *Clowns,* Hawthorn, 1976.

Towsen, John H. "Sources in Popular Entertainment." *The Drama Review* 18 (T-61, March 1974): 118-23.

Truzzi, Marcello, ed. "Circuses, Carnivals and Fairs in America." *Journal of Popular Culture* 6, no. 3 (Winter 1972).

Turner, Willis L. "City Low-life on the American Stage to 1900." Ph.D. dissertation, University of Illinois, 1956.

Vail, Robert William Glenroie. *Random Notes on the Early American Circus.* Barre, Mass., Barre Gazette, 1956 (repr. of 1933 essay in *Proceedings of the American Antiquarian Society*).

Wallace, Irving. *The Fabulous Showman, the Life and Times of P. T. Barnum.* Knopf, 1959.

Watson, Margaret. *Silver Theatre, Amusements of the Mining Frontier in Early Nevada, 1850-1864.* Glendale, Calif., A. H. Clark, 1964.

Webber, Malcolm. *Medicine Show.* Caxton, 1941.

Welsford, Enid. *The Fool: His Social and Literary History.* London, Faber & Faber, 1935.

Werner, Morris Robert. *Barnum.* Harcourt, Brace, 1923.

Willeford, William. *The Fool and His Scepter: A Study in Clowns and Jesters and Their Audience.* Northwestern, 1969.

Willson, Clair. *Mimes and Miners: Theater in Tombstone.* Arizona, 1935.

Wilmeth, Don B. "The American Stage to World War I." Gale, forthcoming.

Winter, Marian Hannah. "'Juba and American Minstrelsy." *Dance Index* 6 (1947): 28-47.

Wittke, Carl. *Tambo and Bones: A History of the American Minstrel Stage.* Greenwood, 1968 (repr. of 1930 ed.).

Wortley, Richard. *A Pictorial History of Striptease: 100 Years of Undressing to Music.* Seacaucus, N.J., Chartwell Books, 1976 (distr. by Book Sales).

Young, William C. *American Theatrical Arts: A Guide to Manuscripts and Special Collections in the United States and Canada.* American Library Association, 1971.

Zanger, Jules. "The Minstrel Show as Theater of Misrule." *Quarterly Journal of Speech* 60 (February 1974): 33-38.

Zeidman, Irving. *The American Burlesque Show.* Hawthorn, 1967.

Zellers, Parker. "The Cradle of Variety: The Concert Saloon." *Educational Theatre Journal* 20 (December 1968): 578-585.

Zellers, Parker. *Tony Pastor: Dean of the Vaudeville Stage.* Eastern Michigan, 1971.

Journals

Amusement Business. 1961-   Billboard Publications, Inc. (subscriptions: P.O. Box 2150, Radnor, PA 19089).

Bandwagon. 1939- . 2515 Dorset Rd., Columbus, OH 43221.

Billboard. 1894- . (Outdoor show news section merged into *Amusement Business*.) Billboard Publications, Inc. (subscriptions: P.O. Box 2150, Radnor, PA 19089).

Le Cirque dans L'Univers. 1950- . Club du Cirque, 11 Rue Ch-Silvestri, 94300 Vincennes, France.

The Drama Review. 1955- . New York University, School of the Arts, 50 W. 4th St., Rm. 300, New York, NY 10012.

Educational Theatre Journal. 1949- . American Theatre Assoc., 1317 F St. N.W., Washington, D.C. 20004.

Journal of Popular Culture. 1967- . Modern Language Assoc. of America, Popular Literature Section, Bowling Green State University, Bowling Green, OH 43402.

Nineteenth-Century Theatre Research. 1973-   . Dept. of English, University of Arizona, Tucson, AZ. 85721.

Theatre Quarterly. 1971-   . T.Q. Pubs. Ltd., 30 Prince of Wales Crescent, London NW1 8HA (dist. by University of Southern California, Parkview 301, Los Angeles, CA 90007).

Variety, 1905-   . Variety, Inc., 154 W. 46th St., New York, NY 10036.

White Tops: Devoted Exclusively to the Circus. 1927-   . Circus Fans Assoc. of America, 4931 Rosslyn. Indianapolis, IN 46205.

Index

About the Contributors_____

Ralph G. Allen is Professor of Theatre at the University of Tennessee and founding director of the Clarence Brown Company, a regional professional theatre. A former editor of *Theatre Survey*, he is co-author with John Gassner of *Theatre and Drama in the Making*, as well as other works of theatre history, poems, translations, and plays, including *Rip Van Winkle* (with Joshua Logan) and *The Sugar Babies* (an entertainment based on traditional burlesque materials). Professor Allen is a Fellow of the American Theatre Association and a member of the National Theatre Conference.

Helen Armstead-Johnson is Professor of English at York College of the City University of New York and Professor of Theatre at the CUNY Graduate Center. She is also the founder and curator of the Armstead-Johnson Foundation for Theatre Research, whose exhibitions have included "Traveling Through History with Black Performers" at the World Trade Center, and "Dixie to Broadway" at the Metropolitan Museum of Art. Her publications include: "Blacks in Black: Genuine Colored Minstrels" (*Encore*), "Black Influences in the American Theater: Part II, 1960 and After" (*Black American Reference Book*), and "Paul Robeson on Stage" (*First World*).

Clifford Ashby (Ph.D., Stanford University) is a Professor of Theatre Arts at Texas Tech University, and served as director of the bicentennial revival of the Harley Sadler Tent Show. His articles have appeared in such publications as the *Educational Theatre Journal*, *Quarterly Journal of Speech*, *Southern Speech Journal*, *Drama Survey*, *Theatre Survey*, the *Dictionary of American Biography*, and the *Pennsylvania Magazine of History and Biography*. A full-length biography of Harley Sadler is to be published by Popular Press.

James H. Bierman has written articles on the performing arts that have appeared in *The Yale Review*, *The Drama Review*, *Comparative Drama*, *Dance Scope*, and *The Soho Weekly News*. His play, *Heartaches*, was presented at the Performing Garage in New York City during the summer of 1978. He is currently teaching at the University of California at Santa Cruz.

William Brasmer is a Professor in the Department of Theatre and Cinema at Denison University in Ohio. He was Chairman, Department of Theatre, 1959-1976; Managing Director of Denison Summer Theatre, 1949-1963; a member of the AETA Board of Directors, 1954-1957; and Chairman of the International Theatre and Liaison Project of AETA, 1954-1957. His major recent publications include: *John O'Keeffe and William Shield: The Poor Soldier (1783)* (1978); "The Wild West Exhibition and the Drama of Civilization" *(Western Popular Theatre,* 1977); and *Black Drama, An Anthology* (1970).

Ray B. Browne, Chairman of the Popular Culture Department at Bowling Green State University, was founder of the Popular Culture Association and serves as its Secretary-Treasurer. He founded and edits *Journal of Popular Culture,* and began and co-edits *Journal of American Culture.* He is the author of more than 100 articles and the author and editor of thirty books, among them: *Melville's Drive to Humanism: Humanism in the Works of Herman Melville; Icons of America; Heroes of Popular Culture; Lincoln Lore: Lincoln in the Contemporary Popular Mind; Themes and Directions in American Literature;* and *The Alabama Folk Lyric: A Study in Origins and Media of Dissemination.*

Paul Antonie Distler is currently Head of the Department of Performing Arts and Communications and Professor of Theatre Arts at Virginia Polytechnic Institute and State University. He received his B.A. *cum laude* in English from Williams College and his M.A. and Ph.D. degrees in Theatre from Tulane. A past president of the American Theatre Association, Dr. Distler has published or spoken about ethnic comedy in vaudeville and burlesque, and he has served as managing editor of the *Tulane Drama Review* and consulting editor of *Southern Theatre Magazine.* He is a member of Phi Beta Kappa and Actors' Equity.

Joey Faye appeared in Billy Minsky's and other burlesque productions from 1931 to 1938. Subsequently, he toured with national companies of hit plays and acted in many New York productions, including *Man of La Mancha* (1965, as Sancho) and *Waiting for Godot* (1971, as Estragon; he had received the 1959 West Coast Critics Award for his Gogo, in the same play). Joey Faye has also performed in night clubs, films, and television; he is the author, director, and producer of *The Anatomy of Humor,* which he has toured nationally. At the Conference, he talked about his career and performed "Floogle Street" and some of his other comic sketches.

Judi Faye, who married Joey Faye in 1973, is an actress who has performed also under the name of Judith Karlin.

Richard W. Flint is Assistant Curator at the Margaret Woodbury Strong Museum in Rochester, New York, where he organized the 1977 exhibition and authored the catalog for "Step Right Up! Show Business at the Turn of the Century." Formerly research assistant at the State Historical Society of Wisconsin's Circus World Museum in Baraboo, he held a Youthgrant fellowship in 1973-1974 from the National Endowment for the Humanities for a study on the history and traditions of the circus and its people. He earned his M.A. degree in Museum Administration from the Cooperstown Graduate Programs, and is Vice-President of the Circus Historical Society.

Denis Gontard is Director of the Institut d'Etudes Théâtrales at the Université Paul Valéry of Montpellier, France. Born in the South of France, he attended the universities of Aix-en-Provence and Paris, where he specialized in history of the theatre, both classical and modern. During the past few years Dr. Gontard has lectured at most of the leading European and American universities on the contemporary directions of the French classical plays, on Jacques Copeau and the training of the actor, and on the main young companies of France. He has published *The French Decentralized Theatre* (Paris, S.E.D.E.S., 1973) and *The Journal de Bord des Copiaus* (Paris, Seghers, 1974).

Monroe Lippman holds the A.B., M.A., and Ph.D. degrees from the University of Michigan and has studied additionally at Iowa and Harvard. He is a past president of the American Theatre Association and has headed theatre departments at several universities, including Tulane, N.Y.U., and the University of California (Riverside). He is the author of numerous articles, and has been the recipient of a Guggenheim Fellowship and a Ford award. He is currently Professor Emeritus of Theatre at the University of California, on whose Riverside campus he teaches part time.

The editor of this book, **Myron Matlaw**, Professor of English at Queens College of the City University of New York, received his Ph.D. at the University of Chicago. He is the author of *Modern World Drama: An Encyclopedia*, the co-author of *Pro and Con*, and the editor of *Story and Critic* and *The Black Crook and Other Nineteenth-Century American Plays*. His articles on literature, the theatre, and popular entertainment have appeared in numerous scholarly and popular journals, and his studies of early vaudeville won an award from the American Council of Learned Societies. Currently he is writing a biography of James O'Neill.

Morton Minsky is the last surviving member of the family that controlled burlesque entertainment until its demise in 1939, when Mayor Fiorello H. La Guardia finally succeeded in having the last New York Minsky theatre closed. Mr. Minsky describes these and other historical, professional, and personal events in his Conference talk.

Max Morath is a distinguished spokesman for American popular music and history and a well-known entertainer. A pianist and vocalist, he has frequently appeared on the stage and television, as well as in night clubs, and he has made many recordings. He is the foremost champion of ragtime and a historian of American popular music.

Born to show biz parents in 1914, **Mae Noell** made her stage debut singing "I'm Forever Blowing Bubbles" at the age of three. At seven, she was cast in the tragic role of Little Mary Morgan in *Ten Nights in a Bar Room*, soon after playing the Ghost in *Three O'Clock Train* and performing in other farces. She married Robert Noell in 1931, has a son and a daughter, six grandchildren, and two great-grandchildren.

Since 1940, she has been foster mother to great apes (gorillas, orangutans, and chimpanzees). Probably the longest run of any small outdoor show was enjoyed by "Noells' Ark Gorilla Show" from 1940 through 1971.

Nahma Sandrow is the author of *Surrealism: Theater, Arts, Ideas*; and of *Vagabond Stars: A World History of Yiddish Theater*, which was awarded honorable mention for the George Freedley Prize for the best theatre book of 1977. With Allen Albert, she created a show, *Vagabond Stars*, for the Berkshire Theatre Festival in the summer of 1978. In addition, she has written for periodicals and newspapers and she lectures widely. A graduate of Bryn Mawr, she received her doctorate from the Yale School of Drama. She is on the faculty of the City University of New York.

Caroline Schaffner is a graduate of the Horner Institute of Fine Arts in Kansas City. She has toured with the Redpath-Horner Lyceum and trouped with musical tabloid companies. In 1925, she married Neil Schaffner and with him organized The Schaffner Players, a repertoire company that played in the Midwest from 1925 to 1963. The Schaffners wrote and appeared in the radio serial "Toby's Corntussle News." Caroline Schaffner is Vice-President of the Society for the Preservation of Tent, Folk, and Repertoire Theatre; Curator of the Museum of Repertoire Americana; and an honorary Doctor of Humane Letters.

Gretchen Schneider has B.A. and M.A. degrees in Dance and is completing her Ph.D. at the University of California (Davis). She was a Predoctoral Fellow with the Smithsonian Institution and an ASTR Research Fellow. She has taught at New York University, and was Associate Curator of History at the Oakland Museum, choreographer for Interlochen National Music Camp, and on the board of directors of (and performed with) the Sacramento Ballet. Her articles appeared in *Dance Perspectives* and *Southern Theatre Quarterly*, and she delivered a paper at the 1978 CORD-ADG meeting in Hawaii.

Laurence Senelick is Associate Professor of Drama at Tufts University, a former Associate of the Russian Research Centre at Harvard, and a member of the Advisory Board of *19th Century Theatre Research*. A frequent contributor to *Theatre Quarterly*, *Theatre Survey*, *Theatre Research International*, and other scholarly journals, he is currently working on a bibliography of British music hall 1840-1930, and a biography of the Russian actor Mikhail Shchepkin. His most recent books are *A Cavalcade of Clowns* and translations of Chekhov's *The Cherry Orchard* and *The Seagull*.

Suzanne Shelton is a dance critic for *Texas Monthly* magazine and Texas correspondent for *Dance Magazine*. A doctoral candidate in American Civilization at the University of Texas at Austin, she has taught courses in American Studies and The Artistic Woman in America. She is preparing a critical biography of Ruth St. Denis to be published by Doubleday and Company, Inc. Other work by her has apepared in *Dance Research Annual*, *Notable American Women*, *New York Dance Calendar*, and elsewhere.

William L. Slout grew up in a dramatic tent show that was owned and operated by his father. He became an actor, stake driver, and all-around handyman, and later graduated to stage manager and boss canvasman. Thereafter, he was an actor and manager of his own summer stock theatre for several years. He has a Ph.D. from the University of California at Los Angeles, and is currently Professor of Theatre Arts at California State College, San Bernardino. He is the author of the book *Theatre in a Tent*.

Bill Smith, educated at C.C.N.Y. and Columbia, is a former newspaperman and critic who covered all phases of the entertainment field. As the senior associate editor of *The Billboard*, he was that publication's last editor to cover vaudeville. While with *The Billboard*, he was on the faculty of the New School in New York, where he lectured weekly for almost four years on "The Individual in Showbusiness," sharing his platform with David Merrick, Hal Prince, Mike Nichols, executives from all the TV networks, and others. Mr. Smith resigned from *The Billboard* to become the editor of *Radio-TV Daily*. At the same time, he also edited the Overseas Press Club's official organ.

Joe Smith, now in his mid-nineties and a semi-retiree in the Actors Fund Home in Englewood, New Jersey, is best remembered for his famous partnership with Charlie Dale, which started at the turn of the century. Their most celebrated act was the comedy sketch "Dr. Kronkhite," which Mr. Smith still performs occasionally before high school audiences and other groups. In the remarks that follow the text of "Dr. Kronkhite" as performed at the Conference, Mr. Smith reminisces about his professional career as an entertainer.

George Speaight, FRSA, is past chairman of The Society for Theatre Research. He is the author of *The History of the English Toy Theatre, The History of the English Puppet Theatre*, and *Punch and Judy: a History*; is currently completing a history of the circus; and is the editor of *The Memoirs of Charles Dibdin the Younger* and *Bawdy Songs of the Early Music Hall*. He is past editorial director of The Rainbird Publishing Group. He is an active partner in the London Puppet Players.

Robert C. Toll, a Berkeley Ph.D. in American History, is the author of *Blacking Up: The Minstrel Show in Nineteenth-Century America* (1974), *On with the Show: The First Century of Show Business in America* (1976, both published by Oxford University Press), and several articles on show business history. He is a free-lance writer now working on an interpretative overview of the form and content of twentieth-century show business in America.

Eleonore Treiber is a dancer and an actress. A frequent performer of classical ballet, a choreographer, and a dance teacher, she has also acted in many Broadway and national tour company productions.

Marcello Truzzi is Department Head and Professor of Sociology at Eastern Michigan University. His numerous publications cross disciplinary lines, with books ranging from *Chess in Literature,* to *The Humanities as Sociology,* to *Sociology: The Classic Statements,* and articles dealing with sociological theory, experimental social psychology, folklore, and popular culture. He has been editor of the journal *The Zetetic* for the Committee for the Scientific Investigation of Claims of the Paranormal, and is currently the editor of the *Zetetic Scholar.* He has written a number of articles dealing with the American circus and, more recently, the American carnival.

Don B. Wilmeth, Professor of Theatre and English at Brown University, received his Ph.D. from the University of Illinois. He is the author of *The American Stage to World War I: An Information Guide* and of articles in *Theatre Notebook, Theatre Survey,* and other journals. He is theatre editor and a member of the board of trustees for *U. S. Today,* book review editor for *The Theatre Journal,* an advisory editor for *Nineteenth-Century Theatre Research,* a member of the executive board of the American Society for Theatre Research, and chairman of the TLA and George Freedley Book Award committees of the Theatre Library Association.

Jenifer Pashkowski Winsted was born in Olympia, Washington, and received her B.A. and M.A. in dance from the University of Oregon. She was an Assistant Professor in the University of Oregon Dance Department (1973-1976), and has been a Senior Lecturer in the University of Southern California Dance Program since 1977. At both universities she has taught dance history courses and dance technique, and she choreographed for concert performing groups. Currently she is a Ph.D. candidate in Physical Education Administration at USC, where she is continuing her investigation of Oregon dance history for her dissertation.